IN THE SHADE OF THE SUNNA

SALAFI PIETY IN THE TWENTIETH-CENTURY MIDDLE EAST

Aaron Rock-Singer

Salma,
I hope that you enjoy this book and that you get your Dad to read it!

UNIVERSITY OF CALIFORNIA PRESS

University of California Press
Oakland, California

Library of Congress Cataloging-in-Publication Data

Names: Rock-Singer, Aaron, author.
Title: In the shade of the Sunna : Salafi piety in the twentieth-century Middle East / Aaron Rock-Singer.
Description: Oakland, California : University of California Press, [2022] | Includes bibliographical references and index.
Identifiers: LCCN 2021049403 (print) | LCCN 2021049404 (ebook) | ISBN 9780520382565 (cloth) | ISBN 9780520382572 (paperback) | ISBN 9780520382589 (ebook)
Subjects: LCSH: Salafiyah—History—20th century. | Salafiyah—History—21st century. | Salafiyah—Social aspects—History—20th century.
Classification: LCC BP195.S18 R63 2022 (print) | LCC BP195.S18 (ebook) | DDC 297.8/3—dc23/eng/20220202
LC record available at https://lccn.loc.gov/2021049403
LC ebook record available at https://lccn.loc.gov/2021049404

Manufactured in the United States of America
28 27 26 25 24 23 22
10 9 8 7 6 5 4 3 2 1

Mom and Dad: This book would have been impossible without your love and support.
Cara: How did I get so lucky?
Liora: I know that you have already written 50 books this year, but this is mine, OK?
Eli: May you one day be as passionate about your job as you currently are about monkeys and the color yellow.

CONTENTS

Acknowledgments *ix*
The Ethics of an Orphan Image *xv*
A Note on Transliteration and Spelling *xix*

Introduction 1
1. The Roots of Salafism: Strands of an Unorthodox Past, 1926–1970 31
2. Conquering Custom in the Name of *Tawhid:* The Salafi Expansion of Worship 66
3. Praying in Shoes: How to Sideline a Practice of the Prophet 102
4. The Salafi Mystique: From *Fitna* to Gender Segregation 137
5. Leading With a Fist: The Genesis and Consolidation of a Salafi Beard 170
6. Between Pants and the *Jallabiyya:* The Adoption of *Isbal* and the Battle for Authenticity 196

Conclusion 229

Bibliography 233
Index 251

ACKNOWLEDGMENTS

The seeds of this book project were planted during my time as a graduate student in Princeton's Department of Near Eastern Studies. When I arrived at Princeton, I planned to study lay religious authority in the twentieth-century Middle East and considered myself unqualified to engage with questions of Islamic theology or law. I had never opened a *fiqh* text or biographical dictionary and knew little of the vast universe of digital Islamic texts, whether Waqfeya or Shamela. My first thanks go to my advisor, Muhammad Qasim Zaman, who guided me through the study of modern Islam and helped me develop my first book on the Islamic Revival in 1970s Egypt. His deep commitment to both scholarship and mentorship have been formative. In tandem, Michael Cook's legendary "Introduction to the Islamic Scholarly Tradition"—if ever a class title understated its depth and rigor!—was both the most challenging and exhilarating class that I have ever taken. Yet, while Michael exudes a commitment to intellectual rigor, he also models a deep form of human decency in academia that is as rare as it is impactful. In a classic case of the rich getting richer, I was also fortunate enough to study with both Bernard Haykel and Hossein Modarressi.

As a graduate student at Princeton, I first delved into Salafism while trying to understand the origins of calls to gender segregation in 1970s Egypt. Muhammad Qasim Zaman offered me deft feedback at the time and support as I worked to place the article in an appropriate journal. Publishing in *Islamic Law & Society* vaulted this project forward as David Powers offered multiple rounds of line-edits to the article before sending it out for review. This was my first experience of David's commitment to mentorship and clear writing. As I worked to bring this article to its final form, I was also fortunate to receive generous comments from Daniel Lav, Cyrus Schayegh, and Suzie Ferguson.

My early research for this project occurred during my year as a postdoctoral fellow at the University of Pennsylvania's Perry World House and as a Visiting Assistant Professor at Cornell. At Penn, I wish to thank Bill Burke-White and Mike Horowitz for their support (and ample writing time!), as well as for their willingness to provide extra money to allow me to purchase Salafi periodicals. During the year in Philadelphia, I benefited greatly from an academic and social community around me, particularly Julia McDonald and two graduate school friends, Sam Helfont and Megan Robb, who fortuitously had also ended up at Penn. Finally, I was able to reunite with Heather Sharkey, the mentor who introduced me to the study of the Middle East as an undergraduate back in the fall of 2004 and supported may first research experience by advising my undergraduate thesis on Amr Khaled.

It was at Cornell, however, that research kicked into high gear and my writing really began. I presented an early version of chapter 1 to participants in the Brett de Bary Interdisciplinary Writing Group and wish to thank David Powers, Ben Anderson, Jeff Eden, Raashid Goyal, and Patrick Naeve for their comments. I then presented my research on the Salafi beard as part of a workshop on Islam and Politics co-organized with David (again!), who agreed to publish the proceedings as a theme issue in *Islamic Law & Society*. I am also grateful to the other contributors to this theme issue (Joel Blecher, Amira Mittermaier, and Lev Weitz), as well as to participants in the workshop. Furthermore, I have had the pleasure of discussing this project at length with Ibrahim Gemeah, who generously shared his experience with Salafis in Egypt and is well on his way to becoming a successful scholar in his own right. At Cornell, I would also like to thank Chiara Formichi, Deborah Starr, Suman Seth, Eric Tagliacozzo, and Seçil Yılmaz, who collectively made me feel like a part of an intellectual community during a challenging professional period.

The History Department at the University of Wisconsin-Madison has been the perfect place to finish this book and to chart the next stage of my career. To begin with, I am fortunate to have an extraordinary set of colleagues. Though much of my first two years have been defined by the Covid-19 pandemic and remote work, I never cease to be impressed by their collective combination of kindness and intellectual intensity. I'm particularly grateful to Mou Banerjee for her wry sense of humor; Marla Ramírez for her thoughtfulness and easy laugh; Tony Michels for his unselfish commitment to scholarly community (and expertise in Madison's lunch dining scene); Fran Hirsch for her unceasing support of junior faculty; Sarah Thal for her understated excellence and kindness; and Leonora Neville, who has guided the department through a challenging time with grace and wisdom. I also wish to thank Jennifer Ratner-Rosenhagen and Lee Wandel for providing generous comments on grant proposals related to this book. This book has also benefited from my participation in the Middle East Studies program at UW directed by Nevine el-Nossery. I am particularly grateful to have Steven Brooke, Marwa Shalaby, Dan Stolz, and Daniel Williford as colleagues.

I also owe a great debt to fellow scholars of Islamic and Middle East History. In particular, I wish to thank Walter Armbrust (whose fault it is that I am fascinated by social practice), Samy Ayoub, Nathan Brown, Cole Bunzel, Suzie Ferguson, Simon Wolfgang Fuchs, Richard Gauvain, Emad Hamdeh, Meir Hatina (who hosted me at Hebrew University during the 2013–14 academic year), Hilary Kalmbach, Yasmin Moll, Jacob Olidort, Christian Sahner, and Arthur Zárate. I benefitted from the feedback of fellow panelists, workshop participants, and audiences at Tel Aviv University (2014 and 2017), Harvard University (2015, organized by Ari Schriber), Columbia University (2016), multiple meetings of the Middle East Studies Association (2016, 2019), Cornell (2017) and finally, a conference at Oxford University co-organized by Masooda Bano and Saud al-Sarhan (2018), entitled "The Future of Salafism." I am also very grateful for the help of Mike Farquhar and Ahmed Said Diop in obtaining the full run of *al-Hadi al-Nabawi* and to Umar Ryad and Maxim Abdulatif for their assistance in accessing *al-Tamaddun al-Islami*. I am also very fortunate that many of the individuals whom I acknowledge here as colleagues are also dear friends.

This book benefited from the keen eye of (at least) half a dozen readers. Omar Anchassi, Alex Thurston, and Simon Wolfgang Fuchs all read the entirety of a first draft of this book in the midst of the early months of the pandemic, challenging me to conceive of the project more broadly and to deepen my analysis. Whether Omar's incredible recall of secondary and primary sources of relevance, Simon's continued push to consider Salafism beyond the Arab world, or Alex's attention to the ways in which my analytical assumptions about Salafism carried traces of this movement's self-perception, all three of these readers drove me to produce a better book. Thanks to the generosity of the UW-Madison History department, particularly Leonora

Neville, I was then able to convene a virtual workshop during which I spent the day with Joel Blecher, Henri Lauzière, and Emilio Spadola working through the weakest parts of my argument and pushing my analysis further. This experience would have been intellectual nirvana in normal times, but was all the more so in the midst of a pandemic that has rendered normal scholarly interaction difficult if not impossible. I am particularly grateful to Emilio for pushing me to think more expansively about visibility and ethics.

At the University of California, Eric Schmidt saw potential for this book to be a broadly relevant story of religion in modernity. I am grateful for his belief in the project, support, and ability to somehow conjure extraordinary reviewers not once but twice! I also wish to thank LeKeisha Hughes for all she has done to shepherd this book to publication, Catherine Osborne for her attention to detail and precise editorial suggestions, and Cindy Fulton for making the proof stage straightforward and low-stress. Chapters four and five of this book were published, in revised version, in *Islamic Law and Society*. I would like to thank David Powers for permission to reprint these articles.

Friends who know nothing about Salafism have also played a huge role in the journey that has been this book. First, a shout out to Pete Silberman (and his better half, Sylvia!), who has been my closest friend since we were in elementary school fighting over ownership of whatever piece of junk we had found in either of our backyards. When I married Cara, I also gained her two best friends, Lilly Hubschmann-Shahar and Lisa Rosenfeld, as lifelong friends, as well as their respective husbands, Yoni Shahar and Bryan Beaudreault. We have also been fortunate to build a community of wonderful friends here in Madison, particularly Josh Garoon and Michal Engelman, Judy Greenberg (along with Dan Stolz, already mentioned!), Kirsten Kiphardt and Sean Ronnekleiv-Kelly, Keesia and Tom Hyzer, Brian Schneirow and Kelly Eagen, Jason and Colleen Deal, and so many other folks, especially at Beth Israel Center.

Finally, as I worked on this book, my family supported me every step of the way. I wish to thank my in-laws Craig Singer, Judy Singer, Ellen Singer Coleman, and Michael Coleman, as well as my siblings Patrick and Miriam and Patrick's wife, Rachel. I am also grateful for the support and love of my extended family (Baron, Levy, Wohl, Rock, Busman, and Rosen), as well as the love and care that my children have received from a succession of nannies: Abby Anello (New York), Heidi Neuhauser (Ithaca), and Anna Volkman (Madison).

It is my parents, Cara, and my children who will see their fingerprints—real and literal—all over this book. My parents, Ed and Andrea Rock, now know more about praying in shoes and Salafi beards than they ever might have imagined, and have given me their full love and support for every personal and professional adventure. One of the defining memories of my childhood is their embrace of my learning style, which can accurately be summed up by the title of the classic children's book *Leo the Late Bloomer*. Another defining memory, however, is my father's comment to the ten-year-old version of me that if I ever found a professional passion that I enjoyed half as much as following baseball and basketball then I'd have a successful career. Though I suspect that he made this claim out of exasperation at having to listen to me drone on about sports statistics rather than as a prediction of the future, I believe that my discovery of a passion for Salafi social practice has proved him right.

The person who has listened to me drone on most, however, has been my wife Cara, who has filled the past eleven years of my life with love, laughter, and joy. As we progressed from graduate students living in a tiny New York apartment to multiple moves in the midst of unclear career prospects to settling in Madison, she has been my ultimate supporter. In the midst of all of this, she brought our two kids, Liora and Eli, into the world, while balancing an ambitious professional path with deep devotion to our family. I thus dedicate this book to my parents, Cara, and our kids who, in ways big and small, both made it possible and life meaningful.

Aaron Rock-Singer
Madison, Wisconsin
November 2021

THE ETHICS OF AN ORPHAN IMAGE

As I searched for an appropriate image for this book's cover, I alternated between recent photographs of Salafi men taken by the photographers of Western media agencies and images of key Salafi texts, particularly periodicals. Neither perspective was satisfactory: while photographs of Salafi men showed them from an angle chosen by the photographer (and did not compensate those depicted), a reproduction of the cover or contents of a Salafi periodical would have risked replicating the faulty assumption that Salafism must be understood as emerging directly from canonical texts.

Having exhausted both of these options, I returned to the cover of a 1980 pamphlet that figures prominently in chapter 4 of this book. Entitled *Flaunting and the Danger of Women Joining Men in Their Workplace,* this text first appeared as a series of articles in Salafi and Islamist periodicals in Egypt, Saudi Arabia and Kuwait and is the work of a leading Saudi Salafi scholar, ʿAbd al-ʿAziz b. Baz (d. 1999). This particular pamphlet, produced by the now-defunct Egyptian publishing house Maktabat al-Salam, is unusual among editions of this text, as it is the only version that I found that contained a cover image. Even more significant, it is an exception among Salafi print media more broadly, which generally eschews the depiction of men (let alone women). Specifically, the cover depicts a faceless yet alluring brunette clad in a cloak in the background, and a glass and wine bottle and deck of cards in the foreground. In doing so, the cover offers a vivid depiction of Salafism's concern with visibility and its focus on regulating public behavior, and summons affective responses that range from enthusiastic agreement (the presumed intended reaction) to anger (among those who oppose the Salafi social project). If a picture is worth a thousand words, this illustration reveals how Salafi scholars came to articulate a public vision of piety premised on a linkage between ethics and visible practice.

This image, however, is of unknown origin. The text itself contains no indication of the illustrator. This could not have been Ibn Baz himself, since he lost his sight as a young man. I searched for other editions of this title, yet could find none that contained this illustration (or any illustration at all). I then went looking for Maktabat al-Salam—which according to this pamphlet was based in Cairo—and contacted a Salafi-leaning Egyptian publishing house with a similar name, Maktabar Dar al-Salam. The latter, however, stated that it had no relationship to Maktabat al-Salam, which it believed to be defunct. Indeed, the address listed on the pamphlet for this publisher now houses a medical diagnostic imaging center. Furthermore, a search of the WorldCat database found fifteen texts published between 1980 and 1985, but none after this date. Finally, Egypt's current copyright law (Law 82 of 2002) does not address the status of such "orphan works."

While this searching solved a legal question, it did not exhaust the broader ethical question of using such an "orphan work." An easy answer would have to find an alternative image with a clear copyright holder yet, after nearly a decade of working with Salafi print media, I could think of no comparable image. Thus, in line with recent work by librarians and archivists to balance between the educational and potential economic value of orphan works,[1] I use this pamphlet's cover in a transformative fashion; far from competing with the original (which was published only once by Maktabat al-Salam over four decades ago), *In the Shade of the Sunna* casts light on how and why the original work emerged. Put differently, even if this book were still in print, its audience and that of my book differ completely, while the use of this image carries educational value for an academic audience.

More broadly, the use of this image reflects the methodological and ethical mission of this book: to depict Salafis as three-dimensional human beings rather than as direct descendants of the seventh century's models, as both their members and critics often depict them. The goal of this book, in short,

1. For example, see the "Statement of Best Practices in Fair Use of Collections Containing Orphan Works for Libraries, Archives, and Other Memory Institutions" (2014), available at https://cmsimpact.org/wp-content/uploads/2016/01/orphanworks-dec14.pdf.

is to ask the same questions about Salafis as one would about any other movement, religious or otherwise, and in doing so, to cast light on their origins, development, and impact on the world around them. I thus hope that this book's cover image will bring readers to the text and illustrate this work's central argument.

A NOTE ON TRANSLITERATION, SPELLING, AND DATING

Transliteration of Arabic terms follows a modified version of the style of the *International Journal of Middle East Studies*. I employ full diacritical marks for technical terms, and, for non-technical terms, indicate the *ʿayn* and *hamza* alone. Accordingly, I will render the robe worn by Egyptian men as *jallābiyya* when citing an Arabic-language reference to this form of dress but as *jallabiyya* when it appears more generally. In the case of personal names, I also follow this system. Furthermore, when referring to individuals by their patronym, I write out "Ibn" (for example, Ibn Baz) while elsewhere, in other contexts, I render the patronymic link with a "b." (for example, ʿAbd al-ʿAziz b. Baz). Finally, when I provide two dates (e.g., 1400/1980), it refers to the Hijri and Gregorian years, respectively.

Introduction

In the Spring of 1978, a leading Saudi Salafi scholar by the name of ʿAbd al-ʿAziz b. Baz (d. 1999) staked a claim to the necessity of gender segregation in the Islamic University of Medina's official journal (*Majallat al-Jamiʿa al-Islamiyya*).[1] In the article, entitled "The Danger of Women Joining Men in Their Workplace," Ibn Baz argued that individual modest behavior by women could not safeguard public morality and that both domestic seclusion and gender segregation were necessary. A few months later, Ibn Baz turned to *al-Tawhid*, the flagship publication of Egypt's leading Salafi organization, Proponents of the Muhammadan Model (*Anṣār al-Sunna al-Muḥammadiyya*, henceforth Ansar al-Sunna). In this journal, Ibn Baz published a revised version of the original article, serialized in three installments, that made the same case for domestic seclusion and gender segregation.[2] The appearance of this argument in publications on either side of the Red Sea reflected the centrality of Saudi Arabia and Egypt to Salafism's development, while Ibn Baz's concern with gender mixing indexed a key concern of this global Islamic movement.

The Salafi claim to the necessity of separating men and women is often understood by both academics and Salafis themselves to derive directly from this movement's "literalist" approach to the Quran and the authoritative account

1. Ibn Baz, "Khatar Musharakat al-Marʾa li-l-Rajul fi Maydan ʿAmalih," *Majallat al-Jamiʿa al-Islamiyya bi-l-Madina al-Munawwara*, Spring 1398/Spring 1978, 15:334–46.

2. ʿAbd al-ʿAziz b. Baz, "Khatar Musharakat al-Marʾa li-l-Rajul fi Maydan ʿAmalih," *al-Tawhid*, Ramadan 1398/August 1978, 14.

of the Prophet Muhammad's life (known as the *Sunna*). In this book, by contrast, I show that Ibn Baz's call to gender segregation does not hearken back to a traditional model of Islam (whether that of the seventh century or later), nor does it reflect the logical endpoint of a particular interpretative method. Instead, the Salafi position on this question—which is central, though not unique, to this movement[3]—emerged in the 1970s out of a transnational debate between Egyptian and Saudi scholars as they sought to respond to Islamist and Secular Nationalist challengers alike. As Salafi elites worked to meet this challenge and to navigate social and economic pressures, they cited not only the Prophetic model but also sources as varied as the writings of nineteenth-century German philosophers and early-twentieth-century American suffrage activists.

This story of gender segregation was striking not merely because of its unorthodox intellectual genealogy, but also because of the considerations about female sexuality that animated it. Among scholars of Islamic law (*fiqh*), the concern that women's sexuality poses a threat of strife (*fitna*) goes back at least to the ninth century, yet the focus was on preventing sexual relations outside of marriage.[4] Put differently, the longstanding commitment to preventing illicit sexual relations depended on and sought to protect the existence of marriage as a social structure. By contrast, the notion that women mixing with men could corrupt society more broadly simply through their physical presence primarily reflects a modernist view of society in which each person is responsible for him or herself and is equally capable of transmitting virtue or vice.

It is the latter view that would define Salafism's development. Most fundamentally, such an approach assumes a broad, anonymous, and homogenous space bereft of stabilizing social structures, yet filled with individuals tasked with regulating themselves as they communicate ethical positions and political allegiances alike. This approach to the social world, an outgrowth of the claims that modern states make to regulate their citizens, explains not merely efforts by Middle Eastern states to regulate bodily comportment and social space alike,

3. Other examples include the Twelver Shi'i Islamic Republican of Iran and Saudi Arabia, which is split between Wahhabi-Hanbali and Salafi scholars. On gender segregation in Iran, see Nazanin Shahrokni, *Women in Place: The Politics of Gender Segregation in Iran* (Berkeley: University of California Press, 2020). On gender segregation in Saudi Arabia, see Amelie Le Renard, *A Society of Young Women* (Stanford, CA: Stanford University Press, 2014).

4. Marion Katz, *Women in the Mosque: A History of Legal Thought and Social Practice* (New York: Columbia University Press, 2014), 103–4, and Judith Tucker, *Women, Family and Gender in Islamic Law* (New York: Cambridge University Press, 2008), 175–99.

but also why varied social movements embraced such models of individual and collective regulation. Accordingly, Salafi calls for gender segregation did not reflect a historically-continuous Islamic social order, whether that of the seventh century or subsequent to it. Rather, leading lights of this movement sought to solve a distinctly modern challenge—that of society—by physically separating men from women's allegedly irresistible sexual powers and by asking men and women to comport themselves in a manner that served this broader goal.

In this book, I move beyond the discrete question of gender segregation to chart the origins and consolidation of self-consciously Salafi social practices in the twentieth-century Middle East with a focus on Egypt. I tell the story of Salafi movement and its often-ahistorical efforts to replicate the golden model of the early Islamic community in seventh century Arabia. Just as importantly, I argue that the development of Salafism is a lens to the broader transformation of the Islamic thought and practice in modernity. In particular, I emphasize how communication becomes an ethical project and a key consequence of this shift: the increasing centrality of visible practices to understandings of piety.

THE RISE AND CONSOLIDATION OF SALAFISM

In the modern Middle East, the question of who has the rightful claim to the normative authority of the Prophetic model is inescapable. Over the course of the twentieth century, movements as varied as the Muslim Brotherhood (*al-Ikhwān al-Muslimūn*, e. 1928), Ansar al-Sunna al-Muhammadiyya (e. 1926), and the Secular-Nationalist Baʿth party (e. 1947) sought both inspiration and legitimacy for their endeavors by citing the Prophet Muhammad and the first three generations of the Islamic community, known as the "pious ancestors" (*al-salaf al-ṣāliḥ*).

This book is focused on a subset of these movements, such as Ansar al-Sunna, who adopted the term Salafism (*al-Salafiyya*) and today can be found from the Middle East to South Asia to Western Europe and the United States. Members of this movement, in turn, distinguish themselves by articulating an interpretative commitment not only to neo-Hanbali theology (known as *Madhhab al-Salaf*)[5]

5. Neo-Hanbali theology sets out God's oneness through three core concepts: The Unity of Lordship (*Tawḥīd al-Rubūbiyya*), the Unity of Lordship or Worship (*Tawḥīd al-Ūlūhiyya* or *Tawḥīd al-ʿIbāda*) and the Unity of God's Names and Attributes (*Tawḥīd al-Asmāʾ wa'l-Ṣifāt*). As Joas Wagemakers notes, "The Salafi position is virtually the same as the Hanbali one. . . .

and to deriving law from the Quran and Sunna, but also through distinct social practices.[6] While this movement is not limited to the Arab world, this region's most populous country, Egypt, was a dynamic space of religious contestation in which it emerged. Specifically, it was during the 1920s that Egypt saw a cacophony of religious appeals, ranging from the Muslim Brotherhood to the Young Men's Muslim Association (*al-Shubbān al-Muslimūn*) to the Lawful Society For Those Who Work According to the Quran and Sunna (*al-Jamʿiyya al-Sharʿiyya li-Taʿāwun al-ʿAmilin bi-l-Kitāb waʾl-Sunna*, henceforth the Jamʿiyya Sharʿiyya). In the midst of this vibrant religious competition, al-Fiqi, a graduate of Egypt's leading religious institution, al-Azhar University, and former student of the noted Islamic reformer Muhammad Rashid Rida (d. 1935), founded Ansar al-Sunna.[7]

Salafis do believe God has a certain form based on the relevant verses, but they do so without descriptive designation (*bi-lā takyīf*). Instead, they accept that God must be different from the human form that they are familiar with." These debates are not merely theoretical, bearing on the status of Quranic revelation and the role (or lack thereof) of rationalism (*ʿaql*) in engaging with the Quran. See Joas Wagemakers, *Salafism in Jordan: Political Islam in a Quietist Community* (Cambridge, UK: Cambridge University Press, 2016), 41–42. Furthermore, Henri Lauzière notes that "in scholarly parlance . . . a Salafi was an adherent to Hanbali theology who could follow any school of Islamic law or none in particular. The term did not have a legal connotation [prior to the early twentieth century]" (*The Making of Salafism: Islamic Reform in the Twentieth Century* [New York: Columbia University Press, 2016], 28). While Islamic Modernists such as Jamal al-Din al-Afghani and Muhammad ʿAbduh have long been categorized as Salafis, there is no evidence that they used this term to describe themselves. See Lauzière, *The Making of Salafism*, 6.

6. My usage of the term Salafism and periodization follows Lauzière's groundbreaking 2016 book on this topic (*The Making of Salafism*, 28, 96). What is distinctive about Salafism is that it fuses longstanding theological and legal approaches, the latter of which involves the rejection of the legal schools. This position can also be found beyond the Arab world, most notably in the Indian *Ahl-i Ḥadīth* movement. See Martin Riexinger, "Ibn Taymiyya's Worldview and the Challenge of Modernity: A Conflict Among the Ahl-i Ḥadīth in British India," in *Islamic Theology, Philosophy and Law: Debating Ibn Taymiyya and Ibn Qayyim al-Jawziyya*, ed. Birgit Krazietz and Georges Tamer (Berlin: Walter de Gruyter, 2013), 493–517. In the late twentieth century, scholars from this movement have also claimed the attribution (*nisba*) of al-Salafi. For example, Muhammad Luqman b. Barakallah b. Muhammad Yasin b. Salamat Allah b. ʿAbd al-ʿAzim Siddiqi (d. 2020), a member of this movement and author of a prominent Urdu Quranic commentary, *Taysir al-Rahman li-Bayyan al-Quran*, is known as Muhammad Luqman al-Salafi. I wish to think Muhammad Qasim Zaman for pointing me to this naming practice.

7. For example, see "Jamaʿat Ansar al-Sunna al-Muhammadiyya bi-l-Sudan," *al-Hadi al-Nabawi*, Jumada al-Ula 1360/~May 1941, 27, and "Sawt min Jamaʿat Ansar al-Sunna al-Muhammadiyya bi-l-Sudan," *al-Hadi al-Nabawi*, Shawwal 1364/~September 1945, 360. The approximate Gregorian dates (indicated by a tilde) correspond to the fact that the magazine

Scholarship on Salafism in Egypt and beyond has tackled questions of theology, legal method,[8] ritual practice,[9] political participation,[10] and military conflict.[11] Salafism's broader impact, however, lies in its emergence as a social movement that has reshaped Islamic thought and practice in Muslim-majority and Muslim-minority settings alike. This book, accordingly, explores an ostensibly secondary question that cuts to the heart of Salafism's development: the history of the daily practices through which Salafis have sought to emulate the Prophet Muhammad.[12] In the following six chapters, I trace the emergence of distinctly Salafi social practices between 1936 and 1995 and argue that, far from seamlessly replicating either the model of early Islamic Arabia or established models of Islamic piety, these embodied routines emerged out of the assumed communicative power of the body that is characteristic of modernity. It is certainly the case that Salafis competed with and were shaped by their ideological rivals, whether secular nationalists, Islamists, or traditionalist scholars committed to a legal approach based on existing schools of law (s. *Madhhab*, pl. *Madhāhib*). What is crucial, however, is that they have done so *not* because of their fundamental differences, but rather because they share the same field of competition: a commitment to shaping the ideas and practices of a communal body known as "society."

---

was published on the first day of each Hijri month. See "al-Majalla fi Thawb Jadid," *al-Hadi al-Nabawi*, Dhu al-Hijja 1369/~September 1950, 12.

8. Daniel Lav, "Radical Muslim Theonomy: A Study in the Evolution of Salafī Thought" (Ph.D diss, Hebrew University of Jerusalem, 2016) and Emad Hamdeh, *Salafism and Traditionalism: Scholarly Authority in Modern Islam* (Cambridge, UK: Cambridge University Press, 2020).

9. Richard Gauvain, *Salafi Ritual Purity: In the Presence of God* (London: Routledge, 2013) and Pieter Coppens, "Jamāl al-Dīn al-Qāsimī's Treatise on Wiping over the Socks and the Rise of a Distinct Salafi Method," *Die Welt Des Islam* (2021, first view), 1-34.

10. Joas Wagemakers, *A Quietist Jihadi: The Ideology and Influence of Abu Muhammad al-Maqdisi* (Cambridge, UK: Cambridge University Press, 2012); Wagemakers, *Salafism in Jordan*; and Zoltan Pall, *Salafism in Lebanon: Local and Transnational Movements* (Cambridge, UK: Cambridge University Press, 2018).

11. Daniel Lav, *Radical Islam and the Revival of Medieval Theology* (Cambridge, UK: Cambridge University Press, 2012).

12. The Salafi committment to emulating Muhammad is sometimes classified as an example of Fundamentalism. On the broader applicability of the term for Islamic movements, see Michael Cook, *Ancient Religions, Modern Politics* (Princeton, NJ: Princeton University Press, 2014), 377–98. In the case of Salafism, the framework of fundamentalism reveals a great deal regarding how Salafis understand themselves, yet tells us comparatively little about how they act in practice.

Most fundamental to the development of Salafi practice would be the relationship between ethics and communication that secular nationalist visions, too, had absorbed from the operating logic of modern states. In this formulation, bodily practice came to be both a tool of regulating the self and an incontrovertible symbol of allegiance to or rejection of particular political projects. By carefully tracing the genesis and consolidation of four practices—praying in shoes, gender segregation, a distinctly Salafi beard, and shortened pants or robes—I show the centrality of the assumptions and demands of communication in the emergence and consolidation of Salafism and, more broadly, in the transformation of the Islamic tradition in the twentieth century.

The challenge in writing a history of the emergence of distinctly Salafi practices is that both Salafi elites and rank-and-file members are deeply committed to the proposition that such embodied acts represent a precise reproduction of the model of Islam bequeathed by Muhammad and his Companions in seventh-century Arabia. Salafis insist that their interpretation of early Islamic history is superior to that of other Muslims because it is based exclusively on the Quran and Sunna, and they castigate Islamic modernists and Islamists alike for their adoption of self-consciously modern questions and concerns. By contrast, Salafis proceed on the epistemological premise that they have succeeded in inoculating themselves not merely from "non-Islamic" influences but also from what they understand to be the faulty interpretations of the *madhhab* tradition.

A focus on a set of practices which Salafi elites claim emerge directly from the Quran and Sunna requires an ambitious approach to sources. In line with recent scholarship that emphasizes the role of transnational linkages in the movement's development,[13] I draw on leading Salafi periodicals published across the Middle East, including in Egypt, Syria, Lebanon, Saudi Arabia, Kuwait, and Yemen as well as pamphlets, some digitized and others culled from archives in Egypt, Saudi Arabia, and Israel. When it is relevant, I also use mosque lessons and sermons recorded on audiocassette and digitized as

13. See Laurent Bonnefoy, *Salafism in Yemen: Transnationalism and Religious Identity* (Oxford: Oxford University Press, 2012); Michael Farquhar, *Circuits of Faith: Migration, Education, and the Wahhabi Mission* (Stanford, CA: Stanford University Press, 2016); Raihan Ismail, *Rethinking Salafism: The Transnational Networks of Salafi ʿUlama in Egypt, Kuwait, and Saudi Arabia* (Oxford: Oxford University Press, 2021); Pall, *Salafism in Lebanon*.

audio files. Collectively, these sources reflect and reveal an interconnected transnational arena of Salafi debate in which it is not uncommon to see the same writer appear in multiple publications, for one magazine to quote or excerpt another, or for a print debate to be echoed in audiocassette sermons and vice versa.

The choice to rely primarily on print media reflects not only the available source base, but also the suitability and centrality of this medium to the promotion of strict models of embodied practice. The ease of reproducing printed material in the modern period facilitated a call to standardized religious practice,[14] while magazines and pamphlets constitute what Wilson Chacko Jacob terms "a performative cultural space in which the making and potential unmaking of subjects was accorded an iterative structure. . . ."[15] Furthermore, as Benedict Anderson argues, print created an imagining of simultaneous readings that allows it to be both a structure for otherwise-unstructured social space, and to reflect particular dynamics of authority.[16] Print media thus served as a site not merely for the transmission of particular models of piety, but also as a space for those outside the Salafi scholarly elite to understand themselves as Muslims committed to replicating the model of the first three generations of the Muslim community. As these readers read about the ostensibly unchanging and timeless model of this golden period, they worked to translate a theoretical commitment into an ethical project of embodied self-regulation. Finally, the medium of print reflected and reinforced broader dynamics of authority within the Salafi movement by enabling editors –who were also elites within the movement more broadly –to police the boundaries

14. In his classic study of the roots of legal stringency in Jewish Ultra-Orthodoxy during the second half of the twentieth century, Haym Soloveitchik similarly highlights the importance of print in creating standards of precise religious practice that did not reflect this community's lived history. See "Rupture and Reconstruction: The Transformation of Contemporary Orthodoxy," *Tradition* 28, no. 4 (1994): 68–69.

15. Wilson Chacko Jacob, *Working Out Egypt: Effendi Masculinity and Subject Formation in Colonial Modernity, 1870–1940* (Durham, NC: Duke University Press, 2011), 70.

16. Indeed, Anderson quotes Hegel to draw an explicit parallel with religious practice: "The significance of this mass ceremony—Hegel observed that newspaper serve the modern man as a substitute for morning prayers—is paradoxical. It is confirmed in silent privacy . . . [y]et each communicant is well aware that the ceremony he performs is being replicated simultaneously by thousands (or millions) of others of whose existence he is confident, yet of whose identity he has not the slightest notion" (Benedict Anderson, *Imagined Communities: Reflections on the Origin and Spread of Nationalism* [New York: Verso, 1991], 35–36).

of acceptable discourse and practice not only by selecting articles but also by accepting or rejecting fatwa requests and letters to the editor.[17]

In this book, I draw on the insights of historians of nationalism, on the one hand, and gender, on the other, to offer an alternative approach to the history of Islamic reformism and reformist movements. Historians of Islamic reformism tend to focus disproportionately on the development of abstract concepts over time,[18] while those who study the Muslim Brotherhood emphasize the political and intellectual dimensions of this movement's development.[19] Scholars of nationalism and gender, by contrast, highlights the centrality of social practice and embodied performance to social movements that span the ideological spectrum, including nationalist movements that subsequently rise to power and use state institutions to further regulate such practice.[20] As such, this history of Salafi piety brings the history of Islamic reform into broader

17. While Ansar al-Sunna's periodicals included fatwa sections, they differed from their Islamist competitors in that they did not include letters to the editor.

18. Malcolm Kerr, *Islamic Reform: The Political and Legal Theories of Muhammad ʿAbduh and Rashīd Riḍā* (Berkeley: University of California Press, 1966); David Dean Commins, *Islamic Reform: Politics and Social Change in Late Ottoman Syria* (New York: Oxford University Press, 1990); Itzchak Weismann, *Taste of Modernity: Sufism, Salafiyya, and Arabism in late Ottoman Damascus* (Leiden: Brill, 2001); Muhammad Qasim Zaman, *The Ulema in Contemporary Islam: Custodians of Change* (Princeton, NJ: Princeton University Press, 2002) and *Modern Islamic Thought in a Radical Age: Religious Authority and Internal Criticism* (Cambridge, UK: Cambridge University Press, 2012); Bernard Haykel, *Revival and Reform in Islam: The Legacy of Muhammad al-Shawkānī* (Cambridge, UK: Cambridge University Press, 2003); Indira Gesink, *Islamic Reform and Conservatism: Al-Azhar and the Evolution of Modern Sunni Islam* (New York: I.B. Tauris, 2009); Florian Zemmin, *Modernity in Islamic Tradition: The Concept of 'Society' in the Journal al-Manar* (Cairo, 1898-1940) (Berlin: De Gruyter, 2018).

19. Richard P. Mitchell, *The Society of the Muslim Brothers* (New York: Oxford University Press, 1993); Brynjar Lia, *The Society of the Muslim Brothers in Egypt: The Rise of an Islamic Mass Movement* (Ithaca, NY: Ithaca Press, 2006); Victor Willi, *The Fourth Ordeal: A History of the Muslim Brotherhood in Egypt, 1968–2018* (Cambridge, UK: Cambridge University Press, 2021).

20. James Gelvin, *Divided Loyalties Nationalism and Mass Politics in Syria at the Close of Empire* (Berkeley: University of California Press, 1993); Max Weiss, *In the Shadow of Sectarianism Law, Shiʿism, and the Making of Modern Lebanon* (Stanford, CA: Stanford University Press, 2010); Wilson Chacko Jacob, *Working out Egypt*; Ilham Khuri Makdisi, "Fin de siècle Egypt: a Nexus for Mediterranean and Global Radical Networks," in *Global Islam in the Age of Steam and Print, 1850–1930*, ed. James Gelvin and Nile Green (Berkeley: University of California Press, 2013), 78–100.

historiographical debates over the relationship between ideological change and bodily practice.

This history of the rise of distinctively Salafi practices also seeks to reorient the study of Salafism towards the social. Rather than approaching this trend's history primarily as a story of scholarly engagement with past authorities, a focus on religious ritual, or political participation, I argue for the centrality of daily practice to both the movement's development and impact. Put differently, to be a Salafi is not merely to hold specific theological or legal commitments but also to engage in particular visible practices. In this book, I show that the social practices that distinguish Salafis were formulated in the twentieth century in order to enable this movement to compete with its ideological foes, thus casting light on the balance among theology, law, and social contestation in the formation of this Islamic movement.

The emergence and consolidation of varied Salafi social practices also reveals how Salafi efforts to shape society are inescapably animated by a modern logic of communication and related linkage of ethics and visible self-regulation. The Salafi movement constitutes a valuable lens to the transformations of the Islamic tradition in modernity precisely because it understands its mission as direct and unmediated preservation. While previous scholarship acknowledges that Salafism emerges *in* the modern period,[21] I show that modernity is constitutive of Salafism and, indeed, of today's Islamic movements more broadly.[22] To make this point more concrete, such an approach

21. For example, see Bernard Haykel, "On the Nature of Salafi Thought and Action," in *Global Salafism: Islam's New Religious Movement*, ed. Roel Meijer (New York: Columbia University Press, 2009), 33–57. Other scholars, however, argue that "Salafism has deep roots in Islamic religious development, with various movements throughout history championing the revival of Islamic tradition based upon a return to the ways of *al-Salaf al-Salih* (the pious ancestors)." (Ismail, *Rethinking Salafism*, 28).

22. In making this argument, I build on Thomas Bauer's study of the shift from ambiguity to a commitment to Cartesian-inspired certainty in Islamic history, which includes analysis of the Saudi Salafi scholar Ibn al-ʿUthaymin. As Bauer rightly declares, "The Salafist position . . . is the kind of reform that is based on an *intolerance of ambiguity*. Thus, it must be understood as the most radical attempt so far to *modernize* Islamic law." (*A Culture of Ambiguity: An Alternative History of Islam*, trans. Hinrich Biesterfeldt and Tricia Turnstall [New York: Columbia University Press, 2021], 128). My argument, which foregrounds the adoption of distinctly modern logics of identity and social organization, is distinct from the linked claim that Salafis engage in modernity's political, social and economic processes as they mediate social change. See Ousman Kane, *Muslim Modernity in Post-Colonial Nigeria: A Study of the Society for the Removal and Reinstatement of Tradition* (Leiden: Brill, 2003), 1–7.

explains not only why Salafis lay claims to models of facial hair or pants that distinguish them from those of their secular-nationalist and Islamist competitors alike, but also why all these factions are concerned with controlling their communication as a form of ethical practice in the first place. By contrast, a focus on Salafi theology reveals little about the world in which theological principles are cited, and is thus of limited value in understanding why Salafi calls for the exclusive worship of God (*al-Tawḥīd*) have powerfully challenged entrenched models of sovereignty and society alike in the twentieth-century Middle East.

My emphasis on social practice also challenges existing scholarship on Islamic piety that separates moral cultivation from social performance. Influential ethnographic studies, most notably by Saba Mahmood and Charles Hirschkind, foreground the continued relevance of a discursive tradition of ethical cultivation to varied Muslim communities in Egypt and beyond.[23] Most notably, Mahmood draws on Foucault's understanding of Aristotelian ethics to emphasize the capacity of individuals to act on their own bodies in a way that transforms them into willing subjects of a moral discourse.[24] In this study, I consider embodied ethical practice not as separate from social performance, but rather as intimately linked to it.[25] It is not that Salafism's

23. Saba Mahmood, *The Politics of Piety: The Islamic Revival and the Feminist Subject* (Princeton, NJ: Princeton University Press, 2005), and Charles Hirschkind, *The Ethical Soundscape: Cassette Sermons and Islamic Counterpublics* (New York: Columbia University Press, 2006). Other scholars that have adopted this approach include Jeanette S. Jouili, *Pious Practice and Secular Constraints* (Stanford, CA: Stanford University Press, 2015); Arsalan Khan, "Pious Sociality: The Ethics of Hierarchy in the Tablighi Jamaat in Pakistan," *Social Analysis: The International Journal of Anthropology* 60, no. 4 (2016): 96–113, esp. 100; and Rachel Rinaldo, *Mobilizing Piety: Islam and Feminism in Indonesia* (New York: Oxford University Press, 2013), 24–26.

24. Mahmood, *The Politics of Piety,* 27–31, 120–22. Indeed, while Mahmood notes the prominence of "outward markers of religiosity—ritual practices, styles of comporting oneself, dress, and so on," –she sees them as oriented inward (31). Jeannette Jouili makes a similar argument that offers a greater emphasis on the limits to such projects of self-cultivation in a European context (*Pious Practice and Secular Constraints,* 14–22).

25. Jouili is an exception to this literature in that she takes seriously "the complicated connections between . . . [pious] practices as communicable identity markers and their embeddedness in long-standing traditions of self-cultivation. . . ." (*Pious Practice and Secular Constraints,* 13). Her argument, however, is that a concern with visual signification is a consequence of these Muslims' "diasporic context," rather than an outgrowth of broader shifts of modernity. Arsalan Khan, too, emphasizes "pious sociality structured by hierarchical relationships," yet he is not concerned with questions of visual signification ("Pious Sociality," 105).

ethical project demands visibility, but rather that its ethics take into account the inescapable social condition of constant visibility.[26]

This study also bridges practices of piety and intellectual history by casting light on how Islamic scholars (the *ʿulamāʾ*) engage with social practice. Muhammad Qasim Zaman and Junaid Quadri have shown how scholarly use of longstanding discourses and methods of Islamic law can mask significant shifts in argumentation.[27] By focusing on practice rather than discourse, I bring out the social conditions that animate Islamic legal reasoning, particularly the citation of past authorities, in the modern period.[28] Specifically, I explore how a claim to the binding nature of a particular practice based on citation of reports of the Prophet Muhammad's statements and actions (s. *ḥadīth*, pl. *aḥādīth*) is a response to particular political, social and economic conditions and an effort to extend scholarly authority into society in a manner that mirrors state efforts to regulate individual citizens.[29]

In line with my argument that communication is central to Salafi social practice, I approach citation not merely as a verbal or text-based claim (for example, a reference to a particular hadith report), but also as a practice of embodied knowledge that echoes, but is distinct from, pre-modern Islamic models of embodiment.[30] As Salafi men pray in shoes or adopt particular

26. This approach follows Emilio Spadola's 2014 argument about Islamic exorcism in Morocco; see *The Calls of Islam: Sufis, Islamists, and Mass Mediation in Urban Morocco* (Bloomington: Indiana University Press, 2014), 119–36.

27. On the expanded usage of appeals to the "Common Good" (*al-maṣlaḥa al-ʿāmma*) between medieval and modern Islam, see Muhammad Qasim Zaman, *Modern Islamic Thought in a Radical Age: Religious Authority and Internal Criticism* (Cambridge, UK: Cambridge University Press, 2012), 108–39. On the claim by twentieth century scholars to "expertise" in the field of religion, see Zaman, *The Ulama in Contemporary Islam* (Princeton, NJ: Princeton University Press, 2002), 99–102. Also see Junaid Quadri, *Transformations of Tradition: Islamic Law in Colonial Modernity* (Oxford, UK: Oxford University Press, 2021).

28. For a recent work that takes seriously the material conditions of Islamic thought, see Leor Halevi, *Modern Things on Trial: Islam's Global and Material Reformation in the Age of Rida, 1865–1935* (New York: Columbia University Press, 2019).

29. In his study of the Babylonian Talmud, Mouli Vidas argues that "quotation is 'destructive' and 'aggressive' in the sense that is destroys continuity. Applied to the Talmud, the transformation of tradition into quotations disrupts the chain of tradition" (*Tradition and the Formation of the Talmud* [Princeton, NJ: Princeton University Press, 2014], 15).

30. On pre-modern Islamic embodiment, see Rudolph T. Ware III, *The Walking Qurʾan: Islamic Education, Embodied Knowledge and History in West Africa* (Chapel Hill, NC: University of North Carolina Press, 2014), 7–9.

styles of dress and facial hair, and as both Salafi men and women observe gender segregation, they collectively use their bodies to reference what they understand to be the Prophetic model. A focus on social practice—and the way that bodies are used to cite Muhammad's model in novel fashion—may appear to be a counterintuitive approach to the study of an Islamic movement that distinguishes itself through its commitment to continuity with the past. Yet, I argue that it is precisely by turning Salafism's normative paradigm on its head that one can trace not merely how this movement emerged but also how it shapes and is shaped by the world around it.

THEOLOGY, LAW, AND POLITICS

In his groundbreaking *The Making of Salafism: Islamic Reform in the 20th Century*, Henri Lauzière charted the development of the term Salafism (*al-Salafiyya*) as referring not only to a specific approach to theology (a neo-Hanbali view of the attributes of God held by scholars such as Ibn Taymiyya, d. 1328), but also to a commitment to deriving law exclusively from the Quran and Sunna. In doing so, Lauzière challenged the widespread use of this label to describe Islamic modernist thinkers such as Jamal al-Din al-Afghani (d. 1897) and Muhammad ʿAbduh (d. 1905), an approach which pivoted on the inaccurate claim that these figures used this term to describe their approach to Islamic reform.[31] This argument has been met with furious responses by scholars who argue that "Salafism" remains a valuable analytical framework for understanding disparate religious approaches.[32]

In this work, however, I follow Lauzière's definition of Salafism, as well as his use of the adjective "Purist" to describe groups such as Ansar al-Sunna, as distinct from those who embraced "balanced reform" (*al-iṣlāḥ al-muʿtadil*),

31. Lauzière, *The Making of Salafism*, 18, 40–49.

32. For example, see Frank Griffel, "What Do We Mean By 'Salafī'?: Connecting Muḥammad ʿAbduh with Egypt's Nūr Party in Islam's Contemporary Intellectual History," *Die Welt des Islams* 55, no. 2 (2015): 186–220; Henri Lauzière, "Rejoinder: What We Mean Versus What They Meant by 'Salafi': A Reply to Frank Griffel," *Die Welt des Islams* 56, no. 1 (2016): 89–96; and Frank Griffel, "Rejoinder: What is the Task of the Intellectual (Contemporary) Historian?—A Response to Henri Lauzière's 'Reply,'" *Die Welt des Islams* 56, no. 2 (2016): 249–55. Also see Itzchak Weismann, "New and Old Perspectives in the Study of Salafism," *Bustan* 8, no. 1 (2017): 22–37.

such as the Muslim Brotherhood.[33] I further qualify the category of Purist with "Quietist" when discussing groups such as Ansar al-Sunna or scholars such as Muhammad Nasir al-Din al-Albani (d. 1999), who abstained from formal participation in politics or explicit critique of ruling regimes.[34] Finally, in focusing on social practice, I draw on Bernard Haykel's observation that

> Salafis are first and foremost religious and social reformers who are engaged in creating and reproducing particular forms of authority and identity, both personal and community. . . . [They] are determined to create a distinct Muslim subjectivity . . . with profound social and political implications.[35]

It is precisely because of the linkage between the individual and the collective that communication is central to Salafism (and to other modern social movements). The Salafi subject, male and female, is thus produced out of the discourse that this community both transmits and performs.

I further place Salafis within a broader category of "Neo-Traditionalist" movements. In the field of Islamic Studies, "Traditionalist" generally refers either to scholars who remain committed to established schools of Islamic law[36] or to adherents of the Hanbali school and, before them, Ahl al-Hadith (not to be conflated with the South Asian Salafi movement Ahl-i Hadith).[37] "Neo-Traditionalist" not only avoids confusion with these groups, but also emphasizes the rupture—conceptual and chronological—in this claim to

33. Lauzière, *The Making of Salafism*, 40–49.

34. Jan Peter-Hartung has challenged the use of "Political Quietism" as an antonym of "Religious Activism." In its stead, he argues for the use of an alternative contrast: "governance-orientation" vs. "guidance-orientation." This alternative formulation expresses a focus on state or society, rather than an engagement or lack thereof with politics. While I retain the term Quietist, my use of this term is consistent with this critique. See Jan Peter-Hartung, "Making Sense of 'Political Quietism': An Analytical Intervention," in *Political Quietism in Islam: Sunni and Shi'i Perspectives*, ed. Sarhan al-Saud (London: I. B. Tauris, 2020), 23.

35. Haykel, "On the Nature of Salafi Thought and Action," 34–35.

36. Jonathan A. C. Brown, *The Canonization of al-Bukhārī and Muslim: The Formation and Function of the Sunnī Ḥadīth Canon* (Leiden: Brill, 2007), 305. Brown describes Salafis as either "Modernists" or "Traditionalists." His definition of Traditionalist Salafis, however, is not consistent with Lauzière's conceptual history of the term, including figures who preceded the twentieth century, most notably Ibn ʿAbd al-Wahhab, Muhammad b. Ismaʿil al-Sanʿani, and Jamal al-Din al-Qasimi, as well as figures like al-Albani who emerged later (see 309–34).

37. For example, see Ahmed El Shamsy, *The Canonization of Islamic Law: A Social and Intellectual History* (Cambridge, UK: Cambridge University Press, 2013), 195–201.

tradition.[38] Like their competitors for religious authority, Salafis make a claim to authenticity (Arabic: *aṣāla*). Unlike their middle-class and self-consciously modern *efendi*[39] counterparts who offered a "local modernity grounded in and organically linked to 'authentic' roots" in early twentieth-century Egypt,[40] Salafi authenticity pivots on a categorical rejection of modernity. Put differently, Salafis claim continuity with the ideas and practices of the first three generations of the Muslim community, while seeking to sidestep the transformations of modernity in which they are inextricably enmeshed.

The Salafi approach to piety also depends on the rejection of race as a category. Recent ethnographic scholarship has emphasized Salafi efforts to make clear that racial origin has no bearing on one's capacity for piety.[41] Yet, even if members of this movement were to transcend a tendency towards ethnic division that is evident in Muslim-majority and Muslim-minority contexts alike,[42] it remains the case that the Salafi call to deracialized piety in an age of ethno-nationalism—whether territorial or Pan-Arab—responds to and is shaped by nationalist claims that ethnicity constitutes a primary basis for identity. Furthermore, the Salafi movement glorifies skills, most notably a command of classical Arabic and knowledge of Arabic-language scholarship, which disproportionately privilege the members of a particular ethno-linguistic community.

Definitional questions regarding Salafism, however, remain. The Salafi claim to worship God is often conflated with the state-sponsored religious project of Saudi Arabia, known as Wahhabism, Wahhabi-Hanbalism, or the

38. For a similar approach, see Adis Duderija, *Constructing a Religiously Ideal 'Believer' and 'Woman' in Islam: Neo-Traditionalist Salafi and Progressive Muslims' Methods of Interpretation* (New York: Palgrave Macmillan, 2011), 49–50.

39. While this term should technically be transliterated *afandī*, I follow the commonly used version of *Efendi*.

40. Lucie Ryzova, *The Age of the Efendiyya: Passages to Modernity in National-Colonial Egypt* (Oxford: Oxford University Press, 2014), 3. Also see Walter Armbrust, *Mass Culture and Modernism in Egypt* (Cambridge, UK: Cambridge University Press, 1996), 22–23.

41. Joel Blecher and Josh Dubler, "Overlooking Race and Secularism in Muslim Philadelphia," in *Race and Secularism in America*, ed. Vincent Lloyd and Jonathan S. Kahn (New York: Columbia University Press, 2016), 134–40; Anabel Inge, *The Making of a Salafi Muslim Woman* (Oxford: Oxford University Press, 2016), 201.

42. For example, see *Inside Mecca* (New York: National Geographic, 2006).

"Najdi Call" (*al-Daʿwa al-Najdiyya*).[43] While these approaches share a theological vision that was consolidated by and transmitted through the Hanbali *madhhab*, they differ on the influence of this legal tradition and its relative weight vis-à-vis proof texts from the Quran and Sunna.[44] If we are to understand Salafism within the post-1920 conceptual history of this term, then the theological approach that it shares with the Hanbali *madhhab* is secondary to a distinctly Salafi legal approach of deriving all law from the Quran and Sunna.[45] Put differently, while figures such as Muhammad b. ʿAbd al-Wahhab

43. Although Wagemakers acknowledges legal differences regarding *ijtihād* and *taqlid* between Wahhabis and non-Wahhabi Salafis, he argues that "Salafism represented the international trends whose adherents claim to emulate the *salaf* as strictly and in as many spheres of life as possible, while Wahhabism is its Najdi version, being (at least initially) more local than Salafism and also perhaps somewhat less tolerant" (*Salafism in Jordan*, 34). Similarly, Michael Farquhar situates Wahhabi-Hanbalism within a "broader Salafi tradition," though he does note its commitment to the rulings of the Hanbali school (*Circuits of Faith*, 6–7). Similarly, Raihan Ismail states that the Kingdom of Saudi Arabia "has long been an advocate of Salafism and is responsible for the spread of Salafi ideals throughout the Muslim world" (*Rethinking Salafism*, 2). Finally, Masooda Bano merges the two concepts, embracing the term "Salafi-Wahhabi" ("Introduction," in *Salafi Social and Political Movements: National and Transnational Contexts*, ed. Masooda Bano [Edinburgh, UK: Edinburgh University Press, 2021], 13). While I acknowledge the theological overlap between Wahhabi-Hanbali scholars and their Salafi counterparts, as well as the late-twentieth century effort by the former group to lay claim to the mantle of Salafism, I consider the Wahhabi-Hanbali commitment to previous rulings of the Hanbali school and regular use of interpretative tools such as "the common good" (*al-maṣlaḥa al-ʿāmma*) and "blocking the pretexts of sin" (*sadd al-dharīʿāt*) as distinguishing them from Purist Salafis.

44. Cole Bunzel argues that, early in his career, Ibn ʿAbd al-Wahhab considered a more thorough critique of the legal schools by rejecting the typology of water for ritual purification. See "Manifest Enmity: The Origins, Development, and Persistence of Classical Wahhābism (1153–1351/1741–1932" (Ph.D. diss, Princeton University, 2018), 38–40. More recently, Wahhabi-Hanbali scholars have argued that the eponym of the Hanbali school, Ahmad b. Hanbal, derived all his rulings from the Quran and Sunna in an attempt to buttress their claim to Salafism. See David Commins, "From Wahhabi to Salafi," in *Saudi Arabia in Transition: Insights on Social, Political, Economic and Religious Change*, ed. Bernard Haykel, Thomas Hegghammer, and Stéphane Lacroix (Cambridge, UK: Cambridge University Press, 2015), 161–63.

45. I am consciously making this distinction between Salafis and those committed to particular legal schools in conceptual terms, in line with Lauzière, rather than as a statement of consistent legal methodology. On the latter front, see Emad Hamdeh, "Qurʾan and Sunna or the *Madhhabs*?: A Salafi Polemic Against Islamic Legal Tradition," *Islamic Law and Society* 24, no. 3 (2017): 211–53.

(d. 1792) and the Yemeni Muhammad al-Shawkani (d. 1834) are indisputably "Salafi in theology" (*Salafī al-ʿAqīda*, that is, belonging to *Madhhab al-Salaf*), they are not Salafi in the dual theological/legal meaning of the term that developed in the twentieth century. Conversely, it is problematic to use this theological overlap to construct a "big tent" of the Salafi tradition in which Wahhabi-Hanbalism is a prominent player.[46]

One must also distinguish these two groups from the proponents of "balanced reform" (*al-iṣlāḥ al-muʿtadil*) who claimed the term Salafism in the 1930s and 1940s. While some members of this trend shared a commitment to neo-Hanbali theology (that is, they defined themselves as *Salafī al-ʿAqīda*), others did not.[47] In the interest of clarity, I will refer to such individuals as Islamic Modernists in this book, while acknowledging, *pace* Lauzière, that in the 1930s and 1940s, the line between Islamic Modernism and Purist Salafism remained permeable.

MODERN ISLAM BETWEEN RUPTURE AND DISCURSIVE CONTINUITY

Over the past four decades, the study of Modern Islam has been divided between two major trends, the first of which emphasized ruptures within Muslim intellectual, social and cultural life, while the second argued for the continued integrity and, for some, primacy of a distinctly Islamic discursive tradition of ethics. In the former case, historians and anthropologists alike have highlighted the ways in which the political, economic and social forces associated with modernity reordered Muslim-majority societies as varied as those of Egypt and Yemen,[48] a

46. A focus on relationship to the legal schools helps us to distinguish not merely between Salafism and Wahhabi-Hanbalism, but also, in the Saudi case, to clarify the existence of a Salafi minority within a broader Wahhabi-Hanbali majority. By way of example, ʿAbd al-ʿAziz b. Baz, Muhammad b. al-ʿUthaymin and ʿAbd al-Razzaq al-ʿAfifi, though prominent, are also an interpretative minority in the Saudi religious establishment. As David Commins notes, however, Wahhabi-Hanbalis have laid increasingly claim to the term "Salafism" since the 1970s (see "From Wahhabi to Salafi," 161–65).

47. Lauzière, *The Making of Salafism*, 40–41.

48. Most notably, see Brinkley Messick, *The Calligraphic State: Textual Domination and History in a Muslim Society* (Berkeley: University of California Press, 1992); Timothy Mitchell, *Colonising Egypt* (Berkeley: University of California Press, 1988); Gregory Starrett, "The Hexis

shift that would only grow more significant with the spread of mass and small media.[49]

It is the latter approach to the study of Modern Islam, however, that has become axiomatic. First articulated in a landmark 1986 article, "The Idea of the Anthropology of Islam," anthropologist Talal Asad's conceptualization of multiple Islamic discursive traditions provided the analytical space for tracing continuity, rather than merely rupture, in Islamic forms of reasoning and debate.[50] Asad then expanded on and refined this approach in his 1994 *Genealogies of Religion* and 2003 *Formations of the Secular.* While the first book pushed back against a view of modernity that made non-Western peoples into objects of Western-driven change,[51] the second challenged debates over Islam's alleged relationship to terrorism and incompatibility with democracy.[52] In *Formations of the Secular,* Asad also traces an Islamic ethical tradition centered on embodied practice.[53] Building on Asad's theoretical interventions, Saba Mahmood, Charles Hirschkind, and Hussein Ali Agrama have each argued

of Interpretation: Islam and the Body in the Egyptian Popular School," *American Ethnologist* 22, no. 4 (1995): 953–69; Gregory Starrett, *Putting Islam to Work: Education, Politics and Religious Transformation in Egypt* (Berkeley: University of California Press, 1998). Messick's second book (*Shari'a Scripts,* 2018), however, shifts emphasis to tracing the continued vitality of the Islamic discursive tradition and situates itself squarely within the Asadian approach. Still other scholars acknowledged the significance of these ruptures yet sought to make the case for the persistence of traditional forms of knowledge and authority. See Richard Antoun, *Muslim Preacher in the Modern World: A Jordanian Case Study in Comparative Perspective* (Princeton, NJ: Princeton University Press, 1989); Patrick Gaffney, *The Prophet's Pulpit: Islamic Preaching in Contemporary Egypt* (Berkeley: University of California Press, 1994); Gaffney, "The Changing Voices of Islam: The Emergence of Professional Preachers in Contemporary Egypt," *Muslim World* 81, no. 1 (1991): 27–47; and Jakob Skovgaard-Petersen, *Defining Islam for the Egyptian State: Muftis and Fatwas of the Dār Al-Iftā* (Leiden: Brill, 1997).

49. See Dale Eickelman and James Piscatori, *Muslim Politics* (Princeton, NJ: Princeton University Press, 2004); Dale Eickelman and Jon W. Anderson, *New Media in the Muslim World: The Emerging Public Sphere* (Bloomington: Indiana University Press, 2003).

50. Talal Asad, "The Idea of an Anthropology of Islam" (Washington, DC: Georgetown University Center for Contemporary Arab Studies, 1986).

51. Talal Asad, *Genealogies of Religion: Discipline and Reasons of Power in Christianity and Islam* (Baltimore, MD: Johns Hopkins University Press, 1994), 1–5.

52. Talal Asad, *Formations of the Secular: Christianity, Islam, Modernity* (Stanford, CA: Stanford University Press, 2003), 5–11.

53. Asad, *Formations of the Secular,* 249–51.

for the existence and continued relevance of a discursive Islamic tradition of ethical formation.[54]

As they argued for the continued centrality of a discursive Islamic tradition of ethics in late-twentieth-century Egypt, Mahmood and Hirschkind engaged with Islamic institutions and communities distinguished by a Salafi orientation.[55] In *The Politics of Piety,* Mahmood argues for a discursive tradition of Islamic ethics in which Muslims act on their bodies through exegesis of Islamic texts as well as through ritual practice with the *telos* of living in accordance with the Prophet Muhammad's example.[56] By way of complement, in *The Ethical Soundscape,* Hirschkind explores a discursive tradition of ethical listening derived from "classical Islamic moral doctrine"[57] and highlights the significance of the "undisciplined discipline" of cassette tape listening in modern Islamic ethics.[58]

Crucially, although they each acknowledge the influence of contemporary conditions,[59] such conditions do not appear to impinge upon, let alone structure, the basic logic of piety. For example, Mahmood argues that "Piety activists seek to imbue each of the various spheres of contemporary life with a

54. Hussein Ali Agrama, *Questioning Secularism: Islam, Sovereignty and the Rule of Law in Modern Egypt* (Chicago, IL: University of Chicago Press, 2012); Hirschkind, *The Ethical Soundscape;* Mahmood, *The Politics of Piety.* In particular, Agrama argues for the persistence of an "asecular" space within al-Azhar's Fatwa Council (*Questioning Secularism,* 186–87). For Agrama's use of the concept of a discursive tradition, see *Questioning Secularism,* 43–45.

55. Neither Mahmood nor Hirschkind specifically acknowledge studying Salafi movements yet, based on the contents of their work, it appears that the members of such movements significantly overlapped with those individuals with whom each engaged. Specifically, Mahmood describes Ansar al-Sunna, the Jam'iyya Shar'iyya and Da'wat al-Haqq as "Islamic nonprofit organizations," while Hirschkind classifies the first two groups as "Islamic charitable associations." Although there is considerable debate as to the Jam'iyya Shar'iyya's Salafi credentials, the other two groups understand themselves and are understood by others to sit squarely within the Egyptian Salafi movement. See Mahmood, *The Politics of Piety,* 72, and Hirschkind, *The Ethical Soundscape,* 57.

56. Mahmood, *The Politics of Piety,* 30–31.

57. Hirschkind, *The Ethical Soundscape,* 74–78.

58. Hirschkind, *The Ethical Soundscape,* 83–85.

59. Mahmood notes the significance of "contemporary social and historical conditions" (*The Politics of Piety,* 117) while Hirschkind situates the auditory practices of the Islamic Revival within a "social and political context increasingly shaped by modern structures on secular governance, on the one hand, and by styles of consumption and culture linked to a mass media of global extension, on the other" (*The Ethical Soundscape,* 9).

regulative sensibility that takes its cue from the Islamic theological corpus rather than from modern secular ethics."[60] Although neither framed Salafism as the object of ethnographic analysis and the piety movement in Egypt far exceeds the ranks of those who identify as Salafi, the significance of Salafi organizations and sites to both studies is inescapable. Yet, I argue, in contrast to Mahmood, that the "regulative sensibility" of Salafism emerges primarily from outside, rather than with, the discursive Islamic tradition which she identifies.

My argument regarding the regulative sensibility of Salafi practice centers on visibility. In their studies, both Mahmood and Hirschkind placed visual signification as a secondary rather than primary consideration, an approach that reflects a longer anthropological debate over the utility of symbolic ethnographic analysis.[61] Most explicitly, Mahmood observes that:

> [A] key line of fracture between the piety movement (of which the mosque movement is an integral part) and Islamist political organizations . . . [is that] for Islamists . . . religious ritual should be aimed towards the larger goal of creating a certain kind of polity, and the mosque movement fails precisely to make this linkage, keeping matters of worship and piety incarcerated within what for them is a privatized world of worship.[62]

60. Mahmood, *The Politics of Piety*, 47.

61. As Clifford Geertz, a prominent proponent of this approach, declared, "Culture . . . is public, like a burlesqued wink or a mock sheep raid" ("Thick Description: Toward an Interpretative Theory of Culture," in *The Interpretation of Cultures: Selected Essays by Clifford Geertz* [New York: Basic Books, 1973], 10). For critiques of this approach, see Asad, *Genealogies of Religion*, 55–82, esp. 73–77; Catherine Bell, *Ritual Theory, Ritual Practice* (Oxford: Oxford University Press, 1992), 182–96; and Daniel Martin Varisco, *Islam Obscured: The Rhetoric of Anthropological Representation* (New York: Palgrave Macmillan, 2005), 21–52. On the longer history of symbolic reading, see Aria Nakissa, *The Anthropology of Islamic Law: Education, Ethics, and Legal Interpretation at Egypt's al-Azhar* (Oxford: Oxford University Press, 2019), 25–27. Building on Geertz, Nakissa proposes "that it is useful to treat the Islamic tradition as, in part, a system of 'signs' (i.e., symbols) . . . [yet] breaks from the existing scholarship by conceptualizing signs as effects of mental attributes" (34). Nakissa's interest in symbols, however, derives from the relationship between internal and external states, rather than the latter's communicative function (91–122).

62. Mahmood, *The Politics of Piety*, 52–53. Two core issues that recur in critiques of Geertz's approach relate to the way that symbolic analysis obscures how power produces symbols, and that such an approach assumes particular internal states based on external signs. Mahmood's claim here also expands on an earlier critique of what she understood to be Gregory Starrett's "evaluation [of] the body largely as a signifying medium that can be read differently by

In parallel, Hirschkind's lack of engagement with visible practice stems from his challenge to ocular-centric understandings of modern Islam; accordingly, he argues that "taped sermons . . . now constitute a new signifying practice, one oriented to the emergent forms of ethical and political community being forged by the Islamic Revival."[63] For Hirschkind, publicly observable behavior, what he terms "ethical sociability," constitutes a reflection of an internal state rather than a mode of social performance and the relevant signification is auditory, not visual.[64]

In contrast to Mahmood and Hirschkind, my approach to Islamic piety generally and Salafism in particular begins not within a discursive tradition of Islamic ethics, but rather in late-nineteenth-century Egypt. In his 1988 book *Colonising Egypt,* Timothy Mitchell explored the disciplinary mechanisms of colonial power in Egypt during the latter period, emphasizing how colonial influence and later rule introduced new models of spatial order, whether in schools, the army, or in the countryside. Collectively, these processes facilitated a government effort to better organize and thus control the population in the service of political quiescence, revenue extraction, and military conscription.[65] This project also introduced two conceptual shifts that proved central to the emergence of Salafism, as well as other Islamic and non-Islamic movements: a "politics of the self" (*al-siyāsa al-dhātiyya*) dependent on indi-

---

different sociopolitical actors in accord with their ideological interests. . . ." Instead, she argues for understanding "the body and its behavioral forms not only in its capacity as a signifying medium, but also as a tool for becoming a certain kind of person and attaining certain kinds of states." Even the secondary focus on signification, however, falls away in *The Politics of Piety.* See Saba Mahmood, "Rehearsed Spontaneity and the Conventionality of Ritual: Disciplines of Salat," *American Ethnologist* 28, no. 4 (2001): 837. The claim that Mahmood attributes to Starrett, however, is not precisely the argument that he made, with the latter centered on the ways in which the significance of embodied religious practices was reconfigured between colonial and post-colonial rule. See Starrett, "The Hexis of Interpretation," especially 954–62.

63. Hirschkind, *The Ethical Soundscape,* 10.

64. Hirschkind, *The Ethical Soundscape,* 130–32.

65. Mitchell, *Colonising Egypt.* Neither was the process analyzed by Mitchell distinct to Egypt: both Benedict Anderson (Indonesia) and James Scott (Germany and France) have argued for a linkage between the expanded power of the modern state and the centrality of visible representation to the regulation of territory and the individual citizen alike. See Anderson, *Imagined Communities,* 163–86, and James C. Scott, *Seeing Like a State: How Certain Schemes To Improve the Human Condition Have Failed* (New Haven, CT: Yale University Press, 1998), 9–84.

vidual hygiene, education, and discipline[66] on the one hand, and the abstraction of authority, expressed through the association of particular uniforms with state power, on the other.[67] While cognizant of the limits of a Geertzian symbolic reading to cast light on internal states, my claim to the centrality of visibility to Salafi practice derives from the argument, elaborated in chapter 1, as to the centrality of visibility to modern social movements and the related necessity of the observable performance of ethical positions.[68] In telling the history of Salafi practices of piety, I give greater weight to the contemporary conditions acknowledged by both Mahmood and Hirschkind, while also taking seriously the limits of a discursive traditions approach for framing the development of Salafism.[69]

An emphasis on a "politics of the self," on the abstraction of authority through symbols, and on the legacies of colonial rule is not a claim that the pre-modern Islamic tradition (or discursive Islamic traditions that drew from it) lacked expectations of public comportment that often depended on visible identification. Pre modern models of comportment (*adab*) set forth broad expectations of appropriate behavior, whether relations with one's parents and neighbors, etiquette within the mosque, or how to engage in acts as mundane as eating or sneezing,[70] part and parcel of a broader project of cultivating a virtuous individual and, by extension, a virtuous collective.[71] Visible practices also served to distinguish Muslims from Jews and Christians, most famously

66. Mitchell, *Colonising Egypt*, 104.

67. Mitchell, *Colonising Egypt*, 37–40.

68. Such as emphasis on the visible does not preclude engagement with the ways in which power is used to construct orthodoxy, nor does it assume public symbols to be unequivocal indications of internal states.

69. As Junaid Quadri notes in his recent book, "the sustainability and ongoing relevance of the concept of tradition demands drawing distinctions between a given tradition and other streams of thought—often traditions in their own right—as well as an account of when that given tradition ceases to be one. . . . Ḥanafism of the late nineteenth and early twentieth centuries experienced a shift from . . . a tradition-guided enquiry to one informed by key presuppositions of modernity: a progressivist history, a scientistic ontology and epistemology, and a new conception of religion" (*Transformations of Tradition*, 12–13).

70. Katharina Anna Ivanyi, *Virtue, Piety and the Law: A Study of Birgivī Meḥmed Efendī's al-Ṭarīqa al-muḥammadiyya* (Leiden: Brill, 2020), 116–59; Megan Reid, *Law and Piety in Medieval Islam* (Cambridge, UK: Cambridge University Press, 2013).

71. Zahra Ayubi, *Gendered Morality: Classical Islamic Ethics of the Self, Family and Society* (New York: Columbia University Press, 2019), 187–200.

in the "distinguishing signs" (*ghiyār*) code promulgated under the rule of the Caliph ʿUmar b. ʿAbd al-ʿAziz (r. 99–101/717–20).[72] Finally, Muslim jurists expressed concern regarding "dissimulation" or "sanctimonious behavior" (*al-riyāʾ*) in which the individual embellishes religious practice in order to attract attention.[73] The late nineteenth century, however, saw the diffusion of a distinctly modern logic of social life in which personal practice could pose a threat to an abstraction known as "society," and by which particular practices signified belonging not only to a particular religious community but also to a broader religio-political project.

The significance of the body to the formation of communities, religious and non-religious, extends beyond comportment and social identity. As media scholar Bernadette Wegenstein argues, the body has historically served as a site of "inscription" through practices as varied as jewelry, cosmetics and masks.[74] The body's communicative power stems not merely from its availability to all, but also from the process of "naturalization that makes one's own embodiment seem 'natural' and the style of embodiment characteristic of different historical periods comparatively alien."[75] A crucial shift of modernity, in turn, lies in not only state efforts to form the individual subject, but also in the ways that "[t]he medium of the body becomes the subject's own vehicle for communicating gender, age, class . . . [and] religion. . . ."[76]

The formation of distinct communities also depends on bodily imitation. In his study of communication in the long nineteenth century, sociologist

72. Milka Levy-Rubin, *Non-Muslims in the Early Islamic Empire: From Surrender to Co-Existence* (Cambridge, UK: Cambridge University Press, 2011), 88–96, 154–57.

73. Ivanyi, *Virtue, Piety and the Law*, 189–92. On the criticism of medieval Muslim preachers for feigning tears, see Linda G. Jones, "'He Cried and Made Others Cry': Crying as a Sign of Pietistic Authenticity or Deception in Islamic Preaching," in *Crying in the Middle Ages*, ed. Elina Gertsman (London: Routledge, 2012), 104. I wish to thank Yasmin Moll for this citation.

74. Bernadette Wegenstein, "Body," in *Critical Terms for Media Studies*, ed. W. J. T. Mitchell and M. Hansen (Chicago: University of Chicago Press, 2010), 20.

75. Wegenstein, "Body," 22.

76. Wegenstein, "Body," 24. Wegenstein's observation holds true for Islamic movements, too. As Shenila Khoja-Moojli argues in the case of the Taliban, "In the absence of territory . . . bodies become the landscape onto which Taliban sovereign power is etched" (*Sovereign Attachments: Masculinity, Muslimness, and Affective Politics in Pakistan* [Berkeley: University of California Press, 2021], 103). Khoja-Moojli further argues that "Sartorial practices become a way for the Taliban to tie themselves to the Prophetic example and visually assert authentic Muslimness" (110).

Armand Mattelart cites the writings of Gabriel Tarde (d. 1904), a French scholar of crowd psychology:

> Imitation is a social bond; any social relation, any social fact, is a relation of imitation. It is what makes a society into a "group of people who present among themselves many similarities produced by imitation or counterimitation." There are many varieties of imitation: imitation by custom, by fashion, by sympathy or obedience, through training or upbringing; it can be naïve or thoughtful. Imitation cannot be conceived without invention and individual initiative . . . [yet] one of the fundamental laws of imitation is that it functions from top to bottom, from the center to the periphery.[77]

Tarde's invocation of imitation as a conscious and even inventive form underscores the centrality of visual communication to social practice, as well as the structural tension between reproducibility and local performance.

Media is central to both the diffusion of distinct models of public performance and to the creation of a broader modern public that understands itself as bound to engage in particular practices of imitation. Citing Mattelart, anthropologist Emilio Spadola argues that, for reformist movements who sought to reshape national communities through the articulation of particular understandings of society, the "communicative networking of a national territory would guarantee not only its political-economic unity, but more importantly, the very possibility of the social, that is, the *moral-spiritual* coherence of its citizens as a collective."[78] This aspirational vision of "moral-spiritual coherence," in turn, could only be preserved through communication. As Spadola notes with regard to twentieth-century Morocco:

> [Mass media] established novel conditions by which to judge what *constituted* apt performance. The forming and *performing* of unified national societies were inseparable in nationalist and reformist Muslim politics. Nationalists' concern with mass communicative spread of underclass Sufi performances concerned, literally, a public *image* of Morocco.[79]

77. Armand Mattelart, *The Invention of Communication*, trans. Susan Emanuel (Minneapolis: University of Minnesota Press, 1996), 254–55. Mattelart does not specify, however, whether Tarde is discussing crowds or publics in this instance.

78. Mattelart, *The Invention of Communication*, 26, and Emilio Spadola, "The Call of Communication: Mass Media and Reform in Interwar Morocco," in *Middle Eastern and North African Societies in the Interwar Period*, ed. Kate Fleet and Ebru Boyar (Leiden: Brill, 2018), 108.

79. Spadola, "The Call of Communication," 119–20. As Spadola notes in his 2014 monograph, "[T]he reformist interpretation of piety as a function of communication, of subjectivity

The spread of media, particularly print, facilitated not merely the greater standardization of social practice in the service of a particular vision of society, but also the conceptual shift that acts could be praised or denigrated primarily based on the public message that they communicated. These assumptions undergird the reconceptualization of social practice as a form of public performance that reflects particular ideological commitments.[80]

In this book, I analyze Salafism as a reformist movement that is grounded in both the possibility and necessity of communication through visible signs.[81] In analyzing how Salafism is shaped by the forces of modernity, I understand the latter concept to contain three intertwined dimensions: 1) a set of material and perceptual conditions; 2) a historically-specific reform project shared by Salafis and secular nationalists; and 3) a focus on communication as an ethical hinge point between individual piety and collective reform. In unpacking the first, I emphasize the material conditions of a powerful centralizing state, mass media (particularly print), and mass urban society alongside the perceptual conditions of both anonymity and visibility within a horizontal society.[82]

---

as receptivity to the proper call, is an effect of distinctly modern mass mediation. . . . The promise of mass-mediated communications as the realization of community, however, generates its own conflicts. From the earliest nationalist efforts to the present, this imaginary has refigured prior or opposing ritual practices as themselves communicative acts and more precisely as competing calls generating divergent subjects. Islamic exorcists, for all their oppositional logic, share with Sufi nationalists and the state a mass-mediated desire for uniform or orderly practice within a field of the call defined by national 'society'" (*The Calls of Islam*, 120). Max Weiss makes a related argument about how the "publicity" of religious practice shapes their performance. See Weiss, *In the Shadow of Sectarianism*, 61-2, 87-91.

80. On the mediatization of Islam more broadly, see Ian Vandermeulen, "Electrosonic Statecraft: Technology, Authority, and Latency on Moroccan Qur'ānic Radio," *American Ethnologist* 48, no. 1 (2021): 80–92, and Yasmin Moll, "The Idea of Islamic Media: The Qur'an and the Decolonization of Mass Communication," *International Journal of Middle East Studies* 52 (2020): 623–42.

81. Spadola, *The Calls of Islam*, 127. Here, I also build on Starrett's 1995 argument that "the em-bodying of ideology is in part an explicit, public, and discursive process, not merely an unconscious and practical one" ("The Hexis of Interpretation," 964).

82. This is not to suggest that all social spaces in the pre-modern period yielded easy identification, or that all social spaces in the modern period are anonymous. Instead, it is to note the structural shift, linked to broader trends of urbanization and employment, in which men and women's daily routines increasingly came to involve passing through public spaces—such as mass transportation and crowded streets—in which the majority of the individuals whom they encountered did not know them as individuals, let alone their connection to particular genealogical networks.

Regarding the second, I argue that Salafism is shaped by a distinctly modern conceptual vision of reform of individual subjects for the sake of a broader whole that is governable at the level of the individual and visible both horizontally (to fellow members) and to those in positions of leadership (whether that of the state or that of Salafi movements). The call (*daʿwa*) to emulate the Prophet Muhammad is necessarily transmitted and received within the communicative space of mass society.

Finally, in a social order that foregrounds visibility, ethics, too, must be observable. In contrast to the discursive tradition approach, which would categorize such forms of visibility as a form of instrumentalism, I read embodiment as a mode of communication that models a commitment to the *telos* of living like the Prophet Muhammad through a visual register. My argument is not that Salafis make a conscious decision to emphasize visible signs; rather, it is that modernity's material conditions make ethics and visibility inseparable. Specifically, as I will argue in the second chapter, the Salafi conception of worship (*ʿibāda*) brings visible daily practice under the control of the individual who orients his or her life to the worship of God. Yet, the power of such practices to facilitate ethical rectitude and the public signaling of virtue is far from assured. Instead, to quote Wilson Chacko Jacob's study of masculinity in late-nineteenth- and early-twentieth-century Egypt, each performance "poses the risk of communicative and pedagogical failure. . . ."[83] Visible performance is thus a potent form of social activism whose basic medium also poses the continued risk of miscommunication.

In Egypt, the Salafi project of communication emerged in the shadow of the state's twentieth-century efforts to lay claim to citizens' bodies—whether through school, the media, or the government bureaucracy—in a manner that assumed that these bodies must signal or distort a particular nationalist project. On the religious front, the Ministry of Endowments (*Wizārat al-Awqāf*) and al-Azhar University and its nationwide network of institutes (*maʿāhid*) loomed large in Egypt, yet equally important is the role played by the Ministry of Education (*Wizārat al-Tarbiyya waʾl-Taʿlīm*) in transmitting a model of pious nationalism to hundreds of thousands of Egyptian students yearly.[84] These state-sponsored efforts of religious regulation collectively defined the arena in which religious contestation took place in twentieth-century Egypt.

83. Jacob, *Working Out Egypt*, 6.

84. Starrett, "The Hexis of Interpretation," 960–62.

In the face of a state claim to its citizens' bodies, Ansar al-Sunna has focused on sustained contestation of "cultural codes."[85] In contradiction to the Muslim Brotherhood's highly structured system of internal organization and regulation, this is a project that is undergirded less by particular organizational structures than by a shared social world of prominent scholars, mosques, and periodicals. In line with this scholarship that emphasizes the informality of Salafi networks in which teacher-student relationships are at least as significant as organizational membership,[86] I focus on social practices that neither depend on nor directly reflect formal membership in a group such as Ansar al-Sunna. Instead, I see Salafism as a diffuse movement that is united by shared debates and practices, while it is spearheaded and regulated by religious elites through their control over periodicals, mosques, and affiliated branches.

Two methodological qualifications are necessary. First, although the Salafi movement is transnational, I have made the methodological decision to center this study on Egypt. This choice reflects Egypt's historical significance to the Salafi movement,[87] the availability of print media from this country, and the existence of sources representing alternative ideological voices (most notably from competing Islamic movements such as the Muslim Brotherhood and the Jamʿiyya Sharʿiyya) that can be used to critically read and contextualize Salafi periodicals. In sum, this is a story of the emergence of transnational Salafism's signature practices from the vantage point of a key center. While an alternative geographic base such as Syria, Yemen or Saudi Arabia could hypothetically yield an alternative story, the extent to which consensus on Salafi social practices emerges transnationally suggests that such a story would not be radically different. Second, this work is primarily one of intellectual, rather than social, history. While I follow historians of Islam by reading fatwa

85. In order to accurately describe Ansar al-Sunna, I modify Sidney Tarrow's definition of social movements as "characteristically mount[ing] *contentious* challenges through disruptive direct action against elites, authorities, other groups, or cultural codes" (*Power in Movement: Social Movements and Contentious Politics* [New York: Cambridge University Press, 2011], 9–12, quotation at 9).

86. Gauvain, *Salafi Ritual Purity*, 34–35.

87. The inaccurate historical claim that Salafism emerges in Egypt in the 1970s in part due to Saudi oil money and that it lacks an institutional infrastructure persists despite significant evidence—including Ansar al-Sunna's existence for over four decades—to the contrary. For example, see Nakissa, *The Anthropology of Islamic Law*, 261.

requests critically,[88] Salafi periodicals generally lack rich letters-to-the-editor sections that would allow a more comprehensive social history.[89]

CHAPTER OVERVIEW

My argument unfolds across six chapters. I begin by situating the emergence of Salafism within two crucial developments of the nineteenth century: efforts by the Egyptian state to promote models of subjectivity that privileged visibility and the rediscovery of early texts of the Islamic legal tradition through the linked spread of print and literacy during this period. Pushing back against the assumption, often implicit, that Salafism emerged either directly out of a defined Islamic legal corpus *or* primarily in competition with other Islamic movements, I trace the material and perceptual shifts that shaped not only Salafism but also its Islamist and Secular Nationalist competitors.

In chapter 2, I move from material and perceptual transformations to the intellectual infrastructure of the Salafi movement, with a focus on Ansar al-Sunna. In an age in which ideologically diverse competitors sought to offer comprehensive visions of state and society, how could Salafis move beyond questions of theology and ritual practice? To answer this question, I probe a Salafi legal innovation: the expansion of the category of non-negotiable devotional or ritual acts (known as *ʿIbādāt*) into domains previously considered customary and thus determined by local practice. Specifically, I reconstruct the process by which leading Salafi scholars and activists developed these claims from the 1930s through 1980s. In the process, these actors produced a model of pious subjectivity that responded to the challenges of Secular Nationalism and Islamism alike while departing in significant ways from longstanding categories of Islamic law.

Transitioning from legal and institutional infrastructure to social practice, the next four chapters chart the development of distinctly Salafi practices of praying in shoes, gender segregation, facial hair, and shortened pants or robes. I begin chapter 3 with a counterintuitive question: how do Salafis work to

88. For example, see Katz, *Women in the Mosque*, and Brinkley Messick, Muhammad Khalid Masud and David Powers, eds., *Islamic Legal Interpretation: Muftis and Their Fatwas* (Cambridge, MA: Cambridge University Press, 1996).

89. For example, see Rock-Singer, *Practicing Islam in Egypt: Print Media and Islamic Revival* (Cambridge, UK: Cambridge University Press, 2019).

avoid following the Prophet's model? To do so, I focus on the first central practice of Purist Salafism: praying in shoes (*al-ṣalāt bi-l-niʿāl*). While authoritative texts in the hadith corpus make clear that the Prophet prayed in shoes, how is it that many Purist Salafis today, like other Muslims, take off their shoes to pray, despite having once insisted on praying in shoes? In this chapter, I tell a story of a practice that had largely fallen by the wayside with the expansion of the Islamic state beyond Arabia in the first centuries of Islam,[90] and of how, in the 1940s, Egyptian Salafis reclaimed it as a signature practice of Ansar al-Sunna. The costs of visible distinctiveness in Egypt, however, grew as Salafis navigated both social opprobrium for their perceived unhygienic behavior as well as the pressures of the ʿAbd al-Nasir period (1952–70). In response, scholars in both Egypt and Saudi Arabia turned to invocations of the common good (*al-maṣlaḥa al-ʿāmma*), which was common among their Islamic Modernist competitors, to justify marginalizing a practice that had a strong basis within the authoritative corpus of Sunni hadith collections and that had previously been declared to be praiseworthy. By charting the rise and fall of praying in shoes, I show how Salafis came to marshal the intellectual methods of their competitors as they sought to marginalize a practice that they had once trumpeted.

In the fourth chapter, I move from shoes to gender segregation, tracing the process through which Egyptian Salafis, in dialogue with their Saudi counterparts, came to argue for the wholesale separation of men and women in public space. I argue that, far from representing either the inevitable product of a defined hermeneutical approach or a ready-made model, Egyptian and Saudi Salafis showed little interest in gender segregation outside of ritual space prior to the 1970s. Yet, as opportunities for mobilization in Egypt grew and the balance between Salafis and the Wahhabi-Hanbali establishment shifted in the 1970s, Salafi elites sought to craft a program of gender relations that necessitated both the reinterpretation of the Quranic injunction "do not flaunt" (*wa lā tabarrajna*, Q 33:33) and the citation of Western anti-suffrage thinkers from the early twentieth century. Scholarly interpretation, however, was also shaped by access to state power: Egyptian Salafis who lacked access to power came to tacitly accept and sometimes even justify men and

90. The exception to the shift away from praying in shoes is the Hanbali school, which maintained this practice. See M. J. Kister, "'Do Not Assimilate Yourselves . . .': *Lā Tashabbahū*," *Jerusalem Studies in Arabic and Islam* 12 (1989): 345.

women sharing public space, while their Saudi counterparts allied with their Wahhabi-Hanbali counterparts on a successful mission to reorganize Saudi society.[91]

Gender segregation may seek to divide men and women, but laid limited claim to men in homosocial spaces. In the fifth chapter, I explore the genesis of a Salafi beard that consciously seeks to emulate the Prophetic model. The Prophet Muhammad is described in multiple hadith reports as possessing a "bushy" or "thick" beard (*kathth* or *kathīth al-liḥya*), but such a description would have done little to distinguish Salafis from their religious competitors, whether segments of the Azhari scholarly community, Islamic student activists, or Muslim Brothers in Egypt and Syria. In this chapter, I show why Egyptian Salafis came to emphasize the significance of facial hair and then how, between 1979 and 1993, they determined that a properly Islamic (that is, Salafi) beard was a minimum of a fist (*qabḍa*) in length. Emphasis on the beard and the consolidation of a distinctly Salafi project of facial hair, however, produced new complications, whether the demands for men to be clean-shaven upon military conscription, aspirations to fashion, or continued confusion between Salafi and non-Salafi jihadi groups.

In chapter 6, I tell the story of the rise of the observance of the prohibition against *isbal*, or the practice of wearing one's pants or robe above one's ankle, in the 1980s. The power of this prohibition was its capacity to enable Salafi men to signal their commitment to this project even as they donned vastly differing uniforms, whether the soldier who rolled up his pants, the student activist who shortened his white robe (*jallābiyya*), or the businessman who subtly signaled his allegiances through his choice of tailored trousers. Deployed in this manner, a minor yet unmistakable sartorial adjustment could either confirm the impression given by a beard, or provide independent verification for those who were forbidden from maintaining facial hair or physically unable to do so. This chapter also documents how the term *isbal* shifted from being a verbal noun (*maṣdar*) associated with growing out one's beard (*isbāl al-liḥya*) to a negative term that denotes a man whose pants hang down out of arrogance,

91. Gender segregation, at first glance, constitutes an exception to this study's focus on embodied practice, as it primarily concerns structural changes to social space. Yet, as this chapter shows, it represents a project of ordering society vertically. Moreover, adherence to gender segregation depends on the visible self-regulation characteristic of other distinct Salafi practices.

and how this changing meaning paralleled the growing normativity of this practice in Salafi communities across the Middle East.

I then conclude the book by examining the implications of this history of Salafi practice for understanding the reconstruction of varied Islamic traditions in the twentieth century. Eschewing the common popular and scholarly assumption that the Salafi movement is more continuous with Islamic history than its Islamist and Islamic Modernist counterparts, I argue that this movement's distinct practices constitute highly selective excavations of the Islamic legal tradition in the service of a distinctly modern project of subject formation centered on visible communication. While Salafis have reshaped understandings of theology, legal interpretation, and piety for Muslims across the world by offering a model of Islam whose authenticity rests on its continuity with seventh-century Arabia, this book will show that these claims obscure radical rupture and are reflective of the broader changes to Islamic thought and practice produced by the transformations of modernity. It is to the conditions that made this project possible that I now turn.

CHAPTER 1

The Roots of Salafism

Strands of an Unorthodox Past, 1926–1970

During the second half of the twentieth century, Ansar al-Sunna laid claim to four signature practices: praying in shoes, gender segregation, a distinctive approach to facial hair, and shortened pants or robes. As chapters 3 through 6 of this book will show, Egyptian Salafis understood these practices to emerge directly from the Quran and Sunna. This chapter seeks to answer a question that lies behind this story of practice: what are the historical conditions under which Salafi pious practice came to center on communication? Specifically, what are the material and perceptual shifts that made this project not merely technologically viable but also socially thinkable?

Previous scholars have emphasized Salafism's engagement with a diachronic Islamic legal tradition, particularly an authenticated corpus of Sunni hadith reports[1] and pre-modern authors such as Ibn Taymiyya and his student Ibn Qayyim al-Jawziyya (d. 1350).[2] In this chapter, by contrast, I will explore the conditions under which Salafis came to cite these sources in the service of a distinctly twentieth-century project of social change. To do so, I will trace Ansar al-Sunna's emergence at the intersection of nineteenth-century projects of subject formation and abstraction, the printing and distribution of classical legal texts of the Islamic tradition, and a rapidly changing social world in which traditional structures of religious authority and longstanding markers of piety

1. For example, see Duderija, *Constructing a Religiously Ideal 'Believer' and 'Woman' in Islam*, 49–68.

2. For example, see Lav, "Radical Muslim Theonomy."

held less sway. My goal is not merely to chart Ansar al-Sunna's development, but also to explain the shared conceptual roots that bind Salafis to ideologically diverse competitors.

Accordingly, in the first section, I will synthesize secondary scholarship on late-nineteenth- to early-twentieth-century Egypt to set the stage for the rise of Salafism as a social movement, with particular attention to questions of communication and textual production. In the second section, I will explore the material conditions that both made possible and facilitated Ansar al-Sunna's rise, most notably the production of a canon of approved Islamic texts and the development of a national network of mosques and branches through which these and other texts could be taught and distributed. The third section then situates Ansar al-Sunna among Islamic movements during this period, emphasizing its commitment to a particular interpretative approach and a related effort to marginalize if not eliminate longstanding and widespread religious practices that it considered to be unlawful innovations (*bid'a*). In the final section, I sketch the transition from monarchical to secular-nationalist rule, with an emphasis on the ways in which Ansar al-Sunna maintained a quietist approach while focusing on the development of grassroots institutions. The chapter concludes at the end of the 1960s, with Ansar al-Sunna having established both the material and perceptual basis for an expansive project of Salafi piety, an achievement that proved crucial to its move beyond defined institutions from the 1970s on.

SALAFISM'S UNORTHODOX PAST

In the late nineteenth century, a call to precise bodily regulation emerged in Egypt alongside a valorization of the capacity of the individual to shape society's broader moral state. This exhortation, however, came not from Islamic reformers but rather from British colonial rulers as they introduced new methods of discipline and subject formation. Timothy Mitchell draws on Michel Foucault's theory of discipline as he argues that "Political order was to be achieved not through intermittent use of coercion but through the continuous instruction, inspection and control,"[3] and individuals were asked to regulate their own bodies in a manner that upheld broader societal goals.[4]

3. Mitchell, *Colonising Egypt*, xi.
4. Mitchell, *Colonising Egypt*, 19.

Schools were central to this project, modeling both the ideal individual subject and a broader entity of society as students moved in a highly organized fashion through social space.[5]

A new system of visual representation was central to British colonial influence and rule. As Mitchell states:

> The methods of organisation and arrangement that produce the new effects of structure . . . also generate the modern experience of meaning as a process of representation. In the metaphysics of capitalist modernity, the world is experienced in terms of an ontological distinction between physical reality and its representation in language, culture, or other forms of meaning. Reality is material, inert, and without inherent meaning, and representation is the non-material, non-physical dimension of intelligibility.[6]

While Mitchell's argument has been critiqued for assuming the uncomplicated translation of theory into practice,[7] the broader enframing effects of colonial influence and rule would shape subsequent ideological projects.

British colonial influence also introduced new notions of political and textual authority. As Mitchell explains:

> Politics was a field of practice, formed out of the supervision of people's health, the policing of urban neighbourhoods, the reorganisation of streets, and, above all, the schooling of the people, all of which was taken up—on the whole from the 1860s onward—as the responsibility and nature of government.[8]

Of particular significance to the calls to piety that followed, however, was the "'governance of the self' (*al-siyāsa al-dhātiyya*) . . . expressed in terms of hygiene, education, and discipline."[9] In short, by the end of the nineteenth century, a model of subjectivity premised on observable self-regulation had been established.

This model of self-regulation in the service of communal imperatives, though initiated by an external power, was consonant with aspects of the

5. Mitchell, *Colonising Egypt*, 68–71.

6. Mitchell, *Colonising Egypt*, xiii.

7. For example, see Khaled Fahmy, *All the Pasha's Men: Mehmed Ali, His Army, and the Making of Modern Egypt* (New York: AUC Press, 2002), 31–32, 158, 317.

8. Mitchell, *Colonising Egypt*, 103. In offering this periodization, Mitchell distinguishes between British colonial rule (which began in 1882) and colonial influence (which emerged from the early nineteenth century on) (14).

9. Mitchell, *Colonising Egypt*, 104.

Islamic ethical tradition.[10] In her recent study of Classical Islamic ethics, Zahra Ayubi argues that this tradition "focuses on inculcating virtue ethics within individuals, with the larger goal of creating ethical conditions in the household and broader society."[11] As in Mitchell's case, the conceptual framework for ethics is that of governance (Arabic: *Siyāsa*; Persian: *Siyasāt*).[12] This tradition pivots on the assumption that communal success is dependent on the "collective skills and trades" of its inhabitants.[13] In the Islamic Classical tradition, however, virtue is achieved not through self-regulating order but through the performance of particular affective practices of love, compassion, and forgiveness, as well as the maintenance of boundaries of modesty.[14] Furthermore, this tradition does not assume that the individual's efforts to successfully regulate him or herself will corrupt the broader social order, and is comparatively unconcerned with the visible performance of virtue.[15]

The British colonial project also advanced notions of textual authority that stood in stark contrast to the traditional Islamic model, which pivoted on human relationships. Whether in the case of the recitation of hadith reports, the teaching of key texts of Islamic law (*fiqh*), or the adjudication of legal cases, the reliability of any given source—and the authority to transmit it—depended on its attribution to a chain of individuals deemed trustworthy.[16] By contrast, colonial notions of writing assumed a mechanical understanding of authorial meaning that made human chains of transmission secondary if not irrelevant,[17]

10. On this point, see Ellen McLarney, "Freedom, Justice, and the Power of *Adab*," *International Journal of Middle East Studies* 48 (2016): 25–46. Though McLarney is right to claim that the project identified by Mitchell "did not supplant Islamic models," this chapter argues that this shift—as adopted by Islamic movements—was significant in that it made communication a central form of ethical practice.

11. Ayubi, *Gendered Morality*, 29.

12. Ayubi, *Gendered Morality*, 222.

13. Ayubi, *Gendered Morality*, 204.

14. Ayubi, *Gendered Morality*, 187–200.

15. Scholars of Islamic law, by contrast, expressed concern regarding the particular danger to public morality posed by the commission of public (rather than private) violations of Islamic law, as the former harms "the public at large." For a Hanbali example, see Michael Cook, *Commanding Right and Forbidding Wrong in Islamic Thought* (Cambridge, UK: Cambridge University Press, 2001), 171–72.

16. Messick, *The Calligraphic State*, 15–28; William A. Graham, "Traditionalism in Islam: An Essay in Interpretation," *The Journal of Interdisciplinary History* 23, no. 3 (1993): 495–522.

17. Mitchell, *Colonising Egypt*, 142–56.

an assumption that reflected the ambitions of a political project that sought to order Egyptian society in uniform fashion.[18] This approach to the balance between textual clarity and human relationships, in turn, was successful not merely due to the political power of colonial authorities, but also because it had been preceded by a homegrown modernization project under the Ottoman governor of Egypt Muhammad ʿAli (d. 1839), which privileged written over oral evidence in legal proceedings.[19]

Ottoman efforts to regulate dress also contributed to the association of visual signs with particular allegiances and positions. Whereas the Egyptian army had previously donned varied garments, Muhammad ʿAli instituted a new system by which "soldiers were . . . to be set apart from the civilian community by their confinement and by the wearing of a uniform dress."[20] Uniforms further served to distinguish various ranks of soldiers *within* the army, reflecting the intersection of hierarchy and communication in a system that sought to anonymize its constituent members.[21] Similarly, students in state institutions were expected to don distinct uniforms, including a dark blue shirt with a single row of buttons, bright red trousers, badges attached the collar's front, and a *tarbush* on the head.[22] The regulation of dress thus reflected not only the emergence of state-sponsored projects of subject formation, but also a linkage between clothing and membership in or allegiance to an abstract entity, here institutions controlled by the Egyptian state.

Just as modernization enabled the state to reach deeper into society, so too did it connect previously far-flung areas of Egypt. Beginning in the mid-nineteenth century under the reign of Muhammad ʿAli's fourth son, the Khedive Saʿid (r. 1854–63, d. 1863), Egyptians came to experience a world in which the country's population was linked by the railroad.[23] Similarly, the development of a national postal system facilitated the circulation of print

18. By contrast, in Yemen, the implementation of this model did not involve foreign colonial intervention. See Messick, *The Calligraphic State*, 234–50.

19. Khaled Fahmy, *In Quest of Justice: Islamic Law and Forensic Medicine in Modern Egypt* (Berkeley: University of California Press, 2020), 81–131.

20. Mitchell, *Colonising Egypt*, 39.

21. Fahmy, *All the Pasha's Men*, 143.

22. Mitchell, *Colonising Egypt*, 79.

23. Ziad Fahmy, *Ordinary Egyptians: Creating the Modern Nation Through Popular Culture* (Stanford, CA: Stanford University Press, 2011), 24–26.

media, particularly periodicals.[24] In his study of Egyptian nationalism, Ziad Fahmy shows that these technological shifts, alongside urbanization, promoted the rise of Egyptian national identity, while enhancing the influence of key cities such as Cairo.[25] In sum, as Thomas Bauer argues, the modernization efforts stimulated in large part by colonial challenge produced a "demand for coming up with unambiguous texts—and for promoting totally consistent ideologies and conceptions, constantly attuning social behavior to stable norms, and submitting to the process of growing bureaucracy and technology . . ."[26]

Technological change and urbanization also contributed to the expansion of preexisting forms of religiosity. The spread of railroads in the first half of the twentieth century enabled popular participation in varied mass religious practices: while the most prominent of such practices was the Hajj pilgrimage to Mecca, the availability of train travel also made it possible for thousands of Muslims to flock to celebrations of the Prophet Muhammad's birthday (s. *Mawlid*, pl. *Mawālīd*),[27] well as for greater numbers of Muslims, Christians, and Jews alike to engage in the longstanding practice of seeking intercession from saints across Egypt.[28] Trains served not only to transport thousands of Egyptians to longstanding sites of pilgrimage, but also to spatially structure national projects of religious change, with the Muslim Brotherhood's branches hewing closely to the path of railroad lines.[29] With transportation knitting together cities large and small within national borders, the Egyptian state worked to assert control over religious discourse and practice nationally, whether by establishing a self-consciously "national" religious space through the creation of an official State Mufti in 1895,[30] or by regulating prayer times in mosques beginning in the 1920s.[31]

24. Fahmy, *Ordinary Egyptians*, 27.

25. Fahmy, *Ordinary Egyptians*, 27–29.

26. Bauer, *A Culture of Ambiguity*, 32–33.

27. For example, in July 1895, "115,594 people traveled by railway to . . . al-Badawī mawlid in Ṭanṭa . . . [and] during the 1901 mawlid of Aḥmad al-Badawī, 800,000 people visited Ṭanṭa. The same year also saw a congregation of 250,000 visitors at the mawlid of Sīdī Ibrāhīm al-Dasūqī." See On Barak, *On Time: Technology and Temporality in Modern Egypt* (Berkeley: University of California Press, 2013), 92.

28. Barak, *On Time*, 93.

29. Steven Brooke and Neil Ketchley, "Social and Institutional Origins of Political Islam," *American Political Science Review* 112, no. 2 (2018): 376–94.

30. Skovgaard-Petersen, *Defining Islam for the Egyptian State*, 103–6.

31. Daniel A. Stolz, *The Lighthouse and the Observatory: Islam, Science and Empire in Late Ottoman Egypt* (Cambridge, UK: Cambridge University Press, 2018), 207–42, esp. 219–21.

The increasingly connectivity of Egypt as a political space expanded the social world of its inhabitants. The shift was not simply that a segment of the population could travel with relative ease, but the fact that improved transportation, alongside urbanization, made mass cultural projects, including religious projects, possible.[32] Urbanization, however, also destabilized the social world of Egyptians who had previously lived in local communities in which one's consanguineous relationships served as a primary form of identification. As rural residents moved to cities, bonds of local community frayed and migrants reconstituted themselves in dense urban environments where anonymity was the rule, rather than the exception. In this setting, communal identity was increasingly formed primarily on the basis of a common national culture, rather than through local ties.[33]

This period also saw the emergence of mass politics in Egypt. Since 1882, British colonial rulers had spearheaded an effort to reorganize rural governance through the Ministry of the Interior by exerting greater control over the local headman or mayor (*al-ʿumda*), a process that led peasants to increasingly turn to national institutions for redress of their grievances.[34] The economic crisis of 1907, in turn, shattered the British claim that occupation would lead to economic improvement, and economic critiques of colonial rule increasingly came to be couched within a broader nationalist project. In this context, Egyptians drew on varied practices of protest, ranging from petitioning the Khedive to authoring editorials in newspapers and journals to popular strikes that transcended class lines, to express their rejection of colonial occupation and to articulate a vision of Egyptian nationalism.[35]

The political, economic and social transformations of the early twentieth century posed a stark challenge to the *ʿulamaʾ*. The spread of religious education within public schools and increasing popularity of Islamic print media destabilized their monopoly on religious interpretation, while the expansion of the state bureaucracy and seizure of their endowments infringed on their

32. Fahmy, *Ordinary Egyptians*, 26.

33. Israel Gershoni and James P. Jankowski, *Redefining the Egyptian Nation, 1930–1945* (Cambridge, UK: Cambridge University Press, 1995), 216.

34. Aaron Jakes, *Egypt's Occupation: Colonial Economism and the Crises of Capitalism* (Stanford, CA: Stanford University Press, 2020), 77–82.

35. Jakes, *Egypt's Occupation*, 167–92.

political and economic independence.[36] These scholars' normative commitment to *Taqlīd* –literally "imitation," but better understood as conscious continuity with *madhhab*-based legal traditions –was mocked by new political elites and Islamic activists alike as "frozenness" (*jumūd*).[37]

In the specific case of political contestation, the rise of mass movements undermined the capacity of scholars to mediate between the ruler and the population by offering an alternative model for negotiation with the state, whether colonial officials or the Egyptian monarchy. Indeed, protests even reached al-Azhar: in January 1909, thousands of students protested the reorganization of this flagship institution of Sunni Islam by Khedive ʿAbbas Hilmi II (r. 1892–1914, d. 1944).[38] The source of protest ranged from a request for higher stipends and guaranteed basic employment for graduates, to the provision of qualified instructors to teach this material, to greater input in the governance of al-Azhar itself.[39] This was a world in which longstanding strategies for the reproduction of social and economic privilege had shifted, in which the capacity of scholars to act as guardians of the faith from within an educational institution such as al-Azhar was increasingly circumscribed, and in which tried-and-true models of political mediation had frayed.

The spread of print also transformed the historical tradition with which the *ʿulama*ʾ could engage. In the late nineteenth century, Egyptian and Syrian editors and printers revived Islam's classical legal heritage (exemplified by the works of the eponym of each *madhhab*) by transferring it from manuscript form, available to only a fortunate few, to print.[40] These efforts entailed the selective reproduction of a textual corpus of Classical works, and challenged institutions such as al-Azhar that relied on post-Classical commentaries and

36. For the rise of public religious education, see Starrett, *Putting Islam to Work*, 23–61. On the challenges to authority faced by *ʿulama*ʾ in late-nineteenth- and early-twentieth-century Egypt, see Meir Hatina, *ʿUlama*ʾ*, Politics, and the Public Sphere: An Egyptian Perspective* (Salt Lake City: University of Utah Press, 2010), 32–44.

37. Indira Falk Gesink, *Islamic Reform and Conservatism: Al-Azhar and the Evolution of Modern Sunni Islam* (London: I. B. Tauris, 2010), 59–88, 96; Hatina, *ʿUlama*ʾ*, Politics, and the Public Sphere*, 99–104.

38. Jakes, *Egypt's Occupation*, 184–88.

39. Jakes, *Egypt's Occupation*,185–86.

40. In the process, these scholars also made key (and unacknowledged) editorial choices as they distilled varied manuscripts into a single "master" text. See Ahmed El Shamsy, *Rediscovering the Islamic Classics: How Editors and Print Culture Transformed an Intellectual Tradition* (Princeton, NJ: Princeton University Press, 2020), 93–122.

glosses.[41] In the process, previously marginalized figures, such as the Damascene Hanbali scholar Ibn Taymiyya, found new popularity.[42] This development, though, was not merely an internal matter: the effort to revive this heritage followed early-nineteenth-century efforts by Orientalist collectors to purchase vast numbers of rare Islamic manuscripts, thus rendering many early works of Islamic law practically inaccessible for Egyptian scholars for decades.[43]

In the shadow of a fragmented if not fractured order, two Azharis—Muhammad Hamid al-Fiqi (d. 1959) and his colleague ʿAbd al-Razzaq al-ʿAfifi (d. 1994)—chose not to follow many of their classmates in pursuing a career within al-Azhar's sprawling national network of educational institutions. Al-Fiqi was born in 1892 and grew up in a village of the Egyptian Delta, Shubrakhit. He memorized the Quran as a child and begun studying in al-Azhar's nationwide network of institutes in 1904, progressing through this system to receive his degree as a scholar (known as the *ʿālimiyya*) by the age of twenty-five.[44] Al-ʿAfifi, born in 1905, was over a decade younger, but like al-Fiqi, began his education in the Nile Delta, specifically in in the village of Shanshur, near the Ashmun Center in the Delta governorate of Egypt. His father taught him to memorize the Quran at an early age, before enrolling him first in the local Quranic schools (s. *kuttāb*, p. *katātīb*) in Shanshur, and then in Azhari institutes for his primary and secondary education. Al-ʿAfifi then went on to complete his university education at the Seminary's central campus in Cairo in 1932, and the equivalent of a doctorate in the Principles of Islamic Jurisprudence (*Uṣūl al-Fiqh*) in 1936.

Yet, instead of pursuing conventional scholarly careers, al-Fiqi and al-ʿAfifi made their marks as leading members of Egypt's first and most prominent Salafi organization. As a matter of interpretative methodology, such a decision was not altogether surprising: al-Azhar was still dominated by proponents of a post-Classical approach who emphasized the study of glosses on each

41. El Shamsy, *Rediscovering the Islamic Classics*, 40. I follow El Shamsy in dating the classical period to the ninth through the fifteenth centuries and the post-classical period as referring to the sixteenth through the nineteenth centuries (31–32).

42. El Shamsy, *Rediscovering the Islamic Classics*, 56–57, 182–90.

43. El Shamsy, *Rediscovering the Islamic Classics*, 8–30.

44. Ahmad Muhammad al-Tahir, *Jamaʿat Ansar al-Sunna al-Muhammadiyya: Nashʾatuha –Ahdafuha –Manhajuha –Juhuduha* (Cairo/Riyadh: Dar al-Hadi al-Nabawi li-l-Nashr waʾl-Tawziʿ/ Dar al-Fadila li-l-Nashr waʾl-Tawziʿ, 2004), 54.

madhhab's eponyms' most significant works rather than direct engagement with these sources. Indeed, this emphasis had been a source of deep frustration for earlier reformist scholars such as Muhammad ʿAbduh and Muhammad Rashid Rida.[45] The challenge of change through mass politics, however, went far beyond interpretative differences. It is to this story—and Ansar al-Sunna's rise—that we now turn.

THE RISE OF ISLAMIC MOVEMENTS IN THE SHADOW OF MASS POLITICS

The 1920s was an era of political tumult and action. It a was world order defined by the end of the First World War in 1918 and a local order reconfigured by both the 1919 Egyptian revolution and the 1924 abolishment of the Ottoman Caliphate. The following decade would be shaped not merely by semicolonial rule in Egypt and a tripartite struggle among colonial officials, the Egyptian monarchy, and the secular-nationalist Wafd party for primacy,[46] but also by the economic effects of the Great Depression.[47] The growth of mass politics both reflected and furthered the breakdown of traditional political, economic, and religious structures, and varied movements laid claim to alternative identities and public space alike.

Most significant to the origins of Salafism would be the rise of a sociocultural middle class stratum known as the *Efendiyya*.[48] Individual participants in this project used particular garments such as a suit and red hat (the *tarbush*) to signal their rejection of the old scholarly order of al-Azhar and to embrace a fusion of "authenticity" (*aṣāla*) and modernity.[49] While many of this segment's members worked in white-color bureaucratic positions,[50] its

45. El Shamsy, *Rediscovering the Islamic Classics*, 151–58. Nonetheless, one should not overstate the opposition between these two scholars and their *alma mater*: a significant portion of al-ʿAfifi's graduate education at al-Azhar occurred once he had already assumed a prominent role in Ansar al-Sunna.

46. Charles D. Smith, *Islam and the Search for Social Order in Modern Egypt* (Albany: State University of New York Press, 1983), 71–72.

47. Robert L. Tignor, *State, Private Enterprise and Economic Change in Egypt, 1918–1952* (Princeton, NJ: Princeton University Press, 2017), 113.

48. Ryzova, *The Age of the Efendiyya*, 8.

49. Ryzova, *The Age of the Efendiyya*, 38–41.

50. Ryzova, *The Age of the Efendiyya*, 8.

distinctive visual cues were not a result of state regulation as in the case of military or school uniforms, nor were they limited to those employed by or studying in these institutions. Just as importantly, such visual cues were insufficient on their own; membership also required "a mastery of the habitus and embodied cultural capital that was shared by group members and required to work as a bureaucrat or religious leader. . . ."[51]

Structurally, the formation and reproduction of the *Efendiyya* was premised on the existence of a self-regulating citizen who was formed and formed him or herself through both the pursuit of education and the consumption of media. Schools were a key site for transmission under both colonial and postcolonial rule as the latter's "precise methods of inspection, coordination and control . . . [sought t]o change the tastes and habits of an entire people . . . [thus creating] a modern political subject—frugal, innocent and, above all, busy."[52] In this context, religious education was a key site of reform as successive governments, colonial and postcolonial, sought to produce an industrious and politically quiescent population.[53]

The *Efendiyya's* understanding of social change derived from a reformist project that had first emerged in the mid-nineteenth century. In the shadow of social and economic transformation produced by both a rapidly modernizing state and the increased incorporation of Egypt and other Eastern Mediterranean countries into a capitalist world economy, the "social" emerged as a central object of reform. As Ilham Khuri-Makdisi argues, "The social, as it was conceptualized starting in the 1860s, was inextricably linked to an obsession with a sense of reform. . .reform was conceived of as a total project. . . ."[54] In the early twentieth century, a secular-nationalist subset of the *Efendiyya*—represented by the lawyer-turned-nationalist activist Mustafa Kamil (d. 1908)—worked to contest the colonial narrative that Egyptians were unable to govern themselves. In this context, Kamil modeled a self-

51. Hilary Kalmbach, *Islamic Knowledge and the Making of Modern Egypt* (Cambridge, UK: Cambridge University Press, 2020), 21–22.

52. Mitchell, *Colonising Egypt*, 74–75.

53. For British efforts to uses education as a means of political control at home and in Egypt, see Starrett, *Putting Islam to Work*, 23–61. For colonial and post-colonial Egyptian efforts that followed a similar logic, see 62–86.

54. Ilham Khuri-Makdisi, "The Conceptualization of the Social in Late-Nineteenth and Early Twentieth-Century Arabic Thought and Language," in *A Global Conceptual History of Asia, 1860-1940*, ed. Hagen Schulz-Forberg (London: Lickering & Chatto, 2014), 93.

discipline premised not merely on avoiding particular vices but on engaging in a set of "productive" actions, whether prayer, exercise, work, reading, or socializing.[55]

Other segments of the *efendi* project sought to offer a model of Islamic authority, intellectual and social, that contrasted itself with both the old scholarly order and the increasingly popular secular-nationalist vision. The key transmission point of this model was Dar al-ʿUlum (DU), a teachers' training college in Cairo established in 1872 that would merge with Cairo University in 1946. At DU, students acquired a hybrid education composed of both the traditional Arabic and Islamic sciences such as grammar and language, Quranic interpretation (*tafsīr*) and Islamic jurisprudence (*fiqh*), as well as mathematics, geography, history, drawing, chemistry, physics, astronomy and the natural or physical sciences.[56]

Dress was central to the *efendi* challenge. While scholars had long worn the turban (*ʿimāma*) combined with either a gown with full-length sleeves (the *qabāʾ*) or an open-front gown with wide sleeves (the *jubba*), members in this new sociocultural formation donned the suit and *tarbush* to signify their orientation to a new modern order. Most notable for Ansar al-Sunna in this respect would have been the practice of a particularly prominent graduate of Dar al-ʿUlum: the Muslim Brotherhood's founder, Hasan al-Banna (d. 1949). Al-Banna's memoir claims that, beginning in his fourth and final year at DU,

> The desire to change clothing (*taghyīr al-ziyy*) intensified [among the students] . . . a shift that was assisted by prominent graduates (*kibār al-mutakharrijīn*) of Dar al-ʿUlum. . . . In [just] a few months . . . the number of tarbush-wearing men (*al-muṭarbashūn*) increased and the number of turban wearers (*al-muʿammamīn*) decreased. . . . Slightly before graduation, we donned the suit (*badla*) and tarbush (*al-ṭarbūsh*) rather than the open-front gown with wide sleeves (*jubba*) and turban (*al-ʿimāma*).[57]

Yet, during other periods of his tenure as a student, al-Banna wore the open toe sandals popular during the Hajj (*naʿl al-iḥrām fi al-Ḥājj*) and a white cloak

55. Chacko Jacob, *Working Out Egypt*, 63.

56. Kalmbach, *Islamic Knowledge and the Making of Modern Egypt*, 107.

57. Hasan al-Banna, *Mudhakkirat al-Daʿwa waʾl-Daʿiyya* (Kuwait City: Maktabat Afaq, 2012), 54.

on top of his robe (*ridāʾan abyaḍ fawqa al-jilbāb*).[58] As al-Banna used these sartorial markers to perform an Islamic identity that both moved beyond the traditional order of *ʿulamaʾ* and challenged secular-nationalist visions of Egyptian state and society, he contributed to the destabilization of ostensibly clear social indicators of knowledge, authority and piety.[59]

Competing Boy Scout organizations also emerged from the *Efendiyya* project. As Wilson Chacko Jacob notes, "[although] Egyptians had begun seeing these strange boys [from Egypt's foreign communities] in uniforms marching through their city streets before the First World War," the first indigenous troop would be established in 1918 as the Royal Egyptian Boy Scouts Associations.[60] After the 1920 founding of the National Scouting Society, the two competed for participants as they reflected political battles between the Palace and Nationalists during this period.[61] As among the *efendiyya* more broadly, self-regulation was central to the scouting project: while colonial officials saw scouts' self-discipline as a necessary step *prior* to self-government, the Wafd-led nationalist movement argued that such activity constituted *proof* of the capacity for self-government.[62] The Muslim Brotherhood, too, laid claim to scouting through the establishment of a "rover troop" (known as the *jawwāla*) clad in their own "official clothing" (*bi-malābisihim al-rasmiyya*).[63]

58. al-Banna, *Mudhakkirat al-Daʿwa waʾl-Daʿiyya*, 26. Also see Kalmbach, *Islamic Knowledge and the Making of Modern Egypt*, 177. Unlike the *jallābiyya*, which was and is worn by Egyptian men of different backgrounds, the *jubba* is specific to the Azhari scholarly outfit. I wish to thank Hilary Kalmbach for this observation.

59. As I will discuss in chapter 5, however, al-Banna's use of visual signs stood in tension with a commitment to avoid appearing distinct and thus "foreign" (*gharīb*) to the society which he sought to transform. See Fatima ʿAbd al-Hadi, *Rihlati maʿa al-Akhawat al-Muslimat: Min al-Imam Hasan al-Banna ila Sujun ʿAbd al-Nasir*, ed. Hussam Tammam and Farid ʿAbd al-Khaliq (Cairo: Dar al-Shuruq, 2011), 16. I wish to thank Mathias Ghyoot for bringing this source to my attention.

60. Jacob, *Working Out Egypt*, 93.

61. Jacob, *Working Out Egypt*, 95.

62. Jacob, *Working Out Egypt*, 100–2.

63. Yusuf ʿAbd al-Hadi, "Fi Jamʿiyyat al-Ikhwan al-Muslimin," *al-Ikhwan al-Muslimun*, Rabiʿ al-Awwal 1354/25 June 1935, 24. I wish to thank Steven Brooke for this reference. Gudrun Krämer notes the Brotherhood's use of "honorific titles, badges, and other insignia . . . [was] designed to create a corporate identity. In the early years, a silver ring was given to all new members. On certain occasions, members wore a green sash with the name 'the Muslim Brothers' written on it" (*Hasan al-Banna* [Oxford: Oneworld, 2010], 37). Also see Richard

Visible markers would also prove central to paramilitary conflict among a "shirts movement" in 1930s Egypt, which similarly emerged from the *efendiyya*.[64] Modeled after the European trend of the same name,[65] the "Blue Shirts" (*al-Qumṣān al-Zarqāʾ*) were allied with the Wafd, and the "Green Shirts" (*al-Qumṣān al-Khaḍrāʾ*) with the Fascist Young Egypt Party (*Miṣr al-Fatā*). The Blue Shirts' uniform included "grey trousers, and the Egyptian *ṭarbūsh* . . . [along with] badges . . . [and a] salute . . . [of] a clenched right hand placed on the heart and then thrust to the sky,"[66] while that of the Green Shirts replicated the pants and headgear choice of their competitors along with a salute that involved "an outstretched arm, palm open and fingers pointing to the sky."[67]

These two groups clashed between 1935 and 1938, a battle that only ceased when the Muhammad Mahmud Pasha government (r. 1937–1939) disbanded all paramilitary organizations.[68] In these clashes, visual cues were central: following the first broad outbreak of violence between the two groups in 1936, Young Egypt's founder, Ahmad Husayn (d. 1982), called on his followers to abstain from wearing their uniforms in public "in order to restore calm in the country."[69] Uniforms and bodily gestures thus communicated membership in a broader movement and, in the case of the Blue Shirts, the backing of a leading political party.

It was in the shadow of these momentous global, regional, and local transformations that Ansar al-Sunna arose. Its genesis, however, was decidedly modest and built off existing social and religious institutions. At the time, al-Fiqi worked in the Ministry of Endowments, which appointed him to lead

---

P. Mitchell, *The Society of the Muslim Brothers* (New York: Oxford University Press, 1993), 200–3. On the Brotherhood's broader focus on communication, see Krämer, *Hasan al-Banna*, 37, and Mitchell, *The Society of the Muslim Brothers*, 190–91.

64. Ryzova, *The Age of the Efendiyya*, 18–19.

65. On Hitler's "Brownshirts" in Germany, see Daniel Simens, *Stormtroopers: A New History of Hitler's Brownshirts* (New Haven, CT: Yale University Press, 2017). On the "Blackshirts" in the United Kingdom, see Stephen Dorril, *Blackshirt: Sir Oswald Mosley and British Fascism* (London: Thistle Publishing, 2006).

66. James P. Jankowski, "The Egyptian Blue Shirts and the Egyptian Wafd," *Middle Eastern Studies* 6, no. 1 (1970): 82.

67. James P. Jankowski, *Egypt's Young Rebels: "Young Egypt" 1933–1952* (Stanford, CA: Hoover Institution Press, 1975), 15.

68. Jankowski, *Egypt's Young Rebels*, 26–27.

69. Jankowski, *Egypt's Young Rebels*, 24.

prayers and deliver Friday sermons at the al-Hadara mosque in the Cairene neighborhood of ʿAbidin. In the months after the organization's establishment but prior to the purchase of a building to serve as its official headquarters in December 1926, Ansar al-Sunna's founder delivered religious lessons (*durūs*) based on "Books of the Sunna" (*kutub al-Sunna*) at the ʿAli Qasim Coffeehouse on Bustan Street, near Ismaʿiliyya (now al-Tahrir) square.[70]

Yet, in the 1920s, al-Fiqi was more concerned with establishing his own scholarly networks and securing employment than building a movement. ʿAli al-Qadi, who chronicled the rise of Ansar al-Sunna in *al-Hadi al-Nabawi* roughly a decade later, notes that al-Fiqi's three-year absence in the Hijaz (1928–1930)—a period during which he taught at the Great Mosque of Mecca (*al-Masjid al-Ḥarām*)[71]—forced the small group of men who had gathered around him to persevere until his return.[72] Despite this slow start, however, the organization's membership grew over the following decade into a movement, still small in comparative terms, of roughly one thousand.[73]

Growth went hand-in-hand with infrastructural expansion. In 1936, with al-Fiqi now back in Egypt and focused on the organization, Ansar al-Sunna began to publish an official journal, *al-Hadi al-Nabawi* (*The Prophetic Guide*).[74] This was not al-Fiqi's first experiment with print media: while in Mecca, he had published an Islamic reformist journal, *al-Islah* (*Reform*, 1928–29) that trumpeted theological concepts shared by Salafi and Wahhabi-Hanbali scholars. By highlighting alleged polytheism (*shirk*), unlawful innovation

70. Muhammad ʿAli al-Qadi, "Nashʾat al-Jamaʿa," *al-Hadi al-Nabawi*, Rabiʿ al-Thani 1356/~July 1937, 22–3.

71. Chanfi Ahmed, *West African ʿulamāʾ and Salafism in Mecca and Medina: Jawāb Al-Ifrīqī—The Response of the African* (Leiden: Brill, 2015), 86.

72. "Jamaʿat Ansar al-Sunna," *al-Hadi al-Nabawi*, Shawwal 1356/~December 1937, 28.

73. Muhammad ʿAli al-Qadi, "Nashʾat al-Jamaʿa," *al-Hadi al-Nabawi*, Rabiʿ al-Thani 1356/~July 1937, 22–3. By comparison, the Young Men's Muslim Association (YMMA) claimed a membership of 15,000 by the end of the 1920s, while the Brotherhood had approximately 20,000 registered members in 1937. For the YMMA's membership, see Gershoni and Jankowski, *Redefining the Egyptian Nation*, 21; for the Brotherhood's membership, see Brynjar Lia, *The Society of the Muslim Brothers in Egypt*, 96. For the article in *al-Fath* on which these numbers are based, see Mustafa Ahmad al-Rifaʿi al-Liban, "al-Jamʿiyyat al-Islamiyya," *al-Fath*, 4 Rajab 1356/~10 September 1937, 12–13, at 13.

74. "Jamaʿat Ansar al-Sunna," *al-Hadi al-Nabawi*, Shawwal 1356/~December 1937, 28.

(*bid'a*) and superstitions (*khurāfāt*),[75] al-Fiqi warned his readers of the danger of deviating from a narrow reading of Islamic theology and law alike.[76] Al-Fiqi's utilization of print followed a strategy that Islamic reformers had pursued over the previous half-century. Most prominently, the 1884–85 publication by Jamal al-Din al-Afghani and Muhammad 'Abduh of *al-'Urwa al-Wuthqa* (*The Firmest Bond*) and the subsequent publication by Muhammad Rashid Rida of *al-Manar* (*The Lighthouse*, 1898–1935) had enshrined print media as a central tool of religious debate and outreach.

In the 1930s, however, the role of print expanded as varied Islamic movements turned to this medium to reach out not only to literate Muslim Arabic speakers generally (as al-Afghani, 'Abduh, and Rida had previously done), but also to members of their respective movements in particular. Most prominently, the Young Men's Muslim Association (*al-Fath*), the Muslim Brotherhood (*al-Ikhwan al-Muslimun*), and the Jam'iyya Shar'iyya (*al-I'tisam*),[77] all began to publish periodicals which appeared either biweekly or monthly. This tactic mirrored that pursued by their secular-nationalist counterparts such as the Wafd (*Majallat al-Shubban al-Wafdiyyin*), and Young Egypt (*al-Sarkha*) during this period.[78] As *al-Hadi al-Nabawi* appeared, its leadership structure reflected that of Ansar al-Sunna, with al-Fiqi taking on the role of editor-in-chief (*ra'īs al-taḥrīr*).[79] Yet, even if one accounts for the possibility of the dif-

75. For example, see "al-Wathaniyya fi al-Islam," *al-Islah*, 15 Rabi' al-Awwal 1347/31 August 1928, 13–14; Abu al-Walid al-Baji, "Hukm al-Bid'at al-Ijtima'iyya fi Mawlid al-Nabi Salla Allah 'Alayhi Wa Salam," *al-Islah*, 15 Sha'ban 1347/26 January 1929, 14–17; and "al-Bayan al-Mufid," *al-Islah*, 15 Muharram wa 1 Safar 348/22 June and 8 July 1929.

76. Salafis and Wahhabi-Hanbalis share a commitment to God's attributes (*al-asmā' wa'l-ṣifāt*) dominant in Hanbali theology, known as *Madhhab al-Salaf*. The key distinction is that, prior to the twentieth century, one could pledge allegiance to *Madhhab al-Salaf* on matters of theology (as Wahhabi-Hanbalis have long done) while simultaneously remaining committed to a particular legal *madhhab*. See Lauzière, *The Making of Salafism*, 27–32.

77. The title of the Jam'iyya Shar'iyya's periodical refers to Surat Al 'Umran 3:103, which reads: "And hold tight to the rope of God (*wa-a'taṣimū bi-ḥabl Allāh*) all together and do not become divided."

78. The practice of tying papers to parties also reflected the reverberations of the 1907 financial crisis, in which papers had been funded by the sale of stock shares, whose value plummeted. By contrast, parties could fund papers based on membership dues. See Jakes, *Egypt's Occupation*, 172–73.

79. al-Tahir, *Jama'at Ansar al-Sunna al-Muhammadiyya*, 96. For a primary source example, see the opening page of the Rabi' al-Thani 1356 issue.

fusion of print media through reading aloud in coffee shops,[80] the reach of such journals was limited by broader literacy rates in Egypt during this time.[81]

Ansar al-Sunna's ambition to bypass the postclassical tradition of Islamic scholarship required it not only to craft a model of religious authority premised on public engagement, but also to define and transmit a textual canon.[82] While the organization would soon mirror state institutions and political parties in its focus on establishing sites that could serve as a model for a broader social project, the particular goal of "holding tight to the authentic Prophetic model" (*al-tamassuk bi-l-Sunna al-ṣaḥīḥa*)[83] depended on the possibility of transmitting foundational classical works of Islamic law. In this vein, an unsigned article in the December 1937 issue of *al-Hadi al-Nabawi* announced that Ansar al-Sunna had established a publishing house to "print texts submitted to it that agree with its principles" (*bi-ṭabʿ mā yuqaddam ilayhā wa-yataffiq mabādiʾhā*).[84]

Such a goal was easier to define than accomplish and, early on, Ansar al-Sunna focused on a medium that required limited technological access and literacy: regular lectures by leading scholars in the movement. Beginning with twice-weekly events at the organization's original Cairo base in ʿAbidin,[85] it expanded outwards, first to Alexandria,[86] and then to the Nile Delta cities of

80. Ami Ayalon, *Reading Palestine: Printing and Literacy, 1900–1948* (Austin: University of Texas Press, 2004), 3–4.

81. In 1927, total literacy stood at 11.8 percent, with the rate for men (19.6 percent) far exceeding that of women (3.9 percent). See Fahmy, *Ordinary Egyptians*, 33.

82. Alexander Thurston has previously drawn attention to canonization processes within Salafism through the ideas of Dr. Muhammad Aman al-Jami (d. 1996), a leading Nigerian Salafi. In doing so, he highlights the centrality of pre-modern scholars such as Ahmad b. Hanbal (d. 855), Ibn Taymiyya (d. 1328), Ibn ʿAbd al-Wahhab (d. 1792), Muhammad al-Shawkani (d. 1834), and Siddiq Hasan Khan al-Qannuji (d. 1890), as well as modern revivalists such as Nuʿman Khayr al-Din al-Alusi (d. 1899), Tahir al-Din al-Jazaʾiri (d. 1920), ʿAbd al-Razzaq al-Baytar (d. 1916), and Jamal al-Din al-Qasimi (d. 1914). While Thurston's overview of the Salafi canon as it eventually emerged in the late twentieth century is persuasive, this canonization process was far from complete in the 1930s and 1940s. See Alexander Thurston, *Salafism in Nigeria: Islam, Preaching and Politics* (Cambridge, UK: Cambridge University Press, 2016), 31–66.

83. "Min Mabadiʾ Jamaʿat Ansar al-Sunna al-Muhammadiyya, *al-Hadi al-Nabawi*, Dhu al-Hijja 1380/~May 1961, 51.

84. "Jamaʿat Ansar al-Sunna," *al-Hadi al-Nabawi*, Shawwal 1356/~December 1937, 28.

85. "Jamaʿat Ansar al-Sunna," *al-Hadi al-Nabawi*, Shawwal 1356/~December 1937, 28.

86. "Muhadarat Jamaʿat Ansar al-Sunna al-Muhammadiyya bi-l-Iskandariyya," *al-Hadi al-Nabawi*, Rabiʿ al-Thani 1357/~May 1937, 4.

Monuf, Damanhur, Port Said, Bani Swayf, Quwaysna, and Shibbin al-Kum,[87] as well as to key cities in Upper Egypt such as Minya.[88] By 1939, it was increasingly common for these centers to host multiple lectures during the week.[89]

In the early 1940s, Ansar al-Sunna also begin to print works that reflected its commitment to neo-Hanbali theology (that is, *Madhhab al-Salaf*) on the one hand, and a commitment to deriving all law from the Quran and Sunna, on the other. At this time, the category of Salafism remained open-ended and the well-known Salafiyya Bookstore (*al-Maktaba al-Salafiyya*) continued to print a theologically-diverse set of works.[90] By contrast, the back cover of the May 1941 issue of *al-Hadi al-Nabawi* listed the publishing house's budget, which included costs associated with the printing of 556 copies of a book on the correct method to interpret the ambiguous verses of the Quran (*Mutashābih al-Qur'ān*), 518 copies of Ibn Taymiyya's *The Creed of Ahl al-Sunna* (*'Aqīdat Ahl al-Sunna*)[91] and *Thulathiyyat al-Bukhari*, an extract from al-Bukhari's canonical hadith collection of reports that have been transmitted by three narrators (and were thus considered reliable). Based on this budget, it appears that Ansar al-Sunna intended to distribute these texts free-of-charge.[92] The February 1943 issue, by complement, listed a text on hadith criticism authored by the Damascene Shafi'i hadith scholar, Shams al-Din Muhammad b. Ahmad

87. al-Mu'tamar al-'Amm li-Jama'at Ansar al-Sunna al-Muhammadiyya, *al-Hadi al-Nabawi*, Dhu al-Qa'da 1357/~December 1938, 21–25.

88. al-Mu'tamar al-'Amm li-Jama'at Ansar al-Sunna al-Muhammadiyya, *al-Hadi al-Nabawi*, Dhu al-Qa'da 1357/~December 1938, 46.

89. "Jama'at Ansar al-Sunna," *al-Hadi al-Nabawi*, 15 Dhu al-Qa'da 1358/~27 December 1939, 46–48, at 48. Also see "Jama'at Ansar al-Sunna," *al-Hadi al-Nabawi*, 15 Dhu al-Hijja 1358/~25 January 1940, 31.

90. Henri Lauzière, "The Construction of Salafiyya: Reconsidering Salafism from the Perspective of Conceptual History," *International Journal of Middle East Studies* 42, no. 3 (2010): 377–78.

91. Though *al-Hadi al-Nabawi* does not specify the author of this text, it published a book authored by Ibn Taymiyya (and edited by 'Abd al-Razzaq al-'Afifi) with this title around in either 1939 or 1940. See Ahmad b. Taymiyya al-Harani, *'Aqidat Ahl a-Sunna wa'l-Firaq al-Najiyya*, ed. 'Abd al-Razzaq al-'Afifi (Cairo: Matba'at Ansar al-Sunna al-Muhammadiyya, 1358/~1939–40). Based on this bibliographic information, it appears that the text was published prior to this advertisement in *al-Hadi al-Nabawi*.

92. "Mizaniyyat Matba'at Ansar al-Sunna al-Muhammadiyya," *al-Hadi al-Nabawi*, Jumada al-Ula 1360/~May 1941, back cover.

al-Dhahabi (d. 748/1348).[93] Yet, notwithstanding the May 1941 budget, it does not appear that Ansar al-Sunna distributed complimentary books to any significant degree or that it had the financial flexibility to do so. A July 1945 notice instructed readers to request "all Salafi books" (*kull al-kutub al-Salafiyya*) from the organization's headquarters but warned that book orders required a deposit in order to be processed.[94]

The late 1940s saw further expansion of the publishing house's offerings. A November 1946 notice described the decision to print "Salafi texts" (*rasāʾil Salafiyya*) such as Ahmad b. Hanbal's (d. 241/855) collection of authenticated hadith (*Musnad al-Imam Ahmad*), the Yemeni Muhammad b. Ismaʿil al-Sanʿani's (d. 1768) *The Purification of Thought* (*Tahtir al-Iʿtiqad*), and Muhammad b. ʿAbd al-Wahhab's (d. 1703) *The Clearing of Doubts* (*Kashf al-Shubuhat*), the last of which centered on an issue of shared concern for Wahhabi-Hanbali and Salafi scholars: efforts to justify acts that both understood to be polytheism (*shirk*).[95]

Ansar al-Sunna also moved beyond printing classical works or texts of later authors whose scholarship supported either neo-Hanbali theology or critical engagement with the hadith corpus. An early example of this broadened focus was a July 1945 advertisement for multiple volumes of the *al-Manar* commentary—written by Muhammad Rashid Rida based on both his and Muhammad ʿAbduh's interpretation—which had quickly emerged as a key reference point for varied transnational Islamic legal debates.[96] Similarly, the November 1946 issue of *al-Hadi al-Nabawi* promoted an anthology of writings by leading Ansar al-Sunna member Abu-l-Wafaʾ Muhammad Darwish, and a text entitled *The Facilitation of Revelation Through Reliance on the Quran and Two Authoritative Hadith Collections* (*Taysir al-Wahyayn bi-l-Iqtisar ʿala al-Qurʾan maʿa al-Sahihayn*) by the Wahhabi-Hanbali migrant to Egypt and member of Ansar al-Sunna ʿAbd al-ʿAziz b. Rashid (d. 1982).[97] Nonetheless, pre-modern luminaries remained prominent: the December 1949 issue

93. "Kitab al-ʿAlu al-Ulli al-Ghaffar," *al-Hadi al-Nabawi*, Safar 1362/~February 1943, back cover.

94. "Jamaʿat Ansar al-Sunna al-Muhammadiyya," *al-Hadi al-Nabawi*, Shaʿban 1364/~July 1945, 287–8.

95. "Akhbar al-Jamaʿa," *al-Hadi al-Nabawi*, Muharram 1366/~November 1946, 47–49, at 48.

96. "Fursa Nadira li-Tullab al-ʿIlm," *al-Hadi al-Nabawi*, Shaʿban 1364/~July 1945, 286.

97. See ʿAbd Allah b. Muhammad b. Ahmad al-Turayqi, *Muʿjam Musannafat al-Hanabila* (Riyadh: Maktabat al-Malik Fahd al-Wataniyya, 2001), 8:190–92. Ibn Rashid's story will be told in greater detail in chapter 3.

advertised works by Ibn Taymiyya and his student Ibn Qayyim al-Jawziyya, among others.[98]

During this period, it also appears that Ansar al-Sunna's printing capabilities improved. The November 1946 issue noted an upgrade to the publishing house's printer,[99] though it did not specify the nature of this upgrade or its implications for the organization. The April 1947 issue, however, gave a concrete example of these capabilities: a report noted that Darwish had delivered a lecture on Divine Will and Predestination (*al-Qaḍā' wa'l-Qadar*) at the local Ansar al-Sunna headquarters in the Delta city of Sohag on 28 November 1946, and that the publishing house had then assembled and produced a copy of it for purchase.[100] Efforts to provide these and other texts to a larger audience also persisted: the August 1952 issue of *al-Hadi al-Nabawi* reported efforts to establish a "comprehensive Salafi library" (*maktaba Salafiyya shāmila*).[101]

These publishing efforts served as the intellectual linchpin of a broader project of institutional development. In September 1945, the organization announced the opening of a night school to teach reading, writing, and theology (*Uṣūl al-Dīn*); a charitable fund to treat the sick and aid those in need; and a program to "put unemployed individuals to work" (*tashghīl al-aydī al-'āṭila*).[102] Similarly, in 1946, Ansar al-Sunna provided supplementary Islamic education to children of members,[103] and touted a library of approved religious texts that could be borrowed from its headquarters in Cairo.[104] Finally, in 1948, *al-Hadi al-Nabawi* featured an advertisement for the medical clinic of a doctor by the name of Ahmad Fadil Ratib: although not officially affiliated with Ansar al-Sunna, this clinic offered a 40 percent discount for members and promised male and female doctors depending on the gender of the patient.[105] While

98. "Min Akhbar al-Jama'a," *al-Hadi al-Nabawi*, Rabi' al-Awwal 1369/~December 1949, 48–49, at 49.

99. "Akhbar al-Jama'a," *al-Hadi al-Nabawi*, Muharram 1366/~November 1946, 49.

100. "Akhbar al-Jama'a," *al-Hadi al-Nabawi*, Muharram 1366/~November 1946, 49.

101. "Akhbar al-Jama'a," *al-Hadi al-Nabawi*, Dhu al-Hijja 1371/~August 1952, 29–30.

102. "Ansar al-Sunna al-Muhammadiyya-Shu'bat al-Jiza," *al-Hadi al-Nabawi*, Shawwal 1364/~September 1945, 395.

103. "al-Jam'iyya al-Umumiyya li-Jama'at Ansar al-Sunna al-Muhammadiyya," *al-Hadi al-Nabawi*, Jumada al-Ula 1365/~April 1946, 173–4, at 174.

104. "Jama'at Ansar al-Sunna al-Muhammadiyya," *al-Hadi al-Nabawi*, Rabi' al-Thani 1365/~March 1946, 168.

105. "al-'Iyada al-Shamila," al-Hadi al-Nabawi, Safar 1368/~December 1948, back cover.

committed first and foremost to the transmission of religious knowledge, Ansar al-Sunna's social services thus ranged from education to employment to discounted medical services.

The organization was also concerned to enhance the skills of its most active members. In 1947, it announced the establishment of a preaching school at its headquarters in the Cairene neighborhood of ʿAbidin to be called the House of Preaching and Guidance (*Dār al-Daʿwa waʾl-Irshād*),[106] and a few months leader reported that "an elite group of youth have already agreed to attend this school."[107] Nonetheless, calls for further institutional development persisted: in the summer of 1948, Ansar al-Sunna's General Conference included a proposal delivered by members from the Upper Egyptian city of Minya to establish a parallel educational system equivalent to that of al-Azhar,[108] as well as the provision of regular lessons regarding "morals and the biography of the Prophet, peace be upon Him" (*al-akhlāq wa sīrat al-Nabī sallā Allāh ʿalayhi wa-sallam*).[109]

Ansar al-Sunna also sought, in limited ways, to expand its public profile beyond these institutions. Most prominently, it organized collective prayers, said to include thousands of members, at the Qasr al-Nil barracks (*thaknāt Qaṣr al-Nīl*) during both ʿId al-Fitr and ʿId al-Adha over the summer and fall of 1947. This site was not merely spatially central but also symbolically significant, as it previously had housed Ottoman-Egyptian troops and then their British colonial successors.[110] Ansar al-Sunna organized this event again in the summer of 1948 as it celebrated ʿId al-Fitr, using a microphone to project the holiday sermon for attendees who filled up the adjacent Ismaʿiliyya Square.[111] Similarly, during the ʿId al-Adha celebrations in the fall of 1948, Ansar al-Sunna's leaders used microphones to "amplify their calls of God's

106. "Akhbar al-Jamaʿa," *al-Hadi al-Nabawi*, Jumada al-Thaniyya 1366/~April 1947, 47–48. This name was likely chosen as homage to Rashid Rida's short-lived seminary of the same name, which functioned between 1912 and 1914. See Lauzière, *The Making of Salafism*, 72.

107. Suliman Hasuna, "Kalimat Sikratir al-Jamaʿa," *al-Hadi al-Nabawi*, Shaʿban 1366/~June 1947, 38–40, at 40.

108. While the text does not specify the precise meaning of equivalency, the likely intended meaning is "equivalency of degrees," so as to allow graduates of this system to enroll at al-Azhar for undergraduate studies.

109. al-Muʾtamar al-ʿAmm li-Jamaʿat Ansar al-Sunna al-Muhammadiyya, *al-Hadi al-Nabawi*, Dhu al-Qaʿda 1357/~December 1938, 21–25, 46–47, at 46.

110. "Akhbar al-Jamaʿa," *al-Hadi al-Nabawi*, Muharram 1367/~November 1947, 45–48, at 45.

111. "Akhbar al-Jamaʿa," *al-Hadi al-Nabawi*, Ramadan 1367/~July 1948, 40–50, at 48; "Akhbar al-Jamaʿa," *al-Hadi al-Nabawi*, Shawwal 1367/~August 1947, 48.

greatness" (*yuwaṣṣil aṣwātahum bi-l-takbīr*) in front of a banner that identified the event with Ansar al-Sunna.[112]

Mass celebrations were not limited to religious ritual and, in November 1950, a reported eight hundred Egyptians gathered in the Sayyida Zaynab neighborhood of Cairo to celebrate the organization.[113] At this event, Rashad al-Shafiʿi, then Secretary of Ansar al-Sunna (and later the President between 1972 and 1975), declared that religious leadership "falls on the shoulders of Ansar al-Sunna al-Muhammadiyya. . . . Returning to the Quran and Sunna (*al-ʿawda ilā al-Qurʾān waʾl-Sunna*) will serve as the treatment for all of society's political, social and moral ills."[114] The following month, Ansar al-Sunna's Cairo branch welcomed the doyen of the Wahhabi-Hanbali establishment Muhammad b. Ibrahim (d. 1969) along with leading scholars from the Ministry of Endowments and al-Azhar.[115]

Ansar al-Sunna had also become an organization that could hold multiple large events in quick order. That same month, the Qalyubiyya branch, located in the Nile Delta roughly twenty-five miles from Cairo, gathered a reported one thousand participants,[116] while the Nakla branch (located in the Giza governorate, adjacent to Cairo), celebrated its establishment with a "cultural party" (*ḥafla thaqāfiyya*) attended by five hundred.[117] Thus, in the twilight years of monarchical rule, Ansar al-Sunna had established the building blocks for a mass project of piety. Ansar al-Sunna was not alone in turning to textual transmission and institutional development in its first two decades, however, and it is to the story of competition among Islamic movements—and their relationship to prior models of Islamic leadership and piety alike—that we now turn.

ISLAMIC MOVEMENTS, INTERPRETATIVE METHOD, AND SOCIAL CHANGE

As Ansar al-Sunna laid claim to Islamic leadership during the 1930s and 1940s, it both cooperated and competed with an internally diverse Islamic scene

112. "Salat al-ʿId," *al-Hadi al-Nabawi*, Dhu al-Hijja 1367/~October 1948, 48.

113. "Akhbar al-Jamaʿa," *al-Hadi al-Nabawi*, Rabiʿ al-Awwal 1370/~December 1950, 65–67.

114. "Akhbar al-Jamaʿa," *al-Hadi al-Nabawi*, Rabiʿ al-Awwal 1370/~December 1950, 66.

115. Ibn Ibrahim had come to Cairo for medical treatment and, following this, al-Fiqi escorted him back to Saudi Arabia. "Akhbar al-Jamaʿa," *al-Hadi al-Nabawi*, Rabiʿ al-Thani 1370/~January 1951, 46–47.

116. "Akhbar al-Jamaʿa," *al-Hadi al-Nabawi*, Rabiʿ al-Thani 1370/~January 1951, 46–50, at 47.

117. "Akhbar al-Jamaʿa," *al-Hadi al-Nabawi*, Rabiʿ al-Thani 1370/~January 1951, 50.

which ranged from the Jamʿiyya Sharʿiyya and Muslim Brotherhood to a Brotherhood splinter group known as Muhammad's Youth (*Shabāb Sayyidinā Muḥammad*), the al-Azhar Scholars' Front (*Jabhat ʿUlamāʾ al-Azhar*), and the Islamic Education Association (*Jamʿiyyat al-Tarbiya al-Islāmiyya*). While these groups were divided on questions of theology, legal method, and the legitimacy of borrowing foreign political models and educational approaches, they were united by common opponents. Accordingly, in the early 1940s, they came together to form "the Islamic Association" (*al-Hayʾa al-Islāmiyya*) to face domestic and international challenges, including the pro-British policies of King Faruq, secular-nationalist political movements such as the Wafd, and Westernizing cultural trends.[118]

This is a story that begins, formally speaking, in October 1942, when the Islamic Association declared that all its members shared a commitment to the Quran and Sunna and the use of revelation (*naql*) over reason (*ʿaql*) in interpreting Islam's core sources, as well as an opposition to the practice of declaring other Muslims beyond the pale of the faith based on sinful actions (*takfīr*).[119] While the Association issued a joint statement calling on then Prime Minister Mahmud Fahmi al-Nuqrashi (d. 1948) to take action to stem the spread of "indecent periodicals" (*al-majallāt al-khalīʿa*) in March 1947,[120] it only formulated a more broad-based articulation of its core concerns in September 1947.

The September 1947 declaration was notable for the breadth of its signatories and concerns. Its signature line suggested a burgeoning alliance, including members of the previously mentioned groups as well as representatives of the Islamic Morals Association (*Jamʿiyyat Makārim al-Akhlāq*) and the Young

118. "Wujub Taʿawun al-Hayʾat al-Islamiyya fi Muqawamat al-Batil," *al-Iʿtisam*, 28 Rajab 1366/~May 1947, 8.

119. On the surface, a concern with *takfīr* appears odd, given that it was only popularized in the 1960s under the ideological influence of Sayyid Qutb (d. 1966). The source of concern may have been King Faruq's religious legitimacy: a June 1939 article in *al-Hadi al-Nabawi* implicitly acknowledges serious challenges on this front by counseling against declaring rulers illegitimate (*al-khurūj ʿalayhim*). See Muhammad Bahjat al-Baytar, "Asʾila wa Ajwibatiha," *al-Hadi al-Nabawi*, Jumada al-Ula 1358/ June 1939, 50–52, at 50. In the cited article, the term is used not to make a determination about whether the King had committed major sins, but rather to simply signal that he was not Muslim.

120. "Mudhakkirat al-Hayʾat al-Islamiyya ila Raʾis Majlis al-Wuzaraʾ," *al-Iʿtisam*, 27 Jumada al-Ula 1366/~March 1947, 16.

Men's Muslim Association. This text also offered a catchall statement of concerns ranging from poverty to public and private immorality, to the battle against "unlawful innovation and superstition" (*al-bidaʿ wa'l-khurāfāt*).[121] Nonetheless, we should not overstate the significance of this alliance: its varied priorities may be read less as a coherent program than as a minimal consensus of Islamic groups during this period.

Just as importantly, the September 1947 statement evinced a political quietism characteristic of Islamic movements at this time.[122] Specifically, it rejected all engagement in "political partisanship" (*al-siyāsa al-ḥizbiyya*) in favor of work in "pursuit of the good of Islam and the nation" (*li-khayr al-Islām wa'l-waṭan*).[123] In this effort, the Muslim Brotherhood sought to position itself as first among equals: in a July 1947 meeting, Salih ʿAshmawi (d. 1983), a leading Brotherhood member, declared that the movement's headquarters and periodicals were always open to the input of the Association's members.[124]

This statement, though, also masked the persistence of competing claims to authenticity. Most notably, in a January 1941 article, an author in *al-Hadi al-Nabawi* had taken aim at the Jamʿiyya Sharʿiyya, referring to the organization as "the people strongest in their opposition to the Sunna of the Messenger of God and those who advocate it" (*ashadd al-nās ʿadāwa*[an] *li-Sunnat Rasūl Allāh wa anṣārihā*).[125] Yet Ansar al-Sunna's indictment of its competitor did

121. "Ittihad al-Hay'at al-Islamiyya," *al-Iʿtisam*, 21 Shawwal 1366/~7 September 1947, 5.

122. The Brotherhood displayed more ambivalence in its internal debates about whether to field candidates for parliament. See Mitchell, *The Society of the Muslim Brothers*, 17, 309–10.

123. "Ittihad al-Hay'at al-Islamiyya," *al-Iʿtisam*, 21 Shawwal 1366/~7 September 1947, 5.

124. "Harakat Islah al-Hay'at al-Islamiyya," *al-Iʿtisam*, 16 Shaʿban 1366/~5 July 1947, 20.

125. "Hani'[an] li-l-Jamʿiyya al-Sharʿiyya," *al-Hadi al-Nabawi*, 1 Dhu al-Qaʿda 1359/1 December 1940, 24. The issue at hand was a recent book, *al-Fath al-Mubin fi al-ʿAmal bi-l-Din al-Matin* (*The Manifest Victory in Acting According to the Firm Religion*), written by ʿAbd Allah al-ʿAfifi. A graduate of al-Azhar, the author was also the leading preacher (*al-wāʿiẓ al-awwal*) of the Jamʿiyya Sharʿiyya, and the Imam and Khatib of the main JS mosque. Ansar al-Sunna took the position that, in this text, al-ʿAfifi placed himself on the same level as the prophets of the Islamic tradition (*fī maṣaff al-anbiyāʾ al-mursalīn*). Ansar al-Sunna also criticized the Grand Shaykh's office at al-Azhar for its failure to censor the book. On the latter, see "Min Suwar al-Hayat al-Misriyya," *al-Hadi al-Nabawi*, Dhu al-Qaʿda 1359/~December 1940, 19–22. This critique likely also reflected theological disagreements between Ansar al-Sunna and the Jamʿiyya Sharʿiyya's founder, Mahmud Muhammad Khattab al-Subki (d. 1933), who challenged the former's neo-Hanbali theological approach. See Lauzière, *The Making of Salafism*, 122–25. Al-Subki's standing was a matter of dispute. Rashid Rida, eulogizing al-Subki in *al-Manar*, praised him for his commitment to "worship" (*ʿibāda*) and the fight against "unlawful

not reflect the latter's self-perception, as a September 1942 article in *al-I'tisam* reiterated the Jam'iyya Shar'iyya's commitment to "the limits set by the Quran and the purified Sunna" (*ḥudūd al-Qur'ān wa'l-Sunna al-muṭahhara*).[126] It also appears that, to at least some degree, the Jam'iyya Shar'iyya's claim found acceptance: a 17 June 1947 article in *al-I'tisam* reported that Muhammad's Youth had declared that

> Islamic associations . . . [work] to spread Islam's virtuous teachings, to fight destructive calls, and to protect traditions inherited from the Pious Ancestors (*al-taqālīd al-mawrūtha 'an al-Salaf al-Ṣāliḥ*) . . . and the Jam'iyya Shar'iyya is at the forefront (*fī muqaddamat*) of these efforts. . . .[127]

In other words, Ansar al-Sunna's professed commitment to the Prophetic model did not categorically distinguish it from its competitors at a time when its elites were engaged in an effort to pit longstanding markers of learning and comportment against reconstructed understandings of Islam's early decades.

As it challenged inherited religious practice and the legal tradition that undergirded it, Ansar al-Sunna's critique of the status quo was both interpretative and social. In August 1937, 'Abd al-Zahir Abu-l-Samh, a leading member of Ansar al-Sunna who was at this time employed as the Imam and Khatib of the Great Mosque of Mecca, sounded the alarm. Specifically, he noted the danger to Islam posed by "the distance of the *'ulamā'* from the Quran and Sunna . . . and distancing of the people from it" (*bu'uduhum 'an al-Kitāb wa'l-Sunna . . . wa ib'āduhum al-nās 'anhā*).[128] Just a few months later, Abu-l-Samh

innovation" (*bid'a*), and for his efforts as an author of scholarly works and teacher. A reader from the Hijaz then wrote to challenge the depiction of al-Subki as one of "the proponents of the Sunna" (*anṣār al-Sunna*), and critically noted al-Subki's disagreement with neo-Hanbali theology. For Rida's article, see "Wafayat al-A'yan," *al-Manar*, Rabi' al-Awwal 1352/~June 1933, 33:320. For the reader's response, see "Intiqad wa As'ila min Jadda (al-Hijaz)," *al-Manar*, 14 Dhu al-Qa'da 1352/28 February 1933, 33:676–77.

126. "Nabdha 'an Nash'at al-Jam'iyya al-Shar'iyya li-Ta'awun al-'Amilin bi-l-Kitab wa'l-Sunna al-Muhammadiyya," *al-I'tisam*, 13 Ramadan 1361/22 September 1942, 3–5, at 5. Similarly, a 26 October 1946 article declared that the Jam'iyya Shar'iyya's mosques carry the "flag of the purified Sunna" (*liwā' al-Sunna al-muṭahhara*). See Muhammad Naji al-Bajuri, "Ahl al-Sunna," *al-I'tisam*, 1 Dhu al-Hijja 1365/26 October 1946, 6–7.

127. "Wujub Ta'awun al-Hay'at al-Islamiyya fi Muqawamat al-Batil," *al-I'tisam*, 28 Rajab 1366/17 June 1947, 8.

128. 'Abd al-Zahir Abiual-Samh, "al-Din al-Khalis," *al-Hadi al-Nabawi*, Jumada al-Thaniyya 1356/~August 1937, 9–14, at 13.

elaborated on this critique, asking rhetorically why al-Azhar's religious institutes and teachers' college "impose conditions . . . regarding the complete memorization of the Quran without possibility of flexibility . . . but the Prophetic model (*al-Sunna al-Nabawiyya*) does not receive this type of attention (*hadhahi al-ʿināya*)."[129]

Ansar al-Sunna's critique of the status quo, however, was not limited to al-Azhar. As an unsigned article in the May 1939 issue declared that

> [True] jihad can only come from an Islamic community in which true Islam has swept away the remnants of polytheism and paganism (*al-shirk wa'l-wathaniyya*) . . . and benefits from correct Islam, in knowledge and theology, action, ethics, wisdom and order . . . [yet] 99 percent of the Islamic community [currently] exists in a state of pre-Islamic barbarism (*jāhiliyya*).[130]

In the face of this challenge, Ansar al-Sunna promised to "translate the view of the Pious Ancestors in the law of the Quran and Sunna. . . . God's oneness (*al-Tawḥīd*) is the first goal. . . ."[131]

The most notable disagreement produced by this approach would be Ansar al-Sunna's position on the turban (*al-ʿimāma*), a longstanding visible marker of Islamic identity in Egypt and beyond.[132] During the interwar period, competing Islamic movements and state institutions debated this form of headgear, a conversation that was part and parcel of a broader negotiation of the relationship among religion, national identity, and dress across the Middle

129. ʿAbd al-Zahir Abu al-Samh, "al-Din al-Khalis," *al-Hadi al-Nabawi*, Ramadan 1356/November 1937, 20–4, at 21.

130. "Jihad Ansar al-Sunna al-Muhammadiyya," *al-Hadi al-Nabawi*, Rabiʿ al-Awwal 1358/~April 1939, 36–8, at 36–7. On the translation of this term as barbarism rather than ignorance, see Ignac Goldziher, *Muhammedanische Studien* (N.P.: Halle A. S., Max Niemeyer, 1889), 225.

131. Muhammad Sadiq ʿArnus, "al-Tawhid," *al-Hadi al-Nabawi*, 15 Muharram 1359/~24 February 1940, 13–18, at 13.

132. According to the Sunni hadith corpus, both Muhammad and his Companions wore turbans. For example, see Abu ʿAbd Allah Muhammad b. Yazid b. Maja, *Sunan al-Hafiz Abi ʿAbd Allah Muhammad Ibn Yazid al-Qazwini Ibn Maja 207–275 H*, ed. Muhammad Fuʾad ʿAbd al-Baqi (Cairo: Dar Ihyaʾ al-Kutub al-ʿArabiyya, 1952–53), 1:1186. The turban remained in use among Sunnis up through the late nineteenth century. See Charles Issawi, *The Fertile Crescent, 1800–1914: A Documentary Economic History* (New York: Oxford University Press, 1988), 390–91. Finally, the black turban has long been used by Shiʿi Muslims to signal descent from the Prophet Muhammad, who is said to have worn a turban of this style.

East.[133] While chapter 6 will analyze debates over proper dress in greater detail, this section explores a narrower matter: is it permissible to pray without a turban?

On one side of the question stood Ansar al-Sunna and the Muslim Brotherhood. In May 1949, Abu-l-Wafa' Muhammad Darwish explained that the practice of covering one's head during prayer is a "custom of the people" (*ʿādat al-nās*).[134] In December 1949, Darwish went further, proudly proclaimed that his organization's members "pray in shoes while their heads are uncovered" (*yuṣallūn bi-aḥdhiyatihim wa-ruʾūsuhum ʿāriya*).[135] Neither was this position vis-à-vis bareheaded prayer a one-time affair: *al-Hadi al-Nabawi* published fatwas permitting this practice in both February and July 1965.[136] Yet, in taking this position, Ansar al-Sunna was joined by a seemingly unlikely bedfellow: the Muslim Brotherhood. In both April and May 1948, the latter's magazine featured fatwas that reserved the categorization of disfavored status (*karāha*) to the practice of praying bareheaded out of laziness (*bi-l-kasal*), while permitting the practice more broadly.[137]

133. The Salafi debate over legitimate dress, while centered in Egypt, was tied to debates in Turkey and Iran during the early twentieth century. On Turkey, see Jenny White, *Muslim Nationalism and the New Turks* (Princeton, NJ: Princeton University Press, 2013), 27–28, and on Iran, see Ali M. Ansari, *Modern Iran: The Pahlavis and After* (New York: Routledge, 2007), 57–59.

134. "Bab al-Fatawa," *al-Hadi al-Nabawi*, Shaʿban 1358/~May 1949, 30–41, at 40–41.

135. Abu-l-Wafa' Muhammad Darwish, "Nahnu wa Majallat Liwa' al-Islam" *al-Hadi al-Nabawi*, Rabiʿ al-Awwal 1369/~December 1949, 21–5. However, Ansar al-Sunna's rejection of the turban during prayer and their agnostic view of its use beyond prayer did not dominate the Salafi debate: in a May 1956 article in *al-Tamaddun al-Islami*, Muhammad Nasir al-Din al-Albani challenged a hadith report that stated that one's prayers are considered more valuable by a factor of 10,000 if performed in a turban. Nonetheless, according to al-Albani "a Muslim needs a turban outside of prayer far more than inside because [such practices] distinguish him from the infidels (*tumayyizuhu ʿan al-kāfir*), particularly in an age in which the clothing of believers has grown similar to that of the infidels." He then notes that many Muslims were wearing "false turbans" (*al-ʿimāma al-mustaʿāra*) just as they wear "false beards" (*al-liḥya al-mustaʿāra*). See Muhammad Nasir al-Din al-Albani, "al-Ahadith al-Daʿifa wa'l-Mawduʿa," *al-Tamaddun al-Islami*, Shawwal 1375/Ayyar (May) 1956, 517–21, at 517–18.

136. "Bab al-Fatawa," *al-Hadi al-Nabawi*, Shawwal 1384/~February 1965 33–39, at 33–34, and "Bab al-Fatawa," *al-Hadi al-Nabawi*, Rabiʿ al-Akhar 1385/~July 1965, 32–7, at 32–33.

137. See Muhammad al-Ghazali, "Istiftaʾat," *al-Ikhwan al-Muslimun*, 15 Jumada al-Thaniyya 1367/24 April 1948, 8, 20; Jadd Subh, "al-Istiftaʾat," *al-Ikhwan al-Muslimun*, 29 Jumada al-Thaniyya 1367/8 May 1948, 19–20.

By contrast, the dominant opinion within the Jamʿiyya Sharʿiyya was that such a practice is disfavored (*makrūh*) regardless of intent, based on authenticated hadith reports that chronicle the Prophet Muhammad's practice of "wiping" (*al-masḥ*) the turban as part of a regime of ritual purity (*wuḍūʾ*). Furthermore, according to the organization's Mufti and leading preacher,[138] ʿAli Hasan Hulwa, donning a turban has the effect of increasing the efficacy of one's prayers.[139] A minority opinion in the organization, by contrast, held that it is praiseworthy (*mustaḥabb*) to pray while wearing a turban but permissible (*jāʾiz*) to pray without one.[140] Hulwa's concern, however, was not limited to ritual: he also sought to dispute the claim, advanced by a man who presumably had removed his turban in favor of either a brimmed hat (*qubʿa*) or red felt hat (*ṭarbūsh*), that the turban was a mere "custom" (*ʿāda*).[141]

What united Ansar al-Sunna and the Brotherhood on the turban was not textual methodology but rather a shared rejection of an older scholarly order and attendant markers of status for this order's representatives. While the third chapter of this book addresses the rise and fall of praying in shoes and the fifth and sixth chapters explore Ansar al-Sunna's challenge to Western-inspired fashion trends, the rejection the turban, articulated in the context of ritual practice, casts light on the social clashes that emerged from Ansar al-Sunna's efforts to question normative models of ritual rectitude. In this context, a claim to continuity with the Sunna was *also* a challenge to over a millennium of Islamic legal debate and practice, preserved by *madhhab*-aligned traditionalist scholars in early-twentieth-century Egypt. Both Ansar al-Sunna's differences with these scholars as well as the Brotherhood, however, would soon extend far beyond this dismissal of the old order.

138. While Hulwa is regular identified as the organization's Mufti, a 1 March 1947 article further describes him as the head preacher of the Jamʿiyya Sharʿiyya branches in Cairo (*wāʿiẓ al-Jamʿiyyāt al-Sharʿiyya bi-l-Qāhira*). See ʿAli Hasan Hulwa, "Asʾila wa Ajwiba," *al-Iʿtisam*, 8 Rabiʿ al-Thani 1366/~1 March 1947, 12.

139. ʿAli Hasan Hulwa, "Asʾila wa Ajwiba," *al-Iʿtisam*, 20 Ramadan 1365/17 August 1946, 2, 4.

140. Kamal Muhammad ʿIsa, "al-ʿImama Sunna li-l-Rijal wa fi al-Salat Akad, *al-Iʿtisam*, 7 Safar 1370/17 November 1950, 17–18.

141. ʿAli Hasan Hulwa, "Asʾila wa Ajwiba," *al-Iʿtisam*, 20 Ramadan 1365/17 August 1946, 2, 4.

THE CHALLENGE OF SECULAR NATIONALISM: QUIETISM, REPRESENTATION, AND INSTITUTION BUILDING

In 1951, ʿAbd al-Rahman al-Wakil (d. 1971), a graduate of al-Azhar[142] who would serve as al-ʿAfifi's Vice-President between 1959 and 1960 and subsequently as president himself, reiterated the organization's position on politics:

> Ansar al-Sunna does not engage in politics or patriotism (*al-siyāsa aw al-waṭaniyya*) . . . [because] politics is defined by corruption and division (*al-fasād wa'l-shiqāq*). . . . [Instead] we work to unite Muslims with their Lord in worship. . . .[143]

Previously articulated concerns regarding the spread of immorality had not vanished, and al-Wakil called on the government to declare a war on wrongdoing (*ḥarb ʿalā al-munkarāt*).[144] The political winds, however, would soon change dramatically.

In July 1952, the Free Officers Revolution, led by Muhammad Najib and Jamal ʿAbd al-Nasir, overthrew King Faruq and offered a promise of potential alliance between Islamic movements and the new Revolutionary Command Council (RCC). At this time, little appears to have changed for Ansar al-Sunna: in late 1952, the organization's board announced plans to build a new mosque in downtown Cairo "at a transportation meeting point" (*ʿinda multaqā al-muwāṣalāt*) and asked members to contribute towards this effort.[145] Neither was al-Fiqi alone in making peace with the post-1952 order: an August 1952 declaration in *al-Iʿtisam* signed by the organization's President (and son of the founder) Amin Muhammad Khattab praised the "the glorious Egyptian army" (*al-jaysh al-Miṣrī al-majīd*).[146]

142. On al-Wakil's experience at al-Azhar, see Richard Gauvain, "Egyptian Sufism Under the Hammer: A Preliminary Investigation into the Anti-Sufi Polemics of ʿAbd al-Rahman al-Wakil (1913–1970)," in *Sufis and Salafis in the Contemporary Age*, ed. Lloyd Ridgeon (London: Bloomsbury Academic, 2015), 39–42.

143. ʿAbd al-Rahman al-Wakil, "Mawqif Ansar al-Sunna min Ilghaʾ al-Muʿahada," *al-Hadi al-Nabawi*, Safar 1371/November 1951, 5–8, at 5. This is not to say, however, that the organization had no interest in the duty to command right and forbid wrong; a late 1953 article in *al-Hadi al-Nabawi* evinced a provisional interest in such a project, noting the obligation of Muslims to rid society of evil (*munkar*) according to their capability. See "al-Amr bi-l-Maʿruf wa'l-Nahi ʿan al-Munkar," *al-Hadi al-Nabawi*, Rabiʿ al-Thani-Jumada al-Awwal 1373/~December 1953-January 1954, 37–38.

144. ʿAbd al-Rahman al-Wakil, "Mawqif Ansar al-Sunna min Ilghaʾ al-Muʿahada," 6.

145. "al-Masjid al-Jamiʿ," *al-Hadi al-Nabawi*, Jumada al-Thaniyya 1372/~February 1953, 2.

146. "Bayan al-Jamʿiyya al-Sharʿiyya," *al-Iʿtisam*, 1 Dhu al-Hijja 1371/22 August 1952, 4–7.

The alliance between the RCC and the Brotherhood, however, was short-lived: an attempted assassination of ʿAbd al-Nasir in October 1954 was followed by a campaign to repress its onetime ally.[147] The end of colonial rule meant not only the opportunity for independence but also the removal of a justification for unity that had bound Ansar al-Sunna to other Islamic movements that did not share its theological or legal commitments. As thousands of Muslim Brothers toiled in Egyptian prisons and ʿAbd al-Nasir's allies in the bureaucracy revised school curricula to glorify socialism and nationalism alike,[148] al-Fiqi visited the president to congratulate him on the expulsion of the British from Egypt.[149]

Notwithstanding the optics of this warm welcome, the rise of authoritarian secular nationalism in Egypt raised urgent questions not merely regarding the bounds of quietism but also of how to respond to this revolutionary order's claim to political allegiance and public space alike. The most clear-cut manifestation of this question involved the representation of the Egyptian nation. This question was not new: in the 1920s and 1930s, this political community was frequently depicted as a woman on paintings, pictures, posters, statues, and stamps.[150] Early-twentieth-century Egypt also saw the creation of statues showcasing nationalist leaders such as Mustafa Kamil (d. 1908) and Saʿad Zaghlul.[151] The most prominent monument in Egypt during the first half of the twentieth century, however, was Mahmud Mukhtar's *The Awakening of Egypt* (*Nahdat Miṣr*), which commemorated the 1919 revolution and "juxtapose[d] two images: the Sphinx rising and a peasant woman unveiling."[152] Yet, as Beth Baron notes, this statue "fell out of favor among Islamists who denounced 'pagan' symbols in the 1930s,"[153] a position that was mirrored in the 1950s by leading Salafi scholars such as Muhammad Nasir al-Din al-Albani who rejected varied methods of representing humans, whether statues or photographs.[154]

147. Mitchell, *The Society of the Muslim Brothers*, 150–62.

148. Starrett, *Putting Islam to Work*, 79.

149. "Akhbar al-Jamaʿa," *al-Hadi al-Nabawi*, Rabiʿ al-Awwal 1374/~November 1954, 49–51, at 49.

150. Beth Baron, *Egypt as a Woman: Nationalism, Gender and Politics* (Berkeley: University of California Press, 2005), 64.

151. Baron, *Egypt as a Woman*, 65–69, 74–77, 155–56.

152. Baron, *Egypt as a Woman*, 67–68.

153. Baron, *Egypt as a Woman*, 68.

154. Muhammad Nasir al-Din al-Albani, *Tadhir al-Sajid min Ittikhadh al-Qubur Masajid* (Damascus, Syria: al-Maktab al-Islami, 1983), 12–13. The first edition of this text was published

In the shadow of a nationalist tradition of visual and physical representation alike, the September 1954 issue of *al-Hadi al-Nabawi* included a fatwa request by a Cairene resident, Saʿad al-Din Muhammad. Muhammad's question was seemingly straightforward: "What is [Islam's] ruling on the erecting of symbols that signify nationalist messages (*mā ḥukm iqāmat al-rumūz allatī tumathil maʿānī waṭaniyya*)? What is the Shariʿa's position on erecting large statues (*iqāmat al-tamāthīl al-uẓamāʾ*)?"[155] In response, Abu-l-Wafaʾ Muhammad Darwish explained that during the Prophet's time, "the concepts of goodness and obedience to God (*maʿānī al-khayr waʾl-birr*) were present . . . whether bravery, altruism, sacrifice, sincerity or allegiance (*min al-shajāʿa waʾl-īthār waʾl-taḍḥiya waʾl-ikhlāṣ*), yet the Prophet did not erect a physical symbol (*ramz^an mujassam^an*) for them." Darwish further explained that Muhammad forbade his Companions from hanging their swords on trees and seeking intercession as the polytheists (*mushrikūn*) did.[156]

Darwish then proceeded to distinguish between symbols and statues:

> [I]f symbols have [solely] a worldly meaning (*maʿnā dunyawī*) . . . and do not involve excess or waste of money, and do not depict people (*lā tumaththil ashkhāṣ^an*) and do not make a religious claim (*lā tushīr ilā maʿanā dīnī*) . . . and the people do not circumambulate them [as the pagan Arabs did] and do not prostrate themselves to it (*lā yatamassaḥūn bihā*), then there is no objection to erecting them. And the Prophet, Peace Be Upon Him, said: 'You know best in worldly matters.' As for statues (*al-tamāthīl*), the texts of the purified Shariʿa prohibit them absolutely and we should spend the money that would be spent [on statues] on matters that help Muslims. And God knows best.[157]

In this formulation, Darwish distinguishes between national symbols that depict people and those which do not. While statues of particular individuals

---

in 1957. Also see Ondřej Beránek and Pavel Ťupek, *The Temptation of Graves in Salafi Islam: Iconoclasm, Destruction and Idolatry* (Edinburgh, UK: Edinburgh University Press, 2019), 139–40.

155. Abu-l-Wafaʾ Muhammad Darwish, "Bab al-Fatawa," *al-Hadi al-Nabawi*, Safar 1374/~September 1954, 29–34, at 30.

156. Darwish, "Bab al-Fatawa," *al-Hadi al-Nabawi*, Safar 1374/~September 1954, 29–34, at 31–32. According to the Muslim historian Ibn al-Athir (d. 630/1233), this refers to a specific tree in Arabia on which pagan Arabs hung their weapons and then sought intercession from the tree. See ʿAli ʿIzz al-Din b. al-Athir al-Jazari, *al-Nihaya fi Gharib al-Hadith waʾl-Athar* ed. Mahmud Muhammad al-Tanahi (N.P: al-Maktaba al-Islamiyya, 1383/1963), 5:128.

157. Darwish, "Bab al-Fatawa," *al-Hadi al-Nabawi*, Safar 1374/~September 1954, 29–34, at 32.

or representative human images of the nation fall into the former camp, acceptable monuments could range from the national flag to currency that depicts the mythical Sphinx or the Pyramids.

The significance of Darwish's response, however, lies not in line that he draws regarding human depiction, but rather in his acceptance of the assumption that physical symbols could depict abstract values or allegiances as long as they did not become a site of human veneration. His account of early Islamic history noted that the Prophet Muhammad saw little need to create such symbols to represent particular values, and decried the pagan Arabian practice of hanging swords on a tree and imputing power to it. And indeed, Salafis within and beyond Ansar al-Sunna were already predisposed to skepticism regarding physical markers of memorial based on their association of grave-visiting (*ziyārat al-qubūr*) with Sufism.[158] Yet instead of using this precedent as a basis for rejecting monuments, Darwish noted that the Prophet offered Muslims broad latitude in worldly matters.

Indeed, for Ansar al-Sunna more broadly, this was not the time to pick fights over nationalist icons but rather to steer clear of any hint of opposition. Accordingly, an August 1955 article in *al-Hadi al-Nabawi* reiterated the organization's resolutely quietist line:

> [T]he organization's political goals are to preserve security and order (*al-muḥāfaẓa ʿalā al-amn waʾl-amān*) and to communicate the voice of the oppressed to the ruler. Our position is [merely] that of monitoring and holding to account (*al-raqīb waʾl-ḥasīb*) as we have absolutely no desire to rule (*lā naṭmaʿ fi-l-ḥukm muṭlaq^{an}*) in any shape or form.[159]

Although suggestive of a theoretical commitment to public morality, Ansar al-Sunna's elites showed little interest in grassroots religious change at this time.

But even this limited level of accountability was easier declared than achieved. The September 1957 issue of *al-Hadi al-Nabawi* contained a statement of principles that emphasized the necessity of Egyptian Muslims returning

158. Muhammad Hamid al-Fiqi, "Majallat al-Shuʾun al-Ijtimaʿiyya," *al-Hadi al-Nabawi*, 1 Jumada al-Ula 1359/~7 June 1940, 38–40, at 38. This skepticism was not limited to Ansar al-Sunna: Muhammad Nasir al-Din al-Albani stipulated that his grave remain unmarked in order to prevent it from becoming a site of pilgrimage. I thank Emad Hamdeh for this information.

159. "Akhbar al-Jamaʿa," *al-Hadi al-Nabawi*, Muharram 1375/~August 1955, 46.

to proper understanding and observance of their faith.[160] In September 1957, Darwish elaborated on the implications of this quietism, declaring that "[t]he prophetic migration (*hijra*) was an awakening (*baʿth*) in the path of freedom, just as our blessed [Free Officers'] revolution (*thawratunā al-mubāraka*) is an awakening (*baʿth*) in the path of freedom."[161] Ansar al-Sunna was, at best, minimally concerned with the question of whether the state under which it lived applied Islamic law.

This quietism appears to have provided Ansar al-Sunna with a degree of grassroots freedom. While the organization did experience a slowdown in the expansion of its branches,[162] it persisted in the development of institutions to spread a distinctly Salafi call. Most notably, the November 1954 issue, published just a couple months after a mass crackdown on the Brotherhood, noted that the Nakla branch (Giza) had established a "Daʿwa Propagation Council" (*Lajnat Nashr al-Daʿwa*) to coordinate lectures and conferences and to publish relevant texts in tandem with a council of the same name located at Ansar al-Sunna's headquarters in Cairo.[163] Similarly, the February 1956 issue announced the creation of a "High Council" (*Lajna ʿUlyā*) to work with branches in order to "develop programs . . . based on the Quran and the Sunna."[164] Neither did such activity cease during the next decade: the September 1962 issue reported that hundreds had attended a lecture at the Tanta branch by ʿAbd al-Razzaq al-ʿAfifi,[165] while the May 1966 issue, published just a few months before Sayyid Qutb went to the gallows, reproduced the schedule for regular Ansar al-Sunna-sponsored Friday sermons throughout Egypt that included both leading and lesser-known scholars within the organization.[166]

160. "Jamaʿat Ansar al-Sunna al-Muhammadiyya," *al-Hadi al-Nabawi*, Safar 1375/~September 1955, 34.

161. Abu-l-Wafaʾ Muhammad Darwish, "Inbiʿath fi Sabil al-Hurriyya," *al-Hadi al-Nabawi*, Safar-Jumada al-Ula 1377/~August-September 1957, 53–54, at 53.

162. For an exception to this trend, see "Akhbar al-Jamaʿa," *al-Hadi al-Nabawi*, Jumada al-Ula waʾl-Thaniyya 1374/~December 1954-January 1955, 51.

163. "Akhbar al-Jamaʿa," *al-Hadi al-Nabawi*, Rabiʿ al-Thani 1374/~November 1954, 33–35.

164. "Akhbar al-Jamaʿa," *al-Hadi al-Nabawi*, Rabiʿ al-Thani-Rajab 1375/~November-December 1955, 94–96, at 94.

165. "Akhbar al-Jamaʿa," *al-Hadi al-Nabawi*, Jumada al-Ula 1382/~September 1962, 48.

166. "Barnamaj Khutab al-Jumʿa Khilal Shahr Safar 1385 al-Muwafiq Yunyu 1965 Miladi," *al-Hadi al-Nabawi*, Safar 1386/~May 1966, 50–51.

At the same time, we should not confuse institutional development with broad-based activism. While the 1950s and 1960s saw notable development of Ansar al-Sunna's organizational structures, few new branches were established. Just as importantly, 'Abd al-Nasir's embrace of a secular-nationalist vision of modernity and claim to Islam as a source of programmatic legitimacy for this project stood in direct conflict with Ansar al-Sunna's commitment to deriving all law from the Quran and Sunna. Finally, Ansar al-Sunna's quietism could not protect it from eventual repression: following Egypt's defeat in the 1967 Arab-Israeli war, 'Abd al-Nasir ordered the shuttering of *al-Hadi al-Nabawi,* the seizure of Ansar al-Sunna's national network of branches and mosques, and a forcible merger with the Jam'iyya Shar'iyya.[167] In 1972, under the rule of Anwar al-Sadat (r. 1970–81), the organization reemerged legally and regained access to scores of branches and mosques that it had once controlled.[168] As it returned to preaching, Ansar al-Sunna would confront not only new opportunities for activism but also resurgent competitors as ideologically diverse Islamic institutions and movements sought to shape an Islamic Revival in 1970s Egypt.

CONCLUSION

During the 1930s and 1940s, Ansar al-Sunna developed both a national network of branches and mosques and a canon of authoritative Salafi texts to be sold or taught through its new institutions. These efforts, in turn, enabled it to compete with varied movements, Islamic and non-Islamic, to lay claim to textual and social authority alike. This process reveals not only Ansar al-Sunna's priorities, but also the dynamic formation of Salafism as a subtradition within Islam. The privileging of Classical Islamic sources reflected new opportunities for religious production and consumption, as well the significance of the Islamic scholarly tradition for claims to cultural authenticity in the face of political, religious, and economic upheaval. That Ansar al-Sunna's emphasis on this resurrected textual corpus appears obvious or natural reflects the success of Salafism's call to religious authenticity in an age of dislocation.

167. Salah al-Din Hasan, *al-Salafiyyun fi Misr* (Giza, Egypt: Awraq li-l-Nashr wa'l-Tawzi', 2013), 8.

168. "Akhbar al-Jama'a," *al-Tawhid,* Jumada al-Ula 1373/January 1954, 1:54.

The question of transmitting a vision of Salafi subjectivity that could position communication as ethical practice, however, remained unanswered. In its first four decades, Ansar al-Sunna had only moved haltingly beyond the mosque and the educational activities that it hosted in its branches. Furthermore, unlike either its secular nationalist or Islamist competitors, it had yet to articulate a broader project of pious communication through visible social cues, even as it had begun to engage with the broader conceptual questions of abstract representation. In the 1930s, though, Ansar al-Sunna inaugurated a process that would prove essential to moving beyond a focus on precise ritual practice: an unacknowledged adjustment of the longstanding boundary between devotional acts (*ʿibādāt*) that are obligatory and "customs" (*ʿādāt*) that differ across time and space. It is to this transformation—and its implications—that we now turn.

CHAPTER 2

Conquering Custom in the Name of *Tawhid*

The Salafi Expansion of Worship

In 2002, Ahmad Muhammad al-Tahir defended his doctoral dissertation at Umm al-Qurra University in Mecca. This dissertation, which would form the basis of a book of the same name published simultaneously in 2004 in both Saudi Arabia and Egypt, was entitled *The Ansar al-Sunna al-Muhammadiyya Organization: Its Rise, Goals, Approach and Efforts.* In the introduction to this study, al-Tahir's advisor, Dr. ʿAbd Allah Shakir al-Junaydi,[1] praised this work as the first book-length treatment of the organization that explores "its activities, goals, call, actions and most prominent preachers who contributed to its revival and progress." He hoped "that my Muslim brothers generally and members of Ansar al-Sunna in particular will benefit from these blessed efforts. . . ."[2]

While much of this four-hundred-page-plus study dealt with Ansar al-Sunna's political history, al-Tahir noted towards the conclusion that the organization's major contributions lay in the realms of theology (*al-Āthār al-ʿAqadiyya*), "society and behavior" (*al-Āthār al-Ijtimāʿiyya waʾl-Sulūkiyya*), the Islamic sciences (*al-Āthār al-ʿIlmiyya*), and politics (*al-Āthār al-Siyāsiyya*). In the specific field of society and behavior, the author highlighted Ansar al-Sunna's success in "the revival of Prophetic practices" (*iḥyāʾ al-Sunan*) and their

1. Junaydi was not only the President of the Islamic Studies Department at the Faculty of Teachers in Qunfudha, a Saudi city off the coast of the Red Sea, but also the Vice President of Ansar al-Sunna in Egypt.

2. al-Tahir, *Jamaʿat Ansar al-Sunna al-Muhammadiyya*, 7.

commitment to the "sound [performance of] devotional acts" (*siḥḥat al-ʿibādāt*). In this overview, al-Tahir singled out Muhammad Nasir al-Din al-Albani's landmark pamphlet on the details of how this leading Salafi scholar concluded that the Prophet Muhammad prayed, and ʿAbd al-ʿAziz b. Baz's work on the rituals of the Hajj and ʿUmra.[3] Beyond the strict realm of ritual practice, he further noted Ansar al-Sunna's successful effort to combat "many the customs and traditions (*al-ādāt wa'l-taqālīd*) which contravene the rulings and directions of the Shariʿa," such as excessively long funeral processions, the use of musical instruments, and the spread of mixed-gender educational and social spaces.[4]

How did Ansar al-Sunna seek to regulate the diverse practices of the Egyptian society from which it had emerged? While later chapters will trace the process by which Salafi scholars articulated a set of social practices meant to embody their commitment to the Prophetic model, this chapter explores how these scholars constructed an intellectual architecture of Islamic law premised on an expansive definition of acts of worship (*ʿibādāt*) that narrowed the previously broad domain of "custom" (*ʿurf* or *ʿāda*).[5] My argument is not that Salafis discarded the distinction between worship and custom; instead, it is that they fused a minority theological strand within a tradition pioneered by Ibn Taymiyya—the oneness of worship (*Tawḥīd al-Uluhiyya* or *Tawḥīd al-ʿIbāda*)—with an ambitious social vision. It further shows that, while such a conversation had precedents within a longer Islamic legal tradition, the debates of this tradition were not the primary field of contestation. Instead, the move to expand the domain of worship reflected the ambitions of a global universalizing project that sought primacy first over secular nationalism and then over Islamism.

The story of how Salafis transformed the relationship between worship and custom is significant for three key reasons. First, it casts light on the ways in which the Salafi theological and legal project, though it claims intellectual continuity with Islam's foundational era, departs from it in unacknowledged

3. al-Tahir, *Jamaʿat Ansar al-Sunna al-Muhammadiyya*, 433.

4. al-Tahir, *Jamaʿat Ansar al-Sunna al-Muhammadiyya*, 434.

5. Khaled Abou el Fadl has previously noted to the expanding scope of *Uṣūl al-Fiqh* at the expense of the *Furūʿ al-Fiqh* in the modern period more broadly (*And God Knows the Soldiers: The Authoritative and Authoritarian in Islamic Discourses* [Lanham, MD: University Press of America, 2001], 28–29).

and significant ways. While Salafis condemn the spread of "unlawful innovation" (*bid'a*) among Islamists and Islamic Modernists alike, the intellectual fulcrum of this endeavor itself constitutes a radical rupture with a longer Islamic history. Second, the story of worship and custom documents the longer history of the Salafi method (*manhaj*), which has previously been understood as an outgrowth of debates over educational method that emerged during the 1960s and 1970s.[6] Finally, this story casts light on the overlap between Salafism and secular nationalism; while scholars of Islamic law had long used the category of "custom" (*'āda*) to denote human practices that fall outside the purview of *fiqh*, Salafi usage of this term was far more similar to that of their secular-nationalist competitors. As they transformed this longstanding boundary, Salafis integrated communication into the heart of worship.

The changing relationship between worship and custom within Purist Salafism thus casts light on the intersection of theology, law, and identity in this movement. While Salafi scholars continued to prize normative ideals of theological rectitude and source criticism, they also worked to craft a theological-legal vision that could lay the basis for a universal (and universalizing) Salafi project. A distinct identity, while central to distinguishing participants in this movement from their ideological competitors, also constituted the conceptual basis for a call to ethical transformation and the legal commitments upon which such a transformation depended.

The chapter will begin by establishing the persistence of the longstanding distinction between devotional and customary acts in early-twentieth-century Egypt, with reference to two leading Islamic thinkers of this period who

6. For the focus on the 1970s, see Lauzière, *The Making of Salafism*, 199–230. Jacob Olidort emphasizes Muhammad Nasir al-Din al-Albani's articulation of an interpretative *manhaj*—and the intellectual debt it owed to the "academic sphere"—from 1961 on. See "In Defense of Tradition: Muḥammad Nāṣir al-Dīn al-Albānī and the Salafī Method" (Ph.D. diss, Princeton University, 2016), 171–204, 214–15. Olidort argues that it was during his time in Jordan (1981–99) that al-Albani "expanded the application of his *manhaj* beyond a methodology in ḥadīth science . . . into a general orientation for his followers to engage with all matters of life, including social and political events. . . . [P]articularly effective in this task was the new slogan he adopted for his mission, 'purification and education' (*al-taṣfiya wa'l-tarbiya*)" (251). Bernard Haykel similarly foregrounds al-Albani's role in the broader history of *manhaj*; see "On the Nature of Salafi Thought and Action," 47. Finally, see Ismail, *Rethinking Salafism*, 19–20. By contrast, Pieter Coppens dates a "distinct Salafi method" to the late nineteenth century ("Jamāl al-Dīn al-Qāsimī's Treatise on Wiping over Socks and the Rise of a Distinct Salafi method," 30–31).

influenced the Salafi movement, Muhammad Rashid Rida and Mahmud Muhammad Khattab al-Subki (d. 1933). It will then trace the transformation of "custom" (*ʿāda*) from a legal category into a crucial cultural battleground between 1940 and 1970, probing the interaction between Purist Salafis and Islamic Modernists in Egypt and Syria. The third section will analyze the changing boundaries of devotional acts from the 1970s on, as Salafi scholars increasingly turned their attention to articulating a "Salafi method" (*manhaj Salafī*) that embraced the Sunna and rejected "unlawful innovation" (*bidʿa*). In the process, Salafis would maintain their visceral opposition to innovation while embracing a transformed understanding of worship and custom alike.

EARLY ECHOES OF A SOCIAL VISION: WORSHIP AND CUSTOM, 1900–1940

In 1901, the pioneering Syrian Muslim reformer Muhammad Rashid Rida sought to tackle the challenges of western cultural influence and nationalist identity alike in *al-Manar*, the leading Islamic reformist journal which he edited.[7] In an article published in November of that year, Rida laid out the centrality of legal observance to the Muslim community:

> God legislated in order to make the people happy individually and to make peoples happy collectively and therefore some of his [prescribed] actions were devotional (*ʿibādāt*) and related to cultivating individuals (*tahdhīb al-afrāḍ*), and some were distinguishing signs (*shaʿāʾir*) that were collective, such as the performance of the Hajj and the two ʿId holidays and Friday and collective prayer, and these distinguishing signs (*shaʿāʾir*) have an extraordinary impact (*taʾthīr ʿajīb*) on communal and social life (*al-ḥayāt al-milliyya waʾl-ijtimāʿiyya*).[8]

7. While Rida did discuss the distinction between religious and customary practice, this was not his dominant concern. For example, he ruled that one can kiss the hands of scholars (*ʿulamāʾ*) only if one does not claim that it is a religious obligation (*min al-wājibāt al-dīniyya*). Instead, Rida explained, it is considered a permitted custom (*ʿāda min al-ʿādāt al-mubāḥa*). See Rida, "Fatawa al-Manar," *al-Manar*, 1 Rabiʿ al-Awwal 1323/6 May 1905, 8:190–3, at 8:191. Rida was similarly concerned that religious obligations not be rendered customs, disputing the claim that the beard was a matter of custom rather than religion (*min umūr al-ʿādāt lā min umūr al-dīn*). See Rida, "Fatawa al-Manar," *al-Manar*, 29 Muharram 1329/25 January 1911, 14:29–34, at 30.

8. Muhammad Rashid Rida, "al-Shuʿur bi-l-Wijdan wa Shaʿaʾir al-Umam waʾl-Adyan," *al-Manar*, Shaʿban 1319/13 November 1901, 4:641–7, at 4:644.

For Rida, the fundamental question was how religious obligation could communicate a commitment to piety and communal life alike. His concern was not a delineation of human action as it fell along the five-part classification scheme of Islamic law—from obligatory to praiseworthy to permitted to disfavored to forbidden—but rather to explain the social utility of religious practice as an engine of social cohesion. Neither was Rida alone in making this claim: fellow reformists, most notably his teacher Muhammad ʿAbduh, sought to frame European concepts of utility, parliamentary democracy, and public opinion within Islam. In the process, as Albert Hourani notes, "Islam itself becomes identical with civilization and activity, the norms of nineteenth century social thought."[9]

Three years later, Rida would also explicitly uphold a distinction between worship and custom as it pertained to sartorial practice. In a February 1904 column in *al-Manar,* Rida rejected the position, identified with unnamed opponents, that "donning the clothing of infidels is effectively [an act of] apostasy" (*inna lubs ay shay min thiyāb al-kuffār mūjab*[an] *li-l-ridda*). Aside from cases of clothing explicitly identified with a specific religion such as the cummerbund imposed on non-Muslims (the *zunnār*),[10] Muslims were permitted to dress as they chose because clothing could not serve as a sign of disbelief (*kufr*). Indeed, one could adopt a custom from non-Muslims simply because one loved it (*li-ḥubb fī al-ʿāda*), or in search of higher civilizational status (*al-ruqī fī al-wujūd al-madanī*).[11]

Rida was not writing in a vacuum. At this time, the declining prominence of the turban (*ʿimāma*) and growing popularity of Western headwear had driven a debate over Islamic law and cultural authenticity. The question at stake was not merely fidelity to the Islamic tradition, but also the challenge posed by British colonial rule to Egyptian nationalism through the depiction of Egyptian men as feminine and thus weak.[12] Rida, however, showed little

9. Albert Hourani, *Arabic Thought in the Liberal Age: 1798–1939* (Cambridge, UK: Cambridge University Press, 1983), 144.

10. On the significance of distinct social practices to early Islamic identity, see Youshaa Patel, "Muslim Distinction: Imitation and the Anxiety of Jewish, Christian and Other Influences" (Ph.D. diss, Duke University, 2012). On the *Zunnār* in early Islamic history, see 312–13. On the "distinguishing signs" (*ghiyār*) code under the Caliph ʿUmar b. ʿAbd al-ʿAziz (r. 99–101/717–20), see Levy-Rubin, *Non-Muslims in the Early Islamic Empire*, 88–96, 154–57.

11. Rida, "Fatawa al-Manar," *al-Manar,* 16 Dhu al-Hijja 1321/3 March 1904, 6:927–43, at 6:936.

12. Jacob, *Working Out Egypt*, 72.

patience for this question, declaring that the "Islam of the Arab does not reside in his turban . . . and he does not become an infidel if he removes the turban during the ritual ablutions (*wuḍū'*)."[13] Instead, he explained the role of clothing in a manner that echoed the traditional category of custom:

> Often peoples that agree about religion differ substantially on dress . . . as Muslims do between the resident of the Hijaz and Turk and Persian and Egyptian and Tunisian. . . . None wears what the Companions of the Prophet wore (*libās al-ṣaḥāba*) . . . and we have no record of the Caliphs of Islam commanding the Persians to put on Arab garb. . . . [Instead] Muslims distinguished People of the Book (*al-dhimmī*) with particular signs. . . . The clothing of the Prophet (*thiyāb al-rasūl*) was not different than that of the Arab polytheists (*al-mushrikīn al-ʿarab*).[14]

Though Purist Salafis later cited Rida, his implicit claim to dress as a basic form of permissible custom, and explicit rejection of the notion that Muhammad and his Companions maintained a distinctive style of dress, would have placed him in the distinct minority of this movement.

Rida was not the only Islamic reformer in this period to uphold the longstanding balance between worship and custom. In his magnum opus, *The Pure Religion: Guiding the People to the Religion of Truth* (*al-Din al-Khalis: Irshad al-Khalq ila Din al-Haqq*), Mahmud Muhammad Khattab al-Subki bemoaned the religious decline of Muslims in his age: "Sunna has become innovation, innovation has become Islamic law (*Shirʿa*), ritual (*ʿibāda*) has become [conflated with] custom (*ʿāda*), and custom with ritual."[15] This native of the Delta governorate of Monufiyya and founder of the Jamʿiyya Sharʿiyya, however, was primarily concerned with the celebration of Shamm al-Nasim, an Egyptian holiday that marks the beginning of spring and falls on the day after Coptic Easter. Specifically, al-Subki argued that this holiday had become a means to augment observance of the "Day of Annunciation" (*Yawm al-Bishāra*),[16] which marks the announcement by the

13. Rida, "Fatawa all-Manar," *al-Manar*, 16 Dhu al-Hijja 1321/3 March 1904, 6:937.

14. Rida, "Fatawa al-Manar," *al-Manar*, 16 Dhu al-Hijja 1321/3 March 1904, 6:937. Rida's position on this matter was apparently echoed by Muhammad Nasir a-Din al-Albani. Born in 1914, al-Albani recalls that, as a young man in Damascus, he donned both the turban (*al-ʿimāma*) and a white robe (*al-jubba*), before realizing that such clothing was not legally required. See ʿAbd al-ʿAziz b. Muhammad b. ʿAbd Allah al-Sadhan, *al-Imam al-Albani Rahimahu Allah: Durus wa Mawaqif wa ʿIbar* (Riyadh, KSA: Dar al-Tawhid li-l-Nashr, 1429/2008), 19.

15. Mahmud Muhammad Khattab al-Subki, *al-Din al-Khalis aw Irshad al-Khalq ila Din al-Haqq*, ed. Amin Mahmud Khattab (Cairo: al-Maktaba al-Mahmudiyya al-Subkiyya, 1986), 3:286.

16. Al-Subki, *al-Din al-Khalis*, 5:96.

Archangel Gabriel to Mary that she would conceive a son by the power of the Holy Spirit.[17] In a period of intense cultural change—British colonialism had arrived formally in 1882 and its proponents offered not merely a political prescription but a broad-based vision of religious, cultural, and economic transformation—al-Subki's concerns were internal as he expressed his deep concern that the basic categories of religious life had become inverted and sought to reassert the fundamental categories that defined Islam as a living faith.[18]

By delineating black-and-white lines of religious duty at a time of change, al-Subki placed himself within a longer Islamic legal tradition that distinguished clearly among acts of worship (*ʿibādāt*), transactions (*muʿāmalāt*) and customs (*ʿādāt*). While acts of worship primarily encompassed religious rituals such as prayer and tithing (*zakāt*), and transactions pertained to mundane aspects of social life such as divorce and inheritance, customary practices included a diverse array of basic human activities such as eating, drinking, and sleeping that are considered permissible (*mubāḥ*) in the absence of explicit prohibitions in the Quran or Sunna.[19] Indeed, as a historical matter, it was the line between devotional deeds and transactions, not that between devotion and custom, that was an occasional source of dispute.[20]

Overlapping with the threefold division stood a debate over the customs (*ʿādāt*) of the Prophet Muhammad, specifically those that pertained to his role as Prophet, Head of State, and Judge. Scholars of *fiqh* understood verbal (*qawlī*), physical (*fiʿlī*) and tacitly approved (*taqrīrī*) actions or saying of Muhammad and his Companions to constitute legal commands.[21] Beyond the Prophet's actions in these three capacities, however, lay a variety of activities in which he

17. There is no evidence, however, that Coptic nationalists in this period focused on this holiday. I thank Candace Lukasik for this observation (and for searching in vain for evidence that they did).

18. For the persistence of the concern that religious obligation had become a matter of personal choice, see Ahmad ʿIsa ʿAshur, "Khawatir," *al-Iʿtisam*, 7 Jumada al-Ukhra 1365/9 May 1946, 3–4; ʿAshur, "Khawatir," *al-Iʿtisam*, 27 Jumada al-Ula 1366/18 April 1947, 13.

19. Ayman Shabana, *Custom in Islamic Law and Legal Theory: The Development of the Concepts of ʿUrf and ʿĀdah in the Islamic Legal Tradition* (New York: Palgrave Macmillan, 2010), 5.

20. Shabana, *Custom in Islamic Law and Legal Theory*, 132.

21. For an example from the late fourteenth/early fifteenth century by the Ottoman scholar Muhammad b. Hamza al-Fanari (d. 834/1431), see *Fusul al-Badaʾi fi Usul al-Sharaʾi* (Beirut: Dar al-Kutub al-ʿIlmiyya, 2006), 2:286. For a more recent example, see ʿAbd al-Rahim Yaʿqub, *Taysir al-Wusul ila Manhaj al-Usul min al-Manqul waʾl-Maʿqul* (Riyadh: Maktabat ʿUbaykan, 2010), 1:67–68.

engaged that did not constitute legal norms because they did not relate to his core mission. *Fiqh*-based debates regarding a Muslim's obligation pivoted on this distinction between acts of the Prophet that had legal status, whether as obligatory (*wājib*) or praiseworthy (*mustaḥabb*), and those that were simply permitted (but had no positive or negative value). These debates also considered whether a practice had been abrogated by a later practice, and the context in which a given act or practice occurred.[22] Notwithstanding this comparatively open-ended approach to non-religious matters, Sunni scholars prior to the twentieth century restricted ostentatious clothing (*libās al-shuhra*),[23] as well as clothing items associated with other religions such as the *zunnār*.[24]

The Sunni tradition, however, differed internally on the precise boundaries of worship. Ibn Taymiyya, who offered a particularly expansive understanding of this concept, declared that worship (*ʿibāda*) is a "comprehensive term for all that God loves and that pleases Him from among statements and actions, hidden and visible" (*ism jāmiʿ li-kull mā yuḥibbuhu Allāh wa yarḍāhu min al-aqwāl waʾl-aʿmāl al-bāṭina waʾl-ẓāhira*).[25] Similarly, Ibn ʿAbd al-Wahhab embraced a broad definition of *tawhid* that pivoted on the demand that all human action be oriented to the worship of God.[26] The question at hand was not the validity of custom or transactions as categories, but rather the boundaries between worship and these other domains.

22. Mohammad Hashim Kamali, *Principles of Islamic Jurisprudence* (Cambridge, UK: The Islamic Texts Society, 2011), 65–66.

23. For an example from canonical Sunni hadith collections, see Abu Daʾud Suliman bin al-Ashʿath al-Sijistani, *Sunan Abi Daʾud wa Maʿalim al-Sunan*, ed. ʿIzzat ʿUbayd al-Daʿas and ʿAdil al-Sayyid (Beirut: Dar Ibn Hazm, 1997), 4:204; Abu al-Hasan al-Hanafi al-Maʿruf bi-l-Sindi, *Sunan Ibn Maja bi-Sharh al-Sindi wa Misbah al-Zujaja fi Zawaʾid Ibn Maja* (Beirut: Dar al-Maʿrifa, 1996), 12:164.

24. For the claim that wearing the *zunnār* constitutes an act of disbelief, see Muhammad b. ʿAbd al-Rahman al-Khamis, *al-Jamiʿ fi Alfaz al-Kufr* (Kuwait City: Dar Ilaf al-Dawliyya li-l-Nashr waʾl-Tawziʿ, 1999), 83.

25. Ibn Taymiyya specifies a range of actions including the five pillars of Islam, commanding right and forbidding wrong, jihad, respect and love for one's parents, caring for neighbors and orphans, and love of God and his Prophet. See Ibn Taymiyya quoted in Hafiz b. Ahmad b. ʿAli Hakami, *Maʿarij al-Qubul bi-Sharh Sullam al-Wusul ila ʿAlam al-Usul fi al-Tawhid*, ed. ʿUmar b. Mahmud Abu ʿUmar (Dammam, Saudi Arabia: Dar Ibn al-Qayyim, 1415/1995), 1:84. For more on Ibn Taymiyya's expansive vision of worship, see Lav, "Radical Muslim Theonomy," 69–84.

26. Lav, "Radical Muslim Theonomy," 109–20.

The deliberations of Rida and Subki on questions of worship and custom were also inextricably linked to broader debates over cultural change as competing claimants sought to define the present and future of Egyptian nationalism. Egypt's westernizing elites understood modernity to be synonymous with "confident possession of such European customs as were deemed desirable, coupled with a fine discrimination of how far one could go in such behavior and remain truly Egyptian."[27] Customs, though, were far from a static marker; as Lucie Ryzova has observed about *effendi* identity more broadly in Egypt during the first half of the twentieth century, "It is less an objectified identity than an effect created by a performance through an idiom of public signs."[28]

These visions of Westernized modernity were not the only or even necessarily the dominant voice. This period also saw the rise of a hybrid Egyptian-Islamic nationalism, most clearly represented by the Muslim Brotherhood. This approach rejected the modern definition of nation as a central form of identity, arguing for a new framework that balanced particularistic loyalties and a universal Islamic bond. Still others groups, most notably the Young Egypt movement, advanced an integral vision of Egypt that saw supra-Egyptian identity as a necessity means to achieve Egyptian interests, while intellectuals such as Muhammad Husayn Haykel argued that Egypt must be culturally and politically oriented towards the East. Finally, proponents of Egyptian Arab nationalism, which would form the basis of ʿAbd al-Nasir's secular nationalist Pan-Arabism in the 1950s and 1960s, arose, arguing for the historical unity of the Arab world.[29] While these competing visions of national identity differed substantially, they all rejected a traditional order dominated by a "politics of notables" in which a longstanding religious and political elite meditated between the ruler and the population.

In the midst of the cultural tremors of the interwar period, a prominent scholar belonging to Ansar al-Sunna offered a decidedly traditional critique that betrayed little of the momentous transformations of this time. In an August 1937 article, ʿAbd al-Zahir Abu-l-Samh (d. 1952), a graduate of al-Azhar and the Imam and Khatib of the Grand Mosque of Mecca, emphasized his concern with "blind imitation" (*taqlīd*) of the existing legal schools, a standard

27. Armbrust, *Mass Culture and Modernism in Egypt*, 84.
28. Ryzova, *The Age of the Efendiyya*, 8.
29. Gershoni and Jankowski, *Redefining the Egyptian Nation*, 35–144.

Salafi concern with the *madhhab* tradition. Just as concerning to Abu-l-Samh, however, was the secularizing claim made by those who are "well-versed in European culture and sciences" (*al-mutaḍalli'ūn fī al-thaqāfa al-ūrūbiyya wa'l-'ulūm al-ūrūbiyya*) that "alienation" (*tanfīr*) from Islam due to "stagnancy" (*jumūd*) was simply a reflection of broader turn away from religion.[30] By and large, however, Salafis gave little thought to the precise practices that collectively constituted this allegedly alien European cultural vision. As the 1930s came to a close, secular nationalism would grow far more threatening and the category of "custom" far more capacious.

THE TRANSFORMATION OF CUSTOM FROM A LEGAL CATEGORY INTO A CULTURAL BATTLE (1940–1970)

In the 1940s, the question of custom rose to new prominence and efforts to broaden the boundaries of worship based on a commitment to the oneness of God intensified. As Daniel Lav has argued, the Purist Salafi emphasis on the unity of worship (*Tawḥīd al-Ulūhiyya* or *Tawḥīd al-'Ibāda*) was one it had inherited from a "minoritarian Muslim tradition that goes by a number of names: Traditionalist, Ahl al-Ḥadīth, salafī, Ḥanbalī, and Wahhābī."[31] This position should not be understood as exceptional within the broader Islamic tradition: God's oneness more broadly has long been understood across the Islamic theological spectrum as demanding belief and practice alike. Instead, the distinctiveness of this approach lies in its prioritization of action, rather than verbal pronouncements, in the assessment of an individual's faith. For Ibn Taymiyya—and by extension, Ibn 'Abd al-Wahhab and Purist Salafis—practice stands at the center of *tawhid*.[32] This claim to the boundaries of

30. 'Abd al-Zahir Abu-l-Samh, "al-Din al-Khalis," *al-Hadi al-Nabawi*, Jumada al-Thaniyya 1356/~August 1937, 9–14, at 12–13. While Abu-l-Samh was based in Saudi Arabia, the concerns that he expressed reflected Egyptian, rather than Saudi, cultural currents during the interwar period. Specifically, the latter country was not host to a social or political elite engaged in a European-inspired model of modernity.

31. Lav, "Radical Muslim Theonomy," 7.

32. For evidence of Salafi usage of Ibn Taymiyya's understanding of God's oneness, see 'Abd Allah Ahmad Qadiri, "Tawhid Allah," *Majallat al-Jami'a al-Islamiyya bi-l-Madina al-Munawwara*, #32 (~1971), 26–7, at 27. The approximate year date is based on a digital version of issues 1–120 of the journal, with ten issues appearing annually over the course of twelve years between 1968 and 1980. Also known as 'Abd Allah al-Qadiri al-Ahdal, this author and teacher

worship and *tawhid*, however, was also inextricably tied to the ideological contestation and political tumult of the 1930s and 1940s. In this context, the Salafi claim to worshipping one God alone, in a country in which 90 percent of the population was Muslim, constituted a veiled critique of world-making political programs, colonial and postcolonial, and the assertion of a conceptual alternative to the sovereignty of the nation-state.

The debate over *tawhid* also reflected a core Islamic principle that piety, not race, determined religious standing. As a hadith report included in Ahmad b. Hanbal's *Musnad* states: "There is no preference (*lā faḍl*) for the Arab over the Persian, or the White over the Black, except in matters of piety (*illā bi-l-taqwā*)."[33] The question of race and religion during this period, however, was inescapable in the face of nationalist winds: most evocatively, in a lecture delivered on 5 April 1943 at the University of Damascus, the Syrian Christian Baʿthist thinker Michel Aflaq claimed the Prophet Muhammad as an Arab nationalist leader par excellence and, by extension, Islam as an Arab national project.[34] While Salafis would not engage explicitly with questions of race during this period, they sought to offer a model that contrasted with ethnoracial understandings of political community.

It would be a Damascene Salafi, Muhammad Bahjat al-Baytar (d. 1976), who initiated the debate over clothing and communal identity with a 1940 fatwa in *al-Hadi al-Nabawi*. The question at hand was whether it was religiously permissible to wear Western-style hats, specifically brimmed hats for women and men alike (the *burnīṭa* and *qubʿa*, respectively). In response, al-Baytar began by asserting the importance of clothing to communal identity and mutual recognition: "the Muslim must [be able] to identify his co-religionist: by his dress and clothing (*bi-libāsihi wa ziyyihi*), as he knows him by his creed and action . . . (*bi-ʿaqīdatihi wa ʿamalihi*)."[35] Al-Baytar cautioned, however, that

---

studied under Ibn Baz and taught theology in the Faculty of the Noble Qurʾan at IUM following its establishment in 1976. See "Taʿrif bi-Fadilat al-Shaykh al-Duktur ʿAbd Allah al-Qadiri al-Ahdal," https://www.saaid.net/Doat/ahdal/ahdal.htm.

33. For Ibn Taymiyya's citation of this hadith, see Taqi al-Din Ahmad b. Taymiyya al-Harrani, *Majmuʿat Fatawa Shaykh al-Islam Ibn Taymiyya*, eds. ʿAmir al-Jazaar and Anwar al-Baz (Mansura, Egypt: Dar al-Wafaʾ li-l-Tibaʿa waʾl-Nashr waʾl-Tawziʿ, 1997), 11:279.

34. Michel Aflaq, *Dhikra al-Rasul al-ʿArabi* (Beirut: al-Muʾassasa al-ʿArabiyya li-l-Dirasat waʾl-Nashr, 1972), 8–12.

35. Muhammad Bahjat al-Baytar, "al-Fatawa," *al-Hadi al-Nabawi*, 1 Safar 1359/~11 March 1940, 26–9, at 26.

the need for distinct clothing must be balanced with a sociological reality that, in Egypt as elsewhere, Western dress, with the exception of headwear, had become part of the national dress, especially in government institutions. Further, the Prophet's model did not necessitate entirely distinct clothing: Muhammad wore the Byzantine gown (*al-jubba al-rūmiyya*) and the Persian robe (*al-ṭiyālsa al-kisrāwiyya*)[36] even as he commanded Muslims to distinguish themselves from infidels in their "customs and clothing . . . not solely in their religious affairs" (*fī ʿādātihim wa azyāʾihim lā fī umūrihim al-dīniyya faqaṭ*).[37] For al-Baytar, who would later become identified with Islamic Modernism, sartorial similarity and social distinction could co-exist.

Whether a Muslim man was permitted to wear pants was an urgent question for those readers of *al-Hadi al-Nabawi* employed in the growing Egyptian bureaucracy.[38] To answer this question, al-Baytar cited a hadith report of a conversation between Muhammad and his Companion Abu Umama, in which the latter noted that "the People of the Book [that is, Jews and Christians] are wearing pants and do not put on a loin cloth (*Ahl al-Kitāb yatasarralūn wa-lā yataʾazzarūn*). In response, the Prophet instructed his Companion that he should wear both pants and the loin cloth (*izār*) in order to distinguish himself.[39] Based on this report, al-Baytar explained that the goal was for Muslims to maintain "distinct characteristics based on their particular customs (*mushakhkhiṣāt min al-ʿādāt khāṣṣa bihim*) . . . [as] independence in customs (*al-istiqlāl fī al-ʿādāt*) . . . is characteristic of those nations known for independence."[40]

Accordingly, the wardrobe of the modern bureaucrat—"patriotic garments" (*azyāʾ waṭaniyya*) such as the raincoat (*al-maʿṭaf*), the jacket (*satra*), pants

36. Literally the "Khosroian robe," a reference to Khosrow I, a Sasanian King who ruled from 531 to 579.

37. al-Baytar, "al-Fatawa," 29.

38. The Egyptian bureaucracy had first undergone a significant expansion in the mid-nineteenth century. See F. Robert Hunter, *Egypt Under the Khedives, 1805–1879: From Household Government to Modern Bureaucracy* (Cairo: American University in Cairo Press, 1984), 41–54. Roughly a decade after Baytar's fatwa, it would undergo further expansion under ʿAbd al-Nasir. See Carrie Rosefsky Wickham, *Mobilizing Islam: Religion, Activism, and Political Change in Egypt* (New York: Columbia University Press, 2002), 27–28.

39. Chapter 5 will more deeply explore the debates over pants as part of Salafi adoption of the prohibition against *Isbal*.

40. al-Baytar, "al-Fatawa," 29.

(*al-banṭalūn*), or pajamas (*al-bījāma*)—is permissible insofar as such clothing is not excessively revealing or tight, does not prevent the wearer from performing the prayers properly, and does not incite forbidden actions.[41] The issue was not cultural similarity, but basic prescriptions of male modesty long enshrined in Islamic law. Circling back to the men's brimmed hat (*qubʿa*), however, al-Baytar declared that this constituted a "foreign sign (*shiʿār ajnabī*) [and a sign of] moral deterioration and social corruption" by which a Muslim left Islam and entered another community.[42] Al-Baytar's prescription, though it was ostensibly based on Islamic laws of modesty, sought to find a middle ground between religious distinction and cultural borrowing while reckoning with the communicative power of particular headgear.

Al-Hadi al-Nabawi, however, did not hew exclusively to this permissive line. In a January 1943 article, ʿAbd al-Halim Qatit, an imam in the Nile Delta city of Rosetta, sought to reorient al-Baytar's language to argue that distinct customs had become a matter of religious unity:

> Muslims must have distinguishing customs (*mushakhkhiṣāt min al-ʿādāt khāṣṣa bihim*) because the independence of nations [lies] in their customs and clothing and it increases the depth and rootedness of their independence.... Imitation (*taqlīd*) of others leads to the annihilation of the components [of the nation].... Imitation leads to the loss of many of Muslims' interpersonal obligations such as greeting each other with *salām*[43] ... and burial in a Muslim cemetery....[44]

Responding implicitly to al-Baytar, Qatit disputed the "claim that the question of clothing is a national one" (*masʾala qawmiyya*),[45] citing the Prophet's com-

41. al-Baytar, "al-Fatawa," 29.

42. al-Baytar, "al-Fatawa," 29.

43. The greeting performed among Muslims begins with "peace be upon you" (*al-salāmu ʿalaykum*) and is reciprocated by "And peace upon you, and the mercy and blessings of God" (*wa ʿalaykum al-salām wa raḥmat Allāh wa barakātahu*).

44. ʿAbd al-Halim Qatit, "al-Azyaʾ fi al-Islam," *al-Hadi al-Nabawi*, Muharram 1362/~January 1943, 20–24, at 23.

45. Qatit's formulation conflated patriotism (*waṭaniyya*) and nationalism (*qawmiyya*). As Adam Mestyan argues, "Modern nationalism is typically defined as an ideology of solidarity, organized around the idea of 'the nation' ... in a sovereign political unit.... Patriotism, by contrast ... [is] an ideology of solidarity associated with the political use of the 'homeland' ... without the explicit demand for a sovereign polity.... Patriotism can precede nationalism, but it can also instantiate a muted nationalism within an imperial framework that makes allowance for a type of federal state" (*Arab Patriotism: The Ideology and Culture of Power in Late Ottoman Egypt* [Princeton, NJ: Princeton University Press, 2017], 2–3).

mand to Muslims to distinguish themselves from the Jews, Christians, polytheists, and Zoroastrians. For Qatit, the matter at hand was "a religious question, not an Arab one (*masʾala dīniyya lā ʿarabiyya*)."[46] Qatit's position, in turn, would constitute a key piece of the intellectual architecture of Salafism and its claims to an ethic of visibility. By effacing the latitude of local custom set forth by the Islamic scholarly tradition and the flexibility towards foreign clothing evinced by Rida and al-Baytar, Qatit had placed clothing exclusively in the realm of religious practice.

The division between cultural accommodation and rejection, however, did not fall neatly along an Islamic Modernist/Purist Salafi binary. While al-Baytar represented a declining trend towards cultural accommodation within Salafism, his ideological peer Muhammad b. Kamal al-Khatib (1913–2000) contributed to the vast expansion of the significance of custom to the Salafi debate. Al-Khatib, the editor of *al-Tamaddun al-Islami* and a graduate of the Damascus University's Faculty of Law, gravitated towards nationalist politics and scholarly circles alike and, in the latter case, studied under the Mufti of Syria Abu al-Yusr al-ʿAbidin (r. 1952–61, d. 1981). Al-Khatib's focus, however, was on *al-Tamaddun al-Islami* and the association of the same name that published it, and he contributed some 450 articles to the journal.

In an August 1945 article, entitled "Custom and Society," al-Khatib argued that customs, broadly construed, constituted the central battleground of communal reproduction:

> Customs begin with the simplest and extend to the highest manifestations of life. . . . Islam made its norms of comportment and Sunna into widespread customs (*ādābahu wa sunnatahu ʿādāt muntashara*) . . . such as the beard (*al-liḥya*) . . . and the greeting among Muslims (Peace be upon You and mercy, and the mercy of God and His blessings) . . . and one of the bases of its customs (*min uṣūl ʿādātihi*), prayer (*al-ṣalāt*), is one of the five pillars of Islam (*arkān al-Islām*). . . .[47]

Not content to make this conceptual intervention without citing textual proof, al-Khatib further noted that there are narrations documented in "reliable traditions [from the Salaf]" (*aqwāl maʾthūra*) which state that "prayer is a custom" (*al-ṣalāt ʿādat^{an}*) that must be repeated five times daily, thus underscoring

46. Qatit, "al-Azyaʾ fi al-Islam," 23.

47. Muhammad b. Kamal al-Khatib, "al-ʿAda waʾl-Mujtamaʿ," *al-Tamaddun al-Islami*, Shawwal 1365/~August 1946, 321–24, at 321.

"the extent of Islam's concern for and interest in customs" (*miqdār ʿināyat al-Islam bi-l-ʿādāt wa ihtimamihi bihā*).[48] Indeed, for al-Khatib, everything from fasting during the month of Ramadan to obligatory and voluntary charity (*zakāt* and *ṣadaqa*, respectively) constitutes "positive customs" (*al-tayyib min al-ʿādāt*) that strengthen a Muslim's faith.[49] Based on this reinterpretation of the traditional boundary between worship and custom, al-Khatib offered "Islam's Sunna in the organization of customs" (*Sunnat al-Islām fī tanẓīm al-ʿādāt*).[50]

Al-Khatib also evinced concern with the spread of foreign customs, specifically the adoption of Western styles of clothing. Echoing ʿAbd al-Halim Qatit, he declared that "changing a custom affects all that surrounds the custom (*bi-kull mā yuḥīṭ bi-l-āda*). . . . Changing one's style and form of clothing (*taghyīr ʿādat al-thiyāb bi-ashkālihā*) . . . [is] an announcement of the power of one nation over another (*iʿlān*^{an} *li-sulṭān umma ʿalā umma*)."[51] The target of this critique was far from ambiguous: al-Khatib castigated those in society—here, disproportionately associated with the expanding government bureaucracy—who wore modern European garb (*al-libās al-urūbbī al-ḥadīth*) and, in doing so, allegedly took on European morals and customs.[52] Al-Khatib concluded with an exhortation to the communicative power of dress: "May [our] customs be an announcement of Arabism and Islam in this society" (*ḥattā takūn min al-ʿādāt ʿunwān*^{an} *li-l-ʿUrūba waʾl-Islām fī hadha al-mujtama*).[53]

It was also during this time period that leading voices of the Jamʿiyya Sharʿiyya laid claim to their own understanding of the relationship between worship and custom. In a 14 February 1945 article in *al-Iʿtisam*, a leading preacher within the organization who would later grow close to Ansar al-Sunna, ʿAbd al-Latif al-Mushtahiri[54] (d. 1995), sought to move beyond a ritual-

48. al-Khatib, "al-ʿAda waʾl-Mujtamaʿ," 321. While one could conceivably translate the phrase "*al-ṣalāt ʿāda*" as "prayer is a habit," such a translation would not correspond to al-Khatib's understanding of *ʿāda* as custom in the remainder of the article.

49. al-Khatib, "al-ʿAda waʾl-Mujtamaʿ," 322.

50. al-Khatib, "al-ʿAda waʾl-Mujtamaʿ," 323.

51. al-Khatib, "al-ʿAda waʾl-Mujtamaʿ," 323.

52. al-Khatib, "al-ʿAda waʾl-Mujtamaʿ," 323.

53. al-Khatib, "al-ʿAda waʾl-Mujtamaʿ," 324.

54. Al-Mushtahiri, alongside a second Jamʿiyya Sharʿiyya thinker, Mahmud ʿAbd al-Wahhab Fayyad, would later be described in *al-Hadi al-Nabawi* as "inclined to the Salafi Call" (*yumīlūn ilā al-Daʿwa al-Salafiyya*). See "Akhbar al-Jamaʿa," *al-Hadi al-Nabawi*, Ramadan 1380/February 1961, 50.

centered understanding of religion. Specifically, he emphasized that the call to Islam includes not merely "the call to prayer, ritual purity, and prayer and fasting" (*al-adhān wa wuḍū' wa ṣalāt wa ṣiyām*) but also the "common good of the Islamic community and nation (*maṣlaḥat al-umma wa'l-waṭan*) and the spreading of the call to Islam . . . through commanding right and forbidding wrong. . . ."[55] While the Jam'iyya Shar'iyya maintained a steadfast commitment to avoiding the Muslim Brotherhood's entanglement in national politics,[56] it shared the latter's interest in articulating a comprehensive vision of religion change.

The expanding boundaries of worship also cannot be divorced from broader trends, Islamic and westernizing alike. In May 1947, Muhammad Muhammad al-Madani (d. 1968), a professor in the Faculty of Shari'a at al-Azhar, had published an article in *al-Hadi al-Nabawi* in which he sought to elucidate the ideological threats faced by Ansar al-Sunna. The article noted the recent profusion of two groups: the former sought to appear pious (*yuḥāwil al-ẓuhūr amām al-nās bi-maẓhar al-tadayyun*) while the latter "detested all appearances that could bring him closer to religion" (*wa yakraḥ kull maẓhar yuqarribuhu min al-dīn*). While the author makes the identity of the second group clear—the "higher classes" (*al-ṭabaqāt al-rāqiyya*)—he describes the first as "the masses" (*'āmmat al-nās*).[57] Some of the members of this category may have been Sufis, as the author notes practices of visiting the graves of saints (*maqābir al-ṣāliḥīn*).[58] Others, though, draw attention by visibly commanding right and forbidding wrong and seek to divide life into actions that are "disfavored" (*makrūh*) and "forbidden" (*ḥarām*).[59] Though al-Madani is ambiguous, this group could well refer to a variety of Islamic movements that arose and spread in Egypt during this period, especially the Muslim Brotherhood and Jam'iyya

55. 'Abd al-Latif al-Mustahiri, "al-Islam wa'l-'Amal," *al-I'tisam*, 12 Rabi' al-Awwal 1365/14 February 1946, 1–2, at 1.

56. Muhammad Khattab al-Subki took the position that the Jam'iyya Shar'iyya should concerned about politics yet not involved in it (*al-inshighāl bi-l-siyāsa wa 'adam al-ishtighāl bihā*) (Hasan, *al-Salafiyyun fi Misr*, 16).

57. Muhammad Muhammad al-Madani, "al-Din Bayna A'da'ihi wa Ad'iya'ihi," *al-Hadi al-Nabawi*, Rajab 1366/~May 1947, 14–19, at 14.

58. The practice of visiting graves, while identified by Salafis with adherents of Sufi orders, is not exclusive to them.

59. al-Madani, "al-Din Bayna A'da'ihi wa Ad'iya'ihi," 15–16.

Shar'iyya.[60] Most striking for the discussion at hand, though, is a final accusation that these individuals who seek to restrict legitimate practice are themselves guilty of "introducing [novel features] to ritual worship" (*yudkhilū fī al-'ibādāt mā laysa minhā*).[61] The transformation of worship remained, at least in theory, a red line.

Longstanding modes of distinguishing worship and customs also persisted. Most prominently, a speech by the organization's Secretary, Suliman Hasuna, at Ansar al-Sunna's 1949 general meeting reiterated the opposition between the principle of spreading "pure monolatry" (*al-tawḥīd al-khāliṣ*) and the threat posed by the "articles of faith, customs and traditions" (*'aqā'id wa 'ādāt wa taqālīd*) of those whom they encountered.[62] Within Ansar al-Sunna, concern with foreign customs was increasingly prominent: in an article published a few months later, an unnamed author defined "unlawful innovation" (*bid'a*) as including not merely illegitimate additions to Islam but also "falling in love with [the foreigner's] customs and lifestyles" (*gharām*[an] *bi-'ādātihim wa asālīb ḥayātihim*).[63] Nonetheless, as the examples of al-Qatit and al-Khatib underscore, the threat posed by foreign customs and the increasing centrality of the category of custom to Islamic law were intimately linked.

In the midst of religious competition and interpretive shifts, Muhammad Nasir al-Din al-Albani recentered this debate within the specific question of the Prophet Muhammad's practices. A perpetual émigré who had arrived in Damascus from Albania during the final years of Ottoman rule, al-Albani's autodidactic immersion in hadith analysis reflected a lived experience of geographic dislocation and radical political change.[64] The 1950s had been a decade of political tumult in Syria: 1954 saw the overthrow of the military

60. The Jam'iyya Shar'iyya was, like Ansar al-Sunna, defined by its commitment to fighting unlawful innovation and immorality (*muḥārabat al-bid'a wa'l-munkarāt*). See Khalid Muhammad Yunus, "al-Qarn al-'Ishrin wa Juhud al-Harakat al-Da'wiyya fi Misr" (Ph.D. diss., Karachi University, 2006), 39–40.

61. al-Madani, "al-Din Bayna A'da'ihi wa Ad'iya'ihi," 16. This would not be the only time that al-Madani would voice his concern with ritual innovation. See al-Madani, "al-Islam Bayna al-Salaf wa'l-Khalaf," *al-Hadi al-Nabawi*, Jumada al-Ula 1360/~May 1941, 22–29, at 28.

62. Suliman Hasuna, "A'mal Majlis al-Idara," *al-Hadi al-Nabawi*, Sha'ban 1368/~May 1949, 24–26, at 24.

63. "al-Bid'a," *al-Hadi al-Nabawi*, Shawwal 1368/~July 1949, 48.

64. For more on al-Albani's personal trajectory, see Olidort, "In Defense of Tradition," 27–52.

government led by Adib al-Shishkali (d. 1964) and a period of relative openness that would persist until the country's short-lived entrance into political union with Egypt (1958–61).[65]

In the midst of shifting political winds, al-Albani focused on a discrete question of ritual practice: the validity of a hadith which stated that wearing the turban (*al-ʿimāma*) increased the value of one's prayer by a factor of one thousand. In this article, al-Albani rejected the hadith in question while emphasizing that the practice remains praiseworthy (*mustaḥabb*) based on the majority opinion among scholars that is "from the Sunna of customs [of the Prophet Muhammad] rather than that of worship" (*min sunan al-ʿāda lā min sunan al-ʿibāda*).[66] This conceptual approach was far more consistent with the longstanding tradition of distinguishing worship from custom generally, and that of these two categories as they pertained to Muhammad's model.

Notwithstanding this continuity, though, al-Albani, too, voiced anxieties about social identity:

> Muslims need turbans outside of prayer far more than they need them inside because it is the distinguishing sign of the Muslim (*shiʿār al-Muslim*) that distinguishes him from an infidel, particularly in this age in which the clothes of the believer have become mixed up with those of the infidel . . . to the point where it is hard for Muslims to determine whether the people they encounter [on the street] are Muslims or not. . . .[67]

This was a question that cut to the core of communal identity and, while al-Albani's methodological approach differed from that of al-Khatib, their shared focus on communication was clear.

65. For more on Syria's brief period of openness, see Kevin W. Martin, *Syria's Democratic Years: Citizens, Experts, and Media in the 1950s* (Bloomington: Indiana University Press, 2015), 13–25.

66. Muhammad Nasir al-Din al-Albani, "al-Ahadith al-Daʿifa waʾl-Mawduʿa," *al-Tamaddun al-Islami*, Shawwal 1375/May 1956, 517–21, at 517–18. Neither was a standard turban necessarily sufficient: a leading Hanbali scholar Ibn Qudama (d. 620/1223) stated that, for the purpose of ablutions, a properly Muslim turban must have a "tail" (*dhuʾāba*) because only turbans with this surplus cloth hanging down at the end are considered distinctively Muslim. See Muwaffaq al-Din ʿAbd Allah b. Ahmad b. Qudama, *al-Mughni ʿala Mukhtasar al-Khiraqi*, ed. ʿAbd Allah b. ʿAbd al-Muhsin Turki and ʿAbd al-Fattah Muhammad Hulw (N.P., ND), 1:383–84. I thank Omar Anchassi for this point.

67. al-Albani, "al-Ahadith al-Daʿifa waʾl-Mawduʿa," 518.

While Ansar al-Sunna's opportunities for visible activism narrowed under ʿAbd al-Nasir, contestation over the boundary between worship and custom intensified. In June 1963, al-Sayyid ʿAbd al-Halim Malaqi, the Imam and Khatib of the Ibn ʿAnnan mosque in Tal Juwayn, a village within the Sharqiyya governorate, authored an article entitled "Worship in Islam." Most strikingly, this rural religious figure argued that, unlike other religions,

> Islam's conception of worship . . . is not limited to prayer (*maqṣūr^an ʿalā al-ṣalawāt*). . . . Rather, every sound action accompanied by sincerity, commitment to God's orders, and the pursuit of His satisfaction is an act of worship that is rewarded accordingly (*ʿibāda yuthāb ʿalayhā thawwāb al-mutaʿabbidin*).[68]

Indeed, "[even acts of] pleasure and enjoyment can *become* worship through good intention" (*yumkin an tuṣbiḥ ʿibādāt bi-ḥusn al-niyya*).[69] In emphasizing intention, Malaqi drew on an approach within medieval Islamic thought represented by Abu Hamid al-Ghazali (d. 505/1111) and Fakhr al-Din al-Razi (d. 606/1209), which argued that mundane acts, when melded with proper intention, could move from the realm of "secular" (*dunyawī*) to that of "religious" (*dīnī*).[70]

By contrast, ʿAbd al-Nasir offered a model of both theology and action consistent with his secular-nationalist vision. In a July 23 1961 speech commemorating the ninth anniversary of the Free Officers' Revolution, Egypt's President declared: "Religion is work (*al-Dīn ʿamal*), the Prophet worked, and every individual worked. . . ."[71] *Al-Iʿtisam's* editor and a leading figure within the Jamʿiyya Sharʿiyya with Salafi leanings, Mahmud ʿAbd al-Wahhab Fayyad,[72] sought to adopt ʿAbd al-Nasir's framework of action, noting that

68. al-Sayyid ʿAbd al-Halim Malaqi, "al-ʿIbada fi al-Islam," *al-Hadi al-Nabawi*, Safar 1383/~June 1963, 34–38, at 36.

69. Malaqi, "al-ʿIbada f al-Islam," 37, emphasis added.

70. As Rushain Abbasi argues, "Ghazali brings *dīn* and *dunyā* together in claiming that there can be no proper *dīn* without adequately worldly sustenance, and that in fact this can be called worship when it is used towards a *dinī* end" ("Did Pre-Modern Muslims Distinguish the Religious and Secular? The Dīn-Dunyā Binary in Medieval Islamic Thought," *Journal of Islamic Studies* 31, no. 2 [2020]: 209).

71. Cited in Mahmud ʿAbd al-Wahhab Fayyad, "Kalimat al-Iʿtisam," *al-Iʿtisam*, Rabiʿ al-Awwal 1381/August 1961, 3–8, at 3.

72. While Fayyad was a prominent member of the Jamʿiyya Sharʿiyya, he was seen within Ansar al-Sunna, alongside ʿAbd al-Latif al-Mushtahiri, as being "inclined to the Salafi Call" (*yumīlūn ilā al-Daʿwa al-Salafiyya*). See "Akhbar al-Jamaʿa," *al-Hadi al-Nabawi*, Ramadan 1380/February 1961, 50.

"Islam does not accept the existence of individuals who are unemployed [because they] detract from its dignity" (*karāmatahu*).[73] More broadly, as Gregory Starrett argues, ʿAbd al-Nasir's educational reforms sought to repurpose the Islamic tradition towards fulfilling concrete policy ends.[74]

At the end of the 1960s neared, *al-Iʿtisam* also hosted greater discussion of the term *manhaj*.[75] In a April 1966 article, Fayyad declared that "Islam is a complete approach (*al-Islām manhaj kāmil*), a comprehensive constitution, a noble goal, and pure set of means which guides people to the paths of happiness in this world and the next."[76] Yet, while his counterparts in Ansar al-Sunna had sought to redefine the boundaries of worship, this leading member of the Jamʿiyya Sharʿiyya maintained that "worship does not develop (*al-ʿibādāt lā tataṭawwar*) . . . but transactions (*muʿāmalāt*) . . . [do]."[77] Roughly a year later, the 1967 Arab-Israeli war rendered the necessity of a clear *manhaj* even more urgent.

In the shadow of the military defeat of 1967, Fayyad reiterated the scope of his challenge, calling for

> [a] distinct Islamic approach (*manhāj Islāmī mufaṣṣal*) that can protect the Islamic community from atheism and depravity (*al-ilḥād waʾl-radhīla*), from injustice and aggression (*al-baghī waʾl-ʿudwān*), from despotism and tyranny (*min al-istibdād waʾl-ṭughyān*), from poverty, ignorance, and sickness and from humiliation and weaknesses and fear. Indeed, Islam is a religion of life, and its approach is a comprehensive and complete one (*manhāj kāmil wa shāmil*) which sets forth for man the path of success and savior.[78]

The question was no longer whether the term *manhaj* was applicable to Islam, but rather one of competing efforts to define this term.

73. Fayyad, "Kalimat al-Iʿtisam," 3.

74. Starrett, *Putting Islam to Work*, 77–80.

75. This was not the first time that the term *manhaj* had appeared in *al-Iʿtisam*, yet previous references had been formulaic and vague. For example, in the May 1950 issue, Muhammad ʿAbd Allah al-Samman, at this time employed at the Muslim Brotherhood's Cairo headquarters, called for the Islamic community (*umma*) to come to a "correct approach" (*manhāj ṣaḥīḥ*) ("Umma bi-Ghayr Manhaj," *al-Iʿtisam*, 27 Rajab 1369/12 May 1950, 3). On al-Samman's membership in the Brotherhood, see "Muhammad ʿAbd Allah al-Samman," *al-Maktaba al-Shamila*, https://shamela.ws/index.php/author/2596, accessed 3 June 2020.

76. Mahmud ʿAbd al-Wahhab Fayyad, "Kalimat al-Iʿtisam," *al-Iʿtisam*, Dhu al-Hijja 1385/April 1966, 3–8, at 3.

77. Fayyad, "Kalimat al-Iʿtisam," 4–5.

78. Mahmud ʿAbd al-Wahhab Fayyad, "Kalimat al-Iʿtisam," *al-Iʿtisam*, Dhu al-Hijja 1385/April 1966, 3–8, at 3.

What drove this change between the 1940s and 1960s? An extended debate in Egyptian and Syrian periodicals over the importance of social practices generally, and the related shifting boundary between matters of worship and custom, cannot be explained by a longer history of Islamic interpretation. Neither can it narrowly be explained by the organizational needs of Salafi elites; during this period, Ansar al-Sunna's activities were largely confined to its network of branches in Egypt and increasingly Sudan, while the Islamic Civilization Association (*Jamʿiyyat al-Tamaddun al-Islāmī*) engaged in limited institutional development or social outreach.

Instead, the shifting of the boundary between worship and custom is best understood in light of Salafism's aspiration to articulate a global and universalizing project that could meet the ideological challenges posed by rise of secular nationalism and Islamism alike during this period. Furthermore, increasing state-enforced distinction between religious and non-religious spaces, most notable in the separation of education and religious practice,[79] challenged a Salafi call that sought to define daily life through worship. Salafi scholars, whether consciously or unconsciously, would continue to redefine the boundaries of worship in a manner that reflected these challenges.

THE EXPANSION OF WORSHIP AND THE RISE OF A SALAFI *MANHAJ*, 1970–1990

By the end of the 1960s, the basic intellectual architecture of Salafi practice had emerged through an extended legal debate that expanded worship to encompass local practices previously deemed customary. Notwithstanding Ansar al-Sunna's relative success in establishing institutions under ʿAbd al-Nasir, however, Salafism remained primarily an elite and intellectual endeavor.

In their efforts to articulate a vision of applied *tawhid*, Egyptian Salafis were joined by leading Islamist thinkers and actors. Most notably, in 1975 the *Sahwa*-aligned Kuwaiti Islamist publication *al-Mujtamaʿ* published a series of articles by ʿAbd Allah ʿAzzam, the Palestinian Islamist who would become known for his alliance with Usama bin Ladin during the Soviet occupation of Afghanistan (1979–89). ʿAzzam, though, had not yet reached this stage of his career and had, just two years earlier, completed and defended a disserta-

79. Mitchell, *Colonising Egypt*, 82–92.

tion on Islamic law at al-Azhar.[80] Following this educational accomplishment and a short stint in the Jordanian Ministry of Religious Endowments, ʿAzzam was appointed as a lecturer in the Faculty of Shariʿa at Jordan University.[81]

In January 1975, ʿAzzam wrote two articles that sought to elucidate the relationship between theology (*ʿaqīda*) and action (*ʿamal*) in a manner that made obligatory a set of practices that had previously been split between obligation and recommendation (*al-istiḥbāb*).[82] ʿAzzam's call to worship emerged from an Islamist sub-tradition dominated by Abu al-Aʿla Mawdudi and Sayyid Qutb, both of whom sought to harness this concept towards a project of top-down and bottom-up religious change alike.[83]

ʿAzzam's second article, in which he explained the practical implications of his declaration, is of particular note:

> Worship includes all aspects of life so prayer is worship, visiting one's family is worship, averting one's gaze (*ghaḍḍ al-baṣar*) from those from whom one is forbidden (*al-maḥārim*) is worship, just rule (*al-ʿādl fī al-ḥukm*) is worship, women wearing the long robe (*al-jilbāb al-ṭawīl*) is worship, trustworthy behavior in transactions (*al-amāna fī al-bayʿa*) is worship, Jihad in the path of God (*al-Jihād fī sabīl Allāh*) is worship, and indeed [even] eating becomes worship (*bal yuṣbiḥ al-ṭaʿām ʿibādat*[an]) and love (*mawadda*) between husband and wife becomes worship. Indeed, every word, movement, and sentiment (*kull ḥaraka wa kull niyya wa kull khālija*) becomes worship and indeed the good intention (*al-niyya al-tayyiba*) is worship . . . and loving God (*al-ḥubb fī Allāh*) is worship and hatred (*bughḍ*) in the path of God is worship. . . . All of this is merely dependent on one's intention being directed to God (*al-niyya mutajjaha ilā Allāh*). . . . Therefore, the value of actions in Islamic theology (*qīmat al-iaʿmāl fī al-ʿaqīda al-Islāmiyya*) is derived from its motivation,

80. In Cairo, he would also spend time with Muhammad Qutb and Ismaʿil al-Shatiʿ, the latter of whom was the editor of *al-Mujtamaʿ* (and with whom he had previously overlapped in Jordan). See Hegghammer, *The Caravan*, 77–79.

81. Hegghammer, *The Caravan*, 80–81.

82. ʿAbd Allah ʿAzzam, "al-ʿAqida wa Atharuha fi Binaʾ al-Jil," *al-Mujtamaʿ*, 1 Muharram 1395/14 January 1975, 35–41, at 35.

83. Specifically, Daniel Lav has argued that Mawdudi and Qutb facilitated a "thenomic shift" that bridged a longstanding Salafi "monolatric tradition . . . [in] the spheres of ritual worship and traditional jurisprudence . . . [and] the legal-political sphere." Mawdudi's seminal work on this topic would be *Four Fundamental Quranic Terms* (*Qurʾan ki Char Bunyadi Istilahen*). Qutb's vision reached final status in the 1960s in *Milestones* (*Maʿalim fi al-Tariq*) and *Constitutive Elements of the Islamic Conception* (*Muqawwimat al-Tasawwur al-Islami*), the latter of which was published posthumously. See Lav, "Radical Muslim Theonomy," 175–264, quotation on 175.

not from its results (*min bāʾithihā lā min natāʾijihā*), as the results are in the hand of God.[84]

Like al-Sayyid ʿAbd al-Halim Malaqi, ʿAzzam drew implicitly on the legal principle that intention could transport otherwise mundane acts from the realm of secular (*dunyawī*) to that of "religious" (*dīnī*). Accordingly, what is notable about ʿAzzam's argument is not its novelty but rather the ways in which it drew on this precedent to meld Islamist and Salafi debates by asserting that the domain of worship should encompass the entirety of life.[85] This shift, far from an academic point, was practically oriented, as the article title noted, "to build a generation" (*bināʾ al-jīl*).

As Islamist activists emerged in Egypt, Kuwait, Saudi Arabia and elsewhere to lay claim to Islam as a comprehensive ideology,[86] Salafis articulated a society-centered concept of *manhaj*.[87] Some ten months after ʿAzzam, ʿAbd

84. ʿAzzam, "al-ʿAqida wa Atharuha fi Binaʾ al-Jil," *al-Mujtamaʿ*, 8 Muharram 1395/21 January 1975, 19–21, at 20. Hegghammer cites what appears to be an expanded and later version of his article in *al-Mujtamaʿ*, published in the 1980s (*The Caravan*, 293, 594). The website Hegghammer cites, however, is no longer operational so it is not possible to determine the extent of similarity; a basic difference in the two, however, is that the earlier articles do not mention jihad as a form of *Tawhid*.

85. Despite his engagement with Salafi discussions, it would be inaccurate to categorize ʿAzzam as a Salafi. He was first and foremost a Muslim Brother and, in the context of 1980s Afghanistan, adopted a pragmatic approach to the Hanafi religious practices of Afghani Mujahidin, which were opposed by Salafi-Jihadis. As such, he can be understood as an Islamist open to key ideas of Salafism and engaged with broader Salafi debates. See Hegghammer, *The Caravan*, 290–91, 389–93. Despite these commonalities, a leading Saudi quietist Salafi, Rabiʿ b. Hadi al-Madkhali, would later claim that ʿAzzam's "chief preoccupation was making war on Salafiyya" (cited in Hegghammer, *The Caravan*, 474). For more on his engagement with the Brotherhood's intellectual tradition, see Hegghammer, *The Caravan*, 130.

86. For a Saudi Arabian example, see Stéphane Lacroix, *Awakening Islam: The Politics of Religious Dissent in Contemporary Saudi Arabia*, trans. George Holoch (Cambridge, MA: Harvard University Press, 2011), 37–80. In the Egyptian case, the claim to Islam's comprehensiveness dates back to Hasan al-Banna, who declared in his famed "Twenty Principles" (*al-Uṣūl al-ʿIshrīn*) that "Islam is a comprehensive religion that treats all manifestations of life collectively" (*niẓām shāmil yatanawwal maẓāhir al-ḥayāt jamiʿan*). See Jumʿa Amin ʿAbd al-Aziz, *Fahm al-Islam fi Zilal al-Usul al-ʿIshrin li-l-Imam Hasan al-Banna* (Cairo: Dar al-Daʿwa li-l-Tibaʿa waʾl-Nashr, 1990), 23.

87. The claim to a *manhaj* is separate from a distinct approach to the Sunna. For example, Ibn Taymiyya authored a multivolume theological work entitled *Manhaj al-Sunna al-Nabawiyya*. See El Shamsy, *Rediscovering the Islamic Classics*, 184.

Allah al-Sabt (d. 2012) published an article entitled "The Salafi Call" (*al-Daʿwa al-Salafiyya*) in *al-Mujtamaʿ*, arguing for the "Salafi *Manhaj*" (*al-Manhaj al-Salafī*). This Kuwaiti Salafi scholar, who would later be active in the establishment of the Salafi-aligned Association for the Revival of the Islamic Heritage (*Jamʿiyyat Iḥyāʾ al-Turāth al-Islāmī*) and the Salafi Publishing House (*al-Dār al-Salafiyya li-l-Ṭibāʿa waʾl-Nashr waʾl-Tawzīʿ*), defined the Salafi Method by its "direct engagement (*al-ittiṣāl al-mubāshir*) with the Quran and Sunna."[88] The following year, Mustafa Hilmi, an Egyptian philosophy professor with ties to Egypt and Saudi Arabia-based members of Ansar al-Sunna, published the *Rules of the Salafi Method in Islamic Thought* (*Qawaʿid al-Manhaj al-Salafi fi al-Fikr al-Islami*).[89] This text framed Salafism as an ideology of "comprehensiveness" (*shumūl*) that could both reorient Muslim thought, as well as provide a clear set of guidelines for putting an epistemological approach into practice.[90]

Salafis, however, were not the only group that claimed a distinct approach. In the November 1976 issue of the organization's official magazine, *al-Daʿwa*, the Muslim Brotherhood offered its "method for Islamic action" (*manhaj al-ʿamal al-Islāmī*),[91] and the next year, an article in the periodical included the assertion that the organization works along the lines of a "method of following, not innovating (*manhaj al-itbāʿ lā al-ibtidāʿ*) based on the Quran and Sunna."[92] State-aligned scholars also intervened in this debate: an August 1979 article in *Minbar al-Islam*, published by the Supreme Council for Islamic Affairs within the Egyptian Ministry of Endowment, declared that those working at the Council are "preachers in the path of God . . . [following] the

88. ʿAbd Allah al-Sabt, "al-Daʿwa al-Salafiyya," *al-Mujtamaʿ*, 24 Shawwal 1395/28 October 1975, 39.

89. Lauzière, *The Making of Salafism*, 201–2, 218–19.

90. For the discussion of comprehensiveness, see Mustafa Hilmi, *Qawaʿid al-Manhaj al-Salafi fi al-Fikr al-Islami* (Beirut: Dar al-Kutub al-ʿIlmiyya, 2005), 176–8. While Hilmi does not discuss the relationship between worship and custom in *Qawaʿid al-Manhaj al-Salafi*, his explanation of Islam's comprehensive nature notes what he considers to be a false divide among creed (*ʿaqīda*), worship (*ʿibāda*), and transactions (*muʿāmalāt*). See Hilmi, *Qawaʿid al-Manhaj al-Salafi*, 176.

91. "Akhbar al-Shabab waʾl-Jamiʿat," *al-Daʿwa*, Dhu al-Hijja 1396/November 1976, 56–7, at 57.

92. "Muhammad ʿAbd al-Quddus, "Qurraʾ al-Daʿwa Yatahadathun Ilayha," *al-Daʿwa*, Rajab 1397/June 1977, 52–4, at 54.

Method of Islam" (*Manhaj al-Islām*).[93] Similarly, a 1980 lecture by the Egyptian state-aligned preacher and scholar Muhammad Mutwalli al-Sha'rawi (d. 1988) declared: "if people don't have a method (*manhaj*) then the story [of their lives] will be corrupted" (*al-ḥikāya tab'a fāsida*).[94]

Sayyid Qutb's shadow loomed particularly large in debates over *manhaj*. In his landmark 1965 call to action, *Milestones* (*Ma'alim fi al-Tariq*), Qutb had contrasted "a Godly Approach" (*Manhaj Rabbānī*) with that of trans-historical conception of barbarism (*al-Jāhiliyya*) that extended to the 1960s.[95] While Qutb's younger brother Muhammad would become a key member of the Salafi movement,[96] the elder Qutb's theological vision was always an uneasy fit with Salafism's neo-Hanbali theological core.[97] Despite occasional Salafi efforts to explain Qutb's lack of direct engagement with two giants of this tradition, Ibn Kathir and Ibn Qayyim al-Jawziyya,[98] this Muslim Brother's theological leanings were highly idiosyncratic. Just as importantly, the details of a Salafi *manhaj* were still unclear. As Lauzière notes, "Hilmi did not explain what it meant to be a Salafi in law."[99] The legal questions and practical implications of the Salafi *manhaj*, and how it related to the legal categories of worship and custom, would be further clarified through a debate over the religious status of facial hair.[100]

This debate began not in Egypt or Saudi Arabia, but in Kuwait. The August 1977 issue of the *al-Wa'i al-Islami*, published by the Kuwaiti Ministry of

93. "Kalimat al-Tahrir," *Minbar al-Islam*, Ramadan 1399/August 1979, 1.

94. Muhammad Mutawalli al-Sha'rawi, "al-Halqa al-Thaniyya min Tafsir Surat al-Fatiha," *Tafsir al-Sha'rawi*, prod. 'Abd al-Mun'im Mahmud, Channel 1, Cairo, ~June 1980, 27:30.

95. Sayyid Qutb, *Ma'alim fi al-Tariq* (Cairo: Dar al-Shuruq, 1979), 41–42. Qutb also refers to "the manhaj of this religion" (*manhaj hadha al-Dīn*) and "the manhaj of life in Islam" (*manhaj al-ḥayāt fi al-Islām*). See 57 and 97, respectively.

96. For Muhammad Qutb's position in Saudi Arabia, see Lacroix, *Awakening Islam*, 54–56. For the younger Qutb's contribution to the Qutbian legacy, see Scott Bursey, "Finding Muhammad Qutb: Praising Ghosts Online, a Different Qutbian legacy and Islamic Revivalism in the Gulf" (M.A. thesis, Simon Fraser University, 2017).

97. Lav, *Radical Islam and the Revival of Medieval Theology*, 54–55.

98. Isma'il al-Shatti, "Liqa' al-Mujtama' Hawl Sayyid Qutb wa Manhajihi," *al-Mujtama'*, 12 Shawwal 1398/5 October 1978, 10–12, at 11.

99. Lauzière, *The Making of Salafism*, 220.

100. The debate over the beard was not unique to Salafis, or even to Sunnis. For a Shi'i modernist example, see Simon Wolfgang Fuchs, "Failing Transnationally: Local intersections of science, medicine, and sectarianism in modernist Shi'i writings," *Modern Asian Studies* 48, no. 2 (2014): 451–52.

Endowments and Islamic Affairs (*Wizārat al-Awqāf wa'l-Shu'ūn al-Islāmiyya*), included a fatwa request from a lecturer of Engineering at Mansura University, located in the Nile Delta city of the same name. In the request, the author, ʿAdil Ibrahim al-Dasuqi, described the spread of those who imitated the style of the English rock band the Beatles (*al-Khanāfis*) by growing their hair and beards long. The questioner noted that the Prophetic command to "grow the beard," like that of coloring it (*sabgh*), was premised on distinguishing Muslims from their Jewish and Christian counterparts. He expressed his desire to avoid "resembling the Beatles" (*al-tashabbuḥ bi-l-khanāfis*) and wondered how to navigate the situation.[101]

The response of ʿAtiyya Saqr (d. 2006), a leading Azhari scholar and member of the Fatwa Council in the Kuwaiti Ministry of Endowments, sought to marginalize the question of visibility. For Saqr, the issue was not so much similarity but the intention involved in growing one's beard out; if resemblance to such youth was a product of "unintentional similarity" (*al-tawāfuq ghayr al-maqsūd*), then "no harm could be done" (*lā ḍarrar fihi abad*[an]). More broadly, Saqr wrote, "jurists . . . agree that it is required to grow [the beard] (*maṭlūb sharʿ*[an]), but differ on whether it is "obligatory" (*bi-l-wujūb*) or a matter of praiseworthy "election" (*nadb*). According to Saqr, those who argue for the former position claim that this obligation is rooted in the historical conditions of seventh-century Arabia in which growing a beard distinguished Muslims from their religious competitors, while proponents of the latter position proceed based on the principle that it is one of the ten characteristics of human nature (*min al-fiṭra*).[102]

It would only be at the end of the article, however, that Saqr would ignite controversy. In the closing paragraphs of this text, he cited an additional unnamed scholar, who had suggested that the command to grow the beard may simply have been a case of [non-binding] "guidance" (*irshād*). According to this scholar, if one were to take "mere resemblance" (*mujarrad al-mushābaha*) in matters of "temporal customs and appearances" (*al-ʿādāt wa'l-maẓāhir al-zamaniyya*) as sufficient justification, then Muslims today should all shave their beards in order to distinguish themselves. Concluding his analysis, Saqr

101. ʿAtiyya Saqr, "al-Fatawa," *al-Waʿi al-Islami*, Shaʿban 1397/August 1977, 100–2, at 100. "Al-khanafis" literally denotes the common insect, the beetle. Though the Beatles had broken up by 1970, the perception of cultural impact in the Middle East persisted. I thank Simon Fuchs for this observation that demonstrates cultural knowledge beyond his years.

102. Saqr, "al-Fatawa," 101.

counseled that "the truth is that clothing and personal bearing, including shaving the beard, are among the customs" (*ʿādāt*) that the individual must consider "in relation to his environment" (*ʿalā istiḥsān al-bīʾa*).[103]

The August 1977 issue of *al-Mujtamaʿ* featured a response, entitled "A Reaction to a Strange Fatwa" (*Taʿqīb ʿalā Fatwā Gharība*). The author, a reader by the name of Ahmad b. ʿAbd al-ʿAziz al-Husayn, disputed Saqr's ruling, stating that the Prophet had clearly commanded Muslims to grow the beard without reference to "considerations of the local environment" (*istiḥsān al-bīʾa*). More broadly, no one is permitted to challenge or contradict something that God and His Messenger have commanded (*Ḥukm Allāh wa Rasūluhu*).[104] This rebuke, one-sided as it may have been, struck a nerve and, in the next issue, Saqr responded that the offending opinion had been but one of many approaches that he had presented, and that the dominant opinion of scholars (*al-rājiḥ*) was that it was obligatory to grow the beard.[105]

Yet the controversy refused to die down. The next issue of *al-Mujtamaʿ* included a two-page article by Saqr in which he further elaborated on the legal position surrounding the beard. In contrast to his previous article and followup, respectively, Saqr declared that, after "research and contemplation" (*al-baḥth waʾl-taʾammul*), he had determined that the opinion that permitted one to shave the beard depending on local circumstances "is not sound in terms of Islamic law" (*lā tuthbat ṣiḥḥatahu sharʿan*).[106] While people remain free, broadly speaking, in matters of "clothing and personal comportment" (*al-malābis waʾl-hayʾāt al-shakhṣiyya*), Islamic law "pertains to particular matters of clothing and personal comportment (*tadhkhul fī baʿḍ umūr al-malābis waʾl-hayʾāt al-shakhṣiyya*) . . . such as the prohibition against men wearing wool, gold, or women's clothing. . . ." Accordingly, Saqr reiterated that the "claim to the obligatory nature of the beard is the majority one" (*al-qawl bi-l-wujūb rājiḥ*).[107]

103. Saqr, "al-Fatawa," 102. Saqr would reiterate this position, including the language of "considerations of the local environment" (*istiḥsān al-bīʾa*), in January 1996. See Salah Muntassar, "Mujarrad Raʾi," *al-Ahram*, 31 January 1996, 13.

104. Ahmad b. ʿAbd al-ʿAziz al-Husayn, "Taʿqib ʿala Fatwa Ghariba," *al-Mujtamaʿ*, 16 Ramadan 1397/30 August 1977, 35.

105. ʿAtiyya Saqr, "Taʿqib ʿala Taʿqib," *al-Mujtamaʿ*, 23 Ramadan 1397/6 September 1977, 5.

106. "Munaqasha Hadiʾa maʿa Fadilat al-Shaykh ʿAtiyya Saqr Hawl Fatwa al-Lihya," *al-Mujtamaʿ*, 8 Shawwal 1397/20 September 1977, 36–37, at 36.

107. "Munaqasha Hadiʾa maʿa Fadilat al-Shaykh ʿAtiyya Saqr Hawl Fatwa al-Lihya," 37.

Several weeks later, ʿUthman al-Salih, also known as ʿUthman b. ʿAbd al-Qadir al-Safi, published an article in *al-Mujtamaʿ* that challenged al-Saqr's initial article. Attributing the popularization of both shaving and trimming the beard (*taqṣīr al-liḥa aw ḥalqihā*) to the influence of the Western occupation and related "invasion" (*ghazw*) of Muslim society following the first World War (1914–18), al-Salih rejected the claim that the beard was merely a form of "civil appearance" (*min al-maẓāhir al-madaniyya*). Instead, he declared: "We the Salafis (*al-Salafiyyūn*) argue that . . . shaving it is forbidden (*ḥurmat ḥalqihā*). . . ."[108] Al-Salih's concerns were twofold: one to challenge Saqr, and the other to buttress the article that had originally responded to Saqr with relevant proof texts. Accordingly, he went into great detail explaining the beard's role in "protecting human nature" (*ḥimāyat^an li-l-fiṭra*).[109] While al-Salih expressed concern with questions of textual methodology, his focus was not on the distinction between worship and custom but on disputing the claim that the beard was not obligatory.[110] Beyond the beard, al-Salih noted, like Rashid Rida, that Islam does not prescribe a set style of clothing. Instead, it sets forth limitations—avoiding resemblance to competing and antagonistic schools of thought (*aṣḥāb madhhabiyya*), distinction between men and women, covering one's "private parts" (*ʿawra*)—that render specific garments or styles forbidden.[111]

That a debate would break out over the beard and its relation to worship was not mere happenstance. Instead, the beard's status as a matter of custom rather than worship is a longstanding tension within Islamic law because of the ambiguity as to whether it fell within the Prophet's "non-legal" activities such as the way he ate, slept, or dressed, or whether it should be categorized

108. ʿUthman al-Salih, "al-Lihya waʾl-Azya," *al-Mujtamaʿ*, 12 Dhu al-Qaʿda 1397/25 October 1977, 12–14, at 12.

109. The same hadith report also references circumcision, yet jurists differed on whether the practice was obligatory or simply praiseworthy. For the Hanbali jurist Ibn Qayyim al-Jawziyya's (d. 750/1350) overview of the position that male circumcision is obligatory, see Ibn Qayyim al-Jawziyya, *Tuhfat al-Mawdud bi-Ahkam al-Mawlud*, ed. ʿUthman b. Jumʿa Dumayriyya (Jedda, Saudi Arabia: Dar ʿAlam al-Fawaʾid, 1431/2011), 236–61. Most evocatively, the Umayyad Caliph ʿUmar b. ʿAbd al-ʿAziz (r. 99–101/717–20) allegedly declared: "God sent Muhammad as a guide, not as a circumciser" (*Allāh baʿth Muḥammad hādiy^an wa-lam yabʿathahu khātin^an*). See Siham ʿAbd al-Salam, *Khitan al-Dhukur: Bayna al-Din, al-Tibb, al-Thaqafa, al-Tarikh* (Cairo: Ruʾya li-l-Nasr waʾl-Tawziʿ, 2006), 47.

110. al-Salih, "al-Lihya waʾl-Azya," 13.

111. al-Salih, "al-Lihya waʾl-Azya," 14.

within the purview of his acts as Messenger of God.[112] Put differently, was the command to grow the beard merely a highly contextual Arab social practice used to visually distinguish Muslims from non-Muslims at a particular historical juncture, or did it constitute an eternal example for Muslims to follow?

Indeed, even as the beard had served as a key marker of masculinity in Islamic history,[113] Mahmud Muhammad Khattab al-Subki still felt the need in the early twentieth century to excoriate those who claimed "that the beard is a mere custom (*ʿāda*) unconnected to religion."[114] Instead, for al-Subki, the beard is among the characteristics of basic human nature (*fiṭra*) and, as such, is obligatory.[115] Roughly a decade later, Muhammad Hamid al-Fiqi had published an article in *al-Hadi al-Nabawi* on this topic, again mentioning the beard (and mustache) as two of the ten characteristics of human nature.[116] Unacknowledged but crucial in this discussion is the question of religious status. While the dominant opinion is one of obligation to grow the beard, a minority strain within the Islamic tradition argued that shaving the beard was "disfavored" (*makrūḥ*) rather than forbidden.[117]

112. The Shafiʿi school provided widest latitude for those who wished to shave the beard by classifying this act as disfavored. By contrast, Hanafi, Hanbali, and Maliki schools considered it forbidden to shave. See ʿAbd al-Rahman al-Jaziri, *al-Fiqh ʿala al-Madhahib al-Arbaʿa* (Beirut: Dar al-Fikr, 2019), 2:42–43. For a similar view that highlights the view of the Almoravid-era Maliki scholar ʿIyad b. Musa (popularly known as al-Qadi ʿIyad, d. 544/1149), see Yusuf al-Qaradawi, *al-Halal wa'l-Haram fi al-Islam* (Cairo: Maktabat Wahba, 2012), 114.

113. Khaled El-Rouayheb, *Before Homosexuality in the Arab-Islamic World, 1500–1800* (Chicago: University of Chicago Press, 2005), 26–27.

114. al-Subki, *al-Din al-Khalis*, 1:193.

115. al-Subki, *al-Din al-Khalis*, 1:189–90.

116. Muhammad Hamid al-Fiqi, "Ahadith al-Ahkam," *al-Hadi al-Nabawi*, 15 Rabiʿ al-Thani 1359/~23 May 1940, 13–21, at 13. The dominant opinion among the legal schools is that trimming the mustache is required. See Fatriyya Wardi Andunisiyya, *ʿInayat al-Shariʿa al-Islamiyya bi-Nizfat al-Fard wa'l-Biʿa* (Beirut: Dar al-Kutub al-ʿIlmiyya, 2014), 57–58.

117. Muhammad al-Shawkani quotes the Maliki scholar al-Qadi Iyad b. Musa (d. 544/1149) regarding the disfavored status of shaving the beard (*Nayl al-Awtar min Ahadith Sayyid al-Akhyar Sharh Muntaqa al-Akhbar* [Beirut: Dar al-Kutub al-ʿIlmiyya, 2011], 124). For a nineteenth-century Shafiʿi example, see Abu Bakr ʿUthman b. Muhammad Shatta al-Dimyati, *Hashiyat Iʿanat al-Talibin ʿala Hall Alfaz Fath al-Muʿin bi-Sharh Qurrat al-ʿAyn bi-Muhimmat al-Din* (N.P: Dar al-Fikr 2019), 2:386.For an example from the 1970s, see al-Azhar's Islamic Research Academy's position that shaving the beard is disfavored but not forbidden, which relies on an earlier ruling by the former Shaykh of al-Azhar Muhammad Shaltut (d. 1963). See ʿAbd al-Hamid Shahin, "Bab al-Fatawa," *al-Azhar*, Muharram 1401/~November 1980, 188–91.

Neither ʿAtiyya Saqr's interpretative concessions nor ʿUthman al-Salih's vehement insistence on the beard's obligatory status settled this question. In an article published around 1980 in the Islamic University of Medina's flagship journal, ʿAbd Allah Ahmad Qadiri, the supervisor of campus life (*al-mushrif al-ijtimāʿī*) at the university, sought to delineate the legal boundaries and practical implications of *tawhid*.[118]

The question was seemingly straightforward: what constitutes worship and how does the commitment to worship (*ʿibāda*) shapes a program (*manhaj*) for state and society? Arguing that worship represents a life program (*manhaj ḥayāt*) inclusive of all "useful actions" (*kull ʿamal nāfiʿ*), Qadiri included not merely "devotional practices" (*al-shaʿāʾir al-taʿbbudiyya*) but also matters of politics, finance, education, the media, or matters of peace and war, whether internal or external. Lest there be any ambiguity as to the broader ideological environment, Qadiri quoted Sayyid Qutb's declaration in *Milestones* that "There is No God but God is an Approach to Life" (*Lā Illa ilā Allāh Manhaj Ḥayāt*).[119]

Qadiri was particularly concerned to make the case that the Prophet's original community understood worship in this manner. Specifically, he argued that:

> The Pious Ancestors (*al-Salaf al-Ṣāliḥ*) understood worship (*al-ʿibāda*) in such a comprehensive fashion (*bi-hadha al-shumūl*). . . . Their lives were [defined] by worship, whether their prayer in the mosque, their jihad in battle, their adjudication in the court, their commerce in the market, teaching and learning in the mosque, and their fasting during Ramadan and at other times. . . .[120]

This IUM employee explained further that his valorization of worship responded to the growth of the faulty understanding that worship was defined by "performing particular devotional rituals" (*baʿḍ al-shaʿāʾir al-taʿabbudiyya*

118. ʿAbd Allah Ahmad Qadiri, "Tawhid Allah," *Majallat al-Jamiʿa al-Islamiyya bi-l-Madina al-Munawwara*, Issue #32 (~1980), 12:26–7. I base my estimate on the date for the forty-ninth issue of the magazine, which is recorded in the 8 February 1982 issue of *al-Madina* newspaper. See "Majallat al-Jamiʿa al-Islamiyya," *al-Madina*, 14 Rabiʿ al-Thani 1402/8 February 1982, 17.

119. Qadiri, "Tawhid Allah," 12:27. In an article on twentieth-century Islamic thought, Muhammad Qasim Zaman observes that the claim to a commitment to God's sovereignty had become so successful that it was difficult to argue against it. At the same, time, though, its dominance has stripped it of any exclusive association with Islamism. See Muhammad Qasim Zaman, "The Sovereignty of God in Modern Islamic Thought," *Journal of the Royal Asiatic Society* 25, no. 3 (July 2015): 418.

120. Qadiri, "Tawhid Allah," 12:28.

ʿalā wajh khāṣṣ).[121] Instead, he offered a reinterpretation of the boundaries of worship that effaced the domain of custom and transactions alike.

Al-Qadiri was also aware that the expansion of the boundaries of worship could lead to conflict, particularly in the case of visible signs of piety. He singled out facial hair: while acknowledging the importance of "commitment to an Islamic appearance such as growing out the beard" (*iʿfāʾ al-liḥya*) as part of a call to live according to the Quran and Sunna—an implicit acknowledgment of the Saudi *Sahwa*, who like their counterparts in the Egyptian Islamic student movement sported bushy beards—Qadiri suggested that many proponents of this approach overemphasized it to the detriment of ritual practice and the study of Islamic law (*fiqh*).[122] At stake was not the notion that one must grow a beard, but rather the relative importance of outward markers of religiosity in comparison with religious knowledge and ritual practice.

Three years later, ʿUthman al-Salih—using the name ʿUthman b. ʿAbd al-Qadir al-Safi[123]—published a pamphlet-length examination of the beard. The pamphlet appeared as part of a series of al-Maktab al-Islami, the prominent Islamic publishing house headed by Zuhayr al-Shawish (d. 2013), which had edited and distributed many of al-Albani's works. In his introduction, Shawish noted that the cultural and political "invasion" (*ghazw*) faced by the Islamic world had reshaped the lives of Muslims, with the beard becoming a site of contestation.[124] This prominent editor also identified the key legal debate behind arguments over the beard: whether it was a requirement, a praiseworthy practice of the Prophet Muhammad (*Sunna/Mustaḥabb*),

121. Qadiri, "Tawhid Allah," 12:30.

122. Qadiri, "Tawhid Allah," 12:31.

123. In the introduction to *Hukm al-Sharʿ fi al-Lihya waʾl-Azya waʾl-Taqalid waʾl-ʿAdat*, editor Zuhayr al-Shawish notes that the book had emerged out of al-Safi's response to Saqr's fatwa, and had first taken form in an article in *al-Mujtamaʿ* for which he did not have a precise citation. See ʿUthman b. ʿAbd al-Qadir al-Safi, *Hukm al-Sharʿ fi al-Lihya waʾl-Azyaʾ waʾl-Taqalid waʾl-ʿAdat* (Beirut/Damascus: al-Maktab al-Islami 1403/1983), 5. While this article and the pamphlet appear under different names—ʿUthman al-Salih and ʿUthman b. ʿAbd al-Qadir al-Safi, respectively—the first section (11–30) contains significant similarities, whether the association of shaving with World War I (11), the claim that the beard is a characteristic of human nature (13), the legal discussion regarding the beard as a permitted practice (*ibāḥa/nadb*) (15), or the claim that shaving the beard constitutes an alteration of God's creation (*taghyīr khalq Allāh*) (19).

124. *Hukm al-Sharʿ*, 3–4.

or merely a "civil form" (*shakl madanī*) regarding which the Shariʿa has no position.[125]

While I examine this pamphlet and Salafi debates over the beard in greater detail in chapter 5, I will conclude this section by analyzing the logic that undergirds al-Safi's efforts to turn the distinction between worship and custom on its head. After setting forth a series of textual proofs as to the obligatory nature of the beard, al-Safi pivots to an alternative argument that "customs" (*al-ʿādāt*) are a "domain of obligation" (*taklīf*).[126] Castigating the effort to "distance customs and traditions from Islamic law" (*iqṣāʾ al-ʿādāt waʾl-taqālīd ʿan al-sharʿ*),[127] al-Safi asserted that clothing, inclusive of the beard, falls within "the religious and civilizational structure of Muslims" (*al-bunya al-dīniyya waʾl-ḥaḍāriyya li-l-Muslimīn*).[128] More broadly, al-Safi explained, "all societies have their specific customs (*li-kull mujtamaʿ aʿrāfahu al-khāṣṣa bihi*) which correspond to their identities (*wa-allatī tabaʿ li-huwiyyatihi*).[129] Accordingly, Islam offers a distinct vision for everything from clothing and beards to urban architecture to street planning to mosque building.[130] In al-Safi's revamped vision, customs constitute a distinct part of what it means to be Muslim, making possible a comprehensive Islamic political, economic and social project.

The move to expand the boundaries of worship and thus religious obligation by laying claim to an Islamized vision of customs as the basis of political community, however, was not unanimous. A 1987 pamphlet published by students of two leading Saudi Salafi scholars, Ibn Baz (d. 1999) and Ibn al-ʿUthaymin[131] (d. 2001), broaches the question of the beard again:

> [Muhammad] said: grow the beard and trim the mustache and do not resemble the Jews and Christians.... As Islam commands and forbids ... perhaps the wisdom of this hadith was to create a distinct Islamic society (*mujtamaʿ Islāmī mumayyaz*). A practical, venerable, and respected society (*mujtamaʿ ʿamalī muhīb*

125. *Hukm al-Sharʿ*, 3.
126. *Hukm al-Sharʿ*, 32.
127. *Hukm al-Sharʿ*, 33.
128. *Hukm al-Sharʿ*, 34.
129. *Hukm al-Sharʿ*, 34.
130. *Hukm al-Sharʿ*, 53.
131. Ibn al-ʿUthaymin's full name is Muhammad b. Salih al-ʿUthaymin, yet he is known as Ibn al-ʿUthaymin rather than al-ʿUthaymin. I follow this convention when referring to this scholar in the body of the text.

> *wa muḥtaram*).... But in the present time, shaving the beard has become a matter of custom and followed practice (*shay' min al-'āda wa'l-'urf al-muttaba'*)....[132]

The students go on to ask whether the beard is required or Sunna (that is to say, praiseworthy). In response, Ibn al-'Uthaymin explained that the beard is among the practices of the Prophets (*min sunan al-mursalīn*) and that it is a requirement for the presentation of masculine human nature (*fiṭra*).[133] As for the specific question relating to the beard having become a "custom" (*'ādat^{an}*) among many people, Ibn al-'Uthaymin explains that this is a test of the perseverance (*ṣabr*) of God's servants.[134] The striking characteristic of this fatwa is not Ibn al-'Uthaymin's answer, nor is it specifically the invocation of custom. Rather, it is his students' extensive resort to distinctly modern language of social practice and unity, influenced by secular nationalist and Islamist competitors to the Salafi movement, which reveals how questions of worship and custom have becoming increasingly consumed by the broader goal of establishing an Islamic society.

Even with this transformation, however, the line between custom and ritual had not vanished. Four years later, the President of Ansar al-Sunna from 1976 to 1991, Muhammad 'Ali 'Abd al-Rahim (d. 1991), responded to a fatwa request from a male reader in the Delta town of Damietta as to whether "Islam sets forth a particular form of dress for men?" (*hal li-l-rajul ziyy mu'ayy^{an} fī al-Islām*). 'Abd al-Rahim explained that "clothing is a matter of custom, not worship" (*al-thiyāb min al-'ādāt laysat min al-'ibādāt*); the only groups that have a uniform are armies and police forces, in order to "identify themselves" (*min bāb al-ta'rīf*), while no such requirement exists in matters of piety (*laysa min al-tadayyun fī shayy*).[135] While Ansar al-Sunna's President may have sought to uphold the distinction between worship and custom and to deny Salafism's linkage between ethics and visibility, he could hardly escape the centrality of communication to worship.

132. Muhammad b. Salih al-'Uthaymin, *al-Risala fi Sifat Salat al-Nabi Sala Allah 'Alayhi wa Salam* (N.P: N.P, 1987), 30.

133. al-'Uthaymin, *al-Risala*, 30.

134. al-'Uthaymin,*al-Risala*, 32.

135. Muhammad 'Ali 'Abd al-Rahim, "Bab al-Fatawa," *al-Tawhid*, Sha'ban 1411/~April 1991, 8–22, at 20. 'Abd al-Rahim died in September of this year.

CONCLUSION

In the 1980s jihadists, some Salafi and some not, engaged in violence against both organs of the Egyptian state and civilian targets. While such violence was not new—the former Minister of Endowments had been assassinated by Jamaʿat al-Muslimin (also known as al-Takfir waʾl-Hijra) in June 1977, and Anwar al-Sadat by a member of the Jihad organization in October 1981—these events had driven the Egyptian Ministry of Interior to task scholars within the Egyptian state with the responsibility of engaging in a series of public dialogues (*ḥiwār*) with youth of these and other factions. During one such meeting, in October 1986, scholars and youth discussed a recent trend of conflicts within Egyptian mosques over "superficial arguments over religious matters" (*mujādalāt shakliyya fī umūr al-dīn*) that are mistakenly understood to be "from among the practices of the Pious Ancestors" (*min sunan al-Salaf al-Ṣāliḥ*).[136] The meeting, in turn, centered on a wide range of such practices as they were performed in Egyptian mosques, including the Salafi prohibition against reciting the Qurʾan loudly (*bi-ṣawt masmūʿ*), concluding the prayers secretly (*jahr^an aw sirr^an*), whether a blue-collar worker (*ʿāmil*) can pray in the factory while machines are running, and the debate over the soundness of a second call to prayer (*adhān*) on Fridays.[137]

Just a year earlier, however, ʿAbd al-Munʿim Nimr, the previous Minister of Endowments and a member of al-Azhar's research arm, the Islamic Research

136. The debate over the distinction between acts of worship and customs would reoccur in November 1991, in a religious dialogue that included ʿAtiyya Saqr and Jamal al-Din Mahmud, the Secretary General of the Supreme Council for Islamic Affairs. See Sayyid Abu Duma, "Hiwar al-Usbuʿ Bayna ʿUlamaʾ al-Din waʾl-Shabab," *al-Ahram*, 24 June 1983, 12.

137. Sayyid Abu Duma, "Nadwat al-Hiwar al-Fikri maʿa al-Jamaʿat al-Diniyya," *al-Ahram*, 28 October 1983, 13. These youth appear to have taken the position that reciting the Quran audibly (*bi-ṣawt masmūʿ*), the conclusion of the prayer quietly or secretly (*khatm al-ṣalāt jahr^an aw sirr^an*), and the use of a second call to prayer (*al-adhānayn*) were disfavored (*makrūḥ*). These positions would have placed them in a minority vis-à-vis broader practice within Egyptian mosques during the 1980s; by way of example, the use of the second call to prayer—in which the first serves to alert those near the mosque that the time of prayer is nearing and the second to call them to the actual performance of the ritual—had long been justified based on the model of the third Caliph ʿUthman who had responded to the growing size of the Muslim community by seeking to facilitate mosque attendance through the double *adhan*. On reading the Quran loudly in the mosque, see Ibn Baz, "Hukm Qiraʾat al-Qurʾan bi-Sawt Murtafaʿ fi al-Masjid," *al-Mawqa al-Rasmi li-Samahat al-Shaykh al-Imam Ibn Baz*, https://binbaz.org.sa/fatwas/1593/حكم-القران-قراءة-في-مرتفع-بصوت-المسجد.

Academy, had published a study on the question of how one should legislate based on the Sunna. Nimr upheld the distinction between the Prophet's functions as a religious, political, and judicial figure and "context-specific actions and customs" (*al-aʿmāl waʾl-ʿādāt al-bīʾīya*) that were distinct from these roles.[138] Moreover, Nimr argued, the Companions did not simply follow the Prophet's use of critical reasoning (*ijtihād*) on matters of significance to the Muslim community, but rather actively debated him.[139] While Nimr's main focus in this text was on discrediting a recent trend towards relying on Muhammad's medical practices (known as *al-Ṭibb al-Nabawī*),[140] he made clear that outside the domain of worship, and to a lesser extent transactions, local custom could play a significant role in achieving the common good (*maṣlaḥa*) for Muslims.[141]

What is striking about this conversation is not the Salafi debate over ritual practice or the Azhari reaction to it, but rather the youth's claim to be implementing the practices of the first three generations of Muslims. On display in this debate was the chasm produced by Salafism's ideological transformation from the 1930s on: while state-aligned scholars described these matters as secondary or even superficial, Salafi youth argued that they constituted characteristic features of a textual method and social approach alike. While no one in this debate referenced the distinction between worship and custom explicitly, the Salafi effort to render social practice subservient to a distinct method formed the inescapable background to this conversation.

In short, for Salafi youth specifically and for the movement more generally, the Salafi method offered an all-encompassing vision of society that vastly expanded the conceptual domain of religious practice beyond the mosque. While assertion of a Salafi *manhaj* was a key feature of this shift, it was a relatively late development. Instead, the articulation of a Salafi social vision arose out of an effort since the 1930s to expand the boundaries of worship and contract those of custom, creating the legal basis for an uncompromising vision

138. ʿAbd al-Munʿim Nimr, *al-Sunna waʾl-Tashriʿ* (Cairo: Dar al-Kutub al-Misri, 1985), 8–15. For an article highlighting Nimr's study, see Mahmud Mahdi, "Dirasa Islamiyya Jadida Tuthir ʿAdad^{an} min al-Tasaʾulat Hawl al-Sunna waʾl-Tashriʿ," *al-Ahram*, 22 March 1985, 15.

139. Nimr, *al-Sunna waʾl-Tashriʿ*, 24–31.

140. Nimr, *al-Sunna waʾl-Tashriʿ*, 65–79. The debate over the relationship between the Prophetic model and medicine had significant precedent: for a fourteenth-century example, see Muhammad b. Abi Bakr b. Qayyim al-Jawziyya, *al-Tibb al-Nabawi*, ed. ʿAbd al-Ghani ʿAbd al-Khaliq, ʿAdil Zuhri and Mahmud Faraj al-ʿUqda (Beirut: Dar al-Fikr, N.D.)

141. Nimr, *al-Sunna waʾl-Tashriʿ*, 60.

of society in which compulsory and unchangeable religious practice reached further and further beyond ritual.

Although Salafi scholars in Egypt and beyond would appeal to ostensibly unchanging understandings of the Prophet Muhammad's explicit commands, such appeals masked the ways in which secular nationalism and Islamism alike had challenged their religious vision. These two ideological competitors had done so not by engaging on Salafi scholars' home turf—textual methodology—but rather by articulating comprehensive social visions that valorized an understanding of a self-regulating subject that adhered to a visual logic of communication. While secular nationalists sought to do away with custom in the name of modernity and Islamists in the name of the formation of a pure Islamic society, Salafis responded to these challenges by radically reshaping the boundary between worship and custom.

The intellectual history of this process, however, is not of interest simply because it shows the ways in which Salafi invocations of the golden Islamic past invariably reflect intimate concerns of the present, including anxieties of communication. Rather, its significance lies in what it enabled: the articulation of a distinct Salafi method that valorized carefully-chosen social practices once understood as customary in the name of upholding God's oneness. The call to worship God, far from a mere repetition of that made in the past, therefore constituted both a rejection and reflection of modernity as it was lived by scholars and laypeople alike. The remaining chapters of this book will trace the rise of these distinctly Salafi practices and their relationship to the Salafi method. It is to a longstanding ritual act with changing social implications—the practice of praying in shoes (*al-Ṣalāt bi-l-Niʿāl*)—that we now turn.

CHAPTER 3

Praying in Shoes

How To Sideline a Practice of the Prophet

In December 1949, Abu-l-Wafa' Muhammad Darwish penned a furious article in *al-Hadi al-Nabawi*. Darwish's focus was neither the persistence of British influence, nor the perceived impiety of King Faruq. Instead, his target was a group of Azhari scholars, affiliated with a second Islamic journal, *Liwa' al-Islam*, who had allegedly criticized Ansar al-Sunna for "praying with shoes while their heads are uncovered" (*yuṣallūn bi-aḥdhiyatihim wa-ru'ūsuhum 'āriya*). Far from denying the accusation, Darwish argued that praying in shoes was no less than a replication of the Prophetic model.[1] As an early distinctive practice of Purist Salafism,[2] one might expect praying in shoes to have taken its place alongside the observance of gender segregation, a distinct beard, and

1. Abu-l-Wafa' Muhammad Darwish, "Nahnu wa Majallat Liwa' al-Islam," *al-Hadi al-Nabawi*, Rabi' al-Awwal 1369/~December 1949, 21–25.

2. Praying in shoes is not necessarily the first Salafi engagement with ritual norms; it is possible that that arguments over supererogatory *Tarawhih* prayers preceded the claim to praying in shoes. I wish to thank Richard Gauvain for making this point. Pieter Coppens argues that the performance of ritual ablutions over the socks (*al-masḥ 'alā al-jawrabayn*) "became a visual identity marker for Salafis" ("Jamāl al-Dīn al-Qāsimī's Treatise on Wiping over Socks and the Rise of a Distinct Salafi method," 2). How one dates this practice, however, pivots on whether one considers Jamal al-Din al-Qasimi (d. 1914) to be Salafi or whether one must look later to Muhammad Nasir al-Din al-Albani; in contrast to Peters and *pace* Lauziere, I do not consider al-Qasimi to be a Salafi. It is nonetheless the case that one often finds an overlap in the legal positions among ideological distinct Islamic reformists; for example, see chapter 1 for a discussion of Ansar al-Sunna's agreement with the Muslim Brotherhood on praying bareheaded.

the prohibition against pants or robes that stretched below the ankle (*Isbāl*) as key markers of a broader complex of religious authenticity. Instead, by the late 1980s, the question for leading Salafi scholars in Egypt and beyond was not how to observe this practice, but rather how to justify downplaying it.

In this chapter, I tackle the question of Salafism's intellectual and social development from a counterintuitive angle by probing how Salafis came to marginalize a practice of the Prophet Muhammad that they had previously categorized as praiseworthy (*Sunna mustaḥabba*). Specifically, I will trace the process by which Salafis reconsidered the legal status of praying in shoes and the conditions in which one should and should not pray in this manner.

The significance of this practice extends beyond telling a story of how Prophetic practices wax and wane for Salafis. Prayer generally—and praying in shoes specifically—was a means by which some Salafis sought to visually mark their own ritual communities, to challenge those of their competitors, and to assert the supremacy of their mode of emulating the Prophet in face of both non-Salafi scholars and powerful centralized states. This practice also challenged a broader Sunni community beyond Egypt that, with the partial exception of adherents of the Hanbali *madhhab*, adhered to strict concerns with ritual cleanliness (*najāsa*).[3] Instead, for Salafis, the significance of potentially impure shoes paled in comparison with a life oriented around worship of God. Praying in shoes projected an image of salt-of-the-earth piety that stood in contrast to both the ostentatiousness of mosques with expensive plush carpets and modern discourses of hygiene.[4] Just as importantly, it embodied a visible critique of the broader political, social, and scientific order that upheld Sunni mosques within and beyond the Middle East.

The Salafi claim to praying in shoes critiqued the hadith corpus in order to assert scholarly excellence and social distinction alike. Yet, as criticism mounted and opportunities for ritually based mobilization narrowed, Salafi scholars sought to avoid this practice for the precise reason that they had once

3. As Richard Gauvain notes, Salafis seek to place the question of ritual purity (whether substantive, i.e. *najāsa*, or legal/technical i.e., *ḥadath*) "in tokenistic terms" (*Salafi Ritual Purity*, 26). Instead, they "mine the *hadith* and, to a lesser degree, *tafsir* material for sufficiently moralistic readings of purity" which privilege intention (32).

4. For the nineteenth-century history of these discourses of hygiene in Ottoman Egypt, see Fahmy, *In Quest of Justice*, esp. 179–225. For the specific concern of British colonial officials with the sanitary conditions of mosques, see Halevi, *Modern Things on Trial*, 37–38.

glorified it: its distinctive and now divisive function as a visual signifier of communal membership and boundaries. I will begin by laying out Ansar al-Sunna's early claim to praying in shoes. Next, I will trace the performance of and debate over this practice between Egypt and Saudi Arabia, emphasizing the tension between this practice and broader calls towards mosque hygiene from the 1950s through 1970s. I will then turn to the 1980s, charting how Salafi scholars in Saudi Arabia maintained the practice's legitimacy in theory while offering justifications to avoid engaging in it. I will conclude by analyzing how, in the 1990s, Saudi and Egyptian Salafi scholars alike sought to decisively marginalize praying in shoes.

ROOTS AND RUPTURES

In May 1940, Ansar al-Sunna's *al-Hadi al-Nabawi* republished a fatwa by the Egyptian State Mufti, ʿAbd al-Majid Salim (r. 1928–45, d. 1954), which had originally been published in the leading Egyptian daily newspaper *al-Ahram* and then reprinted in March 1932 in the scholarly journal *al-Islam*.[5] A Hanafi scholar of ecumenical leanings,[6] Salim was a product of the Egyptian countryside's Quranic school (*Kuttāb*) system. He had then studied at al-Azhar with the noted Islamic reformer Muhammad ʿAbduh and eventually had served as the Shaykh of al-Azhar during the 1919 revolution. Just as important was his Quietist approach to Egyptian politics during the turmoil of the interwar period: Salim's ascent to the office of State Mufti benefited both from a warm relationship with King Fuʾad, and from British support.[7] As Ansar al-Sunna sought to establish itself as a leading light of Islamic reform, this endorsement of a fatwa by a scholar who straddled the study circles of al-Azhar and the state establishment constituted sound political strategy.

At stake, however, was more than strategic positioning. The topic at hand was the religious status of praying in shoes (known alternately as *al-Ṣalāt bi-l-*

5. See "al-Salat bi-l-Hidhaʾ wa Hukmuha Sharʿan," *al-Islam*, 18 Dhu al-Qaʿda 1350/25 March 1932, 4. According to the 1980 official fatwa collection of Dar al-Iftaʾ, the fatwa was first issued in Rajab 1347/December 1928. See *al-Fatawa al-Islamiyya min Dar al-Iftaʾ al-Misriyya* (Cairo: Supreme Council for Islamic Affairs, 1400/1980), 1:64. For its publication in *al-Hadi al-Nabawi*, see "Bab al-Fatawa," *al-Hadi al-Nabawi*, 1 Rabiʿ al-Thani 1359/~9 May 1940, 40.

6. See "Fadilat al-Shaykh ʿAbd al-Majid Salim," *Dar al-Iftaʾ al-Misriyya*, http://www.dar-alifta.org/ar/ViewScientist.aspx?sec = new&ID = 15&LangID = 1.

7. Skovgaard-Petersen, *Defining Islam for the Egyptian State*, 159–61.

Hidhā', al-Ṣalāt bi-l-Ni'āl, or *Ṣalāt al-Na'layn*) while in the mosque. In the original fatwa, Salim had responded that as long as one's shoes were free of impurities (*al-na'lān ṭāhirān*), then praying in them was permissible (*ṣaḥīḥa*), and cited a series of authenticated hadith reports to buttress this position.[8] As he concluded, Salim argued that praying in shoes must be permitted and noted "[that] many Muslim scholars have determined that [this practice is] praiseworthy (*mustaḥabba*)."[9]

Two years later, in a discussion of the religious status of shorts (known as *al-tabān* or *al-banṭalūn al-qaṣīr*), the question of praying in shoes would arise again. The author of the article was 'Abd al-'Aziz b. Rashid (d. 1982), a native of the Wahhabi-Hanbali heartland of Najd who had made his way first to Oman and then to Egypt to study at al-Azhar.[10] During this period, Ibn Rashid joined Ansar al-Sunna, working alongside Abu-l-Wafa' Muhammad Darwish and Muhammad 'Abd al-Majid al-Shafi'i (also known as Rashad al-Shafi'i) in Alexandria before taking over the organization's branch in this leading Egyptian city in the late 1940s when 'Abd al-Razzaq al-'Afifi moved

8. Salim cited a hadith report from *Sahih al-Bukhari* of a conversation with one of the Prophet Muhammad's Companions, Anas b. Malik (d. 93/711), in which the latter related that the Prophet had prayed while wearing shoes. He also cited a second hadith report, narrated by another Companion, Shaddad b. Aws (d. 58/677), in which the Prophet commanded Muslims to "distinguish yourselves from the Jews" (*khālifū al-Yahūd*) who do not pray in either their shoes or in their leather slippers (*khifāfihim*). Finally, Salim cited a third companion of the Prophet, Abu Hurayra (d. 59/678), who reported that the Prophet would often pray in his shoes and that many of the Companions (*Saḥāba*) and the generation of Muslims that followed them (known as the *Tābi'ūn*) would do so as well. A crucial point here is that the cited proof texts all assume prayer to be performed in the mosque.

9. "Bab al-Fatawa," *al-Hadi al-Nabawi*, 1 Rabi' al-Thani 1359/9 May 1940, 40. The question of praying in shoes is distinct from the issue of wiping over leather slippers (*al-masḥ 'alā al-khuffayn*) during ritual ablutions, which served in the early centuries of Islamic history to distinguish Sunnis (who permitted it) from Shi'is (who did not). For a detailed discussion see Patel, "Muslim Distinction," 344–48.

10. See Turayqi, *Mu'jam Musannafat al-Hanabila*, 8:190–92. While Ibn Rashid is included in the Wahhabi-Hanbali scholarly genealogy, he spent a great deal of his professional career in Egypt, settling in Damanhur, where he established a branch of Ansar al-Sunna, before moving to Alexandria. In Alexandria, he assumed leadership of the city's main branch when 'Abd al-Razzaq al-'Afifi left for Saudi Arabia in 1369/~1949. While he eventually returned to Saudi Arabia to teach at the Great Mosque of Mecca, he died in Egypt and was buried in Alexandria in a graveyard either owned by Ansar al-Sunna or simply disproportionately populated by its members. See Fathi Amin 'Uthman, "Bab al-Tarajim min A'lam al-Da'wa," *al-Tawhid*, Rabi' al-Awwal 1418/~July 1997, 48:1.

to Saudi Arabia.[11] The article, in turn, centered on questions of male modesty raised by this new Western style. Near the end of the article, however, Ibn Rashid turned to a related, if distinct topic of particularism: the practice of praying in shoes. Noting that certain unspecified factions of Muslims claim that praying in shoes (*al-ṣalāt fī al-naʿlayn*) is disfavored (*makrūḥ*), Ibn Rashid argued that it is in fact a praiseworthy practice (*mustaḥabb*).[12]

This position was far from unprecedented in twentieth-century Egypt. In both November 1903 and January 1931, Rashid Rida had issued fatwas in *al-Manar* categorizing this practice as *Sunna*, while noting in the second that this had been the dominant practice in the time of the Prophet Muhammad (*al-aṣl alladhī al-ʿamal al-ghālib fī ʿahd al-nabī*).[13] Though Rida was trained as a scholar, he did not specify a legal classification. Taking Rida one step forward, the founder of the Jamʿiyya Sharʿiyya, Mahmud Muhammad Khattab al-Subki, argued in his landmark work *The Pure Religion: Guiding People to the Religion of Truth*, that the "plain meaning [of the hadith reports regarding praying in shoes] is that this practice is praiseworthy" (*ẓāhiruhā al-istiḥbāb*).[14]

This discussion extended to the Muslim Brotherhood and, just six months after Ansar al-Sunna had reprinted Salim's fatwa, its founder and the final editor of *al-Manar*, Hasan al-Banna,[15] published another fatwa on this topic. Al-Banna stipulated that praying in clean shoes is permitted, while noting (but not commenting on) the debate over whether such a practice was merely

11. See al-Tahir, *Jamaʿat Ansar al-Sunna*, 229–33. Also see "Jamaʿat Ansar al-Sunna al-Muhammadiyya," *Iʿdad al-Nadwa al-ʿAlamiyya li-l-Shabab al-Islami*, http://www.saaid.net/feraq/mthahb/8.htm?print_it = 1, accessed 18 May 2020. Al-Shafiʿi would serve as president of Ansar al-Sunna between 1972 and 1975. See al-Tahir, *Jamaʿat Ansar al-Sunna*, 240.

12. ʿAbd al-ʿAziz b. Rashid, "al-Taban (al-Bantalun al-Qasir)," *al-Hadi al-Nabawi*, Ramadan 1361/ ~September 1942, 29–34, at 34.

13. See Rashid Rida, "Bab al-Suʾal waʾl-Fatwa," *al-Manar*, 1 Ramadan 1321/20 November 1903, 823–8, at 827–8; Rashid Rida, "Fatawa al-Manar," *al-Manar*, Shaʿban 1349/19 January 1931, 442–8, at 444–45.

14. Mahmud Muhammad Khattab al-Subki, *al-Din al-Khalis*, 3:161–63.

15. Muhammad Rashid Rida edited *al-Manar* up until his death in the summer of 1935, at which point the journal passed to his brother, Muhi al-Din Rida, and eldest son, Muhammad Shafiʿ, who published two additional issues in 1936. Hasan al-Banna then purchased the license for the journal and published six additional issues between Jumada al-Ukhra 1358/July 1939 and its final issue in Shaʿban 1359/September 1940. I wish to thank Henri Lauzière for this information.

a dispensation (*rukhṣa*) in the case of hardship[16] or praiseworthy (*mustaḥabb*).[17] As Ansar al-Sunna's president Muhammad Hamid al-Fiqi made the decision to reprint ʿAbd al-Majid Salim's fatwa, he could readily cite religious authorities who permitted praying in shoes and a minority that considered the practice to be unequivocally praiseworthy.

The question, however, is not whether Salafi justifications for praying in shoes were unprecedented—they were not—but rather how and why this came to serve as a signature practice of Ansar al-Sunna. The power of this practice, in turn, proceeded from the fact that, notwithstanding these clear proof-texts, its prominence had receded since the early Muslim community expanded beyond Arabia from the mid-seventh century. In this context, Muslims both encountered mosques whose floors were made of tile or large stone slabs, as well as Jews who, unlike their Arabian coreligionists, prayed in shoes while in their places of worship.[18] In the shadow of new social conditions, and with the development of the Sunni legal tradition in primarily urban environments, the practice of praying in shoes was redefined by prominent

16. As a legal term, *rukhṣa* refers to a "special dispensation from performing an obligatory or from submitting to a prohibition, as a result of mitigating circumstances. . . . An action is properly categorised as rukhṣa only if the obligation or prohibition that it overrides remains in force, although temporarily negated by concrete circumstances. . . . " (Marion H. Katz, "ʿAzīma and rukhṣa," in *Encyclopedia of Islam*, ed. Kate Fleet, et al, http://dx.doi.org/10.1163/1573-3912_ei3_SIM_0261).

17. Hasan al-Banna, "Fatawa al-Manar," *al-Manar*, Shaʿban 1359/September 1940, 644–50, at 644–46.

18. We have little evidence as to the actual practice of Jews of Arabia during this period. In the biblical period, there is evidence for a practice of removing one's shoes while in a holy place, such as the Temple. Exodus 3:5, for example, includes a divine command to Moses to "remove your sandals from your feet, for the place on which you stand is holy ground." This appears to have been mirrored in the behavior of the priestly class (the *Kohanim*), who would walk barefoot within the Temple during the First Temple period (957–587 BCE), though this practice also apparently related to the absence of any mention of footwear in biblical prescriptions of priestly dress, enumerated in Exodus 28, 29, and 39 and Leviticus 8. Evidence in the Jerusalem Talmud for the practice of those outside the priestly elite suggests that Jews in the Land of Israel in the third century did not wear shoes in the synagogue. See *Bava Metzia* 9A. There are other sources in the Babylonian Talmud, however, that privilege wearing shoes more generally. For example, see *Masekhet Shabbat* 129a:13 and *Masekhet Pesachism* 112A:10. For an overview of these and other sources, see David Golinkin, "Ha-im Mutar Le-Hitpalel Yakhef?," *Schechter Institute of Jewish Studies*, 16 August 2020, accessed 4 May 2021, https://schechter.ac.il/article/praying-barefoot/?fbclid = IwAR14Fw-glg_j_7dsE2jvdQZkh_oaFPeo-rUN-MhdV8_vKDXz_KKCOSZn2qsc. Also see Kister, "'Do Not Assimilate Yourselves,'" 356–68.

scholars as a dispensation (*rukhṣa*) reserved for the Prophet Muhammad and his Companions,[19] a position evident in Hasan al-Banna's fatwa on this question. There was, however, a significant exception to this shift: Hanbali scholars continued to uphold praying in shoes within mosques as a Prophetic practice that should be emulated.[20]

As Ansar al-Sunna sought to establish itself in interwar Egypt, challenges abounded under the rule first of King Fu'ad (r. 1922–1936) and then King Faruq (r. 1936–1952). Working on the margins of a tripartite battle among the Palace, the secular-nationalist Wafd and the Muslim Brotherhood, this Salafi organization sought to distinguish itself in a crowded religious field that also included the Young Men's Muslim Association and the Jam'iyya Shar'iyya.[21] The challenge, however, was not merely one of unrepresentative government or of inter-Islamic competition; just as Christian missionary activity in interwar Egypt posed a profound religious and cultural challenge to the Muslim Brotherhood, so too did it challenge Ansar al-Sunna and other Islamic movements.[22]

Just as important was the fact that Salim's very position of State Mufti had itself been created in 1895 as part of a broader effort to expand state control over religious thought and practice. These developments included a new exam

19. Kister, "'Do Not Assimilate Yourselves,'" 344–45. For Maliki examples, see citations of the eleventh-century Maliki scholars Ibn Battal and al-Qadi 'Iyad in Ahmad b. Hanbal, *al-Fath al-Rabbani li-Tartib Musnad al-Imam Ahmad b. Hanbal al-Shaybani wa ma'ahu Kitab Bulugh al-Amani min Asrar al-Fath al-Rabbani*, ed. Ahmad 'Abd al-Rahman al-Banna al-Sa'ati (Cairo: Dar Ihya' al-Turath al-'Arabi, 1976), 1:108. For a Shafi'i example that equates permissibility (*ibāḥa*) with dispensation (*rukhṣa*), see Ibn Daqiq al-'Id b. 'Atiyya b. Muhammad Salim, *Sharh Bulugh al-Maram* (Mawqa' al-Shabaka al-Islamiyya, www.Islamweb.net), 4:46, http://shamela.ws/browse.php/book-7714/page-458#page-458. For a slightly different wording of the same point, see Badr al-Din Mahmud b. Ahmad 'Ayni, *'Umdat al-Qari: Sharh Sahih al-Bukhari*, ed. 'Abd Allah Mahmud Muhammad 'Umar (Beirut, Lebanon: Dar al-Kutub al-'Ilmiyya, 2001), 4:177.

20. Kister, "'Do Not Assimilate Yourselves.'" 345. Kister cites Ibn Qayyim al-Jawziyya, who defines praying in shoes as a "well-established Sunna" (*Sunna thābita*). See Muhammad b. Abi Bakr b. Qayyim al-Jawziyya, *Ighathat al-Lahfan fi Masayid al-Shaytan*, eds. Muhammad 'Aziz Shams and Muhammad b. Sa'id Itim (Mecca, Saudi Arabia: Dar 'Alam al-Fawa'id li-l-Nashr wa'l-Tawzi', 2010), 258–63.

21. Mitchell, *The Society of the Muslim Brothers*, 5–10.

22. On the challenge that missionary activity posed to the Muslim Brotherhood, see Beth Baron, *The Orphan Scandal Christian Missionaries and the Rise of the Muslim Brotherhood* (Stanford, CA: Stanford University Press, 2014), 117–34.

to certify scholars at al-Azhar (known as the *ʿĀlimiyya*) in 1872,[23] the establishment of the Council for the Administration of al-Azhar in 1895, increased state control over preaching and ritual leadership within mosques, and even the production of a standard text of the Quran by the Egyptian Ministry of Endowments.[24] Such ambition was reflected in both the growing ranks of religious functionaries within an expanding state bureaucracy,[25] as well as in the increased regulation of Egyptian mosques.[26]

It was thus little surprise that Islamic magazines evinced significant concern with the state of Egyptian mosques. Most significant would be the conversation in *al-Fath*, which functioned as an intellectual meeting point for members of the YMMA, Muslim Brotherhood, and occasionally Ansar al-Sunna.[27] During this period, the journal included articles that expressed concern over the alleged failure of the Egyptian state to uphold its commitment to preserving popular (*ahliyya*) mosques as it embarked on urban development,[28] to guard mosques from Christian proselytization efforts,[29] and to build new mosques as promised.[30] The author of a June 1927 article even called on the Ministry of Endowments to install wooden racks for shoes so that men did not enter the mosque and then place their (dirty) footwear directly in front of them.[31]

The quest for hygiene and mosque maintenance went hand in hand with the elevation of ritual precision. As Daniel Stolz has shown in his study of timekeeping in early-twentieth-century Cairo, the "synchronization [of prayer times] ... was a problem without a conclusive solution," thus creating new opportunities for state institutions to intervene in determining "proper"

23. Gesink, *Islamic Reform and Conservatism*, 53.

24. Stolz, *The Lighthouse and the Observatory*, 220.

25. Skovgaard-Petersen, *Defining Islam for the Egyptian State*, 103–6.

26. Stolz, *The Lighthouse and the Observatory*, 219–21.

27. For example, see Mustafa Ahmad al-Rifaʿi al-Labban, "al-Sunna waʾl-Bidʿa," *al-Fath*, 16 Jumada al-Ula 1354/16 August 1935, 14.

28. For example, see al-Duktur ʿAli Muhammad, "Fi Sabil al-Masajid," *al-Fath*, 11 Dhu al-Qaʿda 1348/10 April 1930, 8–9.

29. For an article on the alleged activity of a missionary at Masjid al-Fakani near al-Azhar, see Muhibb al-Din al-Khatib, "Ghaflat ʿUlamaʾina wa Hukumatina," *al-Fath*, 20 Dhu al-Qaʿda 1346/10 May 1928, 1–2.

30. For example, see "Fi Masajid al-Awqaf," *al-Fath*, 2 Jumada al-Ula 1346/27 October 1927, 7.

31. Mahmud Subh, "Nazafat al-Masajid," *al-Fath*, 23 Dhu al-Hijja 1345/23 June 1927, 13.

religious observance.[32] As Stolz argues more broadly, it was during this period that "creating 'unity in the order of practice' took on new importance,"[33] a shift which challenged these Islamic movements' control over their own ritual space at a time when they had little access to the levers of state power.

The call for precise ritual practice had effects far beyond the control of the Egyptian state. If the government shift to the Gregorian calendar in 1875 had signaled the adoption of a universal project of European origin,[34] efforts by nationalist secondary students in Cairo in 1908 to celebrate the Islamic (*hijrī*) calendar year underscored how this policy change had set the stage for new forms of self-consciously Islamic temporal challenge.[35] Neither was this challenge limited to annual celebrations: in his study of the history of temporality in modern Egypt, On Barak traces how new means of transportation and forms of media produced *both* a "European" emphasis on "expediency and promptness" and "'countertempos' predicated on discomfort with the time of the clock and a disdain for dehumanizing European standards of efficiency, linearity, and punctuality."[36] It was in this context that "'Egyptian time' retroactively sprouted roots in the Islamic tradition and rural folklore," and the religious calendar came to represent a "sacred" or "authentic" time.[37]

And indeed, Ansar al-Sunna would make claims, based on Islamic temporality, to ritual rectitude in the heart of state institutions. In January 1940, *al-Hadi al-Nabawi* reprinted an article authored by Muhammad Bahjat al-Baytar, which complained that daily prayer was "not required" (*ghayr wājiba*) in primary and secondary schools. While prayer could still be performed "outside of class time" (*fī ghayr waqt al-dars*),[38] the author was troubled by the

32. Stolz, *The Lighthouse and the Observatory*, 209. Hussein Ali Agrama makes a similar argument regarding secularism in Egypt (*Questioning Secularism*, 44).

33. Stolz, *The Lighthouse and the Observatory*, 221.

34. Eviatar Zerubavel, *Hidden Rhythms: Schedules and Calendars in Social Life* (Berkeley: University of California Press, 1985), 98–99.

35. Zachary Lockman, "Exploring the Field: Lost Voices and Emerging Practices in Egypt, 1882–1914," in *Histories of the Modern Middle East*, ed. Israel Gershoni, Y. Hakan Erdem, and Ursula Wokock (London: Lynne Rienner Publishers, 2002), 150.

36. Barak, *On Time*, 5.

37. Barak, *On Time*, 4–5. For an important study of time in the Ottoman context, see Avner Wishnitzer, *Reading Clocks, Alla Turca* (Chicago: University of Chicago Press, 2015). On time in late Ottoman Egypt, see Stolz, *The Lighthouse and the Observatory*, 121–44, 207–42.

38. Muhammad Bahjat al-Baytar, "al-Tarbiyya al-'Asriyya Qatila li-l-Islam," *al-Hadi al-Nabawi*, 15 Dhu al-Hijja 1358/25 January 1940, 11–15, at 11. Concern with daily prayer was not

inability of state-run schools to serve as an engine of piety. The question, though, was not merely praying in school, a practice that did little to distinguish Salafis from other pious Muslims at this time,[39] but a call to praying in shoes that could distinguish the movement.

PRAYING WITH SHOES BETWEEN KING FARUQ AND ʿABD AL-NASIR

In June 1947, Muhammad Zahid b. Hasan al-Kawthari (d. 1952), a prolific Hanafi scholar born in 1879 in the Ottoman city of Düzce adjacent to the Black Sea, published a pamphlet entitled *Removing the Doubt Regarding the Two Questions of Praying Bareheaded and Wearing Shoes in Prayer.* A polymath who had previously served as a deputy (*wakīl*) of the last chief religious official of the Ottoman Empire (A. *Shaykh al-Islām*, Ott. *Şeyhülislam*) before fleeing to Cairo, al-Kawthari explained his study's objective as follows:

> In these days, there is much discussion about the ruling [of Islam] on praying while bareheaded (*ḥāsir al-raʾs*) and in shoes (*fī al-niʿāl*).... These individuals who are engaged in the exercise of independent reason (*mujtahidūn*) and seek discord (*fitna*) by arousing troubles among Muslims in the houses of God, in their worship to God ... are most similar to Kharijites (*Khawārij*) in the [practice of] seeking to emphasize small matters (*istiʿẓām al-saghīr*) and to deemphasize important matters (*istiṣghār al-kabīr*) and there is no need to discuss them [further] here....[40]

Al-Kawthari's disdain could hardly have been more palpable, and reflected not merely a methodological dispute but also a generational conflict between this high-ranking Ottoman scholar and a post-Ottoman era in which the

---

limited to Ansar al-Sunna; the original version of the article appeared roughly six years prior in *al-Manar*. See al-Baytar, "al-Tarbiyya al-Islamiyya waʾl-Taʿlim al-Islami," *al-Manar*, Ramadan 1353/December 1934, 34:544–8. Also see al-Baytar, "Fatawa," *al-Hadi al-Nabawi*, 1 Safar 1359/~10 March 1940, 26–30, at 28.

39. Some four decades later, praying in schools was to serve as a key means by which the Muslim Brotherhood and Jamʿiyya Sharʿiyya laid claim to space within state institutions. See Aaron Rock-Singer, "Prayer and the Islamic Revival: A Timely Challenge," *International Journal of Middle East Studies* 47 (2016): 293–312.

40. Muhammad Zahid b. Hasan al-Kawthari, *Rafʿ al-Ishtibah ʿan Masʾalatay Kashf al-Ruʾus wa Lubs al-Niʿal fi al-Salat* (Cairo: al-Sayyid ʿIzzat al-ʿAttar al-Husayni, 1947), 4.

madhhab system had lost much of its institutional weight.[41] The issue at hand, however, was not solely the *maddhab* system. A 1928 report produced by the Theology Faculty at Darülfünun, a university which was established under Ottoman rule (1900) and persisted under its Turkish Republican successor state, proposed a series of reforms aimed at modernizing religious practice, including "praying in the mosque while wearing shoes. . . ."[42] Finally, this conflict also had a specifically Salafi dimension: during the 1930s and 1940s, al-Kawthari had done battle with leading Salafi scholars, most notably Muhammad Hamid al-Fiqi and Muhammad Nasir al-Din al-Albani, over the legacy of the eponym of the Hanafi school, Abu Hanifa.[43]

Despite this visceral opposition to Salafism, however, this Hanafi scholar did not deny that these two practices of praying in shoes and bareheaded were lawful (*ṣaḥīḥa*).[44] Instead, he sought to challenge basic components of the broader complex of authenticity on which they were based. In the case of head covering, he mocked the argument adopted by Salafis that all head covering during prayer is a form of illicit adornment (*zīna*).[45] Al-Kawthari further saw

41. As Ahmed El Shamsy notes, al-Kawthari encountered a "new world with scant institutional authority, [in which] books were being published by people who . . . lacked the appropriate scholarly training and respect for tradition; worse still, they were using these books to challenge ideas that he held sacrosanct" (*Rediscovering the Islamic Classics*, 216–17). During the early twentieth century, the method of drawing from multiple schools in making a ruling (a process known as *Talfīq*) had become more widespread, most notably in the Family Laws of 1920 and 1929, respectively. Indeed, in 1948, a group of reform-oriented Azharis that included ʿAbd al-Majid Salim founded a "Center for Rapprochement Among the Legal Schools" (*Dār al-Taqrīb bayna al-Madhāhib al-Islāmiyya*). Members of this body sought to forge not only an internal Sunni consensus, but also to engage with Shiʿi *madhhabs* in the service of an "intellectual Pan-Islamism." See Skovgaard-Petersen, *Defining Islam for the Egyptian State*, 154–55.

42. Phil Dorroll, *Islamic Theology in the Turkish Republic* (Edinburgh, UK: University of Edinburgh Press, 2021), 62.

43. Ahmad Khan, "Islamic Tradition in an Age of Printing: Editing, Printing and Publishing the Classical Heritage," in *Reclaiming the Islamic Tradition: Modern Interpretations of the Classical Heritage*, ed. Elisabeth Kendall and Ahmad Khan (Edinburgh, UK: Edinburgh University Press, 2016), 60–65. As Khan argues, "Abū Ḥanīfa had come to represent much of what, to Salafis, was institutionally decrepit about the development of Islam since the High Middle Ages" (64).

44. al-Kawthari, *Rafʿ al-Ishtibah*, 9.

45. The argument, in turn, pivots on citation of the position of the eleventh-century Shafiʿi scholar al-Mawardi that adornment (*zīna*) in one's clothing during prayer is forbidden. While such a stipulation could, in theory, include an ostentatious head covering, not all head coverings fall under this designation. See al-Kawthari, *Rafʿ al-Ishtibah*, 5. Decades later,

this practice as serving as a means of visible distinction, declaring that "revealing the head during prayer has become a distinguishing sign for a faction of [illicit] innovators today" (*shiʿārᵃⁿ li-ṭāʾifa min al-mubtadiʿ al-yawm*). . . ."[46] Al-Kawthari, attuned to questions of visual signification, identified this particular practice with his ideological opponents.

The bulk of this work, however, was concerned with praying in shoes, and al-Kawthari first questioned whether this practice was praiseworthy (*mustaḥabb*) rather than merely licit. Specifically, he argued that the former designation pivoted on its function in distinguishing Muslims from Jews, yet in the present, the distinguishing act would be to pray *without* shoes.[47] Moreover, the insistence by "the deviant Hanbalis" (*al-Ḥanābila al-Shudhdhādh*) on praying with shoes was "not based on legitimate proof texts" (*ghayr qāʾima al-ḥujja*) and was now considered to be "rude" (*suʾ al-adab*).[48] Al-Kawthari did no less than condemn Hanbalism as a school for permitting this practice.[49]

In tandem, this Ottoman jurist embraced a series of arguments as to why the practice of praying in shoes was no longer valid. He employed multiple lines of attack, ranging from the claim that shoes in his time differed from those in the Prophet's era, to the linked arguments that the streets were now

Muhammad Nasir al-Din al-Albani criticized "some of our brothers from Ansar al-Sunna" for praying bareheaded; by contrast, al-Albani took the view that such an act is "disfavored" (*makrūha*). See Muhammad Nasir al-Din al-Albani, *Tamam al-Minna fi al-Taʿliq ʿala Fiqh al-Sunna* (Amman, Jordan: Dar al-Raya, 1988?), 164–65. While I was not able to locate a copy of the first edition of the text, the second edition was published in 1988 and a search of the Arabic Union Catalogue did not turn up an edition published prior to 1987.

46. al-Kawthari, *Rafʿ al-Ishtibah*, 7.

47. al-Kawthari, *Rafʿ al-Ishtibah*, 10–12.

48. al-Kawthari, *Rafʿ al-Ishtibah*, 10.

49. The disagreement over praying in shoes was not al-Kawthari's only conflict with his Hanbali competitors. In the footnotes of his commentary on Ibn ʿAsakir's *Tabyin Kidhb al-Muftari fi-ma Nusiba ila al-Imam Abi al-Hasan al-Ashʿari* (*Making Clear the Lies of Those Who Attack That Which is Attributed to the Imam Abi al-Hasan al-Ashʿari*), al-Kawthari implies that Ahmad b. Hanbal belong to the ranks of the *Ḥashawiyya*, defined by Abu Hamid al-Ghazali as those "believing themselves bound to a blind and routine submission to the criterion of human authority and to the literal meaning of revealed books." For al-Kawthari, see Ibn ʿAsakir, *Tabyin Kidhb al-Muftari fi-ma Nusiba ila al-Imam Abi al-Hasan al-Ashʿari*, ed. Muhammad Zahid al-Kawthari (Cairo: al-Maktaba al-Azhariyya li-l-Turath, 2010), 299. For al-Ghazali's definition of *Ḥashawiyya*, see A. S. Halkin, "The Hashawiyya," *Journal of the American Oriental Society* 54 (1934): 12. Halkin notes that the term was originally directed towards "traditionalists (*aṣḥāb al-ḥadith*) and Ḥanbalīs themselves," 12.

far dirtier and that mosque floors were now carpeted, rather than made of stone.[50] Our concern, however, is not with al-Kawthari's persuasiveness, but rather with what this argument can reveal about religious practice in mid-twentieth-century Egypt. The significance of this text is twofold: it identifies the practice of praying in shoes with an unnamed faction (implicitly Ansar al-Sunna) and includes arguments *against* praying in shoes that would later be used by Salafi scholars.

Yet, even as Ansar al-Sunna was the only movement to proudly lay claim to praying in shoes as a distinctive practice, it was far from the only movement to permit it. Most notably, over the course of the 1940s and early 1950s, the Jamʿiyya Sharʿiyya endorsed this practice as permissible on multiple occasions.[51] Most significant to the story of Salafism, however, would be a series of fatwas published in the May 1948 issue of *al-Iʿtisam*. Authored by the journal's Mufti, ʿAli Hasan Hulwa, these rulings focused on a set of practices that would become highly significant to the Salafi movement: praying in shoes and bareheaded, the beard, and shortened robes or pants.

To be clear, there is no evidence that this May 1948 text, authored by a leading member of the Jamʿiyya Sharʿiyya, served as the inspiration for the choice of social practices that would come to define Purist Salafism. Hulwa did not discuss the minimal length of the fist (*qabḍa*) in his fatwa on the beard, considered bareheaded prayer to be disfavored (*makrūḥ*) and praying in shoes to be permitted (*jāʾiz*) rather than praiseworthy (*mustaḥabb*), and foregrounded the question of intent when assessing the actions of those whose clothing hung down below the ankles (*Isbāl*).[52] But the text's existence and foci suggest that the practices on which Ansar al-Sunna would seize were a matter of broader religious attention at this time.

When it came to praying in shoes, Hulwa's positions situated him not with Ansar al-Sunna, but rather with the latter's critics. Specifically, the Jamʿiyya Sharʿiyya's Mufti was highly skeptical that one could maintain the ritual purity of one's shoes in Egypt's dusty climate, arguing that "in Egypt (*fi arḍ Miṣr*),

50. al-Kawthari, *Rafʿ al-Ishtibah*, 14–24.

51. See ʿAli Hasan Hulwa, "Asʾila wa Ajwibatiha," *al-Iʿtisam*, 12 Jumada al-Thaniyya 1366/~3 May 1947, 8–9; Hulwa, "Safhat al-Istiftaʾat," *al-Iʿtisam*, 14 Safar 1367/~27 December 1947, 8–9, at 8; Hulwa, "Asʾila wa Ajwiba," *al-Iʿtisam*, Rabiʿ al-Awwal 1373/November 1953, 8–10, at 9–10.

52. ʿAli Hasan Hulwa, "al-Mufti Yujib," *al-Iʿtisam*, 20 Rajab 1367/~29 May 1948, 33–5, 37.

impurity (*najāsa*) afflicts the higher part of the shoe just as it afflicts its bottom part . . . [but] the owner of the shoe cannot rub it in the ground if he wishes to maintain its cleanliness" (*naẓāfatahu*).[53] While Hulwa left the precise environmental conditions vague—these could have ranged from flooding that turned dirt into mud to the popular use of dried animal droppings as fuel for rural ovens[54]—the fundamental problem was that impurities in the upper portion of the shoe could not be kneaded out in the way that they could on the shoe bottom through rubbing the latter into the dry ground.

Such criticism was not limited to al-Kawthari or Hulwa. In December 1949, *Liwa' al-Islam*, the scholarly journal populated by Azharis mentioned in the opening anecdote of this chapter, published a fatwa request in which the questioner explained:

> I have seen a group, which identifies itself as Ansar al-Sunna al-Muhammadiyya, praying in their shoes [in mosques] with their heads uncovered . . . and insulting the scholars of Azhar . . . cursing [Sufi] saints (*awliyā' Allah*) and claiming that celebrating the Prophet's birthday (*Mawlid al-musṭafā*) is polytheism (*shirk b-illah*). . . . I request a response.[55]

The response was not especially noteworthy, affirming the principle that prayer in ritually pure shoes is lawful (*ṣaḥīḥa*), that such shoes must allow individuals to prostrate themselves fully,[56] and that the challenge of impure shoes had risen in the face of changing mosque surfaces and increasingly polluted streets alike.[57]

A few months later, apparently in response to the implicit endorsement of this fatwa's premises within *Liwa' al-Islam*, Darwish proudly claimed these two practices as distinct to Ansar al-Sunna. In an article entitled "Us and *Liwa' al-Islam*," Darwish angrily noted that the journal's Mufti had not contested these accusations, thus leading to "the awakening of dormant strife"

53. 'Ali Hasan Hulwa, "al-Mufti Yujib," *al-I'tisam*, 20 Rajab 1367/~29 May 1948, 35.

54. I wish to thank Samy Ayoub for his insights on the challenging of maintaining ritual purity in twentieth- and twenty-first-century rural Egypt.

55. "Fatawa," *Liwa' al-Islam*, Rabi' al-Awwal 1369/December 1949, 67–70, at 68. I wish to thank Yaara Perlman for locating this citation for me from Princeton University's Firestone library.

56. The issue here appears to be in the case of shoes that were too firm to allow full prostration.

57. "Fatawa," *Liwa' al-Islam*, Rabi' al-Awwal 1369/December 1949, 67–70, at 68–69.

(*īqāẓ al-fitna al-nāʾima*).[58] Engaging more specifically with the question of praying in shoes, he then sought to knock down his critic's claim that the nature of shoes and mosques in the Prophet's time differed not in degree but in kind, noting that the Angel Gabriel's warning to the Prophet to check his shoes for impurities would have made little sense if the city of Medina was in fact spotless.[59] Neither did criticism of praying in shoes cow Ansar al-Sunna. In August 1951, *al-Hadi al-Nabawi's* editors reprinted ʿAbd al-Majid Salim's fatwa.[60]

It was in March 1952, however, that elites within the organization went on the offensive. In the article, Amin Muhammad Rida (d. 1998), a leading figure within the organization[61] and the husband of Ansar al-Sunna's most prominent female thinker, Niʿmat Sidqi (d. 1977),[62] began by noting that "some Muslims reproach Ansar al-Sunna for praying in shoes. . . . I was even accused of disbelief (*kufr*) and a lack of manners" (*ʿadam al-taʾaddub*).[63] Rida then made clear why this practice was central to his organization:

> Ansar al-Sunna al-Muhammadiyya pray in their shoes without shame, because they pray based on a belief in God and His Prophet, and in obedience to God and His Prophet. . . . [this] is not affected behavior (*takalluf*^{an}) or a custom (*ʿāda*^{tan}) . . . or blind imitation (*taqlīd*^{an} *aʿmā*) without guidance or vision. . . . It is not merely that praying in shoes is allowed. . . . it is actually praiseworthy (*ʿalā istiḥbāb al-ṣalāt fī al-naʿlayn*).[64]

Moving beyond ʿAbd al-Majid Salim's endorsement of praying in shoes as licit at the minimum and Abu al-Wafaʾ Muhammad Darwish's defense of

58. Abu-l-Wafaʾ Muhammad Darwish, "Nahnu wa Majallat Liwaʾ al-Islam" *al-Hadi al-Nabawi*, Rabiʿ al-Awwal 1369/~December 1949, 21–25, at 21.

59. Darwish, "Nahnu wa Majallat Liwaʾ al-Islam," 21–23.

60. "Bab al-Fatawa," *al-Hadi al-Nabawi*, Dhu al-Qaʿda 1370, 23–26, at 23–24.

61. In a 1999 obituary in *al-Tawhid*, Rida is praised for his "sixty years of Daʿwa and scientific research," with the article on praying in shoes constituting "one of his most widely known pieces of writing" (*min ashhar kitābātihi*). See Fathi Amin ʿUthman, "Bab al-Tarajim," *al-Tawhid*, Dhu al-Qaʿda 1419/~February 1999, 54–57, at 55.

62. According to Rida's obituary, it was his wife who brought him into the fold of Ansar al-Sunna (ʿUthman, "Bab al-Tarajim," *al-Tawhid*, Dhu al-Qaʿda 1419/~February 1999, 54–57, at 55).

63. Amin Muhammad Rida, "al-Salat fi al-Niʿal," *al-Hadi al-Nabawi*, Rajab 1371/~March 1952, 20–23, at 20.

64. Rida, "al-Salat fi al-Niʿal," 20.

Ansar al-Sunna's engagement in this practice, Rida had made an additional claim: that praying in shoes was not just permissible but praiseworthy. Just as importantly, his experience of social tension hints that Ansar al-Sunna performed this practice not merely in their own mosques, where it would not have raised eyebrows, but also in non-Salafi mosques.

There was more than authenticity or legal status at stake. For Amin Muhammad Rida, the question, at its core, concerned the oneness of God, and this medical doctor at the Alexandria University hospital proceeded to lay out and dismiss the argument that mosque carpeting makes it preferable to pray barefoot, describing this argument as an example of "*madhhab*-based traditions and *Jahili* customs" (*al-taqālīd al-madhhabiyya wa'l-ʿādāt al-jāhiliyya*). Far from an innocent mistake, Rida argues that such claims against praying in shoes are propagated by those who "pose as Muslims" (*mutamaslimīn*) and seek to deny the "unity of worship" (*tawḥīd al-ʿibāda*, also known as *tawḥīd al-ulūhiyya*).[65] For him, praying in shoes was a key site of battle both with those *madhhab* scholars whom he saw as mired in the stagnancy of the Islamic scholarly tradition, and with those Westernized segments of Egyptian society who had turned away from Islam's legal obligations.

Yet, at the moment that Ansar al-Sunna's call for praying in shoes appeared most strident, political tumult gripped Egypt. With the toppling of King Faruq in July 1952 by the Free Officers and then the massive repression of the Muslim Brotherhood two years later by Jamal ʿAbd al-Nasir, the cost of calling attention to themselves increased for members of Islamic movements. During the nearly fifteen years that followed until the forced merger of Ansar al-Sunna with the Jamʿiyya Sharʿiyya and the shuttering of *al-Hadi al-Nabawi*, debates over the practice of praying in shoes receded in prominence. This shift in emphasis was not a reflection of broader Salafi winds: Muhammad Nasir al-Din al-Albani's landmark work *Characteristics of the Prophet's Prayer* (which endorsed praying in shoes) was published during this period,[66] and the

65. Rida, "al-Salat fi al-Niʿal," 22.

66. The third edition of this text, which I consulted, was published in 1961. See Muhammad Nasir al-Din al-Albani, *Sifat Salat al-Nabi Min al-Takbir ila al-Taslim ki-Annaka Tara'ha* (Damascus, Syria: al-Maktab al-Islami, 1381/1961), 49–50. The second edition of this work was published in 1375/1955. I was not able to find any discussion of the text in *al-Hadi al-Nabawi* during this period, suggesting that al-Albani's influence in Egypt during the 1950s and 1960s may have been limited.

specific question of whether it was legitimate to pray bareheaded arose in *al-Hadi al-Nabawi* on multiple occasions in the mid-1960s.[67]

Ultimately, however, neither increased state regulation of religious interpretation and practice nor changing scholarly alliances were the primary drivers of the decline of praying in shoes. Instead, as opportunities for activism receded at home and the organization's leadership moved abroad, debates over religious practice would increasingly begin in Saudi Arabia before moving back to Egypt. It is to the Saudi stage, and specifically to the changing religious and cultural winds in this country, that we now turn.

PRAYING IN THE SHADOW OF THE WAHHABI-HANBALI TRADITION

The 1970s oil boom in Saudi Arabia empowered Salafis within the kingdom, and those outside it who could gain access to new oil-fueled pipelines of patronage, to spread projects of ritual piety. To an even greater degree than in Egypt, though, the question of praying in shoes was far from novel in Saudi Arabia: while the Egyptian scholarly community was split among Maliki, Shafiʿi, and Hanafi schools of law—none of which categorized praying in shoes as *mustaḥabb*—Saudi Arabia's powerfully institutionalized tradition of Hanbalism provided inbuilt legitimacy for this practice.

Most prominently, the landmark text of Wahhabi-Hanbali legal scholarship, *The Sparkling Pearls of Najdi Responses* (*al-Durar al-Saniyya fi al-Ajwiba al-Najdiyya*), first published in the early 1930s, contained an entry on this question from a native of Dirʿiyya,[68] ʿAbd al-Rahman b. Hasan (d. 1869). Ibn Hasan argued that condemnation of entering mosques and praying in shoes reflected an "ignorance of the Sunna" (*jahl al-Sunna*) and that this practice served to distinguish Muslims from Jews. This Wahhabi-Hanbali scholar affirmed the permissibility of praying in shoes while in the mosque (*jawāz dukhūl al-masjid bi-l-niʿāl waʾl-ṣalāt fihā*), while deriding those who

67. "Bab al-Fatawa," *al-Hadi al-Nabawi*, Shawwal 1384/~February 1965, 33–39, at 33–34; "Bab al-Fatawa," *al-Hadi al-Nabawi*, Rabiʿ al-Akhar 1385/~July 1965, 32–7, at 32–33.

68. Dirʿiyya was one of the key sites of Muhammad b. ʿAbd al-Wahhab's activities in the Arabian Peninsula. Its scholars would remain prominent within the ranks of the Wahhabi-Hanbali establishment, which was populated disproportionately by those who could trace their lineage to Ibn ʿAbd al-Wahhab.

criticized it.[69] Neither was the endorsement of praying in shoes limited to long-dead scholars. In his official fatwa collection, Saudi Arabia's Mufti and longtime doyen of the Saudi religious landscape, Muhammad b. Ibrahim (d. 1969), affirmed that one could pray with shoes (*yajūz al-ṣalāt bi-l-naʿlayn*) provided that they were pure, and affirmed that "some scholars have even noted that they are Sunna" (*bal qadd dhakar baʿḍ ahl al-ʿilm innahu Sunna*).[70]

This Hanbali-Wahhabi position also appears to have been reflected in practice. ʿAbd al-Munʿim Nimr (d. 1991), a graduate of al-Azhar and former Egyptian Minister of Endowments, recounted that during a 1954 visit to Riyadh, he had noticed how Muhammad b. Ibrahim continued to allow Saudis to pray in their shoes, even as this led to what Nimr viewed as unclean mosques.[71] Similarly, a 23 March 1955 fatwa by the Wahhabi-Hanbali scholar Muhammad b. ʿAbd al-ʿAziz al-Maniʿ (d. 1965) noted that "many people pray without removing their shoes which undoubtedly contain dirt and impurities (*awsākh wa najāsāt*). . . ."[72] These textual justifications and anecdotes underscore the broader sanction that a Wahhabi-Hanbali elite provided for praying in shoes and the way in which this sanction was mirrored by grassroots practice.

Over the course of the 1960s, however, prayer became a site of religio-political challenge as group of young men, inspired by Muhammad Nasir al-Din al-Albani and calling themselves Ahl al-Hadith, emerged in Medina. Challenging both centuries of Hanbali jurisprudence and their contemporaries, this group sought to pray and dress in a fashion which distinguished them not only from a majority of Muslims outside of Saudi Arabia, but also from those within it who followed the Hanbali school.[73] As they pursued

69. ʿAbd al-Rahman b. Muhammad b. Qasim al-ʿAsimi al-Qahtani al-Najdi, *Kitab al-Durar al-Saniyya fi al-Ajwiba al-Najdiyya* (Mecca, Saudi Arabia: Matbaʿat Umm al-Qurra, 1352/~1933), 4:135–36. I wish to thank Cole Bunzel for sharing a scanned version of this source with me.

70. Muhammad b. Ibrahim, *Fatawa wa Rasaʾil Samahat al-Shaykh Muhammad b. Ibrahim*, ed. Muhammad b. ʿAbd al-Rahman b. Qasim (Mecca, Saudi Arabia: Matbaʿat al-Hukuma, 1399), 2:170–71.

71. Nimr, *al-Thaqafa al-Islamiyya Bayna al-Ghazw waʾl-Istighzaʾ*, 87.

72. *Maqalat Kibar al-ʿUlamaʾ fi al-Suhuf al-Saʿudiyya*, ed. Ahmad b. ʿAbd al-ʿAziz Jamaz and ʿAbd al-ʿAziz b. Salih Tawil (Riyadh: Dar Atlas li-l-Nashr waʾl-Tawziʿ, 2010/1431), 2:153.

73. Lacroix, *Awakening Islam*, 88–89.

religious precision, al-Albani's *Characteristics of the Prophet's Prayer* served as a key text.[74]

Following a crackdown by Saudi authorities on Ahl al-Hadith's activities in 1965, a segment of this group sought to establish an organization with direct ties to the religious establishment through 'Abd al-'Aziz b. Baz, who was then the Vice President of the Islamic University of Medina. Unlike Muhammad b. Ibrahim, however, Ibn Baz was not a product of the religious establishment stocked disproportionately by descendants of Muhammad b. 'Abd al-Wahhab (*Āl al-Shaykh*); instead, he was the exceptional scholar who had achieved prominence despite hailing from a non-tribal family.[75] Under the leadership of Juhayman al-'Utaybi, this faction would name itself the Salafi Group for Commanding Right and Forbidding Wrong (*al-Jamā'a al-Salafiyya al-Muḥtasiba*, henceforth JSM) as it moved beyond Medina to establish branches "in practically all major Saudi cities, including Mecca, Riyadh, Taif, Ha'il, Abha, Dammam, and Burayda" by 1976.[76]

Alongside Ahl al-Hadith and the JSM arose the Awakening or *Sahwa* movement. Though not focused on ritual practice, this movement drew from mosques, charitable associations, student groups in schools and universities, and formed Committees for Raising Islamic Consciousness as it sought to spread a call that merged traditional Wahhabi-Hanbali understandings of theology and Islamic law with an activist political stance.[77] Though the *Sahwa* was hardly focused on the intricate details of proper religious practice, its activities threatened the monopoly over religious thought and practice to which the Saudi General Presidency for the Management of Religious Scholarship, Preaching and Guidance (*al-Ri'āsa al-'Āmma li-Idārat al-Buḥūth al-Islāmiyya wa'l-Da'wa wa'l-Irshād*), a key sub-body of the Committee of Grand Ulama (*Hay'at Kibār al-'Ulamā'*), aspired.[78]

74. Although Lacroix accurately notes that al-Albani provided "authorization to wear shoes while praying inside the mosque," I have not encountered evidence from the 1950s and 1960s that members of Ahl al-Hadith pursued this practice. See Lacroix, *Awakening Islam*, 88, cf. 300.

75. Nabil Mouline, *The Clerics of Islam: Religious Authority and Political Power in Saudi Arabia*, trans. Ethan S. Rundell (New Haven, CT: Yale University Press, 2014), 178.

76. Thomas Hegghammer and Stephane Lacroix, "Rejectionist Islamism in Saudi Arabia: The Story of Juhayman al-'Utaybi Revisited," *International Journal of Middle East Studies* 39 (2007): 107.

77. Lacroix, *Awakening Islam*, 126.

78. In 1971, The Committee of Grand Ulama (*Hay'at Kibār al-'Ulamā'*) was tasked with acting "as the country's main legislative body alongside the Council of Ministers, and serv[ing]

Just as importantly, Saudi Arabia faced an ideological challenge from Iran during this period. Following the 1979 overthrow of the Shah, Ayatollah Khomeini sought to export the Iranian revolution, arguing for a universal model of Islamic leadership that stood in contradistinction to the Saudi royal family's claim to serve as guardians of Mecca and Medina.[79] In this context, anti-Shiʿi views, long present within the Wahhabi-Hanbali tradition, gained new prominence.[80]

While Saudi Arabia would turn to the Muslim World League in order to respond transnationally to the ideological challenge posed by Ayatollah Khomeini, it channeled its assertion of power locally through the Ministry of Hajj and Endowments' control over domestic mosques. These efforts included the intensified construction of mosques throughout the Kingdom from the mid-1970s on,[81] the expansion of educational institutions to train mosque functionaries,[82] and the provision of "Preaching and Guidance" (*al-Daʿwa waʾl-Irshād*) groups by the Permanent Committee to preach to Muslims outside the Kingdom's major cities on how to avoid polytheism (*shirk*) and illicit innovation (*bidʿa*).[83] These ambitions extended to minute means of regulation: a 10 August 1985 message distributed to all Ministry officials tasked them with

as an ideological shield to the ruling house" (Mouline, *The Clerics of Islam*, 150). This organization contained three subsidiary bodies: the Council of the Committee of Grand Ulama (*Majlis Hayʾat Kibār al-ʿUlamāʾ*), the General Presidency for the Management of Religious Scholarship, Preaching and Guidance (*al-Riʾāsa al-ʿĀmma li-Idārat al-Buḥūth al-Islāmiyya waʾl-Daʿwa waʾl-Irshād*), and the Permanent Committee on Religious Scholarship and Fatwas (*al-Lajna al-Dāʾima li-l-Buhūth wa-l-Iftāʾ*). While the Council of the Committee of Grand Ulama commented on questions pertaining to political legitimacy and public order, the General Presidency for the Management of Religious Scholarship, Predication and Guidance was tasked with defending Hanbali-Wahhabism in Saudi Arabia and abroad, through both public statements and the publication of *Majallat al-Buhuth al-Islamiyya* (*The Islamic Studies Journal*). See Mouline, *The Clerics of Islam*, 155.

79. On Khomeini's efforts to export Iran's Islamic Revolution to Pakistan, see Simon Wolfgang Fuchs, "A Direct Flight to Revolution: Maududi and the 1979 Moment in Iran," *Journal of the Royal Asiatic Society* (2021, first view): 1–22.

80. Lacroix, *Awakening Islam*, 124.

81. In 1984, the MOHE announced that it had built or renovated 630 mosques in the previous ten years and announced its intention to build 1,908 new mosques. "Wizarat al-Hajj waʾl-Awqaf," *al-Riyad*, 22 Safar 1405/16 November 1984, 2.

82. "Tashkil Lijan Ikthibarat Aʾimmat al-Masajid min Furuʿ Wizarat al-Hajj waʾl-Awqaf," *Al-Riyad*, 2 Dhu al-Hijja 1402/19 September 1982, 3.

83. "Firaq li-l-Daʿwa waʾl-Irshad," *al-Madina*, 17 Dhu al-Qaʿda 1404/14 August 1984, 7.

preventing the distribution of written materials within mosques, the placement of fliers on mosque walls, and ensuring that only those authorized by the Ministry could preach.[84]

These efforts to assert greater control over mosques also included considerations of hygiene. In 1979, the Ministry of Hajj and Endowments announced the hiring of Saudi companies to take over maintenance of the cleaning and upkeep of microphones and air conditioning units at 24 mosques in Riyadh.[85] By 1981, nearly 100 mosques were being cleaned under this arrangement,[86] and this number rose significantly to 926 in 1986.[87] In tandem, the Ministry devoted significant funds to mosque construction and maintenance: in 1979, it announced the provision of 17 million riyals to build 11 mosques in the central (*waṣta*) region of the Kingdom that includes both Riyadh and Qusaym, emphasizing the commitment of the Ministry to monitoring the success of Saudi companies in maintaining the "cleanliness of the mosques" (*naẓāfat al-masājid*).[88] Carpets were a point of emphasis: a 1980 article noted successful efforts to provide carpets for 950 mosques in Riyadh.[89] Neither was this emphasis on hygiene limited to mosques: in 1983, the Municipality of Jeddah announced a five-year, nearly one-billion-riyal program to overhaul public cleanliness throughout all of this leading port city's neighborhoods, and a separate 297-million-riyal fund to maintain this program.[90]

Questions of hygiene and cleanliness would soon extend beyond the Kingdom's political center. A letter in the 11 July 1984 issue of *al-Riyad* declared that "Islam is the religion of cleanliness" (*al-Islām dīn al-naẓāfa*) and that this obligation extends beyond the mosque to the home and the street alike. Indeed, as the reader noted, recent years had seen significant improvement within the

84. Mazin S. Mobatagani, "Islamic Resurgence in the Hijaz Region (1975–1990) (Medina, Saudi Arabia: N.D.), 19.

85. "al-Mujtama'," *al-Riyad*, 22 Safar 1399/20 January 1979, 9.

86. "al-Masajid wa Tajhiziha," *al-Riyad*, 12 Ramadan 1401/13 July 1981, 6.

87. "Isnad Siyanat wa Nazafat 926 Masjid[an] wa Jami'[an] ila Shirkat wa Mu'assasat Wataniyya," *al-Riyad*, 24 Ramadan 1406/1 June 1986, 3.

88. "Mandub al-Riyad: Akthar min 17 Milyun Riyal li-Bina' 11 Masjid[an] bi-l-Mantaqa al-Wasata," *al-Riyad*, 29 Muharram 1400/18 December 1979, 2.

89. "Mahaliyyat," *al-Riyad*, 7 Rajab 1400/21 May 1980, 3.

90. "al-Tarkiz 'ala Mashari' al-Nazafa al-'Amma," *al-Riyad*, 22 Dhu al-Qa'da 1403/30 August 1983, 2.

city more broadly.[91] A few months later, in October 1984, Muhammad Ibrahim Musa, the Mayor (*Raʾīs Baladiyya*) of Haʾil, an agricultural center in the northwest of Saudi Arabia, elaborated on this point. In an interview conducted as part of the annual "Cleanliness Week" (*Usbūʿ al-Naẓāfa*), he declared that "cleanliness derives from faith" (*al-naẓāfa min al-īmān*) and that "Our religion and the Prophet Muhammad guided us to cleanliness in clothing, food, domestic affairs, and in the [maintenance of the] streets of the city."[92] In making this claim, however, Saudi public officials shared more in common with fellow twentieth-century modernizing elites than they did with an allegedly diachronic Islamic tradition of hygiene.[93]

In the shadow of this broader cultural shift, official declarations of mosque policy increasingly came to involve hygiene. In December 1984, the Minister of Hajj and Endowments, ʿAbd al-Wahhab al-Wasiʿ, inaugurated "Mosque Attention Week (*Usbūʿ al-ʿInāya biʾl-Masājid*) by emphasizing the centrality of mosques to Muslim life. As he summarized the Ministry's achievements over the previous year, al-Wasiʿ emphasized the praiseworthy activities of a group of youth who had taken it upon themselves to "clean mosque carpets . . . and to place shelves for Qurans and racks for shoes (*dawālīb liʾl-maṣāḥif waʾl-ahdhiya*) in mosques."[94] Like the call to the Egyptian Ministry of Endowment in the pages of *al-Fath* in 1927, ritual purity and hygiene increasingly went hand in hand.

Yet, this drive towards mosque hygiene also generated pushback. That same day, *al-Riyad* published a critical report that asked rhetorically: "Surely, Mosque Week isn't solely about cleanliness?" (*Usbūʿ al-Masājid . . . .laysa li-l-naẓāfa faqat..?!*) The author described the proliferation of annual week-long celebrations in the Kingdom—whether for trees, traffic or cleanliness—and

91. Fahd Muhammad al-ʿAmmar, "al-Islam Din al-Nazafa," *al-Riyad* 13 Shawwal 1404/11 July 1984, 6.

92. "Ikhtitam Usbuʿ al-Nazafa fi Haʾil," *al-Riyad*, 24 Muharram 1405/19 October 1984, 2. Neither was the shift to conflating ritual purity and hygiene confined to Saudi Arabia: as early as the mid-1950s, Egyptian Salafis, too, had begun to emphasize Muhammad's commitment to "comprehensive hygiene" (*al-naẓāfa al-tāmma*). See "al-Tahara waʾl-Nazafa," *al-Hadi al-Nabawi*, Safar 1375/~September 1955, 20–23, at 22–23.

93. For example, see Cyrus Schayegh, *Who is Knowledgeable is Strong: Science, Class, and the Formation of Modern Iranian Society, 1900–1950* (Berkeley: University of California Press, 2009), esp. 32–52.

94. "Wazir al-Hajj waʾl-Awqaf," *al-Riyad*, 18 Rabiʿ al-Awwal 1405/10 December 1984, 2.

noted with some irritation that this particular celebration had come to focus on "the cleanliness of the mosque" (*naẓāfat al-masjid*) at the expense of reviving its historical role as an educational center (*madrasa li-l-taʿlīm waʾl-tawjīh*)." The author did not hide his frustration: this week "should be about something that is more important and deeper ... than getting rid of dust" (*izālat al-ghubār*).[95] While one could certainly read this statement as reflecting broader frustrations with the government's efforts to regulate mosque preaching, concerns with hygiene were nonetheless significant.

Egyptian religious institutes, too, increasingly embraced considerations of hygiene. In July 1980, the Ministry of Endowments announced a national campaign to "clean Egypt's mosques" (*naẓāfat masājid Miṣr*), aiming to set a standard of cleanliness in the 37,000 mosques managed by the Ministry.[96] Neither was such an effort a one-off affair: in May 1988, the Minister of Endowments Muhammad ʿAli Mahjub (b. 1939) declared a specific focus on cleaning Cairo's largest mosques,[97] and a November 1989 statement reiterated the Minister's commitment to cleanliness in mosques outside Cairo and Alexandria.[98] Indeed, in 1989, Mahjub even announced a national competition for the cleanest mosque.[99]

In the shadow of these political and cultural winds, Salafi scholars wrestled with the legitimacy of a practice that Ansar al-Sunna had long hailed. In 1981, a Yemeni by the name of ʿUmar b. Ghurama b. ʿUmar al-ʿAmrawi tackled this question in a book entitled *Clarifying the Prophet's Views Regarding Praying in Shoes*. A native of the Southern Yemeni governorate of al-Bayda', al-ʿAmrawi had come to the Saudi coastal center of Jeddah for secondary school. When he published this text, however, he had recently moved to Egypt to pursue a degree in geography at ʿAyn Shams University in Cairo and later would earn degrees from Muhammad b. Saʿud Islamic University in the Saudi capital of Riyadh

95. ʿAbd al-Majid al-ʿAmari, "Taqrir al-Yawm," *al-Riyad*, 18 Rabiʿ al-Awwal 1405/10 December 1984, 2.

96. Mahmud Murad, "Hamla Wataniyya Hadafuha: 'Nazafat Masajid Misr,'" *al-Ahram*, 19 July 1980, 3.

97. "Wazir al-Awqaf Yuqarrir," *al-Ahram*, 30 May 1988, 5.

98. Saʿid Hulwa, "Mahjub fi Ijtimaʿ li-l-Aʾimma wa Mudiri al-Awqaf bi-l-Muhafazat," *al-Ahram*, 2 November 1989, 5.

99. "Wazir al-Awqaf Yaʿlan fi al-Monufiyya," *al-Ahram*, 14 November 1989, 5. This emphasis can also be found in Egyptian textbooks from this period. See Starrett, "The Hexis of Interpretation," 960–62.

and Karachi University in Pakistan.[100] While in Egypt, or possibly immediately before his migration from Saudi Arabia, al-ʿAmrawi engaged the challenge posed by those who had deserted the Sunna of the Prophet and committed themselves to "imported Sunnas" (*Sunan mustawrada*) from East and West alike.[101]

Al-ʿAmrawi began by describing how such religiously-alienated individuals would attack those who sought to live according to the Sunna by praying in shoes, instead of confronting other individuals engaged in observable sins (*al-maʿāṣī al-ẓāhira*).[102] Yet, when it came to praying in shoes, the author also set out a series of conditions that were initially the province of anti-Salafi polemics. In particular, al-ʿAmrawi was concerned about the relationship between shoe material and ritual purity. While firm or solid (*ṣulba*) shoes could be appropriately cleansed of dirt (*turāb*) through ablutions, one could not do so with permeable plastic shoes (*al-aḥdhiya al-blāstikiyya*), let alone flip-flops (literally "sponge shoes," *al-aḥdhiya al-asfanjiyya*). Specifically, the latter retained impurities even when wiped and could only be purified by drying under the sun (*bi-l-tajfīf taḥta al-shams*).[103]

In light of these concerns, al-ʿAmrawi sought to downgrade the importance of praying in shoes by refining its legal status and providing justifications to abstain from it. On the surface, al-ʿAmrawi had defined praying in shoes as praiseworthy.[104] Yet, he then explicated two different sets of conditions: those under which one should ideally opt against praying in shoes, and a second set under which one should affirmatively avoid doing so. In the former case, the dirt that proliferates in the streets, ritual baths, markets and even in the area near some mosques make it difficult to preserve pure shoes,[105] while in the latter one should take off one's shoes to avoid causing *fitna* in mosques.[106]

100. "al-Sira al-Dhatiyya li-l-Duktur ʿUmar b. Ghurama al-ʿAmrawi," *Tarbiyatuna*, http://www.tarbyatona.net/include/plugins/article/article.php?action = s&id = 300).

101. ʿUmar b. Ghuarama al-ʿAmrawi, *Fasl al-Maqal fi Kalam Sayyid al-Anam ʿAlayhi al-Salat wa'l-Salam fi Hukm al-Salat fi al-Niʿal* (Riyadh: Matabiʿ wa-Iʿlanat al-Sharif, 1988), 5.

102. al-ʿAmrawi, *Fasl al-Maqal*, 5.

103. al-ʿAmrawi, *Fasl al-Maqal*, 13.

104. Specifically, he noted that it is a "*sunna* that, when performed is a source of reward but when abstained from, is not a source of punishment" (*sunna yuthāb fāʿiluhā wa lā yuʿāqab tārikuhā*). Such a categorization is equivalent to being classified as praiseworthy. See al-ʿAmrawi, *Fasl al-Maqal*, 17.

105. al-ʿAmrawi, *Fasl al-Maqal*, 17.

106. al-ʿAmrawi, *Fasl al-Maqal*, 17.

In conclusion, al-ʿAmrawi counseled his fellow Muslim brothers to "not be extreme" (*ʿadam al-tashaddud*) in their approach to the Sunna, stipulating that abstaining from praying with shoes does not constitute a sin (*maʿṣiya*).[107] As the 1980s dawned, Salafis had begun to make the case against praying in shoes, relying on arguments previously marshaled by their critics. Over the course of this decade, these concerns would take on a higher profile as they migrated to the Saudi Permanent Committee on Religious Scholarship and Fatwas.

FORMALIZING A POLICY ON PRAYER IN SHOES

The Committee of the Grand Ulama's third sub-body, the Permanent Committee on Religious Scholarship and Fatwa, played a key role in the debate over praying in shoes. Tasked with addressing questions of theology and ritual encountered by the Saudi population on a daily basis and available to this population by post and telephone,[108] the Permanent Committee's membership encompassed an all-star list of Salafi scholars, including Ibn Baz, Ibn al-ʿUthaymin, Salih al-Fawzan (b. 1933), ʿAbd Allah b. ʿAbd al-Rahman b. Ghadyan (d. 2010), and Ansar al-Sunna's former president, ʿAbd al-Razzaq al-ʿAfifi.[109] Al-ʿAfifi was a central player, serving as the Vice President of the Permanent Committee from its foundation in 1971 until his death in 1994.[110] The Permanent Committee thus represented a Salafi power center within a larger Wahhabi-Hanbali framework.

As Purist Salafis within the Permanent Committee sought to regulate religious practice broadly while resolving the question of praying in shoes, ritually-based challenges abounded. Although the Committee's purview (matters of theology and practice) might have appeared politically marginal, it was precisely because of the claim of the Saudi religious establishment to regulate belief and practice alike that they were significant. Neither was Saudi Arabia an exception; a focus on religious practice was part and parcel of a broader set of claims to control religious space made by modernizing states across the

107. al-ʿAmrawi, *Fasl al-Maqal*, 21.

108. Mouline, *The Clerics of Islam*, 153.

109. For a partial list of the Permanent Commission's membership, see *Fatawa al-Lajna al-Daʾima li-l-Buhuth al-ʿIlmiyya waʾl-Iftaʾ*, ed. Ahmad b. ʿAbd al-Razzaq al-Darwish (Riyadh: al-Muʾyyad li-l-Nashr waʾl-Tawziʿ, 1411/1991), 1:2–14.

110. al-Tahir, *Jamaʿat Ansar al-Sunna al-Muhammadiyya*, 181.

region. As a result, ritual acts both constituted a target of state power as well as a key means of religio-political contestation.

During the 1980s, fatwas relating to the practice of praying in shoes appeared through two key methods of transmission: the popular radio program *Light on the Path* (*Nur ʿala al-Darb*) and the public rulings of the Permanent Committee. Most notably, in August 1982, a Saudi Salafi scholar named Salih al-Lahidan (b. 1932) dealt with a straightforward fatwa request as to the permissibility of praying in shoes by arguing that the permissibility of this practice in the Prophet's time was premised on the existence of dirt rather than carpeted floors in mosques (*kāna al-muṣallā turāb*^an^ *wa laysa mafrūsh*^an^ *bi-l-sajjād*). As al-Lahidan explained: "If [the mosque] had been carpeted then it would be necessary, as a matter of etiquette (*adab*^an^), to avoid stepping [on the carpet] with one's shoes which accumulate dust (*yuʿallaq bihi turāb*). . . ."[111]

In the face of the growing conflation of purity and cleanliness, Salafi scholars on the Permanent Committee issued a series of rulings on praying in shoes between 1977 and 1991. Over this period, the committee published three primary fatwas on this question, two signed by Ibn Baz, al-ʿAfifi, Ibn Ghadyan, and ʿAbd Allah b. Qaʿud (d. 2005), and a third signed by this group minus Ibn Qaʿud.

In the first fatwa request, the question was straightforward: insofar as the original command to pray in shoes and to grow a beard were justified, at least in part, by the *ratio legis* (*ʿilla*) of distinction from non-Muslims (particularly Jews) in seventh-century Arabia, then does the obligatory nature of such acts vanish when its underlying function no longer holds (that is, when a variety of non-Muslims both wear beards and pray in shoes)? Neither is the reference to the status of the beard coincidental; it is precisely during this period that Salafi scholars in Saudi Arabia (as well as in Egypt) had turned to emphasizing the significance of the beard to religious practice even as they had yet to articulate its precise parameters.

In response, the Permanent Committee's ruling explained:

> The best conduct is that of Muhammad (peace be upon him) and one of the things that he did was to let his beard grow, as well as ordering for this to be done [by others]. As for the justification that the Prophet (Peace Be Upon Him) mentioned [of distinguishing the Muslims from the Jews], it was to show the Jews' disobedience to the Prophets and Messengers before him, and he forbade imitation of them

111. "Fatawa," *al-ʿUkaz*, 6 Dhu al-Qaʿda 1402/25 August 1982, 12.

> by ordering Muslims to behave contrary to them. This does not mean that if the *ratio legis* given for a ruling does not exist, then the ruling should no longer be applied. By letting their beards grow, Muslims were following the tradition of the Messengers and the Seal of the Messengers, Muhammad (peace be upon him). . . . As for performing prayer in shoes (*al-ṣalāt fī al-niʿāl*) . . . if the Jews do not pray in shoes, then they are contradicting the conduct of the Messenger. . . . However, if they do pray in shoes, they are following the tradition of the Prophet (peace be upon him) and we should not abandon his *Sunna* . . . [solely because the Jews] apply one of these rulings. . . .[112]

Here, we see a middle ground between Amin Muhammad Rida's call for praying in shoes and al-ʿAmrawi's efforts to justify avoiding this practice. On the textual front, the signatories of this fatwa seek to draw a line between the initial justification for a practice—distinguishing Muslims from Jews in seventh century Arabia—and the broader authority of the Sunna. While these scholars do not provide an alternative justification for praying in shoes beyond the original *ratio legis*, neither do they offer secondary justifications to abstain from it.

The support evinced by the first fatwa for praying in shoes, which contrasts with al-ʿAmrawi's justifications for avoiding this practice, is underscored by two additional undated fatwas, the first of which was signed by Ibn Baz, al-ʿAfifi, and Ibn Ghadyan and the other of which was written by this group as well as Ibn Qaʿud. In the first fatwa, the Permanent Committee pushes back against the growing trend towards the creation of exceptions to praying in shoes. The questioner had enquired as to whether one is permitted to enter mosques (which are generally carpeted) in shoes, and specifically mentioned that men employed by the military are required to wear their boots at all times. In response, Ibn Baz, al-ʿAfifi, and Ibn Ghadyan wrote that it is permissible (*yajūz*).[113] The second fatwa explained that it is "praiseworthy, or at the very least, permissible to pray in shoes," (*istiḥbāb al-ṣalāt fī al-naʿlayn aw ibāḥiyat dhalik ʿalā al-aqall*), whether in open-air areas (*fī al-khalāʾ fī al-arḍ*) or in covered mosques (*fī al-masjid al-masqūf*).[114]

During this period, a leading Yemeni Salafi, Muqbil b. Hadi al-Wadiʿi (d. 2001), mounted an even more strident case for praying in shoes. A native

112. al-Darwish, *Fatawa al-Lajna al-Daʾima*, 3:309–10.
113. al-Darwish, *Fatawa al-Lajna al-Daʾima*, 6:215–16.
114. al-Darwish, *Fatawa al-Lajna al-Daʾima*, 6:216–17.

of the Northern Yemeni city of Saʿada, the capital city of the governorate of the same name, al-Wadiʿi had fled to Saudi Arabia following the 1962 Yemeni revolution. Once in the kingdom, he had found employment teaching at the Great Mosque of Mecca and studied at the Islamic University of Medina with Ibn Baz, the North African Islamic Modernist-turned-Purist Salafi Taqi al-Din al-Hilali (d. 1987), and the Mauritanian Salafi scholar Muhammad al-Amin al-Shinqiti (d. 1973).[115] The 1970s, however, would see al-Wadiʿi ally himself with the JSM, a decision which ultimately led to his 1979 expulsion from the kingdom. As the 1980s began, al-Wadiʿi sought to reestablish himself in Yemen and to position Saʿada as a heartland of Yemeni Salafism as he founded the Dar al-Hadith institute in the governorate village of Dammaj.[116]

As al-Wadiʿi wielded his pen, he targeted unnamed opponents in Yemen and Saudi Arabia alike. In his 1983 work *The Legitimacy of Praying in Shoes*, published first in Kuwait and then in Yemen,[117] he explained that it was this obligation to avoid "strife" (*fitna*) that had inspired him to "compile some of the hadith reports that [he had] come across regarding the legitimacy of praying in shoes" (*sharʿiyyat al-ṣalāt bi-l-niʿāl*).[118] Like al-Kawthari, albeit to diametrically opposed ends, al-Wadiʿi invoked *fitna* as it pertained to praying in shoes.

As an example of this needless internal strife, al-Wadiʿi described an incident that he had witnessed at a mosque in Yemen where he was the caretaker. A congregant who had previously lived in Saudi Arabia had returned to Yemen and sought to enter the mosque wearing shoes, only to be threatened with bodily harm. The source of this threat, who according to the story claimed to be a scholar (*min ahl al-ʿilm*), was ignorant regarding his own legal school (*jāhil bi-madhhabihi*).[119] Neither were such conflicts limited to Yemen: the author recounted that, in the Prophet's mosque in Medina, men who sought to "act

115. "Muqbil b. Hadi al-Wadiʿi," *al-Maktaba al-Shamila*, http://shamela.ws/index.php/author/1224.

116. Bonnefoy, *Salafism in Yemen*, 56–57.

117. *The Legitimacy of Praying in Shoes* pamphlet was originally published in Kuwait by Dar al-Arqam in 1404/1983, and then republished by the same publishing house in 1406/1986.

118. Muqbil b. Hadi al-Wadiʿi, *Majmuʿat Rasaʾil ʿIlmiyya*, ed. Saʿid b. ʿUmar (Sanaa, Yemen: Dar al-Athar, 1420/1990), 7–8. This pamphlet is the first of five included in this anthology; it also includes short texts that deal with dying the beard black and combining prayers while traveling.

119. al-Wadiʿi, *Majmuʿat Rasaʾil ʿIlmiyya*, 22–23.

according to the Sunna [of praying in shoes] faced strong condemnation [presumably by other Hanbalis] and were forced to vow that they would not seek to pray in their shoes again."[120] His criticism, however, was not directed only at those who might go astray but those who led them there, namely the scholars who "respond to the *sunna* by utilizing personal opinion (*raʾī*) and appeals to discretion (*istiḥsān*)."[121] While it is unclear whom al-Wadiʿi is criticizing specifically, he sought to position himself as a defender of the Prophet's model.

Yet, winds of change had arrived and would soon reach the highest rungs of the Salafi hierarchy in Saudi Arabia. Three years later, Ibn al-ʿUthaymin, who would join the Committee of the Grand Ulama the next year, issued a fatwa that, like al-ʿAmrawi's book, provided a justification for a move *away* from praying in shoes. In this 16 June 1986 ruling,[122] Ibn al-ʿUthaymin defended the legitimacy of praying in a carpeted mosque and dismissed the notion that a man who prostrated himself in prayer while wearing shoes was somehow insulting the individual behind him.[123] In this vein, he noted that people should "live according to the Sunna of the Prophet in accordance with their abilities (*mā istaṭāʿa*), committed to that which is obligatory (*wājib*) [and] seizing the opportunity in matters that are voluntary (*wa-ightinām*^{an} *bi-l-taṭawwuʿ*)."[124] While a classification of praying in shoes as praiseworthy was consistent with Ibn al-ʿUthaymin's ruling, this leading Salafi scholar nonetheless stops short of exhorting his followers to emulate the Prophet in this manner.

By the early 1990s, however, arguments against praying in shoes would grow increasingly prominent. In a fatwa published in 1993, Ibn Baz explained that

120. al-Wadiʿi, *Majmuʿat Rasaʾil ʿIlmiyya*, 23.

121. al-Wadiʿi, *Majmuʿat Rasaʾil ʿIlmiyya*, 29.

122. The ruling was issued on 8 Shawwal 1406/16 June 1986, while the appointment occurred on 3 July 1987. For dates of appointment, see "Hayʾat Kibar al-ʿUlamaʾ," *al-Maʿrifa*, available at https://www.marefa.org/هيئة_كبار_العلماء_السعودية, accessed 16 April 2018.

123. Muhammad b. Salih al-ʿUthaymin, *Majmuʿ Fatawa wa Rasaʾil Fadilat al-Shaykh Muhammad b. Salih al-ʿUthaymin*, ed. Fahd b. Nasir al-Suliman (Riyadh, Saudi Arabia: Dar al-Thurya li-l-Nashr waʾl-Tawziʿ, 1419/1998), 12: 387–92, at 390. The insult would presumably be that the person praying in shoes would reveal the bottom of his feet to the individual behind him. This fatwa collection notes that the ruling was issued on 8 Shawwal 1406, corresponding to 16 June 1986.

124. Ibn al-ʿUthaymin, *Majmuʿ Fatawa wa Rasaʾil*, 12: 387–92, at 392.

"with regard to the Sunna on this matter, it [can be] revived by explaining that the Prophet (peace be upon Him) . . . [prayed in shoes] and that there is no objection to it (*lā ḥarj fīhi*). . . ."[125] Despite this seemingly straightforward directive, Ibn Baz then crafted a significant exception:

> [M]ost people will not pay attention to [the obligation to purify the shoes] and if they are allowed to enter the mosque then the junk and dirt will accumulate on the carpet . . . and some people may then avoid praying at the mosque . . . and this may cause harm to those who do pray. . . . [Thus praying without shoes] is preferable and is consistent with the legal bases (*muqtaḍā al-qawāʾid al-sharʿiyya*).[126]

This fatwa was a far cry from the Permanent Committee ruling, published only a few years prior, to which Ibn Baz was a signatory. Although it upheld the Sunna of praying in shoes in theory, this leading Saudi Salafi scholar couched its preferred status within a set of contextual conditions unrelated to ritual purity.

The 1990s also saw the migration of this shift to the Permanent Committee itself. In a fatwa issued in the early years of the decade, the second generation of the Committee—Salih al-Fawzan[127] (b. 1933), ʿAbd al-ʿAziz b. Al al-Shaykh (b. 1943),[128] and Bakr Abu Zayd[129] (d. 2008)—were joined by Ibn Baz in a ruling that moved beyond the specific question of individual purity to consider carpet care. The scholars explained the balancing act as follows: "Praying in pure shoes is Sunna *except* [emphasis added] if this leads to forbidden [results] such as polluting the mosque's floor (*talwīth farshat al-masjid*) . . . and [in this

125. Muhammad b. ʿAbd al-ʿAziz al-Misnid, *Fatawa Islamiyya* (Riyadh: Dar al-Watan, 1414/1994), 1:281–2. It can also be found in ʿAbd al-ʿAziz b. Baz *Majmuʿat Fatawa wa Maqalat Mutanawiʿ*, ed. Muhammad b. Saʿd al-Shuwayʿir (Riyadh: Dar al-Qasim li-l-Nashr, 1420/~2000), 29:225.

126. al-Misnid, *Fatawa Islamiyya*, 1:281–82, and Ibn Baz, *Majmuʿat Fatawa wa Maqalat Mutanawiʿ*, ed. Muhammad b. Saʿd al-Shuwayʿir (Riyadh: Dar al-Qasim li-l-Nashr, 1420/~2000~), 29:225.

127. See "Salih b. Fawzan al-Fawzan," *al-Riʾasa al-ʿAmma li-l-Buhuth al-ʿIliyya waʾl-Iftaʾ*, http://www.alifta.net/Search/MoftyDetails.aspx?languagename = ar&Type = Mofty§ion = tafseer&ID = 7.

128. "Samahat al-Shaykh ʿAbd al-ʿAziz b. ʿAbd Allah b. Muhammad Al al-Shaykh," *al-Riʾasa al-ʿAmma li-l-Buhuth al-ʿIlmiyya waʾl-Iftaʾ*, http://www.alifta.net/Search/MoftyDetails.aspx?Type = Mofty§ion = tafseer&ID = 8.

129. "al-Shaykh Bakr b. ʿAbd Allah Abu Zayd fi Sutur," *Islamweb*, http://articles.islamweb.net/media/index.php?id = 35517&lang = A&page = article.

situation] one should not pray in [shoes] in order to avoid harm. . . ."[130] Put differently, one could now justify the recommendation not to pray barefoot based on the principle that, even if one's shoes are ritually pure, they can still cause harm to carpets. As these leading members of the Permanent Committee provided yet another justification for abstaining from praying in shoes, they claimed that the Sunnaic status of this practice was itself conditional.

RECONSTITUTING THE SUNNA

How might we explain this shift in religious interpretation from praiseworthiness to permission and increasingly limited practice? While it is possible that this period saw increased clashes around this issue, such tensions were hardly novel. Instead, the most likely explanation has to do with an expansion of government control over mosques from 1993 onward. During this period, the Saudi government faced an insurgent *Sahwa* movement that increasingly took aim at the Royal Family's legitimacy[131] and, in response, the latter sought to assert control over universities and religious institutions alike.[132] On the religious front, a 10 July 1993 royal decree created a new body, the Ministry of Islamic Affairs, Endowments, Preaching and Guidance, which took over the responsibility for preaching and guidance formerly arrogated to the Permanent Committee's sister body within the Committee of the Grand 'Ulama', the General Presidency for the Management of Religious Scholarship, Preaching and Guidance. In the process, the basic function of the General Presidency, like that of the Permanent Committee, came to center on issuing fatwas. Similarly, October 1994 saw the creation of the High Council of Islamic Affairs (*al-Majlis al-A'lā li-l-Shu'ūn al-Islāmiyya*) under the authority of Prince Sultan (d. 2011), a son of Ibn Sa'ud and brother of King Fahd.[133] In the face of these interventions, it appears that Ibn Baz and, in turn, the Committee, sought to clamp down on praying in shoes.

130. Ahmad b. 'Abd al-Razzaq al-Darwish, *Fatawa al-Lajna al-Da'ima li-l-Buhuth al-'Ilmiyya wa'l-Ifta': al-Majmu'a al-Thaniyya* (Riyadh: al-Ri'asa al-'Amma li-l-Buhuth wa'l-Ifta', 2006), 5:160. Though this volume was not published until 2006, Ibn Baz's inclusion suggests that the fatwa itself was issued between 1993 and the scholar's death in 1999.

131. Lacroix, *Awakening Islam*, 166–67.

132. Lacroix, *Awakening Islam*, 207.

133. Lacroix, *Awakening Islam*, 208–10.

The move away from praying in shoes would soon be adopted by Egyptian Salafis, too, yet, like in Saudi Arabia, this question was still open in the mid-1980s. As in the case of the Permanent Committee's fatwa on the comparability of the beard and praying in shoes, the Alexandria-based Salafi Call's Muhammad b. Isma'il al-Muqaddam sought to distinguish these two practices. In a text published in Kuwait, al-Muqaddam argued the beard is among the natural practices of Muslims (*min sunan al-fiṭra) and* serves to distinguish Muslims from non-Muslims, while praying in shoes only carries the latter function.[134] Thus praying in shoes must be classified as praiseworthy or recommended (*nadb*), rather than obligatory (*wājib*).[135] Yet, unlike the Permanent Committee, al-Muqaddam's legal classification harkened back to Amin Muhammad Rida as he classified praying in shoes as a praiseworthy practice.

By contrast, Ansar al-Sunna's president Muhammad 'Ali 'Abd al-Rahim sought to strip this practice of its elevated status. Following a silence of nearly four decades since Rida's article in *al-Hadi al-Nabawi*, 'Abd al-Rahim dealt with this question twice between September 1989 and January 1991 in *al-Tawhid*, the successor to *al-Hadi al-Nabawi*. In the first case, he argued that, while permitted, praying with shoes was not praiseworthy (*mustaḥabb*) but rather merely licit.[136] In the second ruling, 'Abd al-Rahim argued that this practice took on the status of Sunna prior to the carpeting of mosques and later served a form of legal leniency (*taysīr*) for those who experienced cold days, were traveling, and or worked as soldiers or in factories.[137] 'Abd al-Rahim's engagement with this question did not question its historical basis on widely authenticated hadith reports, yet nonetheless sought to downplay its significance by downgrading its legal and thus normative status.

Though it would be overly deterministic to credit this shift in interpretation exclusively to changing political winds in Egypt—this process had been in motion for several decades—the 1980s did see the Ministry of Endowments decisively narrow the domain of legitimate activity in Egyptian mosques. In this vein, an October 1984 article in Ansar al-Sunna's mouthpiece, *al-Tawhid*,

134. Muhammad b. Isma'il al-Muqaddam, *Adillat Tahrim Halq al-Lihya* (Huli, Kuwait: Dar al-Arqam, 1405/1985), 35.

135. al-Muqaddam, *Adillat Tahrim Halq al-Lihya*, 35.

136. Muhammad 'Ali 'Abd al-Rahim, "Bab al-Fatawa," *al-Tawhid*, Safar 1410/~September 1989, 15–25, at 19.

137. Muhammad 'Ali 'Abd al-Rahim, "Bab al-Fatawa," *al-Tawhid*, Sha'ban 1411/~February 1991, 8–22, at 20.

described how the crackdown on independent mosques (*al-masājid al-ahliyya*) since September 1981[138] had limited the ability of Salafi preachers to give the Friday sermon and placed new restrictions on who could preach and what could be discussed. In response, the author of this article alleged, Ansar al-Sunna had turned to focusing on topics such as "hygiene" (*al-naẓāfa*) and "truthfulness" (*al-ṣidq*), and "even discussing paradise and hellfire had become politics" (*wa-ḥatā al-kalām ʿan al-janna waʾl-nār siyāsa*).[139] While this claim overstates the extent to which discourses of truthfulness were distinct to the 1980s, and does not acknowledge the straightforward reality that praying in shoes provoked Egyptians across the political spectrum,[140] it nonetheless underscores the changed boundaries of permitted speech and practice alike as well as the increasing significant of concerns of hygiene in debates over religious practice.

By the mid-1990s, as a jihadi insurgency roiled Egypt through attacks on politicians, police officers, and tourist sites, Salafis within Ansar al-Sunna faced not merely surveillance but also active suspicion of violent activity. Despite these challenges, however, a faction within Ansar al-Sunna continued to insist on the importance of praying in shoes. A December 1994 article in *al-Tawhid* by Saʿd Sadiq Muhammad, who had grown up within Ansar al-Sunna and had known the former President ʿAbd al-Rahman al-Wakil since he was a child,[141] explained:

> [S]ome people blame Ansar al-Sunna al-Muhammadiyya for devoting all their attention to calling for *Tawhid* . . . and [accuse] those who belong to the organization of only speaking of the [evils of] visiting shrines and Sufi saints and the Prophet's Family (*Ahl al-Bayt*) and forbidding [other people] from praying in [such] mosques. . . . Just as they belabor praying in shoes (*al-ṣalāt fi al-niʿāl*) and are excessively harsh regarding vowing by those other than God (*al-ḥalf bi-ghayr Allah*) . . . and seek to fight polytheism (*shirk*) in all of its manifestation . . . [but this] is a superficial perspective on Ansar al-Sunna. . . .[142]

138. This crackdown began in the month prior to Anwar al-Sadat's assassination and continued afterwards.

139. Muhammad al-Haywan, "Ilghaʾ al-Riqaba ʿala al-Masajid," *al-Tawhid*, Safar 1405/~October 1984, 22–3.

140. For an ethnographic analysis of praying in shoes in contemporary Egypt, see Gauvain, *Salafi Ritual Purity*, 125.

141. Saʿd Sadiq Muhammad, *Siraʿ Bayna al-Haqq waʾl-Batil* (Cairo: Matbaʿat al-Sunna al-Muhammadiyya, 1964), 3.

142. Saʿd Sadiq Muhammad, "Hawl Daʿwat Ansar al-Sunna al-Muhammadiyya," *al-Tawhid*, Rajab 1415/~March 1985, 53–6, at 54.

The author did not deny Ansar al-Sunna's commitment to these issues; instead, he sought to couch it within a broader commitment to correcting their fellow Muslims' approach to creed (*ʿaqīda*) and to battling social corruption (*muḥārabat al-fasād al-ijtimāʿī*). Indeed, even as they embraced distinct practices such as "praying in shoes . . . or some praying with their heads uncovered (*yuṣallūn fī al-niʿāl. . . . aw yusālī baʿḍuhum bi-lā ghiṭāʾ raʾs*) . . . which many Muslims have forgotten," they did not forget to introduce other Muslims to questions of morality, comportment, and interpersonal relations.[143] Despite efforts to deemphasize praying in shoes—to create justifications for abstaining from it, or to downgrade its status from praiseworthy to merely permissible or optional—it remained a practice, though no longer a signature one, for segments of Ansar al-Sunna's membership.

CONCLUSION

On the surface, the rise and fall of praying in shoes is a perplexing story of how Salafis in Egypt, Saudi Arabia, and Yemen increasingly formulated justifications for abandoning a practice of the Prophet. It is a case in which the polemical arguments of ideological opponents were adopted by leading Salafi scholars, as well as one in which the inertia of a tradition of praying barefoot in Egypt and historically contingent political shifts short-circuited a Salafi claim to ritual space. The balancing act that followed over the religious status of this practice, the conditions in which it can be set aside, and how to justify these conditions under broader appeals to either religious dispensation (*rukhṣa*) or the discretion (*istiḥsān*) of Muslims, reveals the ways in which a Sunnaic practice reimagined for the twentieth century could simultaneously inspire and constrain religious practice. Salafis, far from inexorably anchored in an epistemological commitment to the seventh century, sought to balance a Prophetic model against the threat of both state repression and popular opprobrium.

This is also a story of the social consequences of religious revival. Ansar al-Sunna's decision to trumpet praying in shoes as a signature practice was not random; in the absence of access to political power and with the organization's social influence centered on mosques, ritual practice was an obvious site of

143. Saʿd Sadiq Muhammad, "Hawl Daʿwat Ansar al-Sunna al-Muhammadiyya," 55.

contestation. The structural incentive to focus on ritual practice, however, did not dictate a focus on praying in shoes; as al-Albani's *Characteristics of the Prophet's Prayer* underscored, Salafi elites had a variety of possible practices that they could place at the forefront of their movement.[144] The choice of praying in shoes, instead, was about offering a practice that was at once undeniably performed by Muhammad and highly socially disruptive. It was about not only following Muhammad's model, but also about visually challenging and physically transgressing mosque norms that had been dominant for hundreds of years. As they emerged from the restrictions of the ʿAbd al-Nasir period, Egyptian Salafis would formulate a project of gender segregation that sought to reorder social norms outside the mosque in a similarly drastic fashion.

144. For example, al-Albani also emphasized raising one's hands in prayer immediately before, during, and after the *takbir*, while the majority Sunni opinion is that this practice is Sunna specifically when done during the ʿId prayers. See Muhammad Nasir al-Din al-Albani, *Sifat Salat al-Nabi Min al-Takbir ila al-Taslim ki-Annaka Taraʾha* (Riyadh: Maktabat al-Maʿarif li-l-Nashr waʾl-Tawziʿ, 1410), 87. For Mahmud Muhammad Khattab al-Subki's explanation of this larger debate, see al-Subki, *al-Din al-Khalis*, 4: 337–8.

CHAPTER 4

The Salafi Mystique

From Fitna *to Gender Segregation*

In 1954, Muhammad Nasir al-Din al-Albani declared that women must cover their heads but are under no obligation to conceal their faces or hands as they move outside the home.[1] By the end of the 1970s, however, the question for Salafi scholars was not the particulars of female modesty, but rather the implementation of gender segregation. How did this shift arise, how was it shaped by contrasting institutional opportunities, and what can this development reveal about the relationship between textual interpretation, state power, and communication in Purist Salafism?[2]

As with the rise and fall of praying in shoes, the emergence of gender segregation is a product of a transnational sphere of Salafi elites that were party to a shared textual discourse and even shared practices, yet also faced distinct local opportunities, challengers, and constraints. This chapter charts the course of Egyptian Salafi efforts to find institutional support for gender segregation, both contextualizing it within conditions specific to Egyptian society and contrasting it with the success of their Saudi counterparts in

1. Muhammad Nasir al-Din al-Albani, *Hijab al-Mar'a al-Muslima fi al-Kitab wa'l-Sunna* (Cairo: al-Matba'a al-Salafiyya, 1954), 21.

2. This chapter, and the book more broadly, includes few female voices because, aside from Ni'mat Sidqi, women did not emerge as prominent figures within Ansar al-Sunna during the period under study. Just as importantly, the organization's periodicals did not include a regular letters-to-the-editor section in which women (and men) could have expressed non-elite positions. Contemporary research, by contrast, allows scholars to tell a dynamic story of women's role in the Salafi movement.

reshaping the topography of the kingdom's society. In order to trace the relationship among textual interpretation, proposed policy, and sociological reality, I will focus on the shifting bounds of the legal category of "flaunting" (*al-tabarruj*) and the growing prominence of the category of gender mixing (*ikhtilāṭ al-jinsayn*).

At first glance, gender segregation constitutes an exception to my broader argument about Salafism and visibility, as it does not appear to pivot on a self-regulating individual's performance of ethical rectitude through visible signs. Yet, like the ordering of students or soldiers in neat rows, gender segregation seeks to spatially regulate individuals so that they collectively constitute a virtuous social order. In Saudi Arabia, where the Salafi argument for gender segregation found support within the Wahhabi-Hanbali elite, this model of separation became a social reality. In Egypt, by contrast, the absence of durable structures of gender segregation meant that Salafi men and women faced the challenge of separating themselves in a manner that performatively set them apart from social peers.

The growth of textual arguments in favor of gender segregation and particular institutions to separate men and women, however, did not occur in lockstep. In Egypt, interpretative shifts ran into practical complications, while in Saudi Arabia, textual claims were used to expand, rather than inaugurate, pre-existing gender segregation. The fate of these efforts, in turn, would also differ: Egyptian Salafis ultimately accepted that women could segregate themselves from men through particular norms of comportment, while Saudi Salafis would ally with their Wahhabi-Hanbali counterparts to drive the creation of largely separate social worlds for men and women. The divergent fates of gender segregation in these two Salafi centers reveals how Salafi elites sought to both map public space and to redefine gender relations by articulating a particular model of visible (and thus observable) separation of men and women in public space.

The significance of gender segregation to Salafism, however, extends beyond sociability. Unlike praying in shoes, gender segregation could serve as a source of visual distinction throughout society, not merely in the mosque. Furthermore, in contrast to both the fist-length beard and shortened pants (chapters 5 and 6), the male/female binary at the heart of gender segregation was, in the Egyptian case, unmistakably associated with the Salafi movement. By contrast, beard and pant length often produced greater challenges of mutual recognition.

I begin by situating Salafi claims to separate men and women within Islamic history, emphasizing both the particular contexts in which gender segregation occurred, as well as the broader fears articulated within the scholarly tradition regarding female sexuality. I then turn to the modern period, highlighting the transformation of Islamic law into a bulwark of religious particularism and the initial Salafi position that individual comportment was sufficient to preserve public morality. In the second half of the chapter, I probe the contrasting trajectories of gender segregation in Egypt and Saudi Arabia, showing how an effort to gender the entirety of public space emerged out of the fusion of a longer Islamic tradition with modernist notions of regulation and, in Egypt, a secular-nationalist project of State Feminism.

SETTING THE STAGE

Salafi debates over mapping public space in the second half of the twentieth century emerged out of the Islamic legal tradition even as they both contributed to and reflected a transformation of Islamic law over the first part of the century. As they examined the very Islamic legal tradition that they sought to bypass through a turn to the Quran and Sunna, Salafi scholars certainly had a body of scholarship on which to draw. The Hanafi scholar Badr al-Din al-ʿAyni (d. 855/1451) sought to restrict gender mixing during the funeral prayer (*al-janāza*),[3] while his fellow Hanafi Ibn ʿAbidin (d. 1252/1836) cautioned against women joining men to welcome the ruler.[4] The Maliki scholar al-Dasuqi warned against gender mixing in celebrations of the Prophet's birthday (s. *Mawlid*, pl. *Mawālīd*),[5] while his fellow Maliki Muhammad ʿIlayash (d. 1299/1882) declared that judges must set aside time each week to adjudicate among women lest they be compelled to mix with men.[6] The Shafiʿi scholar

3. al-ʿAyni, *ʿUmdat al-Qari Sharh Sahih al-Bukhari*, 8:161.

4. Muhammad b. ʿUmar b. ʿAbidin, *Radd al-Muhtar ʿala al-Durr al-Mukhtar li-Khatimat al-Muhaqqiqin Muhammad Amin al-Shahir bi-Ibn ʿAbidin*, ed. ʿAdil Ahmad ʿAbd al-Mawjud and ʿAli Muhammad Muʿawwad (Riyadh: Dar ʿAlam al-Kutub, 2003), 9:511.

5. Muhammad b. Ahmad b. ʿArafa al-Dasuqi, *Hashiyyat al-Dasuqi ʿala al-Sharh al-Kabir li-l-Shaykh Abi al-Barakat Sidi Ahmad b. Muhammad al-ʿAdawi al-Shahir bi-l-Dardir* (Beirut: Dar al-Kutub al-ʿIlmiyya, 2010), 6:492.

6. Muhammad b. Ahmad b. Muhammad ʿIllayash, *Minah al-Jalil Sharh ʿala Mukhtasar al-ʿAllama al-Khalil*, ed. ʿAbd al-Jalil ʿAbd al-Salam (Beirut: Dar al-Kutub al-ʿIlmiyya, 2003), 4:201.

Ibn Hajar al-ʿAsqalani (d. 852/1449), like al-ʿAyni, objected to gender mixing during the funeral prayer,[7] while the Hanbali Ibn al-Jawzi (d. 597/1201) objected to the mixed audiences who gathered around popular preachers and storytellers (*quṣṣāṣ*).[8] Jurists were perhaps most resolute in their efforts to emphasize that women are not obligated to attend Friday prayer,[9] and to enforce gender segregation within the mosque through the provision of separate prayer sections.[10]

The turn to a broad regulation of men and women as they moved through public space arose in the late nineteenth century alongside a broader shift in the social role of Islamic law. In addition to continuing to serve as a tool for scholars in explicating God's intentions and regulating defined communal spaces, *fiqh* increasingly became a central site for the contestation of identity. Legal and political changes, especially the introduction of European legal codes to Egypt in the second half of the nineteenth century and the fall of the Ottoman Empire in 1922, produced a situation in which law came to perceived as a bulwark against the erosion of Muslim particularism.[11] Though this inherited understanding of divine commandment could not be enforced through state-sanctioned coercion, it could be utilized in defining the boundaries, internal and external, of the Islamic community. Just as importantly, it was during this period that colonial rule introduced sexuality as an object of

7. Ahmad b. ʿAli b. Hajar al-ʿAsqalani, *Fath al-Bari bi-Sharh Sahih al-Bukhari*, ed. ʿAbd al-ʿAziz b. Baz and Muhammad Fuʾad ʿAbd al-Baqi (Beirut: Dar al-Kutub al-ʿIlmiyya, 2017), 4:159.

8. Abu al-Faraj ʿAbd al-Rahman b. ʿAli b. al-Jawzi, *Kashf al-Mushkil min Hadith al-Sahihayn* (Riyadh: Dar al-Watan li-l-Nashr, 1997), 4:146. For more on gender mixing in popular preaching and storytelling sessions in the medieval Islamic world, see Jonathan Berkey, *Popular Preaching and Religious Authority in the Medieval Islamic Near East* (Seattle: University of Washington Press, 2001), 31.

9. For an overview of women's legal obligation to attend prayer, see ʿAbd al-Karim Zaydan, *Mufassal fi Ahkam al-Marʾa waʾl-Bayt al-Muslim* (Beirut: Muʾasassat al-Risala, 1994), 1:210–13. Also see Katz, *Women in the Mosque*, 17–109, and Christopher Melchert, "Whether to Keep Women Out of the Mosque: A Survey of Medieval Islamic Law," *Authority, Privacy and Public Order in Islam: Proceedings of the 22nd Congress of L'Union Européenne des Arabisants et Islamisants* (Dudley, MA: Orientalia Lovaniensia Analecta, 2006), 59–70.

10. Separate spaces for male and female prayer are a longstanding feature of Islamic architecture. See Katz, *Women in the Mosque*, 120–26.

11. Muhammad Qasim Zaman has similarly noted how Islamic law served as a boundary for communal identity in colonial India. See Zaman, *The Ulama in Contemporary Islam*, 22–32.

reform, importing Victorian understandings of sexual desire and sin alien to Islamic history.[12]

Yet, notwithstanding the increasing centrality of punctilious legal observance to religious identity, the transmission of Victorian understandings of sexuality, and separate arguments for women's access to public space in the context of nationalist mobilization,[13] Salafi scholars did not initially present a comprehensive blueprint for the gendering of public space. In *al-Hadi al-Nabawi*, Muhammad Bahjat al-Baytar's December 1939 fatwa took the position that that men and women should not shake hands, that women covering their face was praiseworthy (*mustaḥabb*) yet not obligatory,[14] and that men must avert their gaze from women in all situations (*fī jāmiʿ al-aḥwāl*) save for those interactions which sought to achieve a religiously-legitimate goal (*gharḍ ṣaḥīḥ sharʿī*).[15] Collectively, this was far from a comprehensive vision for restricting women's circulation in public space, let alone a call for gender segregation.

It was only during the late 1940s and 1950s that Salafi thinkers began to devote greater interest to the public position of women as it related to interaction with men. This shift was inaugurated by Ansar al-Sunna's leading female thinker, Niʿmat Sidqi, in her book *Flaunting* (*al-Tabarruj*). Sidqi had first met Muhammad Hamid al-Fiqi while traveling to perform the Hajj with her husband, Amin Muhammad Rida, and Ansar al-Sunna's founder came to serve as Sidqi's religious guide and most significant teacher.[16] By the mid-1940s, Sidqi had established her home as an AS branch in which she gave lectures to female members of the organization on Tuesday evenings.[17]

In *Flaunting*, Sidqi tackled the question of women's public conduct. Specifically, she claimed that Egyptian women were exposing themselves on the

12. Bauer, *A Culture of Ambiguity*, 183–213.

13. Baron, *Egypt as a Woman*, 107–34.

14. Those who take this view also take the related position that there is no requirement to cover the face on account of it being classified as part of her nudity. For example, see Muhammad b. Muflih b. Shams al-Maqdisi, *al-Adab al-Sharʿiyya*, ed. Shuʿayb Arnaʾut and ʿUmar Qiyyam (Beirut: Dar al-Risala al-ʿAlamiyya, 2014), 1:296–97.

15. Muhammad Bahjat al-Baytar, "al-Fatawa," *al-Hadi al-Nabawi*, Dhu al-Qaʿda 1358 /~December 1939, 38–43, at 41.

16. Ellen Anne McLarney, *Soft Force: Women in Egypt's Islamic Awakening* (Princeton, NJ: Princeton University Press, 2015), 109–10.

17. Niʿmat Sidqi, "al-Salat," *al-Hadi al-Nabawi*, Jumada al-Ukhra 1363/~May 1944, 15.

beach, in the street and within public institutions, and argued that such female flaunting and male apathy about controlling it was the premier threat to public morality. In this "sea of forbidden pleasures" (*baḥr al-ladhdhāt al-muḥarrama*),[18] how could society remain Islamic? Sidqi was concerned not with the challenge posed by non-Muslims but rather with "the enemy within yourselves, which goes by the name of corruption" (*al-ʿadūw fī nufūsikum ismahu al-fasād*).[19] This text was a call to action, instructing Muslims to "boycott those who have transgressed proper norms of comportment and modesty" (*al-ādāb wa'l-iḥtishām*).[20] Published first in serial form in *al-Hadi al-Nabawi* and *al-Tamaddun al-Islami* beginning in 1947 and then as a full book in Cairo (1951) and Damascus (1954),[21] *Flaunting* challenged Muslim men and women in these two countries in general, and participants in Salafi movements specifically.[22]

Like Sidqi's *Flaunting*, Muhammad Nasr al-Din al-Albani's 1954 pamphlet *The Muslim Woman's Hijab in the Quran and Sunna (Hijab al-Mar'a al-Muslima fi al-Kitab wa'l-Sunna)* laid out the laws that govern female public modesty in an effort to regulate women's visibility and circulation within public space. While al-Albani was concerned with women's presence outside of ritual contexts, he did not discuss gender mixing, let alone its capacity to lead to social disorder. Instead, his focus was on the preservation of femininity and women's access to Paradise.[23] Though the concern for sartorial modesty evinced by

18. Niʿmat Sidqi, *al-Tabarruj* (Cairo: Dar al-Iʿtisam, 1975), 5–6. The original edition of this book was published in Cairo by Ansar al-Sunna; see Sidqi, *al-Tabarruj* (Cairo: Matbaʿat al-Sunna al-Muhammadiyya, 1951).

19. Sidqi, *al-Tabarruj*, 8.

20. Sidqi, *al-Tabarruj*, 8.

21. Parts of the book were first serialized in *al-Hadi al-Nabawi* and *al-Tamaddun al-Islami* beginning in the 1940s. For example, see Niʿmat Sidqi, "al-Tabarruj," *al-Hadi al-Nabawi*, Ramadan-Shawwal 1366/July-August 1947, 34–61 and Sidqi, "al-Tabarruj," *al-Tamaddun al-Islami*, Muharram 1367/Kanun al-Awwal (December) 1947, 502–5. Several years later, advertisements for the full pamphlet appeared in both periodicals. See "al-Tabarruj," *al-Hadi al-Nabawi*, Rajab 1370/April 1951, 51, and "al-Tabarruj," *al-Tamaddun al-Islami*, Shawwal 1373/June 1954, 637.

22. Dating this text to the 1940s and early 1950s rather than to 1967 (contra McLarney, *Soft Force*, 113) suggests that its initial circulation was not to "students . . . mobilizing on university campuses in the late 1960s," but rather to members of Ansar al-Sunna seeking to understand women's role in public two decades earlier.

23. For example, al-Albani cites a popular narration stating that "scantily clad women" (*nisāʾ kāsiyāt ʿāriyāt*) will not enter Paradise. See al-Albani, *Hijab al-Mar'a al-Muslima fi al-Kitab wa'l-Sunna*, 34.

Sidqi and al-Albani points to a greater emphasis on women's visibility, neither scholar understood female conduct to be a collective social concern and neither called for gender segregation. Other Salafi thinkers and activists, in conversation and competition with Wahhabi-Hanbali scholars, Islamists, and secular nationalist proponents of state feminism would soon change the conversation.

BETWEEN ISLAMIST COMPETITORS AND LOCAL PARTICULARITIES

How did gender segregation become a key concern for Salafis, and why did this shift occur? The absence of extended debate on this topic should not be construed as a sign of disinterest: an October 1947 article in *al-Hadi al-Nabawi* noted mixing as one symptom of moral decline,[24] and a March 1963 commentary on popular news articles attributed the spread of extramarital affairs to gender mixing.[25] Concern and sustained textual engagement, however, were two different matters.

In Egypt, it would be Muslim Brothers who would drive this conversation forward. As early as 1933, the Muslim Brotherhood's magazine *al-Ikhwan al-Muslimun* featured articles warning of the dangers of gender mixing.[26] Most vivid, however, was Sayyid Qutb's recollection of his experience in the late 1940s participating in a government-sponsored education mission in Greely, Colorado, during which he witnessing mixed dancing to the midcentury hit "Baby It's Cold Outside."[27] On the legal front, a key work from the 1960s later cited in *al-Tawhid* during the 1970s as a basis for gender segregation[28] was *Fiqh al-Sunna*, a popular legal compendium by a Muslim Brother, al-Sayyid

24. "Min Suwar al-Hayat al-Misriyya," *al-Hadi al-Nabawi*, Dhu al-Hijja 1366/~October 1947, 41–3, at 42.

25. Sa'd Sadiq Muhammad, "Ta'liqat 'ala al-Suhuf," *al-Hadi al-Nabawi*, Dhu al-Qa'da 1382/~March 1963, 50–1, at 50.

26. For example, see Hasanayn 'Abd Allah al-Musalami, "al-Nisa'iyat: Dustur al-Mar'a al-Muslima," *al-Ikhwan al-Muslimun*, 19 Sha'ban 1352/6 December 1933, 21–22, and Muhammad Hilmi Nur al-Din, "al-Nisa'iyyat: Ihtijab al-Nisa' Wajib," *al-Ikhwan al-Muslimun*, 19 Muharram 1353/3 May 1934, 21–22.

27. John Calvert, *Sayyid Qutb and the Origins of Radical Islamism* (Oxford, UK: Oxford University Press, 2013), 150–51.

28. al-Sayyid Sabiq, "Min Qadaya al-Mujtama'," *al-Tawhid*, Dhu al-Qa'da 1396/~October 1975, 10–24.

Sabiq (d. 1968), who had begun his life in the Jamʿiyya Sharʿiyya.[29] In contradistinction to Sidqi and al-Albani, Sabiq emphasized the broader social implications of female flaunting, namely the "corruption of morals and destruction of norms of comportment" (*inḥilāl al-akhlāq wa tadmīr al-ādāb*).[30]

Sabiq's former colleagues in the Jamʿiyya Sharʿiyya also maintained a keen interest in the challenge of gender mixing. The topic would first arise a year into the print run of *al-Iʿtisam*, when Ahmad ʿIsa ʿAshur (d. 1990), a leading scholar within the movement, noted the danger posed by men mixing with women (*ikhtilāṭ al-rijāl bi-l-nisāʾ*) on the beaches of Alexandria,[31] a concern that he would repeat the next month in greater detail.[32] To the extent that the organization's leaders sought to address this matter, however, their legal argumentation was extremely vague: in June 1946, ʿAli Hasan Hulwa opposed men and women mixing in the mosque based on a Prophetic hadith about the virtue of women praying in their homes rather than the mosque,[33] while in February 1947, he invoked the prohibition against "flaunting" (*tabarruj*) as a reason that mixing in cinemas, theaters, and social clubs should be forbidden.[34] As Hulwa raised the threat of flaunting, his fundamental concern was how women might use their sexuality to seek male attention.

As the 1950s progressed and rates of bureaucratic employment among men and women alike expanded,[35] members of the Jamʿiyya Sharʿiyya would also

29. ʿAbd Allah ʿUqayl, *Min Aʿlam al-Daʿwa wa'l-Haraka al-Islamiyya al-Muʿasira* (Amman, Jordan: Dar al-Bashir, 2008), 299.

30. al-Sayyid Sabiq, *Fiqh al-Sunna* (Beirut: Dar al-Kutub al-ʿArabi, 1973), 2:213. After facing political harassment under ʿAbd al-Nasir, Sabiq left Egypt to join the faculty of King ʿAbd al-ʿAziz University in Jeddah, later becoming the Dean of the Faculty of Shariʿa at Umm al-Qura University in Mecca. See ʿUqayl, *Min Aʿlam al-Daʿwa wa'l-Haraka al-Islamiyya al-Muʿasira*, 299–309.

31. Ahmad ʿIsa ʿAshur, "Khawatir," *al-Iʿtisam*, 10 Rabiʿ al-Awwal 1359/18 April 1940, 3–5, at 4.

32. Ahmad ʿIsa ʿAshur, "Khawatir," *al-Iʿtisam*, 16 Rabiʿ al-Thani 1359/23 May 1940, 6–9, at 8.

33. Hulwa was specifically concerned with preventing men and women from interacting within the mosque based on the pretext of feigning old age (*al-tamshīkh*). See Hulwa, "Asʾila wa Ajwiba," *al-Iʿtisam*, 8 Rajab 1365/8 June 1946, 2.

34. ʿAli Hasan Hulwa, "Asʾila wa Ajwiba," *al-Iʿtisam*, 10 Rabiʿ al-Awwal 1366/~1 February 1947, 14–16. Unlike Ibn Baz three decades later, however, Hulwa did not claim that flaunting and mixing were synonymous.

35. Laura Bier, *Revolutionary Womanhood: Feminisms, Modernity, and the State in Nasser's Egypt* (Stanford, CA: Stanford University Press, 2011), 65–68, and Wickham, *Mobilizing Islam*, 25–28.

articulate a pronounced concern with gender dynamics in the workplace. Most notably, in a July 1958 fatwa, Hulwa responded to a reader who noted that "government ministries have become accustomed to appointing many young women (*taʿyīn al-kathīrāt min al-fatayāt*)," leading to extensive mixing in these bodies' offices. In response, Hulwa merely assured the questioner that he must command right and forbid wrong in his heart when faced with "evils" (*munkarāt*) that he is unable to change or speak out against.[36] Similarly, an article in the August 1958 issue of *al-Iʿtisam* expresses concern with the "absolute chaos" (*al-fawḍā al-muṭlaqa*) of women in Egyptian schools and institutes.[37] At this time, though, orderly separation of men and women was not an option even as gender mixing had become an increasing concern among Islamic movements more broadly.

In Saudi Arabia, on the other hand, it would be Muhammad b. Ibrahim, then head of the Committee for Commanding Right and Forbidding Wrong (*Hayʾat al-Amr bi-l-Maʿrūf waʾl-Nahī ʿan al-Munkar*), who helped to make gender segregation a social imperative. An October 1955 fatwa noted the potential threat posed by the Christian wives of foreign engineers mixing with Saudi men,[38] while an August 1960 fatwa again expressed concern over foreign women walking unveiled in the Eastern Saudi city of Khobar, a major area of oil extraction.[39] Increasingly, this concern of gender mixing became more clearly focused on interactions *among* Saudi citizens: an August 1963 fatwa expressed concern regarding men who intentionally visited the zoo in an unnamed Saudi city on the day set aside exclusively for women,[40] a March 1966 fatwa stated that *ḥisba* functionaries (*muḥasibīn*) should not mix with female teachers within the schools at which they are employed,[41] and a 1966 fatwa expressed concern over "lower-class men" (*saflat al-rijāl*) mixing with women at textile markets (*aswāq al-aqmisha*).[42]

36. "Asʾila wa Ajwiba," *al-Iʿtisam*, Dhu al-Hijja 1377/July 1958, 24–6 at 24–5.

37. Mustafa Mujahid, "Lamhat Islamiyya," *al-Iʿtisam*, Muharram 1378/August 1958, 4–6, at 5.

38. Muhammad b. Ibrahim, *Fatawa wa Rasaʾil Samahat al-Shaykh Muhammad b. Ibrahim b. ʿAbd al-Latif Al al-Shaykh*, 10:44.

39. Ibn Ibrahim, *Fatawa wa Rasaʾil*, 10:45.

40. Ibn Ibrahim, *Fatawa wa Rasaʾil*, 10:47.

41. Ibn Ibrahim, *Fatawa wa Rasaʾil*, 10:47.

42. Ibn Ibrahim, *Fatawa wa Rasaʾil*, 10:46–7.

The story of gender segregation would also carry secular particularities. In Egypt, both the Brotherhood focus on public morality and the emergence of nascent Salafi claims to regulate gender relations were shaped by ʿAbd al-Nasir's project of state feminism, in which women were both objects and agents of development.[43] The centrality of women to Egyptian nationalism was not new: the female body had served as a site of nationalist battles under the British colonial (1882–1922) and semicolonial (1923–1952) rule. Yet, state feminism recruited the body to new ends. As Laura Bier argues, "[I]t was the unveiled and active presence of women in an outer sphere of progress that marked the Nasserist public sphere as modern, secular, and socialist."[44] Conversely, managing this female presence—including women's capacity to signal support for varied ideological projects through their clothing—became the new challenge.

In the Egyptian case, the question also emerged because the entrance of Egyptian women into public life aroused male anxieties over professional and domestic authority. The extension of education to females led to a threefold increase in girls' primary school enrollment,[45] while expanded employment of women, particularly as primary and secondary educators and civil servants, challenged men's economic centrality.[46] In both instances, this shift was largely urban; the presence of women in workspaces, especially the fields, was a long-standing reality of agricultural labor.[47] These urban anxieties could only be assuaged through veiling. Though state feminism rejected sartorial veiling as a form of "reactionary traditionalism," it trumpeted the "veiling of conduct" to relieve the tensions of mixed workspaces.[48] This approach to veiling as a "performative boundary"[49] preceded the public performances of piety that came to define gender segregation, yet is tied to them, both spatially and ideologically.

By contrast, Saudi debates over gender segregation reflected the consequences of a project of economic development which brought a flood of non-

43. Bier, *Revolutionary Womanhood*, 24–25.

44. Bier, *Revolutionary Womanhood*, 62.

45. Bier notes the massive expansion of female education under Nasser: the number of girls studying in primary schools increased from 541,712 in 1952 to 1.4 million in 1969 (*Revolutionary Womanhood*, 51).

46. Bier, *Revolutionary Womanhood*, 76.

47. For a Jordanian example, see Richard Antoun, "On the Modesty of Women in Arab Muslim Villages: A Study in the Accommodation of Traditions," *American Anthropologist* 70, no. 4 (August 1968): 682.

48. Bier, *Revolutionary Womanhood*, 92.

49. Bier, *Revolutionary Womanhood*, 98.

Muslims into Saudi Arabia as part of a larger effort to cultivate a robust oil industry. Though Saudi Arabia had first signed an oil concession in 1933, rapid development only began with the 1944 formation of the Arabian American Oil Company (known as ARAMCO) by Standard Oil of New Jersey, Mobil Oil, Standard Oil of California, and Texaco.[50]

While interaction between Western and Saudi ARAMCO employees at sites such as the Eastern Province city of Dhahran was limited by separate living quarters[51] and by a basic aversion against "mixing" (*al-ikhtilāṭ*) with non-Muslims,[52] the number of Saudis it employed in "semiskilled or higher" positions grew from 24 percent of employees (6,932) in 1949 to 66 percent of all such employees (13,400) by 1959.[53] This growth, though in theory limited to compounds, meant that this foreign presence was an increasingly notable aspect of Saudi society in the 1950s and 1960s, with the exception of Mecca and Medina, from which non-Muslims were barred.

Yet, while foreign women may have been an impetus for considering the dangers of gender mixing, their presence was but one piece in a larger puzzle of regulating Saudi society in the face of expanding mass education and employment for women. Article 155 of the 1968 educational policy (*siyāsat al-taʿlīm*) stipulated that "mixing between boys and girls (*al-ikhtilāṭ bayna al-banīn waʾl-banāt*) is to be prevented at all stages of education except in nurseries and kindergartens,"[54] while the 1969 labor law prohibited "mixing between women and men in the workplace or in any related facilities or

50. Previously, the California-Arabian Standard Oil Company had been formed in 1933 to develop the Hasa oil field concession. See Michael Quentin Morton, *Buraimi: The Struggle for Power, Influence and Oil in Saudi Arabia* (London: I.B. Taurus, 2013), x.

51. In 1951, ARAMCO first offered Saudi employees a subsidized loan plan to support home purchases, and in 1954, it began to assist in the establishment of new municipalities, most notably Rahima (on the northwest end of Ras Tunra) and Madinat Abqaiq, in the Abqaiq area. By 1959, a total of almost 2,100 employees had participated in the loan plan. See Roy Lebkicher, *Aramco Handbook* (N.P.: ARAMCO, 1960), 214–16.

52. Madawi Al-Rasheed, *A History of Saudi Arabia* (Cambridge, UK: Cambridge University Press, 2010), 92–93.

53. Lebkicher, *Aramco Handbook*, 210–11.

54. "Wathiqat Siyasat al-Taʿlim 1379," *Manhal al-Thaqafa al-Tarbawiyya*, https://www.manhal.net/art/s/12262, accessed 20 February 2018. In the Saudi system, boys' education fell under the authority of the Ministry of Education and girls' under that of the General Presidency of Girls' Education. See Mona AlMunajjed, *Women in Saudi Arabia Today* (London: Macmillan Press Ltd, 1997), 66.

elsewhere" (*ikhtilāṭ al-nisā' bi-l-rijāl fī amkinat al-ʿamal wa mā yatbaʿahā min marāfiq wa ghayrihā*).[55] The significance of this legislation in the realm of education would only increase as enrollment in girls' education swelled nearly sixfold between 1964 and 1975, from 50,000 to 284,000.[56]

Gender-segregated schools were part and parcel of a broader effort to define distinct male and female circulation, and the 1969 labor law had not succeeded in rooting out mixed-gender offices. More to the point, though, there was still a leap that had yet to be made from arguing that *particular* spaces should be exclusively male or female—a position with significant grounding in the Islamic scholarly tradition—to claiming that society *as a whole* should function according to this logic of visual separation. As the 1970s arrived, Salafi writers on both sides of the Red Sea would seek to articulate a vision of gender relations that moved beyond existing legal precedents or policies. In the process, these thinkers inaugurated a shift that would radically alter women's legal position as public participants in Egypt and support the expansion of the separation of men and women in Saudi Arabia.

A CHANGING SOCIAL TOPOGRAPHY

As the 1970s dawned, Salafi scholars in Egypt and Saudi Arabia turned to making a textual case for comprehensive gender segregation. Such a case, however, was not born fully formed, nor was it immediately dominant. Here, we return to Niʿmat Sidqi, whose pamphlet *Flaunting* was first published in Cairo in 1951 and then in Damascus in 1954. The 1970s and early 1980s, however, would see nearly a dozen separate editions in not only Cairo and Damascus, but also in Morocco, Tunisia, and Kuwait.[57] Indeed, in Cairo alone, no fewer

55. An English language translation of the 1969 Labor Law can be found on the website of the Saudi Arabia Embassy in Washington, DC (https://www.saudiembassy.net/labor-and-workmen-law#Employment%20of%20Women, accessed 20 February 2018). The original Arabic version is available at https://tinyurl.com/yd42bls8.

56. AlMunajjed, *Women in Saudi Arabia Today*, 64–65.

57. For the publication of *al-Tabarruj* outside Egypt, see Sidqi, *al-Tabarruj* (Casablanca, Morocco: Dur al-Furqan li-l-Nashr wa'l-Hadith, 1975); Sidqi, *al-Tabarruj* (Tunis, Tunisia: Dar Bu Salama li-l-Tibaʿa wa'l-Nashr, 1981); Sidqi, *al-Tabarruj* (Kuwait City, Kuwait: Maktabat al-Saha al-Islamiyya, 1983).

than six publishers distributed this book between 1971 and 1976.[58] The notion that female modesty was sufficient to safeguard a neotraditional gender order remained prominent in Salafi circles.

The turn to enforced gender segregation also occurred at a time of significant transition for Islamic movements broadly. While an Islamic Revival that included Muslim Brothers, Salafis, scholars, state bureaucrats, and student activists emerged in Egypt during the second half of the decades, it was student activists alone who defined the early years of the 1970s in Egypt. Most notably, Jamaʿat Shabab al-Islam (The Muslim Youth Group) was established during the 1972–73 academic year, alongside a previously existing movement, al-Jamaʿa al-Diniyya (The Religious Group). Both, in turn, would merge with a third faction, the Jamaʿa Islamiyya (The Islamic Group, also known as the Islamic Student Movement), by 1974.[59] The Jamaʿa Islamiyya would soon distinguish itself by holding summer camps (*muʿaskarāt*), providing subsidized modest clothing to Egyptian women, and even policing public buses to prevent gender mixing.[60]

Yet the infrastructure of Islamic student activists during this period was highly rudimentary. Jamaʿa Islamiyya and later Brotherhood leader ʿAbd al-Munʿim Abu-l-Futuh recounts his experience during 1971–1972 academic year:

> At that time, mentioning the Muslim Brotherhood was prohibited as was [possessing] their books. During this period, the [only] books which were widespread were those of Ansar al-Sunna al-Muhammadiyya and the Jamʿiyya Sharʿiyya, and the books of [the Pakistani Islamist thinker] Abu-l-Aʿla al-Mawdudi. . . . Books of the Salafi orientation (*al-ittijāh al-Salafī*) were distributed free of charge at universities . . . and [we also had access to some] books from the noble al-Azhar.[61]

58. Specifically, Matbaʿat al-ʿAsima (1971), Dar al-ʿUlum li-l-Tibaʿa waʾl-Nashr (1972, 1973), Dar ʿAlam al-Kutub (1972), Dar al-Wahdan li-l-Tibaʿa waʾl-Nashr (1975), and Dar al-Iʿtisam (1975, 1976, 1981).

59. Abdullah al-Arian, *Answering the Call: Popular Islamic Activism in Sadat's Egypt* (Oxford: Oxford University Press, 2014), 59–70, esp. 69.

60. Badr Muhammad Badr, *al-Jamaʿa al-Islamiyya fi Jamiʿat Misr: Haqaʾiq wa Wathaʾiq* (Cairo: N.P., N.D.), 27,111.

61. ʿAbd al-Munʿim Abu-l-Futuh, *ʿAbd al-Munʿim Abu-l-Futuh: Shahid ʿala Tarikh al-Haraka al-Islamiyya fi Misr, 1970–1984*, ed. Hussam Tammam (Cairo: Dar al-Shuruq, 2012), 40.

Though the position of the Jama'a Islamiyya improved in 1975 when the organization's success in the General Union of Egyptian Students elections provided it with access to printing facilities in which it could produce pamphlets,[62] this organization was still limited to university campuses.

Such organizational challenges extended to Islamic movements more broadly. As Khalid ʿAbd al-Qadir ʿAwda, an Islamic student activist in Asyut, noted with regard to the Muslim Brotherhood, "there was no organization (*tanẓīm*). . . . There was merely the 'idea of the Brotherhood'" (*fikrat al-Ikhwān*).[63] The Jamʿiya Sharʿiyya and Ansar al-Sunna, on the other hand, had maintained their educational networks, yet neither had any significant experience in laying claim to public space more broadly.[64] Under al-Sadat, an increasingly open environment for Islamic activism meant that, for the first time, Salafi men and women could explore what a vision of public morality centered on female modesty might look like in practice.

In Saudi Arabia, by contrast, the question of gender mixing came to take center stage at a time of religious tumult. At stake was the religious monopoly of state-aligned scholars, and ʿAbd al-ʿAziz b. Baz sought to maintain his control over religious challengers, some of whom belonged to the *Sahwa* movement, and others of whom, most notably Ahl al-Hadith, strongly opposed this movement for its Islamist-inspired view of the legitimacy of political activity.[65] While Egyptian Salafis worked to upset the status quo, Saudi Salafis attempted to maintain it.

Just as important were changing demographic realities. Between 1947 and 1976, Egypt's population had grown from 18.8 million to 36.6 million, and this growth was primarily urban: the percentage of the Egyptian population living in cities rose from 33 to 44 percent, and the number of urban inhabitants from

62. Gilles Kepel, *Muslim Extremism in Egypt: The Prophet and Pharaoh*, trans. Jon Rothschild (London: al-Saqi Books, 1985), 141.

63. *Hadith Dhikrayat maʿa Khalid ʿAbd Al-Qadir ʿAwda, al-Juzʾa al-Awwal*. Perf. Khalid ʿAbd al-Qadir ʿAwda. Ikhwantube, 2010.

64. These two organizations' reemergence was far from assured: in 1967, ʿAbd al-Nasir had forcibly merged them while placing an ally, ʿAbd al-Rahman Amin, as President. In 1973, however, al-Sadat allowed Ansar al-Sunna and the Jamʿiyya Sharʿiyya to become independent organizations once again. See Tahir, *Jamaʿat Ansar al-Sunna al-Muhammadiyya*, 148, 241, respectively.

65. Lacroix, *Awakening Islam*, 73–109.

6.2 million to 16.1 million.[66] The number of students enrolled in higher education grew even more rapidly, increasing from one to four million between 1951 and 1976, of which 30.4 percent were women.[67] Crucially, these shifts occurred without a proportional expansion of infrastructure. In the university setting, the result was overcrowded lecture halls and classrooms that often were filled to several times capacity.[68] As personal space in public decreased, the threat of physical contact increased.

In Saudi Arabia, by contrast, dramatic demographic change went hand in hand with a newfound expansion of the educational system. Between 1960 and 1981, the population grew from 4.08 million to 10.37 million,[69] and the portion of the population that was urbanized increased from 49 to 66 percent.[70] This growth was mirrored by educational enrollment, male and female and, by the 1982–1983 academic year, the number of female students in primary and secondary institutions had reached 700,000, constituting 39 percent of a total student population of 1.78 million.[71] Unlike in Egypt, the issue was not overcrowding, at least not as a result of co-education: when King ʿAbd al-ʿAziz University opened its doors in 1971, it offered gender segregated campuses to its young male and female students.[72] The fact remained, though, that increasing numbers of Saudi as well as Egyptian women left their homes daily to attend school and to work.

As Salafi scholars began to debate gender segregation, basic questions of female modesty remained unresolved. One internal division among Salafis was whether a woman's face should be classified as part of her nudity (*ʿawra*): al-Albani rejected this claim, and al-Sayyid Sabiq would cite this Salafi lumi-

66. Saad Eddin Ibrahim, *Egypt, Islam and Democracy: Twelve Critical Essays* (Cairo: AUC Press, 1996), 99.

67. Central Agency for Public Mobilization and Statistics, *1976 Population and Housing Census* (Cairo: Central Agency for Publication Mobilization and Statistics, 1980), 1:29.

68. Egyptian universities enrolled approximately four times their capacity, with Arts, Law and Commerce faculties particularly overcrowded. See Mahmoud Abdel-Fadil, *The Political Economy of Nasserism: A Study in Employment and Income Distribution Policies in Urban Egypt, 1952–72* (Cambridge, UK: Cambridge University Press, 1980), 354–55.

69. "Saudi Arabia," *The World Bank*, https://data.worldbank.org/indicator/SP.POP.TOTL?locations = SA, accessed 20 February 2018.

70. Anthony H. Cordesman, *Saudi Arabia Enters the Twenty-First Century: The Political, Foreign Policy, Economic and Energy Dimensions* (Westport, CT: Praeger, 2003), 232.

71. AlMunajjed, *Women in Saudi Arabia Today*, 65.

72. AlMunajjed, *Women in Saudi Arabia Today*, 68.

nary in the pages of *al-Tawhid* as he, too, took this position.[73] By contrast, Niʿmat Sidqi and Ibn Baz both argued that the face and the hands alike fall into this category.[74] This dispute, while unresolved, was not new: al-Albani's position on this matter had reportedly contributed to Muhammad b. Ibrahim's decision to expel him from the Kingdom and from his position at the Islamic University of Medina in 1963.[75] Similarly, the *niqab* had limited social presence at this time: Fatima ʿAbd al-Hadi, a member of the Muslim Sisters (*al-Akhawāt al-Muslimāt*), recounts that, prior to the 1970s, "we did not hear of the *niqab* at all (*ama al-niqāb fa-lam nasmaʿ bihi waqtihā abad*^{an})."[76]

Notwithstanding this interpretative disagreement, the crucial difference among challengers was environmental. In Egypt, Salafi scholars competed with a reconstituted Brotherhood as each sought to lay claim to the mantle of religious authority in the face of a regime that claimed to be pursuing top-down Islamization[77] while simultaneously adopting an open-door economic policy that occasioned despair over the moral decline of Egyptian society.[78] The Brotherhood's advantage as a popular force lay in its religiously-based political program: through the reformation of state and society, everyday life could be rendered "Islamic." By contrast, Ansar al-Sunna did not have a vision of broad-based social change, yet had to compete with an organization that promised not merely ethical and ritual rectitude but also sociopolitical change. A growing Salafi-Islamist faction within the Jamʿiyya Sharʿiyya found itself doubly torn: because the Muslim Brotherhood was the unquestioned premier claimant to Islamism, a successful Salafi claim to Islamism would necessitate a self-differentiation that did not burn bridges with Salafi theological and

73. al-Albani, *Hijab al-Mar'a al-Muslima fi al-Kitab wa'l-Sunna*, 6; al-Sayyid Sabiq, "Min Qadaya al-Mujtamaʿ," *al-Tawhid*, Dhu al-Qaʿda 1396/October 1976, 24.

74. Sidqi, *al-Tabarruj*, 13; ʿAbd al-ʿAziz b. Baz, *Fatawa Nur ʿala al-Darb li-Samahat al-Imam ʿAbd al-ʿAziz b. ʿAbd Allah b. Baz*, ed. Abd Allah b. Muhammad al-Tayyar and Muhammad b. Musa b. ʿAbd Allah Al Musa (Riyadh: Dar al-Watan li-l-Nashr, N.D.), 1:2211–13.

75. Al-Albani's attacks on the Hanbali school of jurisprudence and Muhammad b. ʿAbd al-Wahhab also likely contributed to his expulsion. See Lacroix, *Awakening Islam*, 84–85.

76. ʿAbd al-Hadi, *Rihlati maʿa al-Akhawat al-Muslimat*, 16.

77. The 1971 Constitution set the Islamic Shariʿa as a "principle source of legislation" and a 1980 amendment defined it "*the* principle source" (italics added). See Skovgaard-Petersen, *Defining Islam for the Egyptian State*, 199–200.

78. On discourses of moral decline relating to the *Infitah*, see Relli Shechter, "From Effendi to Infitahi? Consumerism and Its Malcontents in the Emergence of Egyptian Market Society," *British Journal of Middle Eastern Studies* 36, no. 1 (2009): 21–35.

legal commitments.[79] In addition, neither Salafis nor Brothers wanted to challenge al-Sadat directly at this time; their interests were best served through ostensibly apolitical claims to pious practice.

Visible claims to morality thus represented an opportunity for safe yet powerful protest, promising a public reward of authenticity with minimal threat of repression. The basic difficulty, however, was that the Salafi position of condemning flaunting (*tabarruj*) and unveiled dress (*sufūr*) did not distinguish them from the Brotherhood. Instead, the Brotherhood's position on female sartorial piety—that a woman's *ʿawra* does not include her face and hands[80]—did not differ substantially from many of their Salafi counterparts. Though individual Salafi thinkers such as Sidqi may have argued that the face and hands are *ʿawra*, there was little difference between al-Albani's view and that of the Brotherhood on this particular question. Put differently, there was no surefire means of visually distinguishing a Salafi woman from her Islamist counterparts.

By contrast, in Saudi Arabia, the question of gender segregation cut to the heart of the claim made by Wahhabi-Hanbali and Salafi scholars over Saudi society. The Saudi religious establishment and the royal family had struck a deal in the early 1960s for the former to provide a religious sanction for new technologies (radio and television) and female education in exchange for greater say regarding female sartorial practice and gender relations.[81] Ibn Baz's call to expand gender segregation during the second half of the 1970s would solidify and expand this pact not merely between scholars and the King, but also between Salafi and Wahhabi-Hanbali factions within the Kingdom's scholarly elite.

Ibn Baz also sought to channel the challenge posed by Saudi *Sahwa* youth. In his capacity as vice president of the Islamic University of Medina,

79. During the 1970s, the organization was split between those within it, most notably ʿAbd al-Latif al-Mushtahiri and Mahmud ʿAbd al-Wahhab Fayyad, who were recognized by Ansar al-Sunna as being "inclined to the Salafi Call" (*yumīlūn ilā al-Daʿwa al-Salafiyya*), and others who were not. See "Akhbar al-Jamaʿa," *al-Hadi al-Nabawi*, Ramadan 1380/February 1961, 50. Other segments of the Jamʿiyya Sharʿiyya, however, had shifted towards Islamism in a manner that gave priority to religio-political change over theological commitments or legal process. See ʿImad Siyam, "al-Haraka al-Islamiyya waʾl-Jamʿiyyat al-Ahliyya fi Misr," in *al-Jamʿiyyat al-Ahliyya al-Islamiyya fi Misr*, ed. ʿAbd al-Ghafar Shukr (Cairo: Dar al-Amin, 2006), 130.

80. "Bab al-Iftaʾ," *al-Daʿwa*, Rabiʿ al-Awwal 1397/February 1977, 49.

81. Mouline, *The Clerics of Islam*, 211.

he oversaw a largely foreign-born faculty, in which Muslim Brothers from abroad played an increasingly prominent role in everything from instruction to curricular development.[82] The challenge was not merely cross-pollination among Wahhabi-Hanbali, Salafi, and Islamist ideas, but also the question of how to manage the Saudi youth who had adopted them as they sought to "'politicize everyday life.'"[83] It was here that Ibn Baz, as representative of a religious establishment that sought to limit the political thrust of religious activism, would soon lay claim to gender segregation as a state initiative in order to dampen the challenge posed by these youth.[84]

BETWEEN SAUDI ARABIA AND EGYPT: DEBATING THE FUTURE OF GENDER SEGREGATION

As Saudi scholars turned to making a case for gender segregation, their task was facilitated by existing structural realities: educational institutions, from primary schools through university, were already segregated by gender. Yet these discrete spaces were insufficient and, in late 1968, a professor at the Islamic University of Medina, ʿAtiyya Salim, stressed the importance of "preventing mixing not merely in universities, but in all public sites of interaction" (*lā fī al-jāmiʿa fa-ḥasb bal fī kull al-ijtimāʿāt*).[85] A native of Egypt who had studied with Salafi scholars such as Ibn Baz, al-ʿAfifi, ʿAbd al-Razzaq Hamza (d. 1972) and the Maliki scholar Muhammad Amin al-Shinqiti (d. 1973),[86] Salim was nonetheless careful to emphasize that IUM supported female education as long as it occurred separately from men.[87]

Salim's ambitions, however, stood in tension with rulings within the IUM magazine itself. In a 1972 fatwa, an unidentified petitioner asked whether

82. Farquhar, *Circuits of Faith*, 129–56. Brothers would come to play key roles in other leading educational institutions, such as King ʿAbd al-ʿAziz University in Mecca and Imam Muhammad Ibn Saʿud University in Riyadh. See Lacroix, *Awakening Islam*, 43–44.

83. Lacroix, *Awakening Islam*, 60.

84. Lacroix, *Awakening Islam*, 78.

85. ʿAtiyya Salim, "Mashakil al-Tullab al-Jamiʿin wa Halluha ʿala Dawʾ al-Islam," *Majallat al-Jamiʿa al-Islamiyya bi-l-Madina al-Munawwara*, 1:140–44, at 142 (#1).

86. "Hadath fi Mithl Hadha al-Yawm," *al-Bawaba al-Iliktruniyya li-Muhafazat al-Sharqiyya* 19 July 1999, http://www.sharkia.gov.eg/Event/event_dis2017.aspx?ID = 429, accessed 14 May 2020.

87. ʿAtiyya Salim, "Mashakil al-Tullab al-Jamiʿin wa Halluha ʿala Dawʾ al-Islam," 1:144.

women "whose intent is sound" (*niyātunā salīma*) could mix with men in the context of employment. In response, an unnamed mufti ruled simply that "women must not reveal their faces and must not mix with unrelated men while uncovered" (*ʿadam al-ikhtilāṭ bi-l-ajānib wa-hiya mutakashafa*).[88] Implicit in this response, however, was the assumption that if women *were* veiled, they could meet with unrelated men. That efforts to implement comprehensive gender segregation were still incomplete is similarly evident in a March 1976 article by Ibn Baz in IUM's journal, in which he praised Shaykh Ahmad Muhammad Jamal (d. 1993), an author of popular Islamic texts, for calling for the removal of all female employees from cinemas and all businesses in which they are engaged in "male roles" (*al-majalāt al-rijāliyya*) such as high-ranking administrators (*sakratīriyyāt*).[89] As in the case of the 1972 fatwa, the issue for Ibn Baz is not *yet* the segregation of men and women in all public spaces, but rather a specific focus on women at private-sector companies, especially those who worked in positions that elevated them above men.

Sahwa youth, though, were increasingly exposed to debates over gender mixing. While these youth lacked a periodical of their own at this time—*al-Bayan* would only begin to publish in 1986—they frequently received copies of *al-Mujtamaʿ*, a weekly magazine published by The Association of Social Reform (*Jamʿiyyat al-Islah al-Ijtimaʿi*), which was the Kuwaiti branch of the Muslim Brotherhood.[90] *Al-Mujtamaʿ*, in turn, was chock full of articles about the threat of gender mixing in Kuwait, especially at Kuwait University. In this context, an issue of particular concern was that university leisure areas remained mixed, even as the Parliament (*Majlis al-Umma*) had passed a law on 17 July 1967 to separate men and women on a university level.[91]

Al-Mujtamaʿ would also host Ibn Baz's first effort to link flaunting and gender mixing in March 1974. As this prominent Saudi Salafi scholar explained:

88. "al-Fatawa," *Majallat al-Jamiʿa al-Islamiyya bi-l-Madina al-Munawwara*, 7:113–4 (#19).

89. ʿAbd al-ʿAziz b. Baz, "Taʾyid wa-Shukr," *Majallat al-Jamiʿa al-Islamiyya bi-l-Madina al-Munawwara*, Rabiʿ al-Awwal 1396/March 1976, 11:371–12:68, at 11:371 (#32). Jamal taught at King ʿAbd al-ʿAziz and Umm al-Qurra Universities and harbored a particular interest in Islamist thought. See Muhammad Khayr Ramadan Yusuf and Khayr al-Din Zirkili, *Tatimmat al-Aʿlam li-l-Zirkili* (Beirut: Dar Ibn Hazm, 1998), 1:55–58

90. Lacroix, *Awakening Islam*, 60.

91. ʿAli Muhammad, "al-Ikhtilat," *al-Mujtamaʿ*, 21 Shaʿban 1393/18 September 1973, 26.

> [Women flaunting leads to] fornication and obscenities (*al-zinā' wa'l-fawāḥish*), bringing young men and women together in one class or even on one chair (*fī kursī wāḥid*) . . . [and] is one of the greatest cases of temptation (*fitna*) and evil. . . . Mixing is a cause of temptations and battle (*al-qitāl*) and conflicts among families (*al-nizā' bayna al-usar*).[92]

Although Ibn Baz had limited ability to shape the conversation within *al-Mujtama'* as he could within the Saudi religious establishment, he had found a sympathetic outlet, whose editors and writers separately expressed a concern with similar phenomena in Egypt,[93] Yemen,[94] and Qatar.[95] Indeed, a writer in *al-Mujtama'* even took aim at Riyadh University's Faculty of Education, which had allegedly used male teachers for all-female classes.[96] Gender segregation represented both an opportunity for Ibn Baz to expand his reach into society, and a potential source of vulnerability if he failed to do so. In contrast to the debates that followed, however, this leading Salafi scholar did not claim that flaunting and mixing were equivalent, only that one led inexorably to the other.

Four years later, Ibn Baz publishing a lengthy article entitled "The Danger of Women Joining Men in Their Workplaces" in the Islamic University of Medina's flagship journal, *Majallat al-Jami'a al-Islamiyya.* This article, the bulk of which would later be serialized in three parts in Ansar al-Sunna's *al-Tawhid,* sought to prove ironclad textual justification for a Salafi case against gender mixing. As Ibn Baz looked to his Wahhabi-Hanbali peers, he would have undoubtedly been aware of Ibn Ibrahim's previous argument against gender mixing through appeal to the five objectives of the Shari'a (*Maqāṣid al-Sharī'a*).[97] The problem with this case for Ibn Baz, however, was the absence

92. "Liqa'at al-Mujtama'," *al-Mujtama'*, 7 Jumada al-Ula 1394/28 March 1974, 15–18.

93. Ba'da al-Tajriba al-Mut'iba fi Misr 'Awda ila "Adam al-Ikhtilat,'" *al-Mujtama'*, 16 Jumada al-Ula 1395/27 May 1975, 11.

94. "Limadha al-Ikhtilat fi Jami'at San'a'?," *al-Mujtama'*, 3 Dhu al-Hijja 1394/17 December 1974, 42.

95. "al-Dirasa al-Mukhtalita fi Dawlat Qatar al-Shaqiqa," *al-Mujtama'*, 22 Dhu al-Qa'da 1398/24 October 1978, 16–17.

96. "Liqa' al-Mujtama' ma'a Taliba min Kuliyyat al-Tarbiya fi al-Riyad," *al-Mujtama'*, 9 Rajab 1396/6 July 1976, 26–32.

97. The five objectives of the Shari'a are the protection of the faith (*al-dīn*), the soul (*al-nafs*), wealth (*al-māl*), the mind (*al-'aql*), and one's offspring (*al-nasl*). For a prominent example of the use of this justification in modern Islamic thought, see al-Qaradawi, *Dirasa fi Fiqh Maqasid al-Shari'a.* Muhammad b. Ibrahim also sought to inductively demonstrate the prohi

of persuasive proof texts: Ibn Ibrahim had not pointed to a verse in the Quran or hadith report in the Sunna that explicitly forbade, or even mentioned, gender mixing.

The turn to emphasize gender segregation also intervened in a conflict then brewing between the Minister of Interior Prince Nayf b. ʿAbd al-ʿAziz (d. 2012) and the Minister of Labor and Social Affairs, Shaykh Ibrahim al-ʿAnqari (d. 2008). The crux of the disagreement was female employment in mixed gender workplaces. As Nayf sought to limit women's employment to hospitals, schools for girls, women's prisons, and charitable associations, Ibn Baz would fashion a textual justification rooted not in the broader goals of the Shariʿa, but in canonical texts.

In order to elevate the principle of absolute gender segregation above the claim that modest comportment and dress are a sufficient protection against illicit contact and broader social disorder, this leading Saudi Salafi offered a domestically-oriented interpretation of Q 33:33: "And abide in your houses (*wa qarna fī buyūtikuna*) and do not display yourselves (*lā tabarrajna*) as was the custom in the manner of women in the time of Jahiliyya. . . ." Instead of merely stressing the important role that the Muslim woman play domestically, Ibn Baz insisted that the phrase "and abide in your houses" requires domestic seclusion (*al-qarār fi-baytihā*). Ibn Baz emphasized that this injunction was inseparable from the warning to avoid flaunting.[98] Based on this interpretation, the issue at hand was not merely men and women being alone in an office environment, or women dressing immodestly in public. Rather, in order to eliminate the possibility of gender mixing in *any* context, women must remain secluded.

Perhaps sensing the limited textual appeal of this argument, Ibn Baz sought to bolster it through a novel interpretation of the injunction against flaunting

bition of gender-mixing based on the challenge of observing other Quranic commandments such as averting the gaze (*ghadd al-baṣr*). See Ibn Ibrahim, *Fatawa wa Rasaʾil*, 10: 35–41.

98. Ibn Baz, "Khatar Musharakat al-Marʾa li-l-Rajul fi Maydan ʿAmalih," *Majallat al-Jamiʿa al-Islamiyya bi-l-Madina al-Munawwara* Spring 1398/Spring 1978, 15:334–46, at 15:337 (#41). The information about the conflict between Prince Nayf b. ʿAbd al-ʿAziz and Shaykh Ibrahim al-ʿAnqari can be found at 15:345–6. The .Bok file only indicates issue number—here, #41—and I was unable to locate a hard copy or scanned version of the original. I was, however, able to find a scanned version of issue #36, which was published in Dhu al-Hijja 1397/November 1977. Additionally, issue #42 includes reference to an article published on 30 July 1978, which suggests that issue #41 was published somewhere in the Spring of 1978.

in Q 33:33. Specifically, he claimed that "the meaning of the command not to flaunt is a command not to mix" (*nahyuhā ʿan al-tabarruj maʿnāhu: al-nahī ʿan al-ikhtilāṭ*). Put differently, the mere act of women inhabiting the same spaces as men, whether for reasons of work, commerce or travel, constituted flaunting.[99] By contrast, scholars aligned with al-Azhar during this period highlighted the political and economic roles of the Prophet Muhammad's female companions.[100]

Almost as striking as this novel interpretative move to redefine the meaning of flaunting were the non-Islamic justifications that this key Salafi scholar gave for forbidding gender mixing. Ibn Baz cited a work by the founder of the Syrian Muslim Brotherhood, Mustafa al-Sibaʿi (d. 1964), on women, law, and Islam,[101] with the latter having likely found these sources in *al-Manar*.[102] Based on al-Sibaʿi's text, Ibn Baz invoked the ideas of the German philosopher Arthur Schopenhauer (d. 1860), Lady Cook (also known as Tennessee Claflin, d. 1923), Lord Byron (d. 1824), and Samuel Smiles (d. 1904) to support his view that gender mixing should be forbidden. Leaving aside the basic point that Ibn Baz's rendition of these authors was not necessarily consistent with the original intent—Lady Cook, for one, was an advocate of women's suffrage in the United States and opened up a Wall Street brokerage firm with her sister, Victoria Woodhull[103]—what is remarkable here is that this leading Salafi scholar made no effort to base his argument exclusively on canonical sources.

Instead, Ibn Baz explicitly justified drawing on non-Islamic sources:

99. Ibn Baz, "Khatar Musharakat al-Marʾa li-l-Rajul fi Maydan ʿAmalih," *Majallat al-Jamiʿa al-Islamiyya bi-l-Madina al-Munawwara* Spring 1398/Spring 1978, 15:334–46, at 15:336 (#41).

100. Ibrahim al-Fahham, "al-Marʾa waʾl-ʿAmal fi al-Islam," *Minbar al-Islam*, Muharram 1396/January 1976, 162.

101. Ibn Baz, "Khatar Musharakat al-Marʾa li-l-Rajul fi Maydan ʿAmalih," *Majallat al-Jamiʿa al-Islamiyya bi-l-Madina al-Munawwara*, Spring 1398/Spring 1978, 15:334–46, at 15:346 (#41). For the original, see Mustafa al-Sibaʿi, *al-Marʾa Bayna al-Fiqh waʾl-Qanun* (Beirut: Dar al-Warraq, 1420/1999), 141–44.

102. The language that al-Sibaʿi uses is nearly identical the text that appeared in *al-Manar*. See "al-Rijal waʾl-Nisaʾ," *al-Manar*, 1 Jumada al-Thaniyya 1319/15 September 1901, 4:481–9.

103. As Amanda Frisken notes, "Woodhull and Claflin challenged the notion that a female broker was improper because she performed public work in mixed company, unprotected in a world of men" (*Victoria Woodhull's Sexual Revolution: Political Theater and the Popular Press in Nineteenth-Century America* [Philadelphia: University of Pennsylvania Press, 2004], 2).

> We have noted both Islamic proof-texts (*al-adilla al-sharʿiyya*) and tangible reality (*al-wāqiʿ al-malmūs*) . . . but in light of the fact that some people might benefit (*qad yastafīdūn*) from the words of the men of the West and East more so than they benefit from the Word of God and His Prophet (peace be upon him) and the words of Muslim scholars, we have decided to transmit [these sources] in which men of the West and East acknowledge the harm of mixing and its corruptions (*maḍār al-ikhtilāṭ wa mafāsidihi*).[104]

It was not merely that Ibn Baz cited the scholarship of a leading Islamist to make his case; it was that, in doing so, he appeared to accept the persuasive limits of proof texts from the Quran and Sunna for even the students of the Islamic University of Medina as he made a novel case for gender segregation.

During this same time period, Ibn Baz also sought to shape the Egyptian debate over gender mixing. Unlike in Saudi Arabia, however, neither he nor his conversation partners had the power to drive policy within state institutions. In Egypt, the absence of gender segregated educational institutions forced a debate over alternative paths: in an article published in the May 1977 issue of *al-Iʿtisam*, ʿIsa ʿAbduh had proposed a "home university" (*jāmiʿat al-dār*), facilitated by television and radio broadcasts, through which a woman could reach a "scientific level" while remaining in her "religious stronghold."[105] These discussions, however, were short-lived, and nothing came of this program. Similarly, in the August 1977 issue of *al-Tawhid*, Ibrahim Ibrahim Hilal argued that, while women had a right to university education, such education should occur in a private setting in order to avoid gender mixing.[106] Like in Saudi Arabia, the question of education was merely the beginning of a shift towards (re)mapping public space.

Though Hilal had echoed ʿAbduh's proposal for distance learning, he and his colleagues within Ansar al-Sunna also trained their eyes on working women as they sought to distinguish themselves from the Muslim Brotherhood. In a three-part series in the summer of 1977, entitled "The Necessity of Women Returning to the Home," Hilal argued against female employment on social, economic and moral grounds. He began with a social argument:

104. Ibn Baz, "Khatar Musharakat al-Marʾa li-l-Rajul fi Maydan ʿAmalihi," *Majallat al-Jamiʿa al-Islamiyya bi-l-Madina al-Munawwara*, Fall 1398/1978, 15:334–46, at 15:343 (#41).

105. ʿIsa ʿAbduh, "Unshaʾu Jamiʿat al-Dar," *al-Iʿtisam*, Jumada al-Ula 1397/May 1977, 17.

106. Ibrahim Ibrahim Hilal, "Darurat ʿAwdat al-Marʾa ila al-Bayt," *al-Tawhid*, Ramadan 1397/August 1977, 44–45.

women are needed in the home to educate their children, thus protecting not only the welfare of the family, but also, more broadly, the moral and intellectual health of society.[107] In August 1977, Hilal followed up with an economic critique, arguing that female employment in the bureaucracy depresses male wages, thus making it necessary for both men and women to work. He proposed that women withdraw from state employment and, in exchange, the state would raise men's salaries by 50 to 60 percent.[108] The issue was not merely social or economic but also moral. As Hilal argued in September 1977, female employment destabilizes gender relations not only by facilitating illicit sexual contact, but also by placing women under the authority of men other than their husbands.[109] This state of affairs was compounded by the challenge of transportation: Hilal expressed his concern for "the woman who toils in offices and on mass transit" (*al-marʾa al-kādiḥa fī al-dawāwīn waʾl-muwāṣalāt*).[110]

The arguments made by Ibrahim Ibrahim Hilal in *al-Tawhid* were in large part echoed by ʿIsa ʿAbduh in *al-Iʿtisam*. As in the case of distance learning, however, ʿAbduh offered a recommendation rather than a legal prescription. Specifically, ʿAbduh argued that the employment of women to make ends meet harmed both men and women insofar as it limited the ability of women to fully perform their domestic roles while also depressing men's wages.[111] Though these arguments were an extension of previous concerns relating to male/female contact and male social authority, the concern had expanded: gender mixing threatened not only husbands, but also a broader gendered socioeconomic and moral order, whether inside or outside the home.

The position previously represented by Niʿmat Sidqi, by contrast, had become decidedly marginal. Most notably, Zaynab ʿAwad Allah Hasan, who edited *al-Iʿtisam*'s "Muslim Woman's Corner" (*Rukn al-Marʾa al-Muslima*), argued that women's employment as teachers and nurses "brought only good to society" (*mā yaʿūd ʿalā al-mujtamaʿ illā bi-l-khayr*). But this was hardly a carte blanche justification for female employment: Hasan conditioned such work

107. Hilal, "Darurat ʿAwdat al-Marʾa ila al-Bayt," *al-Tawhid*, Shaʿban 1397/July 1977, 87.

108. Hilal, "Darurat ʿAwdat al-Marʾa ila al-Bayt," *al-Tawhid*, Ramadan 1397/August 1977, 44–45.

109. Hilal, "Darurat ʿAwdat al-Marʾa ila al-Bayt," *al-Tawhid*, Shawwal 1397/September 1977, 40–42.

110. Hilal, "Darurat ʿAwdat al-Marʾa ila al-Bayt," *al-Tawhid*, Shawwal 1397/September 1977, 42.

111. ʿIsa ʿAbduh, "Tashghil al-Nisaʾ," *al-Iʿtisam*, Ramadan 1396/September 1976, 12.

on limited domestic responsibilities (whether due to not having children or having relatives who could help care for these children) and adherence to "limits" (*ḥudūd*) of modesty while in public.[112] In the latter respect, Hasan upheld Sidqi's legacy, yet she was a minority voice, in both gender and substance. Notwithstanding this vulnerability, however, Hasan had one advantage: many women who were already employed derived both personal satisfaction and a measure of economic independence from their activities.[113]

The case for segregation soon moved forward, and it is here that Ibn Baz published a revised version of an article that had previously appeared in *al-Mujtamaʿ* (Kuwait) and *Majallat al-Jamiʿa al-Islamiyya* (Saudi Arabia) as he sought to shape Egyptian society. Perched at the top of the Saudi religious hierarchy, far from the economic challenges of working-class Egyptians, he showed little sensitivity to the practical obstacles that his proposal might face. As in his previous article in IUM's journal, Ibn Baz made the case that Q 33:33 required that women remain in their homes and that "do not flaunt" (*lā tabarrajna*) referred not to female dress and comportment but to gender mixing for reasons of work, commerce, or travel.[114] This vision of domestic confinement, highly restrictive in Saudi Arabia, was unsustainable in Egypt.

Ibn Baz's challenge was not merely the precedent of women working; it was also that these prescriptions for female confinement were economically elitist. Indeed, as Ibn Baz and Hilal turned against female employment in the mid-1970s, they ignored the relationship between class and modesty. On the one hand, they sympathized with women who traversed the increasingly long distance between home and work by train, trolley, or bus. They also called for women to be removed from educational or professional environments that

112. Zaynab ʿAwad Allah Hasan, "Hukm al-Islam fi ʿAmal al-Marʾa wa-Taʿlim al-Fataʾ," *al-Iʿtisam*, Shaʿban 1400/June 1980, 40.

113. Though not a sufficient explanation for veiling, economic motives can play a role in the public piety of working and middle-class women. See Arlene Macleod, *Accommodating Protest: Working Women, the New Veiling, and Change in Cairo* (New York: Columbia University Press, 1991), 4–5.

114. ʿAbd al-ʿAziz b. Baz, "Khatar Musharakat al-Marʾa li-l-Rajul fi Maydan ʿAmalih," *al-Tawhid*, Ramadan 1398/August 1978, 14. Unlike the article that appeared in the IUM's journal, this version does not mention internal Saudi disputes over gender segregation. The other articles in this series were Ibn Baz, "Khatar Musharakat al-Marʾa li-l-Rajul fi Maydan ʿAmalih," *al-Tawhid*, Dhu al-Qaʿda 1398/October 1978, 10:14–19, and Ibn Baz, "Khatar Musharakat al-Marʾa li-l-Rajul fi Maydan ʿAmalih," *al-Tawhid*, Dhu al-Hijja 1398/November 1978, 11:11–14.

might threaten their chastity or modesty. This was an effort, all suggested, to protect the Muslim woman in the face of manifold threats.

Yet, some of the social developments that these writers found so odious—especially gender mixing on public transportation—were hardly an issue for those women who could afford private transportation. Other topics of criticism, such as female employment, were again no issue for women of means, yet had concrete consequences for women (and families) outside the Egyptian elite. Finally, the vision of a domestically confined woman who not only did not work but also did not leave the house for regular errands was only possible with the help of domestic servants.

Ibn Baz's claim to redefine flaunting in Egypt was also undercut by Muslim Brotherhood efforts to provide practical solutions for women's presence in public space over the course of 1978, in cooperation with the Jamaʿa Islamiyya. Together, these organizations had negotiated with local government officials to secure gender-segregated seating on a set number of train routes beginning in February 1978, most notably between Cairo and Alexandria, thus protecting female students and workers of limited income who relied on public transportation.[115] Similar challenges related to gender mixing awaited university students inside and outside the classroom, and the Brotherhood, again in cooperation with the Jamaʿa Islamiyya, negotiated with the administration of Cairo University to provide separate spaces for men and women for university events hosted in the university's outdoor stadium.[116]

The goal of separation was also extended to the classroom. Most notably, the Brotherhood's magazine *al-Daʿwa* boasted that the Faculty of Agriculture at Cairo University now provided separate seating in lecture halls for male and female students and, in the near future, the lectures themselves would be separate.[117] Crucially, however, neither the Brotherhood nor the Islamic Student Movement were able to achieve, or arguably even desired, the creation

115. "Tajriba Yajib an Tuʿummam," *al-Daʿwa*, Jumada al-Thaniyya 1398/ May 1978, 44–6. It is unclear whether a gender segregation program was put into broad practice on public transportation, or whether it was another proposal that led to the creation of women-only sections on trains and subway cars in Egypt. Outside of a women-only subway car, however, gender segregation has remained a minority trend and was never instituted on public buses.

116. "Fasl al-Tullab ʿan al-Talibat fi Tijarat al-Qahira," *al-Daʿwa*, Jumada al-Thaniyya 1401/ April 1981, 60.

117. "Akhbar al-Shabab wa'l-Jamiʿat," *al-Daʿwa*, Shaʿban 1397/June 1977, 45–6. It does not appear that classroom gender segregation was implemented prior to the end of al-Sadat's rule.

of comprehensive gender segregation. By contrast, Salafi scholars sought to achieve this end yet, in the face of differing socioeconomic realities and political positions in Egypt and Saudi Arabia, would soon revise their textual claims accordingly.

TRANSNATIONAL SALAFI DIVISIONS

In Egypt, the call to define flaunting as mixing and to advocate domestic confinement clashed with local realities and with the competing programmatic appeal of the Muslim Brotherhood to provide gender segregation in public spaces. The tensions that arose from this competition played out not merely in the lives of individual women, but also on the pages of *al-Tawhid*. A prominent Egyptian Salafi voice on this topic, Ibrahim Ibrahim Hilal, led this shift away from domestic confinement. Following a three-part series of articles in late 1978 on the necessity of women returning to domestic space, Hilal took a more nuanced position in December 1979, qualifying his previous opposition to female education outside the home as a reaction to public pressures on women to dress "unveiled and in immodest dress" (*sāfira ghayr muḥtashima*). If women were free to dress modestly, their public presence would not threaten social order.[118]

Whereas Hilal sought to return to an emphasis on sartorial modesty even as he moved away from the subsequent extension of this claim to female domestic seclusion, Ibn Baz held his ground even as he jettisoned his previous justification. In his 1980 work, *Flaunting and the Danger of Women Joining Men in the Their Workplace*, published in Cairo and featured on the cover of this book, Ibn Baz quietly excised his previous claim that flaunting was equivalent to mixing and pointedly avoided discussing female employment. Instead, Ibn Baz invoked the argument that a permitted action that led to forbidden actions should itself be forbidden (known as damming the pretexts of sin, *sadd al-dharīʿāt*).[119] Based on this logic, Ibn Baz argued that, given that the Quran

118. Ibrahim Ibrahim Hilal, "al-Taʿlim waʾl-Tabarruj," *al-Tawhid*, Safar 1399/December 1978, 4.

119. This legal tool is similar to the Halakhic concept of "building a fence around the Torah" used by Rabbinic scholars to justify legal innovations. See Richard S. Rheins, "Asu Seyag LaTorah: Make a Fence to Protect the Torah," in *Re-Examining Progressive Halakhah*, ed. W. Jacob and M. Zemer (New York: Berghahn Books, 2002), 91–110.

commands women to avert their gaze from men and to cover themselves, then it logically follows that one must forbid mixing in order to avoid situations in which men and women could look at each other.[120] Indeed, Ibn Baz still maintained that the "best Hijab for a woman . . . other than that which covers her face and body with clothing, is her home."[121] This was, conceptually speaking, similar to Ibn Ibrahim's invocation of the objectives of the Shariʿa: an intellectual method to justify a position without the citation of explicit proof texts that were central to the authenticity claims of Purist Salafism.

Why did this vision of social restriction fail to catch on in Egypt? There are two possibilities, one elite-centered, the other society-centered. Female education had exposed a tension in the Salafi vision of public morality: women had to be educated, both to fulfill their domestic role and to realize their textually-grounded right to education. At the same time, however, changing definitions of public space and, beginning in 1977, the technological challenges of distance learning had made female presence in public not merely a luxury but a necessity.

Just as importantly, women were in no hurry to give up their mobility outside the home. From his position at the apex of Saudi religious institutions, most notably the Permanent Committee for Scholarly Research and Iftaʾ, the Islamic Fiqh Academy, and the Islamic University of Medina, Ibn Baz probably did not appreciate the grassroots realities of 1970s Egypt. Similarly, ʿAbduh, who was born in Egypt but was now a resident of Saudi Arabia, was more concerned with elite-level questions of Islamic finance.[122] By contrast, Hilal, an active member of Ansar al-Sunna and a professor of Islamic Studies at ʿAyn Shams University's Women's Faculty (*Kulliyyat al-Banāt*),[123] likely

120. ʿAbd al-ʿAziz b. Baz, *al-Tabarruj wa Khatar Musharakat al-Marʾa li-l-Rajul fi Maydan ʿAmalih* (Cairo: Maktabat al-Salam, 1980), 17. The Arabic Union Catalog suggests that this title was also published in Riyadh and Medina by Dar al-Yaqin li-l-Nashr waʾl-Tawziʿ, Maktabat al-Maʿarif and the Islamic University of Medina over the course of the 1980s. For reference, see https://tinyurl.com/y9vlr4z9. The Ultra-Orthodox Jewish argument against gender mixing rests on similar grounds. See Chaim Saiman, *Halakhah: The Rabbinic Idea of Law* (Princeton, NJ: Princeton University Press, 2018), 135–37.

121. Ibn Baz, *al-Tabarruj wa Khatar Musharakat al-Marʾa li-l-Rajul fi Maydan ʿAmalih*, 18.

122. al-ʿUqayl, *Min Aʿlam al-Daʿwa waʾl-Haraka al-Islamiyya al-Muʿasira*, 1:679.

123. See the introductory note in a book by Muhammad Aman al-Jami about the history of Islam in Africa (*al-Islam fi Ifrīqiyya ʿAbr al-Tarikh*, http://shamela.ws/browse.php/book-8734/page-9).

witnessed the on-the-ground challenges faced by pious women from Ansar al-Sunna's network of mosques and charitable associations, on the one hand, and activism of the Jama'a Islamiyya, on the other.[124]

Indeed, the prominence of women within the Jama'a Islamiyya's activities underscores the ways in which Salafi women within this group regarded the performance of female modesty as not only a right but also a distinct contribution. As in state feminism, women were both objects and agents of transformation; what was non-negotiable was their presence in public space. Within the Jama'a Islamiyya, some women held Muslim Brotherhood sympathies while others supported a wide array of Salafi organizations. All had taken on pious garb—and in the case of many Salafi women, a stringent interpretation of modesty that included covering the face with the *niqab*—and used sartorial choice to challenge the claims of the Egyptian state to define the feminine body and public life. In light of previous efforts by male Salafi scholars to restrict women's appearance in public, however, it appears that these women challenged not only the al-Sadat regime but also Salafi elites.

It is perhaps for this reason that, by the early 1980s, the discussion of female modesty in Egypt came to resemble Ni'mat Sidqi's original call to Egyptian women to abide by modest gender norms, albeit with a greater emphasis on avoiding gender mixing. In a November 1981 article, a preacher within Ansar al-Sunna, Ahmad Taha Nasr, returned to discussing the requirements of women's clothing, almost as though female seclusion was off the agenda.[125] A crucial change, however, had occurred: gender segregation *within* public space was now broadly acknowledged as a key means of facilitating public morality. Women were in public to stay and, if Salafi elites in Egypt were to successfully compete with the Muslim Brotherhood for a popular audience, they had to adapt to this reality.

Yet, even this structural solution was not viable in the long term and, increasingly, gender segregation came to be defined not in terms of separate spaces allocated to men and women respectively, but rather in terms of visible female

124. The precise number of such mosques is unknown, but Salah al-Din Hasan confirms the centrality of mosques and charitable societies to the activities of Ansar al-Sunna. See Hasan, *al-Salafiyun*, 9. As of 1988, Ansar al-Sunna had 120 branches across Egypt with 1500 affiliated mosques. See Siyam, "al-Haraka al-Islamiyya wa'l-Jam'iyyat al-Ahliyya fi Misr," 129.

125. Taha Nasr, "al-Tahdhir min Fitnat al-Azwaj wa'l-Awlad," *al-Tawhid*, Safar 1402/November 1981, 5.

self-regulation. This shift is most notable in a text published some three decades later by the Salafi scholar and Salafi Call founder Shaykh Shahata Muhammad ʿAli Saqr (b. 1969). Entitled *Mixing Between Men and Women: Rulings and Fatwas,* this two-volume work included a preface by a leading preacher of the Alexandria-based Salafi Call (*al-Daʿwa al-Salafiyya*), Yasir Burhami. In this preface, Burhami offered a novel interpretation of gender mixing and, by extension, a path to gender segregation through personal discipline:

> Our brother Shahata Saqr has pointed us in this study to the harms of forbidden mixing. . . . He has brought up well-known issues of our Egyptian society . . . in our universities, schools, and professional workspaces . . . which encompass numerous evil actions (*anwāʿ al-munkarāt*) including illicit looking (*al-naẓar al-muḥarram*), illicit speech (*al-kalām al-muḥarram*), illicit listening (*al-samāʿ al-muḥarram*) and the forbidden touch (*al-lams al-muḥarram*). . . .[126]

Through proper comportment, a woman could quite literally segregate herself from the men in her midst.

By contrast, Muhammad Yusri Ibrahim (b. 1966), an Egyptian Salafi based in Saudi Arabia at the Islamic University of Medina and the head of this volume's publisher, Dar al-Yusr, cautioned the author and his readers alike:

> Let us not say that there are permitted and forbidden forms of mixing (*inna al-ikhtilāṭ minhu mubāḥ wa minhu muḥarram*). . . . Instead, let us say: mixing is unequivocally forbidden by human nature, it is an educational failure that has been discarded by history. It brings down civilizations and is forbidden in the most absolute terms by Islamic law.[127]

From across the Red Sea, an Egyptian scholar who had migrated to Saudi Arabia chastised his counterparts in Egypt for the ideological and practical implications of this choice of words.

Al-Yusri's position reflected the status quo in his adopted country. Although Ibn Baz's vision of domestic seclusion did not come to fruition, his ambition was realized through the expansion of gender segregation in schools, workplaces, and sites of leisure throughout the Kingdom. Within the private sector, women's employment was limited to ARAMCO, which had, since its found-

126. Shahata Muhammad ʿAli Saqr, *al-Ikhtilat Bayna al-Rijal wa'l-Nisa': Ahkam wa Fatawa, Thimar Murra Qisas Mukhziyya, Kashf 136 Shubha li-Duʿat al-Ikhtilat* (Cairo: Dar al-Yusr, 2011), 1:10–11.

127. Saqr, *al-Ikhtilat Bayna al-Rijal wa'l-Nisa'*, 1:14.

ing, constituted an exceptional social space vis-à-vis gender relations.[128] Beyond ARAMCO, however, gender segregation has flourished, whether in charitable associations, on university campuses, or in banking; indeed, the number of women-only bank branches in Saudi Arabia grew from one to thirteen between 1980 and 1982 alone.[129]

By the turn of the century, such gender segregation would extend not only to the workplaces but also to sites of leisure, whether zoos (in which three days are set aside each week for men and women respectively), shopping centers, hospitals, or restaurants.[130] As Amelie Le Renard notes in her ethnography of gender segregation in contemporary Saudi Arabia, "an archipelago of spaces for women has created a parallel city, with its campuses, sections for businesses, administrations, charitable organizations, and religious spaces."[131] While domestic confinement was unrealistic, the creation of gender-segregated public institutions made it largely unnecessary.

New institutional structures did not end the search to more securely establish gender segregation through proof texts. A 1987 study, originally completed as an M.A. thesis at the Higher Institute of Islamic Daʿwa (*al-Maʿhad al-ʿĀlī li-l-Daʿwa al-Islāmiyya*) in Medina and endorsed by Salih B. Ibrahim al-Bulayhi, a Salafi scholar from the central Arabian city of Burayda, defined mixing as a "one of the manifestations of flaunting" (*min maẓāhir al-tabarruj*).[132] Ibn al-ʿUthaymin, by complement, argued in a 1998 study that women were forbidden from mixing with men based on a hadith report in which the Prophet instructed women to walk on the side of the street (*bi-ḥāffāt al-ṭarīq*) in order to avoid mixing with men.[133] In short, Salafi scholars sought

128. AlMunajjed, *Women in Saudi Arabia Today*, 92.

129. AlMunajjed, *Women in Saudi Arabia Today*, 91.

130. AlMunajjed, *Women in Saudi Arabia Today*, 33, 91.

131. Le Renard, *A Society of Young Women*, 36–37.

132. ʿUbayd b. ʿAbd al-ʿAziz b. ʿUbayd al-Silmi, *al-Tabarruj waʾl-Ihtisab ʿAlayhi* (Medina, Saudi Arabia: N.P., 1987), 32.

133. Ibn al-ʿUthaymin, *Tawjihat li-l-Muʾminat Hawl al-Tabarruj waʾl-Sufur* (Riyadh, Saudi Arabia: Dar Ibn Huzayma, 1998), 12. For the original hadith, see al-Sijistani, *Sunan Abi Daʾud*, 565. Al-Albani affirmed Abu Daʾud's designation of the hadith regarding the Prophet instructing women to walk on the side of the street as fair (*ḥasan*), a level below sound (*saḥīḥ*), in his comprehensive assessment of the reliability of hadith reports. See Muhammad Nasir al-Din al-Albani, *Sahih al-Jamiʿ al-Saghir wa-Ziyadatuhu*, ed. Zuhayr al-Shawish (Damascus, Syria: al-Maktab al-Islami, 1988), 955. This report, however, does not appear in either of the two most-cited Sunni hadith collections, *Sahih al-Bukhari* and *Sahih Muslim*.

alternative justifications as institutional gender segregation spread throughout Saudi Arabia, a position that their Egyptian counterparts could have only envied.

CONCLUSION

In the 1970s, gender segregation emerged as a key question for Salafi scholars in Egypt and Saudi Arabia alike as they sought to map public space through a gendered binary. The divergent fates of this project are, on one level, a story of how access to state power (or lack thereof) shapes textual interpretation and vice versa. Calls within Egypt to implement gender segregation ultimately came to reflect their proponents' political position; bereft of the ability to set policy within educational institutions, state bodies, or private businesses, gender segregation through domestic confinement was both impractical and politically unwise. Instead, self-regulation, rather than physical structures of separation, came to define "gender segregation." Whether glossed as modesty or gender segregation, Niʿmat Sidqi's basic vision retained its sway.

By contrast, the Saudi story is one in which state power derives legitimacy from religious conceptions but does not create them. Just as importantly, though, are the internal dynamics that structure the exercise of state power: gender segregation is not merely premised on separating men and women, but also on men asserting control over women's bodies. It is here that we see the limitations of this form of social regulation: despite calls for domestic seclusion, Salafi scholars succeeded in fragmenting, rather than dominating, public space because their ability to assert control was limited by a combination of circumscribed spaces, social pressure and the choices of their followers. This challenge, though novel to these scholars, was a familiar one to state elites in Egypt and beyond who, since the nineteenth century, had sought to produce and maintain a society populated by self-regulating individuals.

When compared with praying in shoes, gender segregation appears to present a series of contrasts: textual roots versus invention, individual practice versus structural change, and finally, failure in Egypt versus success in Saudi Arabia. Notwithstanding these contrasts, however, scholars in both cases reckoned with the opportunities and challenges for shaping social practice through regulation, structural and individual. While the question of praying in shoes involved textual claims to a broadly marginalized practice of the Prophet and his Companions, gender segregation necessitated an active reinterpretation of specific verses of the Quran. Similarly, while Saudi and to a lesser degree Egyptian Salafis came to invoke extratextual justifications of the common good to justify avoiding prayer in shoes, so too did arguments for gender segregation involve arguments for preventing actions that could harm the "common good" (*al-maṣlaḥa al-ʿāmma*) or lead to forbidden acts (*sadd al-dharīʿāt*). Both cases, in turn, reveal how hermeneutics could alternately shape and reflect policy, and the ways in which the practicalities of physical separation (and its communicative value) were as important as the meaning ascribed to canonical texts. Not all practices, however, necessitated access to state power and it is to one of these—the cultivation of a Salafi beard—that we now turn.

CHAPTER 5

Leading with a Fist

The Genesis and Consolidation of a Salafi Beard

In the mid-1990s, 'Abd al-'Aziz b. Baz and Muhammad Nasir al-Din al-Albani were no longer young men; both would pass away in 1999. They had alternated between collaboration and disagreement over the previous decades. At this moment, however, the two octogenarians were locked in a fierce disagreement. This was a time of considerable turmoil, especially for Ibn Baz, who sought to mediate between members of the *Sahwa* and the Saudi Royal Family.[1] Yet, the issue at hand was not Islam's relationship to politics but rather the length of the properly Islamic beard: Ibn Baz argued that even if the beard reaches a minimum of a fist one should not cut it,[2] while al-Albani took the position that such a prohibition was not only unfounded but a case of "additional innovation" (*al-bid'a al-iḍāfiyya*).[3] Despite this division over whether men are permitted to trim their beards, however, these two scholars shared a reference point: the fist (*al-qabḍa*).[4]

1. Lacroix, *Awakening Islam*, 183–85.

2. 'Abd al-'Aziz b. Baz, "Wujub I'fa' al-Lihya wa Tahrim Halqiha wa Qassiha," *al-Tawhid*, Jumada al-Ukhra 1415/November 1994, 34–5.

3. Muhammad Nasir al-Din al-Albani, *Silsilat al-Ahadith al-Da'ifa wa'l-Mawdu'a wa Atharuha al-Sayyi' fi'l-Umma* (Riyadh: Maktabat al-Ma'arif, 2001), 5:5. Al-Albani's accusation was not the first time that the charge of "additional innovation" (*al-bid'a al-iḍāfiyya*) had arisen in Salafi circles: a Rajab 1361/July 1942 article in *al-Hadi al-Nabawi* cited al-Shatibi on this front. See "al-Bid'a," *al-Hadi al-Nabawi*, Rajab 1361/~July 1942, 30–32.

4. The use of the fist as a reference point is not exclusive to Salafis for the simple reason that it is only unit of measurement mentioned in canonical hadith collections. Anecdotally, in conversations with two scholars of Islamic and Middle Eastern history who studied at

How did Salafi scholars come to focus on articulating such a model of facial hair, and what does this debate reveal about the centrality of communication to Salafism generally, and the Salafi ethical project in particular? While Salafis are certainly not the only Muslims who wear long beards or cite the fist as a possible measurement, in the 1980s Salafi scholars appropriated *madhhab*-based deliberations on beard length in an attempt to formulate a model of facial hair that would be recognized as both Sunnaic and distinctly Salafi. Part and parcel of a sustained effort to define the practices of a broader social movement through the active reconstruction of early Islamic history, this project aimed to enable members to signal their commitment to Muhammad's visual model while distinguishing them from both student activists and jihadi groups who also sported bushy beards. Just as importantly, debates on the parameters of the beard reflect separate, if connected, stakes of textual interpretation that cannot be reduced to the imperatives of political competition or communication.

Like praying in shoes and gender segregation, the story of the Salafi beard is both a story of the legal demands of ritual rectitude and the centrality of communication to Salafi ethics. The *obligation* to grow a beard is far from novel and the assumption that this bodily practice represents a manifestation of the Prophet's model is found in canonical texts of the Islamic scholarly tradition. Just as importantly, however, the significance of the beard stems from its accessibility, as men across the ideological spectrum can choose whether or not to use facial hair to signal identification with a cultural trend or movement. The Salafi beard, in turn, reflects a fusion of prior Islamic models of masculinity, secular-nationalist visions of progress, and the symbolic centrality of facial hair to twentieth-century visions of political and cultural change.

Accessibility, though, also produced confusion. As in the cases of praying in shoes, gender segregation, and shortened pants or robes (for which see chapter 6), the call for a Sunnaic beard reflects an effort to reconstruct Prophetic practice in the service of ethical cultivation. This project is premised on social distinction and built on scholarly excellence. The story of the Salafi beard, like these other stories, however, is not one of unmitigated success, as

---

al-Azhar—Samy Ayoub and Ibrahim Gemeah—an opening question about the Salafi beard prompted both to raise their clenched fists to directly underneath the chin while exclaiming "the fist" (*al-qabḍa*).

Ansar al-Sunna would struggle to visually differentiate its members from both violent and nonviolent iterations of the Jamaʿa Islamiyya.

I will begin by sketching the relationship between facial hair, religion, and political change in the Middle East from the 1930s onward. At a time when secular-nationalist elites dismissed a long and flowing beard as a sign of backwardness and offered a clean-shaven face coupled with a mustache as a model of progress, Salafis saw the beard as a basic expression of an Islamic identity. Their focus, at this time, however, was not on analyzing hadith reports to lay out how Muhammad and his Companions wore their beards and mustaches. Instead, between 1930 and 1950, Salafis were more concerned with questions of foreign influence, and between 1950 and 1970 with challenges of political repression by secular-nationalist regimes. It is thus little surprise that, during this period, leading members of Ansar al-Sunna wore beards of vastly varying lengths.

Between the early 1970s and mid-1980s, however, Salafi scholars sought to respond to the efforts by Islamic student groups in Egypt and Saudi Arabia to claim the Sunna by nailing down a specific model of Islamic facial hair based on the reexamination of hadith reports. It was in this context that Salafi scholars initially developed an understanding of a Sunnaic beard to visually distinguish themselves from student activists in both countries and jihadists in Egypt: to resemble the Messenger of God, a Salafi man must trim his mustache so that it does not stretch above the upper lip and must grow the beard so that it exceeds the length of a fist. Why did Salafi scholars turn to the beard, and which textual resources did they find at their disposal?

THE ORIGINS OF SALAFI FACIAL HAIR

In May 1940, Muhammad Hamid al-Fiqi published an article that drew on hadith narrations to explain the beard and mustache as two of the ten characteristics of innate human nature (*fiṭra*) that orients human beings to God.[5] Ansar al-Sunna's founder emphasized that a beard constitutes an "adornment of masculinity" (*zīnat al-rujūla*) that makes it possible for Muslim men to distinguish themselves from both non-Muslim men and from Muslim women. While stipulating the centrality of the beard to masculinity, however, al-Fiqi was vague as to its measurements, specifying that a man "leave it, so that it accumulates

5. For the relevant hadith reports, see Muslim b. Hajjaj al-Qushayri, *Sahih Musilm*, ed. Nazar b. Muhammad al-Faryabi Abu Qutayba (Riyadh, Saudi Arabia: Dar Tayba, 2006), 133–35.

and grows plentiful" (*ḥattā yukhaththira shaʿruhā wa-yatawaffar*).[6] While al-Fiqi regarded the cultivation of an Islamic beard as necessary and valuable, this practice did not distinguish Salafis from other Muslims who grew a beard as a means of signaling piety, masculinity, or a fusion of the two.[7] Al-Fiqi's successors within Ansar al-Sunna, however, would sport significantly more distinct beards.

The definition and maintenance of interreligious boundaries was a far more urgent matter. In April 1938, al-Fiqi had taken aim at the increasing tendency of Muslims to resemble non-Muslims. In an article entitled, "Those Who Resemble a People Belong to It" (*Man tashabbaha bi-qawm$_{in}$ fa-huwa min-hum*),[8] he explained that "visual similarity (*al-tashābbuḥ al-ẓāhirī*) frequently leads to the creation of moral similarity" (*ījād al-tashābbuḥ al-maʿnawī*).[9] In the shadow of unavoidable interaction with Muslims of limited religious commitment and with Egypt's substantial Coptic Christian minority, Ansar al-Sunna's founder noted the linkage between external and internal states and sought to foreground the observance of the "characteristics, actions, states of being, ritual practices, and acts of obedience" enjoined by God and lived by His Prophet.[10] His goal, like Mahmud Muhammad Khattab al-Subki before him, was to combat observance of Shamm al-Nasim, an Egyptian national holiday that celebrates the beginning of spring and falls on the day after Coptic Easter.[11]

6. Muhammad Hamid al-Fiqi, "Min Sunan al-Fitra," *al-Hadi al-Nabawi*, 15 Rabiʿ al-Thani 1359/23 May 1940, 13–21, at 18.

7. For an image of al-Fiqi from Ansar al-Sunna's official twitter account, see https://twitter.com/a_s_almohamadia/status/563230937547161600/photo/1, accessed 14 May 2020.

8. The statement that "those who resemble a people belong to it" is traced to a hadith report ascribed to the Prophet Muhammad by Ibn ʿUmar and recorded in one of the six authoritative Sunni hadith collections, *Sunan Abi Da'ud*. See al-Sijistani, *Sunan Abi Da'ud*, 4:204. For an overview of Sunni texts based on this principle, see Youshaa Patel, "The Islamic Treatises against Imitation (Tašabbuh): A Bibliographical History," *Arabica* 65 (2018): 597–639. Also see Youshaa Patel, "'Whoever Imitates a People Becomes One of Them': A Hadith and its Interpreter," *Islamic Law and Society* 25 (2018): 359–426.

9. Muhammad Hamid al-Fiqi, "Man Tashabbaha bi-Qawm$_{in}$ Fa-Huwa Min-Hum," *al-Hadi al-Nabawi*, Safar 1356/April 1938, 34–9, at 35.

10. al-Fiqi, "Man Tashabbaha bi-Qawm$_{in}$ Fa-Huwa Min-Hum," 37. As with the case of the beard, the importance of visual distinctiveness may be traced back to the articulation of the importance of communal unity in Sunni hadith collections.

11. al-Fiqi, "Man Tashabbaha bi-Qawm$_{in}$ Fa-Huwa Min-Hum," 38. Writers in *al-Hadi al-Nabawi* also voiced a concern with the observance of Shamm al-Nasim elsewhere; see Sadiq Arnaws, "Yawm Shamm al-Nasim," *al-Hadi al-Nabawi*, 1 Rabiʿ al-Thani 1360/28 April 1941, 11–16. For al-Subki, see chapter 2.

Indeed, the most prominent discussion of the beard among Muslim scholars and activists in this period is found in al-Subki's *The Pure Religion* (*al-Din al-Khalis*). In his magnum opus, the Jamʿiyya Sharʿiyya's founder challenged the classification of the beard as a mere "custom" (*ʿāda*) with little relation to Islam, a claim made by secular nationalists who argued for a clean-shaven appearance. Instead, he argued that a distinctly Islamic model of facial hair reflects the authoritative practice of the Prophet Muhammad and the early Muslim community, and serves to tie Muslims to God and to distinguish them from members of other faiths.[12]

Al-Subki's emphasis on the beard expands on that of al-Fiqi in two key respects. First, he regards facial hair as a key site of competition, noting the challenge posed by "armies in our day that require men to shave their beards" (*ḥalq liḥāhim*),[13] as well as by those men who claim the prerogative to shave their beards to make themselves more attractive to female partners, current and potential.[14] The explicit reference to the challenge posed by military service and fashion reflects the secular-nationalist currents of this period: beginning in the interwar period (1918–39), proponents of secular Egyptian nationalism promised to liberate Egyptians from the ostensibly stultifying shackles of (religious) tradition, poor hygiene, and despotic politics. The beard, long considered a marker of masculinity,[15] now symbolized an unhealthy attachment to the past. In this vision, a clean-shaven face and a mustache combined to signal its bearer's orientation to the future as a modern man.[16]

Al-Subki also referenced a key debate within the Sunni legal tradition regarding the beard's length, instructing readers not to shave beyond the "authoritative amount . . . and that is the fist" (*ʿan al-qadr al-masnūn . . . wa huwa al-qabḍa*).[17] This prescription for the beard, which is found among

12. al-Subki, *al-Din al-Khalis*, 1:193 and 1:189–90.

13. al-Subki, *al-Din al-Khalis*, 1:191.

14. al-Subki, *al-Din al-Khalis*, 1:193.

15. El-Rouayheb, *Before Homosexuality in the Arab-Islamic World*, 26–27. Similarly, Afsaneh Najmabadi cites an eleventh-century Persian book of advice to underscore the historical role of beards in distinguishing adult men from their adolescent male counterparts (*Women With Mustaches and Men Without Beards: Gender and Sexual Anxieties of Iranian Modernity* [Berkeley: University of California Press, 2005], 15–16).

16. Ryzova, *The Age of the Efendiyya*, 20.

17. al-Subki, *al-Din al-Khalis*, 1:192; also see 1:196.

scholars of all four Sunni law schools,[18] revolves around a hadith report from al-Bukhari's canonical *Sahih* collection. In this report, the Umayyad-era scholar Nafiʿ (d. 95–6/785) reported the following regarding the son of the second caliph ʿUmar b. Khattab (d. 23/644), ʿAbd Allah b. ʿUmar (d. 73/693): "The Prophet said, 'Distinguish yourselves from the pagans. Grow the beards and trim the mustaches.' Whenever Ibn ʿUmar performed the Hajj or ʿUmra pilgrimages, he used to hold his fist up to his beard and cut whatever exceeded it."[19] While al-Fiqi, like al-Subki, would have presumably learned about this debate during his studies at al-Azhar, his early discussion of the beard did not mention it, likely because the precise length of one's beard was not then a pressing question.

In contrast to Ansar al-Sunna, the Muslim Brotherhood's position on facial hair was already set. In the 1930s and 1940s, Hasan al-Banna had sported a closely trimmed beard that identified him in a manner consonant with the *Efendiyya* project as "Islamic modern."[20] This approach would be reflected in the Brotherhood's magazine, *al-Ikhwan al-Muslimun*, which featured the writings of al-Sayyid Sabiq (d. 2000). In a 15 July 1944 article, this graduate of al-Azhar and member of the Brotherhood explained:

> Grow the beard out and let it accumulate so that it makes its wearer appear dignified. And one should not trim it [to the point] that it is close to shaving (*qarīb^{an} min al-ḥalq*) nor should one let it become indecent (*ḥattā tafḥash*). Rather, moderation (*al-tawassuṭ*) is best as it is in every matter. . . .[21]

18. For a Hanbali example, see Muhammad b. Muflih b. Shams al-Din al-Maqdisi, *Kitab al-Furuʿ*, ed. ʿAbd Allah b. al-Muhsin al-Turki (Beirut: Muʾassasat al-Risala, 2003), 1:151–52. For an example from a leading jurist within the Maliki school, see al-Dasuqi, *Hashiyyat al-Dasuqi*, 1:90. For an example from the Shafiʿi school on the obligation to a grow a beard which notes the measurement of the fist (*al-qabḍa*), see al-Imam Abu Zakariya Muhyi al-Din b. Sharaf al-Nawawi, *Kitab al-Majmuʿ Sharh al-Muhadhdhab li-l-Shirazi*, ed. Muhammad Najib al-Mutiʿi (Jeddah: Maktabat al-Irshad, 1980), 1:342–43. For a discussion within the Hanafi school that notes the beard as obligatory and the fist as a measurement, see Muhammad b. ʿAli b. Muhammad b. Ahmad b. ʿAbd al-Rahman al-Hanafi al-Haskafi, *Al-Durr al-Mukhtar: Sharh Tanwir al-Absar wa Jamiʿ al-Bahhar*, ed. ʿAbd al-Munʿim Khalil Ibrahim (Beirut: Dar al-Kutub al-ʿIlmiyya, 2002), 148.

19. Muhammad b. Ismaʿil al-Bukhari, *Sahih al-Bukhari* (Damascus, Syria: Dar Ibn Kathir, 1423/2002), 1487.

20. Krämer, *Hasan al-Banna*, 90.

21. al-Sayyid Sabiq, "al-Taharat," *al-Ikhwan al-Muslimun*, 24 Rajab 1363/15 July 1944, 18–19.

He then repeated the hadith about Ibn ʿUmar. Al-Sabiq's prescription, which would two years later be enshrined in his *Law of the Sunna* (*Fiqh al-Sunna*),[22] a central legal text for the Brotherhood, sets forth the Brotherhood's standard of a closer-shaven beard. Equally important, it again cites the Ibn ʿUmar hadith report as a means to justify *trimming* the beard to the point of moderation—reflected in Hasan al-Banna's closely trimmed beard—rather than as a basis for the fist as a minimal measurement.

Indeed, it appears that al-Banna specifically opposed significant facial hair. In her memoir of a life spent in the Muslim Sisters (*al-Akhawāt al-Muslimāt*),[23] Fatima ʿAbd al-Hadi (d. 2015), who joined the group in 1942, recounts an exchange between the Brotherhood's founder and Mahmud Suliman, a member of the organization who at that point was a medical student:[24]

> As we were leaving the office, we encountered Brother Mahmud [Suliman] and he had grown out his beard and appeared foreign (*gharīb*ᵃⁿ) and different from what we were used to. . . . When the Imam [al-Banna] saw him, Mahmud gestured to him, saying: 'I follow the Sunna ardently' (*laqad aṣabtu al-Sunna*).[25] The Imam responded: 'You follow the Sunna ardently [but] you have squandered [fulfilment of] the obligation [to do *Daʿwa*] (*aṣabta al-Sunna wa ḍayyʾta al-farḍ*). Go shave your beard and join us . . . you cannot have an effect on people when you [appear] strange to them' (*wa anta gharīb ʿanhim*). And the Imam Hasan al-Banna would refuse to distinguish himself from [other] people through clothing or bearing so as to remain part of society.

22. Sabiq, *Fiqh al-Sunna*, 1:34.

23. This organization is distinct from Zaynab al-Ghazali's Muslim Women's Association (*Jamāʿat al-Sayyidāt al-Muslimāt*), which remained independent from the Brotherhood from its establishment in 1935 until 1949, shortly before al-Banna's assassination. See Euben and Zaman, *Princeton Readings in Islamist Thought*, 276–77.

24. Though the memoir does not specify a university, it is likely that Suliman studied at Cairo University's Faculty of Medicine, as the Brotherhood was particularly active in this faculty during the 1930s and 1940s.

25. This is a reference to a hadith in which two early Muslims were in the midst of a journey and performed ritual purification using the clean earth (*ṣaʿīd*ᵃⁿ *tayyib*ᵃⁿ, a practice known as *tayammum*) rather than water (*wuḍūʾ*) before praying. Following prayer, they found water, with one of these two men then purifying himself with water before repeating the prayer, while the other did not. These two men then approached Muhammad and described their actions, and Muhammad declared: "'you followed the Sunna (*aṣabta al-Sunna*) and the [first] prayer and fulfilled [the obligation] to pray.' He then addressed the man who had purified himself with water and prayed again: 'for you, there is a double reward.'" See al-Sijistani, *Sunan Abi Daʾud wa Maʿalim al-Sunan*, 1:173–74.

In contradistinction to an emphasis on visual signification characteristic of Islamic and non-Islamic movements in interwar Egypt, al-Banna sought to blend in.

For those who wished to maintain a beard, however, the pressing question was not that of beard length but rather one of how to navigate the strictures of the state bureaucracy. In March 1947, the Mufti of the Jamʿiyya Sharʿiyya, ʿAli Hasan Hulwa, counseled readers of *al-Iʿtisam* that they must disobey the order from their bureaucratic superiors or fathers to shave the beard while "meeting his supervisor or defamation by one's father in a civil manner" (*yuqābil isāʾat raʾīsihi aw wālidihi bi-l-ḥusnā*).[26] Similarly, in January 1948 Hulwa responded to yet another reader who sought to find a solution to demands by police and government institutions alike that men employed therein shave their beards. As in the previous fatwa, Hulwa reiterated that it was forbidden to shave the beard and that government and police employees alike must "request from the general administration (*al-idāra al-ʿāmma*) to let them grow their beards. . . ."[27] Stand-alone mustaches were also a source of concern: a May 1950 article in *al-Iʿtisam*, entitled "The Unlawful Innovation of the Mustaches," described the spread of an "epidemic illness with fast infection rates" (*marḍ wabāʾī sarīʿa al-ʿadwā*), namely the fact that 90 percent of Egyptian men had grown mustaches.[28] Prior to 1952, then, Islamic thinkers and movements navigated the twin challenge of Westernizing cultural influences and state power.

In the changing context of the post-1952 secular-nationalist regime in Egypt, alongside some three decades of Westernizing cultural influences, Salafis came to discuss facial hair with greater frequency. In a July 1954 fatwa request in *al-Hadi al-Nabawi*, Abu-l-Wafaʾ Muhammad Darwish explained: "shaving the beard is a sin (*fī ḥalq al-liḥya ithm*) . . . that has spread among Muslims as a result of mixing with non-Muslims . . . [leading them] to abandon the Sunna of their Prophet."[29] Darwish spoke primarily to an Egyptian readership raised on the values of a secular-nationalist vision of masculinity that emphasized a

26. ʿAli Hasan Hulwa, "Asʾila wa Ajwiba," *al-Iʿtisam*, 8 Rabiʿ al-Thani 1366/~1 March 1947, 10.

27. ʿAli Hasan Hulwa, "Safhat al-Istiftaʾat," *al-Iʿtisam*, 28 Safar 1367/~11 January 1948, 8.

28. "Bidʿat al-Shawarib," *al-Iʿtisam*, 27 Rajab 1369/12 May 1950, 22.

29. Abu-l-Wafaʾ Darwish, "Bab al-Fatawa," *al-Hadi al-Nabawi*, Dhu al-Qaʿda 1373/July 1954, 45–47, at 47.

clean-shaven face adorned by a mustache. Just a few months later, however, ʿAbd al-Nasir would crack down on the Muslim Brotherhood following a failed assassination attempt.[30]

The story of contestation over the beard, however, should not be reduced to a two-way battle between ruling regimes and Islamic movements. Al-Azhar University emerged as a third key player in this contest, situated between the ideological and political power of the Egyptian state and its scholarly networks that included members of the Jamʿiyya Sharʿiyya and Ansar al-Sunna alike. The concern with al-Azhar's internal practices, though far from unprecedented,[31] surfaced in the post-1952 period: a June 1953 fatwa in *al-Iʿtisam* confronted the question of the practice of many Azhari scholars and army recruits (*abnāʾ al-jaysh*) of shaving the beard, describing it as "among the remnants of abominable colonialism" (*min āthār al-istiʿamār al-baghīḍ*).[32] Similarly, a March 1954 article, also in *al-Iʿtisam*, challenged al-Azhar's journal—referenced as *Nur al-Islam* but at this point called *al-Azhar*—for its February 1954 ruling that the beard was a praiseworthy action (*nadb*) rather than obligatory. Instead, Amin Muhammad Khattab, son of the Jamʿiyya Sharʿiyya's founder, explained that the beard's status in Islamic law is in fact one of "obligation" (*wujūb*).[33]

Despite these debates, or perhaps because of their political sensitivity, Ansar al-Sunna's scholars wrote little about the beard during the 1960s. This silence cannot be separated from the regime's repression of the Muslim Brotherhood. In a 1 May 1966 speech in the Delta textile town of al-Mahalla al-Kubra, ʿAbd al-Nasir depicted Egypt's leading Islamist organization as a foreign agent and stated: "Someone who grows out his beard (*ba-yurrabī dhaʾnahu*) comes to you and says that Socialism is disbelief (*kufr*). . . . [Someone] who claims that Socialism opposes Religion [Islam] is the person who will take the country's wealth for himself."[34] Indeed, it was during this period

30. Mitchell, *The Society of the Muslim Brothers*, 150–51.

31. For example, in the fall of 1937, ʿAbd al-Zahir Abu-l-Samh expressed concern with the quality of hadith education in Azhari institutes. See Abu-l-Samh, "al-Din al-Khalis," *al-Hadi al-Nabawi*, Ramadan 1356/~November 1937, 20–24, at 21.

32. "Asʾila wa Ajwiba," *al-Iʿtisam*, Shawwal 1372/June 1953, 15.

33. Amin Khattab, "Hawl Iʿfaʾ al-Lihya," *al-Iʿtisam*, Rajab 1373/March 1954, 41–42.

34. "Fidyu ʿAbd al-Nasir Yuhajim al-Lihya wa-Radd Ikhwani ʿAlayhi," *al-Tahrir*, 0:50, *https://www.youtube.com/watch?v = zVOAxxBpysE*, accessed 27 September 2017. For the text of the speech, see http://nasser.bibalex.org/Speeches/browser.aspx?SID=1163&lang=ar.

that guards in the infamous military prison (*al-sijn al-ḥarbī*) are reported to have shaved the heads and beards of imprisoned Muslim Brothers, with some guards amusing themselves by shaving only a portion of these prisoners' heads or beards.[35] Though this threat and coercive shaving in prisons was directly primarily at the Brotherhood, it was not limited to them. Soon thereafter, however, student activists would come to challenge not only secular-nationalist elites but also Salafi scholars by emphasizing a self-consciously Sunna-based beard.

THE RETURN OF ISLAMIC MOVEMENTS AND THE EXPANSION OF SALAFISM

June of 1967 brought ideological and military devastation as the stunning victory of the Israeli Defense Forces posed a lethal challenge to ʿAbd al-Nasir's vision of secular nationalism and the ranks of the Egyptian army alike. On ʿAbd al-Nasir's death in 1970, his Vice President Anwar al-Sadat took the reins, embracing the mantle of "religion and science" (*al-ʿilm waʾl-īmān*) as he positioned himself as the "Believing President" (*al-Raʾīs al-Muʾmin*).[36] Over the course of the next decade, al-Sadat sought to shape the rise of a broader "Islamic Revival" (*Ṣaḥwa Islāmiyya*) as both state institutions and Islamic movements worked to redefine the goalposts of piety and public morality alike. Whether the Brotherhood, Ansar al-Sunna and the Jamʿiyya Sharʿiyya among Islamic movements, or the Supreme Council for Islamic Affairs (*al-Majlis al-Aʿlā li-l-Shuʾūn al-Islāmiyya*) within the Ministry of the Endowments and the Islamic Research Academy (*Majmaʿ al-Buḥūth al-Islāmiyya*) within al-Azhar, the question was not whether Islam should be applied to daily life but *how* to do so. When it came to facial hair, though, the earliest claimants to distinction were the activists affiliated with the Jamaʿa Islamiyya. While some

35. Jabir Rizq, *Madhabih al-Ikhwan fi Sujun Nasir: Asrar Rahiba Tudhaʿ li-Awwal Marra* (Cairo: Dar al-Iʿtisam, 1978), 117. A member of the Brotherhood who was executed in 1966, ʿAbd al-Fattah Ismaʿil, also sought not only to continue to grow his beard but, based on hadith reports of the Prophet Muhammad's actions that would become prominent among Salafis, plucked his mustache in order to trim it (155). I wish to thank Mathias Ghyoot for these citations.

36. Islamists often invoked these phrases to challenge the alleged gulf between the President's rhetorical commitments and his actions. For example, see "Barid al-Daʿwa," *al-Daʿwa*, Shaʿban 1398/July 1978, 62–63.

eventually aligned themselves with Salafi organizations, others would pledge allegiance to the Brotherhood.[37] Regardless of eventual allegiance, the men in this group displayed their substantial beards from Cairo to Alexandria to Asyut.[38]

The battle over facial hair in Egypt, however, only rose to prominence near the end of the 1970s as varied Islamic factions sought to visually communicate ethical rectitude. It would be members of the Jama'a Islamiyya who would first struggle with this issue. In February 1978, a letter from a group of students at a secondary school in Egypt appeared in the Muslim Brotherhood's mouthpiece, *al-Da'wa*. In this short note, the students complained that "we let our beards grow" (*aṭlaqnā liḥyātunā*) only to be denied entrance to the school and to be accused of being members of the Society for Excommunication and Migration (*al-Takfir wa'l-Hijra*).[39] Confusion with this organization, which called itself "The Muslim Group" (*Jamā'at al-Muslimīn*), was no small matter as it had risen to infamy in Egypt in July 1977 with the kidnapping and murder of Muhammad al-Dhahhabi, the former Minister of Endowments.[40]

Neither was such activism, and the potential for confusion with violent claimants to political power, limited to Egypt. In Saudi Arabia, Juhayman al-'Utaybi (d. 1980) led the attack of the Jama'a Salafiyya Muhtasiba (JSM) on the Grand Mosque of Mecca in December of 1979 while sporting a long and bushy beard. A onetime mentee of Ibn Baz, al-'Utaybi had come to the conclusion that his brother-in-law, Muhammad 'Abd Allah al-Qahtani (d. 1979), was the Mahdi, a Sunni messianic figure. Rejecting the religious legitimacy of the Saudi royal family and the political quietism of his mentor, al-'Utaybi and four to five hundred members of the JSM killed hundreds of

37. 'Abd al-Mun'im Abu-l-Futuh, *'Abd al-Mun'im Abu-l-Futuh*, 175.

38. For an overview of the movement's activities, see Kepel, *Muslim Extremism in Egypt*, 129–71. For a late 1970s/early 1980s image of an Islamic Student Movement 'Id celebration in which many students sport beards, yet most are not lengthy and some lack beards, see "Tayyar al-Jama'a al-Islamiyya fi al-Jami'at al-Misriyya," *al-Islamiyyun*, published 4 February 2016, https://tinyurl.com/y6dutbyf. I wish to thank Ibrahim Gemeah for pointing me to this image.

39. "Barid al-Da'wa," *al-Da'wa*, Sha'ban 1398/July 1978, 62–3.

40. *Al-Takfir wa'l-Hijra* (Excommunication and Migration) was a pejorative term used by Egyptian state bodies to challenge Jama'at al-Muslimin's claim to religious legitimacy. On the effort by state-aligned newspapers to discredit this group's demands, see Muhammad 'Abd al-Quddus, "Mawqif al-Sihafa min Qadiyyat al-Takfir," *al-Da'wa*, Shawwal 1397/September 1977, 46.

pilgrims and security forces before being subdued by a joint force that included the Saudi National Guard and French and Pakistani commandos.[41]

The JSM also posed a threat to the Saudi royal family and Salafi scholars alike by laying claim to Salafism. In a January 1980 interview with Salman b. ʿAbd al-ʿAziz (b. 1935), who became King in January 2015, the then-Governor of Riyadh noted that members of the JSM were not *merely* Kharijites (*khārijūn ʿalā al-dīn*) who had rejected the political order, but also were guilty of "concealing themselves by claiming to represent Salafism" (*al-tasattur bism al-Salafiyya*).[42] While the governor did not mention the JSM's distinctive bushy beards, a recent documentary about this attack includes still images of al-ʿUtaybi's full beard and trimmed mustache.[43] In addition, in a photograph taken shortly after the arrest of the surviving members of this group, at least half of the twenty pictured men appear to be adhering to the obligation to trim one's mustache and grow one's beard.[44]

While Egyptian Salafis could hardly escape the rumblings of domestic discord in Saudi Arabia, their concerns were also distinctly local. During this same period, leading figures within the Egyptian Ministry of Endowments, al-Azhar, and Dar al-Iftaʾ convened regular dialogue sessions (*ḥiwār*) with religious youth throughout Egypt, some of whom hailed from jihadist groups.[45] Such events, structured to serve the propaganda needs of the Mubarak regime, often included formerly imprisoned Islamists who had been coerced into attending as a condition of their release. In response, leading scholars, most notably the Jamʿiyya Sharʿiyya's ʿAbd al-Latif al-Mushtahiri, refused to appear.[46]

41. Stéphane Lacroix and Thomas Hegghammer, *The Meccan Rebellion: The Story of Juhayman al-ʿUtaybi Revisited* (Bristol, UK: Amal Press, 2011).

42. "Wahdatuna al-Wataniyya Mawdiʿ Fakhr wa Iʿtizaz," *al-Riyad*, 20 Muharram 1400/9 December 1979, 13.

43. BBC Arabic, *al-Film al-Wathaʾiqi: Hisar Makka* (BBC Arabic, 2017?), https://www.youtube.com/watch?v = hXDQSsLx8qQ, 52:30–52:59.

44. These pictures are taken from the archive of the Saudi historian ʿAbd Allah al-ʿUmrani. For a compilation of these photos, see "Hadithat al-Haram al-Shahira," 31 May 2017, available at https://www.youtube.com/watch?v=6DOSm_-EN44.

45. For example, Sayyid Abu Duma, "Nadwat al-Hiwar al-Fikri maʿa al-Jamaʿat al-Diniyya," *al-Ahram*, 28 October 1983, 13, and Sayyid Abu Duma, "Fikr Dini," *al-Ahram*, 18 December 1987, 13.

46. "Tasaʾulat Hawl al-Barnamaj al-Tilfizyuni Nadwat al-Raʾi," *al-Mujtamaʿ*, 15 Jumada al-Ula 1405/5 February 1985, 26–29.

One such event, convened in November of 1983 at the Workers' Cultural Institute (*al-Mu'assasa al-Thaqāfiyya al-'Ummāliyya*) in the blue-collar Cairene neighborhood of Shubra, discussed the related issues of the beard and the *niqab*. This event featured lectures by a leading member of al-Azhar's premier intellectual body, the Islamic Research Academy, 'Atiyya Saqr (who previously appeared in chapter 2), and by Muhammad al-Ahmadi Abu'l-Nur, Dean of the Girls' branch of the Faculty of Arabic and Islamic Studies at al-Azhar. These two leading scholars, together with less well-known colleagues from al-Azhar and the Ministry of Endowments, counseled these youth that "while some may think that growing a beard is inextricably linked to one's faith" (*iṭlāq al-liḥya qarīn al-īmān*), scholars disagree as to whether a beard is obligatory at all, let alone a basis for declaring someone non-Muslim (*al-takfīr*).[47] Although a broad cross-section of pious youth participated in these dialogues, the association of shaving the beard with *takfir* left little doubt that this point was directed at jihadi youth, some of whom were also Salafi.[48]

As Ibn Baz balanced his role as a leading religious authority in Saudi Arabia and his transnational Salafi commitments, he used the medium of the pamphlet to drive a conversation about facial hair. In 1981, he served as the editor (*muḥaqqiq*) of a short text, *The Obligation to Grow Out the Beard*, written by Muhammad Zakariyya al-Kandhalawi (d. 1982), who had moved to Medina from India in 1973. Most striking about this choice was al-Kandhalawi's organizational and legal affiliations: he was not a Salafi or even a Wahhabi-Hanbali, but rather a Hanafi scholar of significant stature within the Tablighi Jama'at, an Islamic proselytization movement that emerged in South Asia.[49]

47. Sayyid Abu Duma, "Nadwat al-Hiwar al-Fikri ma'a Shabab al-Jama'at al-Diniyya Tunaqish," *al-Ahram*, 25 November 1983, 13.

48. Salafi youth were deeply influenced by the ideas of Sayyid Qutb regarding divine sovereignty (*ḥākimiyya*) and the related necessity of excommunicating those Muslims who lived according to "man-made" law. As Richard Gauvain argues, "the key question [that divided Egyptian Salafism] was simple: to what degree should a Salafi acknowledge the legitimacy of Mubarak's regime (and implicitly any political regime that does not rule through Shari'a)?" (*Salafi Ritual Purity*, 39–40).

49. Like Salafis, members of the Tablighi Jama'at seek to model their lives after the practices of the Prophet Muhammad. See Barbara Metcalf, "Living Hadith in the Tablighi Jama'at," *The Journal of Asian Studies* 52, no. 3 (1993): 584–608. The Tablighi Jama'at was founded in 1927 by Mawla Muhammad Ilyas Kandhalawi (d. 1944), the paternal uncle of Muhammad Zakariyya al-Kandhalawi (d. 1982), who studied with leading Deobandi scholars. See Brannon

In a fifty-eight-page text first published in India in 1976 and then translated into Arabic three years later,[50] al-Kandhalawi emphasizes the significance of the beard as a marker of boundaries between Muslims and non-Muslims, on the one hand, and men and women, on the other.[51] As this South Asian scholar explained, "All people have [distinct] characteristics and we have characteristics that we learned from our Prophet, peace be upon him . . . including growing out the beard and trimming the mustache. . . ."[52] The beard thus serves to signal the "beauty, completeness, respect and dignity of masculinity" (*jamāl al-rujūliyya wa kamāluhā wa'l-hayba wa'l-waqār*).[53]

With regard to the key issue of the precise length of the beard, al-Kandhalawi dispassionately set out the differing positions of the four Sunni legal schools on this matter, noting that there is no report of any Companion ever cutting his beard to *less* than "a minimum of a fist" (*ʿalā mā dūna al-qabḍa*).[54] It is here that Ibn Baz added a footnote, in which he introduced an alternative interpretative approach: the claim that a vague but sound Prophetic hadith trumps a detailed report about the practice of a Companion (*al-sunna muqaddama ʿalā al-jamīʿ wa-lā qawl li-aḥad bi-khilāf al-sunna*). Moreover, for Ibn Baz, the record of the Companions was far from straightforward: to challenge the Ibn ʿUmar hadith, he cited competing narrations from ʿUmar b. al-Khattab, his son Ibn ʿUmar, and Abu Hurayra that prohibited cutting the beard at all. In light of this ambiguous evidence, Muslims must defer to the Prophet's general instruction to "grow the beard."[55]

That same year, the question of the beard's specifications became a matter of discussion in the official journal of the Islamic University of Medina. Ahmad ʿAli Taha Rayyan (d. 2021), an Egyptian graduate of al-Azhar who

---

Ingram, *Revival From Below: The Deoband Movement and Global Islam* (Berkeley: University of California Press, 2018), 10–11, 149–59. Unlike its Salafi counterpart, however, this group includes strong Sufi influences. See Metcalf, "Living Hadith in the Tablighi Jamaʿat," 602.

50. Muhammad Zakariya al-Kandhalawi, *Wujub Iʿfaʾ al-Lihya*, ed. ʿAbd al-ʿAziz b. Baz (Mecca: Maktabat al-Maʿarif, 1981), 6. According to Worldcat records, a 1979 edition of the work was published in Mecca by al-Maktaba al-Imdadiyya without Ibn Baz's comments. I was unable to locate a physical copy of this edition.

51. al-Kandhalawi, *Wujub Iʿfaʾ al-Lihya*, 1 and 23, respectively.

52. al-Kandhalawi, *Wujub Iʿfaʾ al-Lihya*, 27.

53. al-Kandhalawi, *Wujub Iʿfaʾ al-Lihya*, 52.

54. al-Kandhalawi, *Wujub Iʿfaʾ al-Lihya*, 16–17.

55. al-Kandhalawi, *Wujub Iʿfaʾ al-Lihya*, 18–19.

had received his Ph.D. from the University's Faculty of Shariʿa and Law (*Qānūn*) in 1973, was about to conclude a four-year stint (1977–81) teaching in the Faculty of Noble Hadith at IUM.[56] In the first of two articles, this Salafi scholar set out three hadith narrations regarding actions that constitute "practices central to human nature" (*sunan al-fiṭra*), only one of which includes both growing a beard and trimming one's mustache.[57] In the second article, Rayyan explained the division between those jurists who argued that one can cut the beard if it exceeds the length of a fist (*al-qabḍa*) or to the extent that it serves a man's distinguished bearing (*hayʾa*)[58] and those who reject any form of trimming the beard. For Rayyan, "the fist (*al-qabḍa*) or close to it . . . is the measure on which one should rely."[59] More broadly, wearing a beard constitutes a "prominent sign of masculinity" (*ʿunwān^{an} bāriz^{an} ʿalā al-rujūla*) as well as a means of shaping sound behavior and of distinguishing Muslims from non-Muslims.[60] For Rayyan, the beard communicated religious and gendered claims alike.

There is no evidence from this period, however, that Salafi scholars more broadly invoked the fist as a minimal measurement when discussing the beard. In a 1982 pamphlet, the Syrian Salafi ʿUthman b. ʿAbd al-Qadir al-Safi (d. 2002) says nothing about the length of the beard,[61] while in a 1984 work, the Jordanian Salafi and student of al-Albani, ʿAli al-Halabi (b. 1960), states that the beard should stretch from "the hair below the lower lip to the hair that grows under the chin" (*al-shaʿr al-nābit ʿalā al-shafa al-safalī maʿa shaʿr al-dhaqn—ila al-shaʿr al-nābit taḥta al-dhaqn*).[62] This trend extended to Saudi

56. For biographical information on Rayyan, see the Salafi website Ahl al-Hadith ("Tarjama Mukhtasara li-Fadilat al-Shaykh al-Ustadh Ahmad Taha Rayyan," https://www.ahlalhdeeth.com/vb/showthread.php?t = 262939).

57. Ahmad ʿAli Taha Rayyan, "Min Abhath al-Fiqh waʾl-Sunna," *Majallat al-Jamiʿa al-Islamiyya bi-l-Madina al-Munawwara*, #44 (1981), 44: 257–58. I base my estimate on the date of the forty-ninth issue of the magazine, as recorded in the 8 February 1982 issue of *al-Madina* newspaper. See "Majallat al-Jamiʿa al-Islamiyya," *al-Madina*, 14 Rabiʿ al-Thani 1402/8 February 1982, 17.

58. Rayyan, "Min Abhath al-Fiqh waʾl-Sunna," 19:494–6. This citation is from issue #46 of *Majallat al-Jamiʿa al-Islamiyya bi-l-Madina al-Munawwara*.

59. Rayyan, "Min Abhath al-Fiqh waʾl-Sunna," 19:498.

60. Rayyan, "Min Abhath al-Fiqh waʾl-Sunna," 19:494–99 and 20:1–4.

61. al-Safi, *Hukm al-Sharʿ fi al-Lihya*.

62. ʿAli al-Halabi, *Hukm al-Din fi al-Lihya waʾl-Tadkhin* (Amman, Jordan: al-Maktaba al-Islamiyya, 1984), 18.

Arabia: in a 1985 work, the Saudi scholar Hammud al-Tuwayjiri (d. 1993) noted that the Prophet Muhammad himself had a "thick beard" (*kathth al-liḥya*).[63] He further recounted a hadith report in which the Prophet stated that he had seen the Prophet Aaron in the heavens while on his Night Journey (*al-isrāʾ wa'l-miʿrāj*) and that the latter's beard was so long that it nearly reached his navel (*takād liḥyatuhu tuṣīb surratahu min ṭūlihā*).[64] Indeed, even Ibn Baz did not mention this measurement in a 1983 ruling published in the Kuwaiti Islamist magazine *al-Mujtamaʿ*.[65] The fist was not yet a standard among Salafis across the Middle East.

Similarly, leading Salafi scholars of Ansar al-Sunna had yet to embrace this measurement. Most prominently, in a January 1986 fatwa, Ansar al-Sunna President Muhammad ʿAli ʿAbd al-Rahim noted that it is forbidden to shave the beard, yet did not specify the extent to which one should trim it.[66] During this mid-1980s, though, a relatively junior voice in the Salafi movement, Muhammad b. Ismaʿil al-Muqaddam of the Alexandria-based Salafi Call (*al-Daʿwa al-Salafiyya*), cited a series of hadith reports and a twentieth-century Maliki scholar[67] to answer the question of whether the beard should be one fist or two (*qabḍatayn*). According to al-Muqaddam, the "most appropriate" (*al-ansab*) solution is that the beard "not exceed a fist" (*lā tazād ʿalā al-qabḍa*) in order to avoid excess (*al-mughāla*).[68] Apart from al-Muqaddam, however, Egyptian Salafis said little on this topic.

The second half of the 1980s witnessed intensified debates among Salafis over whether the fist is sufficient and, if so, whether one may or should remove hair beyond this length. On the one hand, the debate constituted Salafi engagement with the question of how to understand and apply the hadith

63. Hammud al-Tuwayjiri, *al-Radd ʿala Man Ajaza Tahdhib al-Lihya* (Riyadh: Maktabat al-Maʿarif), 11–12.

64. al-Tuwayjiri, *al-Radd ʿala Man Ajaza Tahdhib al-Lihya*, 7–8.

65. ʿAbd al-ʿAziz b. Baz, "Tasaʾulat wa Ijabat," *al-Mujtamaʿ*, 20 Rajab 1403/3 May 1983, 42–43, at 43.

66. Muhammad ʿAli ʿAbd al-Rahim, "Bab al-Fatawa," *al-Tawhid*, Jumada al-Ula 1406/February 1986, 18–31, at 29.

67. Muqaddam cited the opinion of Muhammad b. Habib Allah b. ʿAbd Allah b. Ahmad al-Maliki (d. 1944), also known as Habib Allah al-Shinqiti. See al-Shinqiti, *Zad al-Muslim fi-ma Ittafaq ʿalayhi al-Bukhari wa Muslim* (Cairo: Dar Ihyaʾ al-Kutub al-ʿArabiyya, 1967), 1:128–9.

68. al-Muqaddam, *Adillat Tahrim Halq al-Lihya*, 90.

corpus to law, a longstanding site for the articulation of normative Islamic practice and the performance of scholarly knowledge. On the other hand, the concern with the beard was also a matter of communicating social distinction, as Saudi and Egyptian Salafis alike sought to make authoritative claims to the mantle of Islamic law. Egyptian Salafis also faced an additional burden: the challenge of differentiating themselves from jihadists in the eyes of security forces, a matter that had grown even more pressing as this period witnessed a spate of violence targeting nightclubs, liquor stores, former government ministers, and journalists.[69]

In a 1987 editorial in Ansar al-Sunna's mouthpiece *al-Tawhid*, the journal's editor vented his frustration that, in the aftermath of incidents of terror and violence in Cairo, writers have "sought to make people fear every bearded man (*kull dhī liḥya*) . . . accusing those who wear the beard and long robe (*jilbāb*) of terrorism."[70] Saudi Salafis took note of this challenge faced by their Egyptian counterparts: in a 1987 article in the *Sahwa*-affiliated *al-Bayan*, entitled "Where is Egypt Going?," Muhammad ʿAbd Allah noted the increasing popularity of the beard and long robe in Egypt and complained that proponents of jihad in Egypt were not necessarily Salafis.[71] Furthermore, as a preacher in Ansar al-Sunna, Ahmad Taha Nasr, explained in 1988, "the beard serves as a noble announcement to introduce society to what it means to be a Sunni" (*li-taʿrīf al-mujtamaʿ bi-kalimat Sunnī*).[72] Whether we read Nasr's invocation of Sunnism as an ecumenical statement or as code word for Salafism, the beard's communicative function is clear.

Just as challenging was the question of how to integrate into Egyptian government institutions that rejected the beard. In the early 1980s, this question was first tackled not by Salafi scholars but by the State Mufti, Jadd al-Haqq ʿAli Jadd al-Haqq (r. 1978–82, d. 1996). In a 21 June 1981 ruling, this leading state religious official fielded a fatwa request from the military's judicial branch (*qiṣm al-qaḍāʾ al-ʿaskarī*) regarding whether it was licit for conscripted soldiers (*mujannadīn*) to shave the beard. In response, al-Haqq

69. Ibrahim, *Egypt, Islam and Democracy*, 62.

70. Ahmad Fahmi Ahmad, "Kalimat al-Tahrir," *al-Tawhid*, Safar 1407/October 1986, 109.

71. Muhammad ʿAbd Allah, "Misr ila Ayna?," *al-Bayan*, Dhu al-Hijja 1407/August 1987, 7:62.

72. Ahmad Taha Nasr, "Iʿfaʾ al-Lihya Sunna Thabita wa Fitra Mustaqima," *al-Tawhid*, Ramadan 1408/April 1988, 52–5, at 54.

described a beard as "a desired command in Islam and the Sunna of the Prophet. . . ." (*amr marghūb fī al-Islām wa innahu min Sunnatihi*).[73] Accordingly, bearded men are simply following "the authoritative model of Islam. . . . It is not necessary to force them remove it or to sanction them for growing it (*ijbārahum ʿalā izālatihā aw ʿiqābahum bi-sabab iṭlaqihā*) . . . and there is no obedience to man in sinning against the creator (*lā ṭāʿa li-makhlūq fī maʿṣiyyat al-khāliq*)."[74] Despite this ruling, however, we have no evidence of a change in army policy at this time.

Instead, in the late 1980s, Salafi scholars would seek to tackle the same question as Jadd al-Haqq, albeit from a position outside the Egyptian state. In a 9 October 1988 fatwa, Ibn Baz responded to an Egyptian enrolled in a school of maritime transportation (*al-naql al-baḥrī*) which required students to shave. According to Ibn Baz, such a challenge was easily surmounted:

> We recommend that you enroll in a Saudi university, such as the Islamic University of Medina or King ʿAbd al-ʿAziz University in Jeddah, or Umm al-Qura University in Mecca. . . . We are ready to help you if you write to us with [these details] and send me a copy of your qualifications and a letter which certifies your religious commitment (*tazkiya*) from the President of Ansar al-Sunna al-Muhammadiyya in Cairo, Shaykh Muhammad ʿAli ʿAbd al-Rahim.[75]

By contrast, Ibn al-ʿUthaymin offered a more confrontational approach, arguing that, if forced to shave, the entirety of the army lower ranks should disobey their superiors and should instruct them that "this sin is the reason for the failure and defeat [of Arab armies]."[76] In short, whatever one's approach, shaving the beard was non-negotiable for these two leading Saudi Salafi scholars.

Yet, if Ibn Baz recommended a move to a more supportive climate and Ibn al-ʿUthaymin counseled resistance, Ansar al-Sunna's leader had other ideas.

73. *al-Fatawa al-Islamiyya min Dar al-Iftaʾ al-Misriyya*, ed. Zakariyya al-Bari, Jadd al-Haqq ʿAli Jadd al-Haqq, and Jamal al-Din Muhammad Mahmud (Cairo: Supreme Council for Islamic Affairs, 1400/1980), 10:3479.

74. *al-Fatawa al-Islamiyya min Dar al-Iftaʾ al-Misriyya*, 10:3480.

75. Ibn Baz, *Majmuʿa Fatawa wa-Maqalat Mutanawiʿa*, 10:71–72.

76. See Ibn al-ʿUthaymin, *al-Sharh al-Mumtiʿ ʿala Zad al-Mustaqniʿ* (Dammam, Saudi Arabia: Dar Ibn Jawzi, 1425), 8:20. By contrast, the 11 April 1997 edition of *al-Ahram* included a fatwa request from a young men who wished to grow his beard but feared the suspicion of state security forces. In response, the State Mufti, Ahmad al-Tayyib (b. 1946), advised him that the beard was praiseworthy rather than required and that he had nothing to fear from the security forces. See "Isʾalu al-Faqih," *al-Ahram*, 11 April 1997, 8.

In a January 1988 fatwa, Muhammad ʿAli ʿAbd al-Rahim noted that he'd received many letters regarding whether it was permissible to shave the beard and that, while growing the beard was indeed obligatory (*yajib al-iltizām bihi*), such an obligation was not absolute. Specifically, in those instances in which the "discord caused by [growing] the beard is greater than that from shaving it" (*qiyām al-fitna bi-sabab al-liḥya ashshad min ḥalqiha*), then shaving was permissible.[77] Whatever the solution, the dilemma for Egyptian Salafi men was clear.

In Saudi Arabia, on the other hand, the threat of transnational (as distinct from local) jihadism had not yet reared its head, and the debate over the beard among Quietist Salafis was primarily one of interpretative approach rather than distinction from jihadis, Salafi or otherwise. At a time when there was broad public support and active government participation in funding the *Mujahidun* in Afghanistan, neither Saudi security forces nor scholars were concerned with the possibility that Saudi members would soon turn their fire on the Kingdom.[78] It was thus little surprise that, far from pushing them away, scholars in key Saudi religious institutions, most notably the Council of Senior Scholars (*Hayʾat Kibār al-ʿUlamāʾ*) and the Permanent Committee for Scholarly Research and Issuing Fatwas, wrote articles and issued fatwas on the topic of the beard in a Salafi-Jihadi magazine published in Afghanistan.[79]

77. Muhammad ʿAli ʿAbd al-Rahim, "Bab al-Fatawa," *al-Tawhid*, Jumada al-Ukhra 1408/~January 1988, 13–21, at 13.

78. I wish to thank Yasir Qadhi for this observation.

79. For a ruling on the beard, see Hayʾat Kibar ʿUlamaʾ al-Saʿudiyya, "Bab al-Fatawa," *al-Mujahid*, Dhu al-Qaʿda-Dhu al-Hijja 1414/May-June 1994, 49–52, at 51–52. On the beard's importance to Muslim identity, see Muhammad Jamil Zaynu, "Man Tashabbaha bi-Qawmin Fa-Huwa Min-Hum," *al-Mujahid*, Jumada al-Thaniyya 1410/January 1990, 46. *Al-Mujahid* published regularly between 1988 and 1994 under the leadership of Jamil al-Rahman (d. 1991), who in the mid-1980s founded a movement known as Jamaʿat al-Daʿwa ila al-Qurʾan wa Ahl al-Hadith. After the withdrawal of Soviet troops in 1988, al-Rahman established a Salafi state in the Kunar Province of Afghanistan. On Saudi support for al-Rahman, see Hegghammer, *The Caravan*, 415. *Al-Mujahid*, however, was a comparatively marginal player within a broader periodical scene that included Islamist, Traditionalist and Nationalist publications. Further, as Simon Wolfgang Fuchs argues, "[t]he marginality of . . . anti-Shiʿi statements also calls into question the suspected Saudi influence on the *jihad* more broadly" ("Glossy Global Leadership: Unpacking the Multilingual Religious Thought of the Jihad," in *Afghanistan's Islam*, ed. Nile Green [Berkeley: University of California Press, 2017], 197). For an analysis of the

As the 1990s began, the question of whether one should trim the beard beyond a fist was still unsettled. The early years of this decade were chaotic: from the 1990 Iraqi invasion of Kuwait and the Saudi decision to welcome American troops, to the *Sahwa*'s explicit challenge to the religious credentials of the royal family and the religious establishment, both Salafi and Wahhabi-Hanbali scholars were on the defensive. This position was a product not merely of the decision by the Council of Senior Scholars to provide religious cover for the arrival of foreign troops, but also of the broader perception that state-aligned scholars were mere appendages of the ruling elite.[80]

The debate over the beard, however, was separate from these contestations, part and parcel of an interpretative debate among Salafis as to how to balance between the authority of the Prophet's general directions and practices and his Companions' more specific instructions.[81] This methodological question was of outsized significance to Salafi scholars: unlike their *madhhab*-aligned counterparts who could cite previous rulings within their school alongside proof texts from the Quran and Sunna, Salafis were committed to the normative and textual centrality of the first three generations of Islamic history.[82] Debate over the authority of the Companions was thus both a method of distinguishing Salafis from non-Salafis and a strategy for internal differentiation among Salafis.

The importance of precise evidence and rulings was only heightened by

---

ambiguity exhibited by Ibn Baz regarding whether participation in the Afghani jihad was obligatory, see Hegghammer, *The Caravan*, 198–99, 305.

80. Lacroix, *Awakening Islam*, 152–53, 158–64.

81. The debate over how to strike the correct balance between Muhammad's general directions and his Companions' statements and practices was hardly unique to Salafis or to the twentieth century. Early Muslim jurists, most notably al-Shafiʿi, had sought to resolve the challenge posed by apparent contradictions both between the Quran and hadith reports, and among hadith reports, so that he and other jurists could use the corpus of authenticated hadith reports to elaborate on the Quran. See David R. Vishanoff, *Islamic Hermeneutics: How Sunni Legal Theories Imagined a Revealed Law* (New Haven, CT: American Oriental Society, 2011), 15–65, esp. 20, 40, 61.

82. I am not suggesting that Salafis have bypassed the subsequent legal tradition all together; what Alexander Thurston terms the "Salafi Canon" includes Ibn Hanbal, Ibn Taymiyya, Muhammad b. ʿAbd al-Wahhab, Muhammad ʿAli al-Shawkani, and Siddiq Hasan Khan al-Qannuji (*Salafism in Nigeria*, 37–52). Rather, I am arguing that Salafis foreground early Islamic history as uniquely authoritative, and assess the truth-value of this canon with reference to its fidelity to the accurate transmission of early Islamic history.

broader educational and intellectual trends that affected Islamic scholars throughout the region. Gregory Starrett has previously noted the "objectification" and "functionalization" of religious knowledge in Egypt, which rendered Islam as a concrete set of pronouncements which was then utilized in the service of discrete political goals.[83] A similar dynamic occurred in the Saudi educational system that developed rapidly during the second half of the twentieth century,[84] and the claim that Islam had defined positions on everything from politics to economics to hygiene could be found in daily Saudi newspapers.[85]

Al-Albani, who was at this point based in Jordan, sought to establish his position clearly. In a lesson delivered on 7 August 1992 entitled "The Proof Texts Regarding the Obligation to Trim the Beard Beyond the Fist,"[86] he claimed that those who argue for the obligation to grow the beard out indefinitely are "innovators . . . who follow their own whims" (*mubtadiʿūn . . . yatabbiʿūn ahwāʾahum*).[87] Declaring his goal of elucidating "the Messenger's practice" (*mā kāna ʿalayhi al-rasūl*), al-Albani stipulated that it is permitted to shave the hair that extends beyond the fist (*al-qabḍa*), based on the Ibn ʿUmar hadith.[88] In a second lesson held on 8 September 1993,[89] al-Albani elaborated on the interpretative difference between him and some of his Salafi colleagues: "Today, it is not sufficient to [just] take from the Quran and Sunna. . . . We must also take from the path of the believers (*al-akdh min sabīl al-muʾminīn*) . . . that is to say, what the Pious Ancestors (*al-Salaf*

83. Starrett, *Putting Islam to Work*, 77–86.

84. For the history of trends of objectification and functionalization in Saudi Arabia, see Farquhar, *Circuits of Faith*, 47–65.

85. For example, the claim that Islam is "the religion of cleanliness" (*din al-naẓāfa*) had become increasingly common. See "Taqrir al-Yawm: Usbuʿ al-Nazafa," *al-Riyad*, 6 Muharram 1405/1 October 1984, 9. The cited article sought to elucidate "the Islamic view on cleanliness" (*mawqif al-Islām min al-naẓāfa*).

86. *Ashritat al-Shaykh al-Albani*, www.thedawa.org, accessed 24 June 2019. These tapes were converted into digital files as part of the *al-Huda wa'l-Nur* (Guidance and Light) series. The audio files themselves provide the data of the lecture.

87. Muhammad Nasir al-Din al-Albani, *Adillat Wujub Akhdh ma Zad ʿan al-Qabda*, 7 August 1992, 62 min., at 3:10.

88. al-Albani, *Adillat Wujub Akhdh ma Zad ʿan al-Qabda*, 8:30–9:05.

89. Muhammad Nasir al-Din al-Albani, *al-Insaf ʿInda al-Imam al-Albani bi-Wujub al-Akdh min al-Lihya ma Zad ʿan al-Qabda*, 8 September 1993, 65 min.

al-Ṣāliḥ) did."[90] This interpretative approach that emphasized engagement with the early Islamic community beyond Muhammad would have significant implications.

The contrasting position in this debate is most visible in a 1994 ruling by Ibn Baz, in which he turned to Ansar al-Sunna's *al-Tawhid* to respond to an article in *al-Madina* newspaper. The offending article, published on 3 July 1994, was written by Muhammad b. ʿAli al-Sabuni, a Syrian graduate of al-Azhar with Ashaʿrite theological leanings. Al-Sabuni had come to Saudi Arabia in the 1960s on a teacher loan program organized by the Syrian Ministry of Education and would spend some thirty years in teaching and research at King ʿAbd al-ʿAziz University (Jeddah) and at Umm al-Qurra University (Mecca), while also serving as an advisor for the premier Saudi international proselytization body, the Muslim World League (*Rābiṭat al-ʿĀlam al-Islāmī*).[91] In this article, al-Sabuni noted that "some among the youth believe that taking anything from the beard is forbidden" (*al-akhdh shayʾ min al-liḥya ḥarām*) and thus grow their beard "so that it nearly reaches the navel . . . [a practice that] frightens children (*tukhīf al-aṭfāl*)."[92]

Al-Sabuni's challenge to Salafism, however, stretched back more than a decade. During the spring and summer of 1983, this scholar had published a series of articles in the Islamist *al-Mujtamaʿ* in which he argued for a "big tent" of Sunni theology that included not only Salafi theology (e.g., *Madhhab al-Salaf*) but also Ashʿarism and Maturidism.[93] In response, leading Salafi scholars, including Salih al-Fawzan and Ibn Baz, challenged these efforts to blur the theological distinctions between Salafi theology on God's attributes

90. al-Albani, *al-Insaf ʿInda al-Imam al-Albani*, 20:50–21:23.

91. "Muhammad ʿAli al-Sabuni," *al-Maktaba al-Shamila*, http://shamela.ws/index.php/author/1318, accessed 5 June 2019.

92. ʿAbd al-ʿAziz b. Baz, "Wujub Iʿfaʾ al-Lihya wa Tahrim Halqiha wa Qassiha," *al-Tawhid*, Jumada al-Ukhra 1415/November 1994, 34–5, at 34. Ibn Baz's ruling also appears in Ibn Baz, *Majmuʿ Fatawa wa Maqalat Mutanawwiʿa*, 8:39–70.

93. al-Sabuni, "ʿAqidat Ahl al-Sunna fi Mizan al-Sharʿ," *al-Mujtamaʿ*, 17 Ramadan 1403/28 June 1983, 34–36; al-Sabuni, "ʿAqidat Ahl al-Sunna fi Mizan al-Sharʿ #2," *al-Mujtamaʿ*, 24 Ramadan 1403/5 July 1983, 34–36; al-Sabuni, "ʿAqidat Ahl al-Sunna fi Mizan al-Sharʿ #3," *al-Mujtamaʿ*, 9 Shawwal 1403/19 July 1983, 34–37; al-Sabuni, "ʿAqidat Ahl al-Sunna fi Mizan al-Sharʿ #4," *al-Mujtamaʿ*, 16 Shawwal 1403/26 July 1983, 34–36; al-Sabuni, "ʿAqidat Ahl al-Sunna fi Mizan al-Sharʿ #5," *al-Mujtamaʿ*, 24 Shawwal 1403/2 August 1983, 34–36.

vis-à-vis their Sunni competitors.[94] As Ibn Baz explained, Ashʿari and Maturidi Muslims would suffer in hellfire (*fī al-nār*) for their theological errors, while Salafis would not.[95] Over a decade later, the terrain of contestation had shifted from theological to legal debate and Ibn Baz sought to strike down the claim that one may trim the beard. While the target of his ire was ostensibly al-Sabuni, who had argued against an absolute obligation to grow the beard, Ibn Baz was equally committed to showing that it is impermissible to trim the beard beyond the fist, as al-Albani had suggested.

To do so, Ibn Baz questioned the soundness of a hadith report in al-Tirmidhi's collection that the Prophet would trim his beard horizontally and vertically (*min ʿarḍihā wa-ṭūlihā*). He acknowledged that such a text, if authentic, would have constituted sufficient proof as to the permissibility of trimming the beard. Yet, he classified it as "weak" (*ḍaʿīf*) because its chain of transmission included ʿUmar b. Harun al-Balkhi, whose reports were considered unreliable (*matrūk al-ḥadīth*).[96] Further, while Ibn Baz accepted the soundness of the Ibn ʿUmar report—not invoked by al-Sabuni but used explicitly by those such as al-Albani who argued for trimming beyond the fist—he argued that a general yet sound Prophetic hadith (here, "grow the beard") takes precedence over a specific report of a Companion's practice. As such, this interpretation would constitute an action of "critical reasoning" (*ijtihād*) based on this hadith, rather than reliance on the narration as a proof text.[97]

While the battle with al-Sabuni appears to have subsided, al-Albani was not finished. In a 1996 study of weak hadith reports, he expanded upon his previous argument that the beard can be trimmed:

> The Sunna attested to by the actions of the pious ancestors (*salaf*) from among the Companions and the Successors (*al-tābiʿīn*) and the eponyms of the legal schools who used critical reasoning (*al-āʾimma al-mujtahidīn*) is that the beard should be the length of a fist and that anything beyond that should be cut. . . . The claim that one should grow the beard in absolute fashion (*iʿfāʾuhā muṭlaqan*) is

94. Salih b. Fawzan, "Taʿqibat ʿala Maqalat al-Sabuni fi al-Sifat," *al-Mujtamaʿ*, 17 Safar 1404/22 November 1983, 36–38; b. Fawzan, "Taʿqibat ʿala Maqalat al-Sabuni fi al-Sifat," *al-Mujtamaʿ*, 24 Safar 1404/28 November 1983, 38–39, 48; Ibn Baz, "Tanbihat Hamma ʿala Ma Katabahu al-Shaykh Muhammad ʿAli al-Sabuni fi Sifat Allah ʿAzza wa Jall," *al-Mujtamaʿ*, 19 Jumada al-Ula 1404/21 February 1984, 41–48.

95. Ibn Baz, "Tanbihat Hamma," 42.

96. Ibn Baz, "Wujub Iʿfaʾ al-Lihya wa Tahrim Halqiha wa Qassiha," 35.

97. Ibn Baz, "Wujub Iʿfaʾ al-Lihya wa Tahrim Halqiha wa Qassiha," 34–5.

what the [leading Maliki scholar Abū Isḥāq] al-Shatibi [d. 790/1388] termed "additional innovation" (*al-bid'a al-iḍāfiyya*).[98]

Far from a necessary product of the Prophetic record, al-Albani used al-Shatibi to argue that the prohibition against trimming the beard when it exceeds the length of a fist is a case of expanding incorrectly upon a legitimate act of worship.[99]

Al-Albani also responded to Ibn Baz's claim that the Prophet's general instruction supersedes the specific practice of a Companion. While acknowledging that he could not locate an authentic hadith in which the Prophet trims his beard or explicitly permits doing so, al-Albani argued that this action is affirmed by Companions beyond Ibn 'Umar—most notably 'Abd Allah b. 'Abbas (d. 68/687–8) and Muhammad b. Ka'b al-Qurazi (d. 108/726)—who asserted that the Prophet permitted trimming the beard based on Q. 22:29 ("and let them end their untidiness"), which specifies how Muslims are to prepare themselves for Hajj.[100]

What should we make of this methodological disagreement between these two heavyweights of Purist Salafism? The disagreement does not concern the requirement to grow the beard, or the relevance of the fist as a measurement. Instead, it pivots on how to apply the principle that a Companion hadith can specify or clarify actions or instructions of the Prophet Muhammad. Ibn Baz sought to sidestep the issue by claiming that the obligation to grow the beard is absolute; by contrast, al-Albani relied on Ibn 'Umar to elaborate on this obligation. For those Salafis such as al-Albani who demonstrated a rigorous commitment to proof-texts,[101] the actions of the Companions constituted a vital source that undergirded the articulation of a communicative ethical

98. al-Albani, *Silsilat al-Ahadith al-Da'ifa wa'l-Mawdu'a wa Atharuha al-Sayyi' fi al-Umma*, 5:5. For further explanation, see 5:375–77.

99. The category of "additional innovation" is distinct from a case of "true innovation" (*al-bid'a al-haqīqiyya*) in which there is no basis for the practice at all. See Abu Ishaq al-Shatibi, *al-I'tisam*, ed. Salim b. 'Abd al-Hilali (Khobar, Saudi Arabia: Dar Ibn 'Affan, 1992) 1:367.

100. al-Albani, *Silsilat al-Ahadith al-Da'ifa wa'l-Mawdu'a wa Atharuha al-Sayyi' fi'l-Umma*, 5:376.

101. Al-Albani's previous rejection of Wahhabi-Hanbali claims to the necessity of the *niqab* due to what he saw as the absence of unequivocal proof texts is said to have contributed to his expulsion from the Kingdom in 1963. His position on this question was part and parcel of a broader argument that Hanbalism is essentially similar to other schools of law because it privileges precedent within the school over proof texts. See Lacroix, *Awakening Islam*, 84–85.

project for modern Muslims based on a reconstruction of early Islamic history. Equally important, al-Albani had spent much of his professional career trumpeting a minority religious position outside established scholarly hierarchies; as with the case of praying in shoes and individually-centered female modesty, al-Albani's concern was to prioritize daily behavior that would visually distinguish his flock from their competitors but did not require access to state power.

By contrast, Ibn Baz, whose Salafism was a minority strand within a larger Wahhabi-Hanbali establishment, was a beneficiary of this establishment's key institutions. As a scholar for whom departing from the rulings of the Hanbali *madhhab* carried potential professional costs, a broader set of sources was not necessarily an advantage. This institutional reality, in turn, is linked to Ibn Baz's interpretative preferences: as discussed in chapter 4, he was generally ready to avail himself of alternative means of justification, such as "blocking the means of sin" (*sadd al-dharīʿāt*), when he could not find persuasive proof texts to justify separating men and women in educational and professional settings, as his Wahhabi-Hanbali counterparts did. Notwithstanding these differing interpretative approaches and institutional positions, however, both agreed on the fist as the relevant point of reference while, roughly a decade prior, there was no such consensus. More importantly, Salafi men across the Middle East now had a clear measurement on the basis of which to emulate the Prophet through facial hair.

CONCLUSION

Beginning in the mid-1970s, Salafi scholars laid claim to the beard as a marker of identity. While the argument for a beard drew on an extensive Islamic legal tradition, the turn to this practice also reflected an ambition to articulate a universal standard of piety, the cultural challenge posed by secular-nationalist understandings of facial hair as markers of community and masculinity alike, and the changes that these trends had wrought on the social world of these scholars and their audiences. Equally important were the visually striking young Islamic activists who sported bushy beards (the length of which exceeded a fist) and some of whom, through spectacular acts of violence, drew the attention not only of a mass Muslim audience but also of state security forces. Faced with a need to differentiate themselves from the secular-nationalist competitors and to visually communicate Salafism's commitment to a *telos* of emulating the Prophet Muhammad, these scholars came to emphasize the fist as a minimal measurement.

What does the history of the Salafi beard teach us about this religious movement? Prior to the 1970s, Salafi scholars gave little thought to the precise parameters of the beard. Though they emphasized their commitment to deriving all Islamic law from the Quran and Sunna, the "Salafi beard" did not arise directly from this movement's hermeneutical approach. Instead, the impulse to emulate the Prophet arose from an effort to craft a model of embodied piety that communicated Salafism's purist commitment to Islam's first three generations. While the seemingly marginal site may have appeared to offer the basis for a powerful visual statement, Salafis also struggled to differentiate themselves on the basis of the beard alone from their jihadi counterparts.

Despite the qualified success of this effort, the centrality of facial hair to Salafi piety underscores the increasing significance of visibility for twentieth- and twenty-first-century participants in an Islamic ethical tradition. As Ahmad Taha Nasr noted in *al-Tawhid*, "The beard serves as a noble announcement to introduce society to what it means to be a Sunni" (*li-ta'rīf al-mujtama' bi-kalimat Sunnī*).[102] Salafis made a claim to define true Sunnism, and by extension true Islam, by embracing a project of Islamic ethical formation that, in inextricably modern fashion, centered on communication.

Faced with ambiguities and interpretative divisions regarding the early textual record of the Prophet's life and challenges of religio-political mobilization, Salafi scholars came together in cooperation and competition to define a model of facial hair as they sought to distinguish adherents to their movement from other Muslims. Within a few years, Salafi scholars would craft an additional means of social distinction: shortened pants and robes. It is to the story of the revival of the prohibition against letting one's clothing extend past the ankle, known as *isbal*, that we now turn.

102. Ahmad Taha Nasr, "I'fa' al-Lihya Sunna Thabita wa Fitra Mustaqima," *al-Tawhid*, Ramadan 1408/April 1988, 52–55, at 54.

CHAPTER 6

Between Pants and the *Jallabiyya*

The Adoption of Isbal *and the Battle for Authenticity*

In May 1989, *al-Tawhid*'s Ahmad Fahmi Ahmad used the periodical's opening editorial to address a broader debate over the causes and solutions to the challenge of radicalism (*al-taṭarruf*) in Egypt. Rejecting the association of radicalism with specific movements or religious approaches—Ansar al-Sunna and Salafism, respectively—Ahmad attributed this trend to "matters specific to the individual who is described as being radical" (*al-umūr al-khāṣṣa bi-dhāt al-shakhṣ alladhī yūṣaf bi-l-taṭarruf*). For Ansar al-Sunna's leader, the actual radicalism coursing through the fringes of Egyptian society could best be explained by limited education in the Quran, Sunna, and Arabic language on the one hand, and the absence of a guide and teacher (*al-murshid waʾl-muʿallim*) who can impart religious culture to the youth (*tathqīf hadha al-shabāb dīniyy*[an]), on the other.[1] Put most simply, the issue was not too much religion in Egyptian society, but rather, not enough.

Ahmad was especially concerned with the ways in which unnamed Egyptian media outlets had framed the question of radicalism and its material manifestations. Specifically, the use of this term to describe youth who engaged in practices of "growing the beard" (*iʿfāʾ al-liḥya*) and "donning short clothing" (*irtidāʾ al-thiyāb al-qaṣīra*) threatened to blur the line between mem-

1. Ahmad Fahmi Ahmad, "Kalimat al-Tahrir," *al-Tawhid*, Shawwal 1409/~May 1989, 1–4, at 1.

bers of the Jama'a Islamiyya[2] who embraced violence as a political tool and the quietism of Ansar al-Sunna.[3] Instead, he sought to reclaim the meaning of radicalism as referring specifically to those who engage in *takfir* of other Muslims for minor disagreements such as growing the beard but removing (rather than trimming) the mustache, or the designation of the *niqab* as praiseworthy rather than required.[4]

In this chapter, however, I tackle a question that looms in the background of Ahmad's description of piety: what is the practice of "donning short clothing" and how did the observance of the prohibition against full length lower-body garments because they communicate arrogance—known as *isbal*—seek to tackle the challenge of misrecognition characteristic of massified societies?[5] Alongside the fist-length beard and trimmed mustache, a lower garment that ends somewhere between the mid-shin and ankle is among the most visually distinct Salafi practices and, when combined with the beard, leaves little doubt as to the religious allegiances of its wearer. Just as importantly, the prohibition against full-length lower body clothing is the last of the key Salafi practices to develop, casting light on the consolidation of practices of piety within the movement near the end of the 1980s and into the 1990s. Finally, the popularization of this practice allows us to probe the process by which legal debates are reintroduced—or perhaps inaugurated—into the social sphere.

Pant or robe length represents an attractive combination of accessibility and visibility. Like the beard, observance of the prohibition against *isbal* was theoretically available to all while communicating commitment to a particular moral order and legal norm alike. Unlike gender segregation, it did not depend on either structural change or significant social sacrifice (for example,

2. Though in the 1970s the name Jama'a Islamiyya referred to the Islamic Student Movement, the movement split in the 1980s and those who retained the name came to embrace violence against civilian and state targets under the banner of jihad.

3. Ahmad, "Kalimat al-Tahrir," *al-Tawhid*, Shawwal 1409/~May 1989, 2–3, at 2.

4. Ahmad, "Kalimat al-Tahrir," *al-Tawhid*, Shawwal 1409/~May 1989, 2–3.

5. I am not suggesting that observance of the prohibition against *isbal* is unique to Salafis, only that it is a key marker within a broader Salafi complex of authenticity. The Deobandi revivalist movement in South Asia, for example, has long emphasized this prohibition, which is reflected in the opinion of a leading Deobandi scholar, Ashraf 'Ali Thanvi (d. 1943) on this matter. Ashraf 'Ali Thanvi, *Imdad al-Fatawa* (Karachi, Pakistan: Maktabat Dar al-'Ulum, 2010), 4:121–2. I wish to thank Brannon Ingram for pointing me to this source.

refusing to frequent mixed spaces such as public transportation, educational institutions, or government offices). And finally, unlike praying in shoes, it was to be performed not merely within the mosque but also beyond it.

This chapter will begin by situating the debate over *isbal* in Egypt during the first half of the twentieth century, as Islamic reformers discussed *either* the prohibition against letting one's pants hang down *or* the broader importance of distinctive dress, but rarely both. It will then turn to the 1950s and 1960s, when ʿAbd al-Nasir's secular-nationalist regime sought to marginalize the traditional Egyptian male attire of the robe (*jallābiyya*) by popularizing a "popular suit" (*badla shaʿbiyya*). With ʿAbd al-Nasir's 1970 death and Anwar al-Sadat's rise to power, however, this robe was reappropriated by the Jamaʿa Islamiyya to lay claim to a highly visible form of male dress on Egyptian college campuses. Moving beyond university campuses, the third section of this chapter will explore how Quietist Salafis navigated both the visual claim to the Sunna made by pious student activists and the increasing association of these shortened robes with radicalism over the second half of the 1980s as they adopted the prohibition against *isbal*.

PANTS AND PIETY BEFORE *ISBAL*

It is not difficult to establish an early Islamic precedent for contemporary Salafi claims to the prohibition against robes or pants that extend past the ankles (*al-kaʿbayn*). As in the case of praying in shoes, this was a practice clearly enshrined in the Sunni textual corpus and encapsulated in a hadith narrated by Abu Hurayra and included in al-Bukhari's canonical collection. In the report, this Companion quoted the Prophet as stating that "he who allows his loin cloth (*izār*) to fall below the ankles (*al-kaʿbayn*) will meet hellfire (*fī al-nār*)."[6] Similarly, the Prophet Muhammad is reported to have said: "he who drags his robe out of arrogance (*man jarra thawbahu khuyalāʾ*), Allah will not look at him on the Day of Judgment."[7] In turn, leading scholars of all four Sunni schools of Islamic law noted the prohibition against letting one's cloth-

6. Ibn Hajar al-ʿAsqalani, *Fath al-Bari Bi-Sharh Sahih al-Bukhari*, ed. ʿAbd al-Qadir Shayba al-Hamd (Riyadh: Maktabat al-Malk Fahad al-Wataniyya, 1421/~2001), 10: 268–69.

7. al-ʿAsqalani, *Fath al-Bari bi-Sharh Sahih al-Bukhari*, ed. ʿAbd al-Qadir Shayba al-Hamd 10:269–80.

ing hang down if done out of arrogance, though they differed on whether such an act was prohibited if done without this intent.[8]

Neither had this question somehow been forgotten in the tumult of colonial occupation. In *al-Din al-Khalis*, Jamʿiyya Sharʿiyya founder Mahmud Muhammad Khattab al-Subki discusses this prohibition in detail, distinguishing the level of punishment incurred based on intent.[9] Similarly, in Saudi Arabia, Muhammad b. Ibrahim's collection of fatwas, published in 1969 but issued over the course of his career, makes clear that *isbal* is not prohibited if done out of arrogance. Ibn Ibrahim adds, however, that one is permitted to let one's robes hang down "out of necessity" (*li-l-ḥāja*).[10] Whatever the extent of this contingency, Ibn Ibrahim retained serious concerns about the practice more broadly, even comparing it to female immodesty, glossed as "flaunting" (*al-tabarruj*), and categorizing it as one of "the observable evils regarding which one must not remain silent" (*min al-munkarāt al-ẓāhira allatī lā yaḥill al-sukūt ʿalayhā*).[11]

8. Malikis are split on whether letting one's clothes hang down is forbidden or merely disapproved if done without the intention of arrogance. For the former view, see Abu Bakr b. al-ʿArabi al-Maliki, *Aridat al-Ahwadhi bi-Sharh Sahih al-Tirmidhi* (Beirut: Dar al-Kutub al-ʿIlmiyya, 2011), 7:238. For the latter view, see al-Hafiz b. ʿAbd al-Birr, *al-Tamhid lima fi al-Muwatta min al-Maʿani wa'l-Asanid*, ed. Muhammad al-Taʾib al-Saʿidi (N.P: N.P, 1971), 3:244–50. Shafiʿis are similarly divided. For the former opinion, see Abu Zakariyya Muhi al-Din Yahya b. Sharaf al-Nawawi, *al-Minhaj bi-Sharh Sahih Muslim Ibn al-Hajjaj* (Cairo: al-Matbaʿa al-Misriyya bi-l-Azhar, 1930), 14:60–65. For the latter opinion, see Ibn Hajar al-ʿAsqalani, *Fath al-Bari bi-Sharh Sahih al-Bukhari*, ed. ʿAbd al-ʿAziz b. Baz, Muhammad Fuʾad ʿAbd al-Baqi, and Muhibb al-Din al-Khatib (Beirut: Dar al-Maʿrifa, 1959?), 10: 258–64. Leading Hanbali scholars upheld the status as forbidden/disfavored based on intent. For example, see Ibn Qudama al-Maqdisi, *al-Mughni*, eds ʿAbd Allah b. ʿAbd al-Muhsin al-Turki and ʿAbd al-Fattah Hulw (Riyadh: Dar ʿAlam al-Kutub, 1997), 2:298. For the Hanafi view that if not done out of arrogance *isbal* is merely disfavored, see Nizam al-Din al-Barnahaburi, *al-Fatawa al-Hindiyya al-Maʿrufa bi-l-Fatawa al-ʿAlamkiriyya fi Madhhab al-Imam al-Aʿzam Abi Hanifa al-Nuʿman* (Beirut: Dar al-Kutub al-ʿIlmiyya, 2000), 5:411.

9. al-Subki, *al-Din al-Khalis*, 6:163–64. Al-Subki then goes on to explicitly note the possibility that one's robe can hang down for reasons other than arrogance (*khuyalā*), in which case the action is merely disfavored (*makrūp*). Al-Subki, *al-Din al-Khalis*, 6:169.

10. Ibn Ibrahim, *Fatawa wa Rasaʾil Samahat al-Shaykh Muhammad b. Ibrahim*, 2:155. Ibn Ibrahim argues that the condition of necessity is met when one does not have a choice in the matter (*bi-ghayr ikhtiyār minhu*), yet specifies that the person must lift it once he realizes (*idhā faṭana lahu*). The crucial matter here, as it pertains to the later Salafi position, however, is that he maintains a distinction between arrogance and an alternative intent.

11. Ibn Ibrahim, *Fatawa wa Rasaʾil Samahat al-Shaykh Muhammad b. Ibrahim*, 13:169.

We have little evidence, however, that the legal status of full-length robes or pants as either forbidden or disfavored shaped social practice, and leading scholars and reformists such as Rashid Rida do not appear to have shortened their robes.[12] More broadly, documentary evidence of Egyptian men up through the 1950s suggests that, while the *jallabiyya* dominated, the prohibition against shortening one's robe so that it did not hang down to the ankle (*al-kaʿb*) was not observed.[13] In the early twentieth century, the legal stipulation against long robes was a scholarly debate but not a social reality, and did not yet relate to questions of ethical formation or visual distinction.

Neither did theoretical awareness of this prohibition necessarily translate into the articulation of a clear vision of Islamic dress for men. As discussed in chapter 2, Rashid Rida showed little patience for this question in a 1904 article, declaring that the "Islam of the Arab does not reside in his turban . . . and he does not become an infidel if he removes the turban during the ritual ablutions (*wuḍūʾ*). . . . Often peoples that agree about religion differ substantially on dress."[14] Ten months later, Rida further declared: "Islam does not legislate a specific form of dress (*libās*^{an} *khāṣṣ*^{an}) nor does it prohibit specific forms of clothing . . . save for the prohibition against silk and gold and silver

12. I was not able to locate any photographs of either Jamal al-Din al-Afghani or Muhammad ʿAbduh that could provide evidence as to whether or not either observed *isbal.* Rashid Rida, on the other hand, does not appear to have done so. A photo of Rida as a young boy in Tripoli, Lebanon shows him wearing a suit and fez alongside his elder brother who is similarly dressed. See Umar Ryad, "A Printed Muslim 'Lighthouse' in Cairo al-Manār's Early Years, Religious Aspiration and Reception (1898–1903)," *Arabic* 56 (January 2009): 53. Furthermore, an image of the 1922 Syrian-Palestinian Conference shows him in the foreground with a long *jallābiyya* and overcoat. For a digitalized version of this photo, see "Aʿdaʾ al-Muʾtamar al-Suri al-Falastini al-Munʿaqad fi Jinif Sayf 1922," https://eltaher.org/docs_photos/1922-Members-of-the-Syrian-Palestinian-Delegation-in-Geneva-01-image929_ar.html, accessed 9 February 2020.

13. The *jallābiyya* was worn prior to the twentieth century as the default male attire in Egypt, especially in its rural areas (where it remains popular today). I was not able to find any evidence, however, of the observance of *isbal* among non-elite Egyptians during the early twentieth century. By way of example, see Ref 199, 387, 765, 1030, and 1173 of the Yasser Alwan Collection, a collection of over 3,000 images taken by the Egyptian photographer of the same name and digitalized by the NYU Abu Dhabi Center for Photography. These photographs can be accessed at http://akkasah.org/results/Yasser%20Alwan%20Collection?filter = collection_title%3EYasser%20Alwan%20Collection;;&queries = &pageid = 1.

14. Rida, "Fatawa al-Manar," *al-Manar,* Dhu al-Hijja 1321/3 March 1904, 6:937.

. . . as well as [the prohibition against] ostentatious clothing (*libās al-shuhra*)."[15] Rida's silence on the question of *isbal* was not a function of widespread observance of this prohibition elsewhere: as he noted in a 1912 article in *al-Manar* that discussed the practices of his co-religionists in India, "most Muslims now wear trousers (*wa akhthar al-Muslimīn yalbasūn al-sarāwīl*), though some poor people do not."[16] In this context, Rida sought to articulate a vision of clothing that both reflected and shaped the practices of Muslims globally.

This leading reformist's dismissal of the claim that clothing was central to religious identity reflected a society in sartorial and ideological transition. A 4 December 1926 image in the Egyptian weekly *al-Siyasa al-Usbuʿiyya* encapsulates this confusion: in an article entitled "The Chaos of Dress in Egypt" (*Fawḍā al-Azyāʾ fī Miṣr*), the author lays out some thirty-three different forms of dress, ranging from the *jallabiyya* and turban to the modern suit and *tarbush*, and encompassing various hybridized forms in between. At the bottom of the image, the author asks rhetorically: "Which one is national dress?" (*al-libās al-qawmī*).[17] Far from a question of clothing alone, these debates reflected the declining social influence of the old scholar-dominated cultural order and indexed broader anxieties of identity in the context of modernity.[18]

Yet, clothing was an unavoidable question for both those invested in a secular-nationalist vision of modernity as well as those opposed to it. During the 1930s and 1940s, the *efendi* model would challenge Egyptians to not only think in a "modern" manner, but also to dress and comport themselves in this vein as they donned the suit and *tarbush*.[19] A state-sponsored project of secular modernity laid claim to the bodies of its citizens, while these same citizens could accept, amend, or subvert the demands of this vision.

15. In the same article, Rida was critical of Ottoman scholars for banning the brimmed hat (*al-burnīṭa*). See Rida, "al-Libas al-Rasmi wa Kasawi al-Tashrif," *al-Manar*, 1 Shawwal 1322/8 December 1904, 7:737. For analysis of further examples of Rida's accommodating approach to foreign dress, see Halevi, *Modern Things on Trial*, 195–203. As Halevi notes, Rida's position on foreign dress would grow more rigid in the mid-1920s, a response to Mustafa Kamal Ataturk's 1925 decision to ban the fez (209–10).

16. Rida further noted the continued use (and diverse styles) of the turban, the *tarbush*, and the *taqiya*, a white skullcap often worn under the *tarbush*. Muhammad Rashid Rida, "ʿUjala fi Rihlat al-Hind," *al-Manar*, Jumada al-Ukhra-Rabiʿ al-Thani/June 1912, 449–58, at 452.

17. "Fawda al-Azyaʾ fi Misr," *al-Siyasa al-Usbuʿiyya*, 4 December 1926, 19. Also see Wilson Chacko Jacob, *Working Out Egypt*, 213.

18. Jacob, *Working Out Egypt*, 220–21.

19. Ryzova, *The Age of the Efendiyya*, 50. Also see Jacob, *Working Out Egypt*, 13.

FIG. 1. “The Chaos of Dress in Egypt,” *al-Siyasa al-Usbu ʿiyya*, 4 December 1926.

The popularization of the secular-nationalist project by state institutions and Westernized intellectuals challenged Islamic scholars to articulate their own vision of clothing. Secular nationalism sought to do away with the old cultural order, including its characteristic male garments, the turban and robe. The task for Muslim reformers, therefore, was to delineate modern yet authentically Islamic clothing in a manner that neither imitated their secular-nationalist competitors nor exposed them to the accusations of stagnancy (*jumūd*) that they often directed towards *madhhab* scholars.[20] The question at this time was one of foreign clothing and how such clothing related to "national dress" (*al-ziyy al-waṭanī*).

This was a matter of visual differentiation not merely from Egypt's Christian occupiers, but from other Muslims as well. It was for this reason that the most heated debates over clothing would erupt regarding the right of Azhari students to wear a suit and *tarbush* rather than a turban and robe. In a 1926 battle on this matter, the leading medical professional body, the Egyptian Medical Association,[21] ruled against the *tarbush* on sanitary and health grounds,[22] while *al-Fath* featured an article that argued in favor of it by a representative of the "Islamic community" (*al-milla al-Islāmiyya*).[23] This journal, edited by Muhibb al-Din al-Khatib (d. 1969), who established the Salafi Bookstore (*al-Maktaba al-Salafiyya*) and promoted the claim of Ibn Saʿud to regional Islamic leadership in the 1920s,[24] was no marginal site of debate: one could have hardly picked a more prominent

20. Gesink, *Islamic Reform and Conservatism*, 59–88 and Hatina, *ʿUlamaʾ, Politics and the Public Sphere*, 99–104. Also see Kalmbach, *Islamic Knowledge and the Making of Modern Egypt*, 213–14.

21. Established first in 1898 and then reestablished in 1924, the EMA reflected broader trends of professionalization in Egypt as well as the increasing unity of Egyptian doctors vis-à-vis their foreign counterparts. See Hibba Abugideiri, *Gender and the Making of Modern Medicine in Colonial Egypt* (New York: Routledge, 2016), 172.

22. For the debate over the *tarbush*, see Jacob, *Working Out Egypt*, 207. The basis of the Egyptian Medical Associations' concern was the fact that the *tarbush*, made of wool (*ṣūf*), would lead to excessive sweating on account of its core material, and due to the lack of air circulation in its design. Instead, the EMA argued that a pith helmet (*al-qalansuwa al-bayḍāʾ*), worn by British soldiers in hot locales and made of cork (*fallīn*), is best for the summer. According to this logic, the *tarbush* is less harmful in the winter, yet it is still preferable to use the brimmed hat (*al-qubʿa*). See "al-Tarbush am al-Burnita," *al-Muqtataf*, August 1926, 140–48, at 147–48.

23. Ahmad Zaghlul, "al-Tarbush waʾl-Qubʿa," *al-Fath*, 12 Muharram 1345/22 July 1926, 12.

24. Lauzière, *The Making of Salafism*, 42, 64.

periodical venue aside from *al-Manar.* In this setting, headgear was claimed as a marker of communal identity and modernity (or lack thereof) alike.

Such debates would have been an opportune time for Salafis to define a model of self-consciously Islamic clothing generally and to reiterate their opposition to full-length pants or robes specifically. There is, however, no evidence of such a claim. As discussed in chapter 5, Ansar al-Sunna founder Muhammad Hamid al-Fiqi's April 1938 article on the importance of Muslim distinctiveness emphasizes "the characteristics, actions, rituals and obedience" modeled by the Prophet, yet does not provide specifics.[25] In the case of the association of specific types of clothing with ostentatious performance and arrogance, a February 1940 article in *al-Hadi al-Nabawi* by Muhammad Bahjat al-Baytar warns Muslims not to dress in a matter designed to "[attract] attention and [communicate] arrogance" (*libs al-shuhra wa'l-makhīla*).[26] What is most remarkable about al-Baytar's warning is that he does not focus on the details of the prohibition most associated in the *Fiqh* literature with ostentatious and arrogant dress, namely garments that cover the lower body. Finally, a September 1946 article in *al-Tamaddun al-Islami* uses the term *isbal* not to designate a prohibition against excessively long pants or robes but rather to emphasize the importance of "growing the beard long" (*isbāl al-liḥya*).[27] Up through the first half of the twentieth century, Salafis neither evinced a clear vision of properly Islamic dress for men, nor did they discuss the prohibition against *isbal.*

Discussions of *isbal* also did not appear in debates over the permissibility of pants. In the shadow of a secular-nationalist vision that offered models of

25. Muhammad Hamid al-Fiqi, "Man tashabbah bi-qawm$_{in}$ fa-huwa minhum," *al-Hadi al-Nabawi,* Safar 1356/April 1938, 34–39, at 37. Al-Fiqi would have also come across discussions of *isbal* in his other publishing activities. In 1950, he published a critical edition of Ibn Taymiyya's *Iqtida' al-Sirat al-Mustaqim: Mukhalafat Ashab al-Jahim* (*The Necessity of the Straight Path in Distinction to the People of Hell*). See Ibn Taymiyya, *Iqtida' al-Sirat al-Mustaqim: Mukhalafat Ashab al-Jahim,* ed. Muhammad Hamid al Fiqi (Cairo: Matba'at al-Sunna al-Muhammadiyya, Dhu al-Qa'da 1369 H/~August 1950). Most notably, Ibn Taymiyya discussed the question of *isbal,* though he did so primarily through the prism of prayer, specifically the question of enveloping oneself in garments while in prayer (known as *al-Sadal*) (130–31). For a definition of *al-Sadal,* see Edward William Lane, *Arabic-English Lexicon* (London: Williams and Norgate, 1863), 4:1333.

26. Muhammad Bahjat al-Baytar, "al-Fatawa," *al-Hadi al-Nabawi,* 15 Muharram 1359/24 February 1940, 27–30, at 28.

27. Muhammad b. Kamal al-Khatib, "al-'Ada wa'l-Mujtama'," *al-Tamaddun al-Islami,* Shawwal 1365/~August 1946, 321–24, at 322.

sartorial presentation that stood in stark contrast with the traditional *jallabiyya*, al-Baytar tackled this question in the 10 March 1940 issue of *al-Hadi al-Nabawi*. He began by noting that in Egypt and elsewhere, "national dress" (*al-azyāʾ al-waṭaniyya*) had become incumbent on all those who worked for the government, including men of religion (*rijāl al-sharʿ*).[28] The matter at hand was ostensibly simple: did Islam permit men to wear pants?

To tackle this question, al-Baytar set forth the broader *ratio legis* (*ʿilla*) of distinguishing Muslims from non-Muslims. As discussed in chapter 1, he noted a hadith report in which a Companion of the Prophet, Abu Umayma, stated that the Prophet explained that one could wear trousers (*sarāwīl*) while still distinguishing oneself from non-Muslims.[29] Far from an injunction to avoid resembling non-Muslims in literalist fashion, the goal was for Muslims to cultivate distinct characteristics (*mushakhkhiṣāt min al-ʿādāt khāṣṣa bihim*) and to not slavishly imitate others (*wa lā yakūnū tābiʿīn li-ghayrihim*).[30] The exception to this ruling, however, was if wearing such clothing violated other requirements of Islamic law, such as revealing men's private places (*ʿawra*)—here, the thigh (*al-fakhidh*)—during prayer.[31] Accordingly, there was no objection to wearing pants in principle as the issue was not the origin of the clothing, but rather the motivation for donning it. Crucially for this story, al-Baytar makes no effort in this instance to problematize pant length as a matter of Islamic law.

While al-Baytar's interpretation might be dismissed as reflective not of the movement as a whole but rather of its moderate branch, such claims cannot be made about ʿAbd al-ʿAziz b. Rashid (d. 1982), a native of the Wahhabi-Hanbali heartland of Najd who had made his way to Egypt and joined Ansar

28. Muhammad Bahjat al-Baytar, "al-Fatawa," *al-Hadi al-Nabawi*, 1 Safar 1359/11 March 1940, 26–29, at 29.

29. For Ibn Hanbal, see Ahmad b. Hanbal, *Musnad al-Imam Ahmad*, ed. Hamza Ahmad al-Zayn (Cairo: Dar al-Hadith, 1416/1995), 16:257–8. Ibn Hanbal, however, cites a second Companion, al-Qasim, as the source. Al-Albani resolves the dispute over narration by noting that al-Qasim had narrated it to Abu Umayma. See Ibrahim Abu Shadi, *al-Ikhtiyarat al-Fiqhiyya li-l-Imam al-Albani* (Mansura, Egypt: Dar al-Ghadd al-Jadid, 1427/2006), 240–41.

30. Muhammad Bahjat al-Baytar, "al-Fatawa," *al-Hadi al-Nabawi*, 1 Safar 1359/11 March 1940, 26–29, at 29. The wording of al-Baytar's citation—and thus the source—matches up with Muhammad Rashid Rida's fatwa on this topic in *al-Manar*. See Rida, "Fatawa al-Manar," 30 Rabiʿ al-Awwal 1344/18 October 1925, 416–24, at 422–23.

31. al-Baytar, "al-Fatawa," *al-Hadi al-Nabawi*, 1 Safar 1359/11 March 1940, 29.

al-Sunna. In an article published some two years after that of al-Baytar, Ibn Rashid noted the spread of shorts (*al-tabān* or *al-banṭalūn al-qaṣīr*) in Egypt. Ibn Rashid was especially concerned with efforts by Egypt's monarch, King Faruq, to promote the shortening of men's clothing (*taqṣīr thiyāb al-rajul*). By contrast, he notes that others advocate for "long pants that go beneath the ankles" (*al-banṭalūn al-ṭawīl alladhī yaṣilu ilā asfal min al-kaʿbayn*).[32] The focus of this text is not on pant length but rather on shorts and the Westernizing cultural effort of which they represented but one manifestation. What is striking about it, nonetheless, is that Ibn Rashid does not invoke the prohibition against *isbal* even as he elaborated precisely the length that would qualify as a violation of its technical parameters.

Roughly a year later, a third article that centered on clothing appeared in *al-Hadi al-Nabawi*. The author was ʿAbd al-Halim Qatit, an imam in the Nile Delta city of Rosetta, and the issue at hand was a 30 November 1942 article in the Egyptian daily *al-Ahram* that had legitimized the increasingly popular practice of Egyptians wearing foreign clothing.[33] Echoing the *ratio legis* of distinguishing Muslims from non-Muslim, Qatit argued that it was permissible to wear pants as long as they were paired with a loin-cloth (*izār*) because this combination would prevent any resemblance to non-Muslims.[34] On the question of the permissibility of pants, Qatit's position differs substantially from that of al-Baytar and Ibn Rashid, yet he too, shows little concern with questions of *isbal*. Neither was this position a product of a wider ignorance of the capacity of clothing to signal arrogance: in January 1947, ʿAli Hasan Hulwa published a fatwa in *al-Iʿtisam* in which he responded to a question about whether the headband (*ʿiqāl*) that secured the characteristic Arabian headdress

32. Abd al-ʿAziz b. Rashid, "al-Taban (al-Bantalun al-Qasir)," *al-Hadi al-Nabawi*, Ramadan 1361/~September 1942, 29–34, at 29–30.

33. The article argued that it is permissible for men to wear a brimmed hat (the *qubʿa*) because Islam does not prescribe a particular form of clothing. While the author, a government inspector (*mufattish*) of Arab historical sites, acknowledged the existence of limited prohibitions relating to the clothing of other religious groups in Islamic history, he explained that "the national question" (*al-masʾala al-qawmiyya*) has rendered such prohibitions superfluous as different nationalists choose among clothing articles to formulate a distinct national dress. See Hasan ʿAbd al-Wahhab, "al-Azyaʾ fi al-Islam," *al-Ahram*, 30 November 1942, 3.

34. ʿAbd al-Halim Qatit, "al-Azyaʾ fi al-Islam," *al-Hadi al-Nabawi*, Muharram 1362/~January 1943, 20–4, at 21. In this article, the garment at hand does not appear to be Western pants but rather the combination of wide trousers and long shirts known as *Shalwar Kameez* in South and Central Asia.

(*al-kūfiyya*) could be made from silk (*al-ḥarīr*). In response, Hulwa explained that while silk was generally forbidden, other material could *become* disfavored (*makrūḥ*) if its use reflected "pride and arrogance" (*al-kibr waʾl-khuyalā*).[35]

Ansar al-Sunna was not alone in providing sanction for a lower garment that was at once distinct from a *jallabiyya* yet also was not equivalent to Western pants. Most notably, Amin Muhammad Khattab, son of the Jamʿiyya Sharʿiyya's founder, wrote in the 16 November 1947 issue of *al-Iʿtisam* to emphasize the praiseworthy status of trousers (*ʿalā istiḥbāb lubs al-sarāwīl*), asserting that the Prophets Abraham and Moses, too, wore trousers.[36] Unlike his counterparts within Ansar al-Sunna, however, Khattab was attuned to the prohibition against *isbal*: just two weeks later, he published a second article that emphasized the Prophet Muhammad's practice of wearing a long shirt (*qamīṣ*) that stopped "above the ankles" (*fawqa al-kaʿbayn*)[37] and cited the hadith report that equated the dragging of the robe with arrogance.[38] Khattab further specified his reason for writing: while historically, men wore their clothing above the ankles and women below them, "the people [today] have reversed the matter" (*al-qawm ʿakasū al-qaḍiyya*).[39] What Khattab sought was no less than the reversion of this social practice to its previous norm.

Yet, in contrast with their counterparts in the Jamʿiyya Sharʿiyya, Salafis during this period showed little interest in questions of *isbal*. It is doubtful that scholars within the movement, most notably Muhammad Hamid al-Fiqi, would have been totally unaware of this legal question. Awareness of and concern with this prohibition, however, are two different matters. And the question at this stage, as with the cases of the beard and praying in shoes during this period, was one of distinguishing Muslims from non-Muslims; questions of internal Muslim distinction had yet to become central. These dynamics would soon change substantially.

35. ʿAli Hasan Hulwa, "Asʾila wa Ajwiba," *al-Iʿtisam*, 25 Safar 1366/18 January 1947, 10, 14, at 10.

36. Amin Muhammad Khattab, "al-Fiqh al-Islami," *al-Iʿtisam*, 2 Muharram 1367/16 November 1947, 6–7.

37. Khattab, "al-Fiqh al-Islami," *al-Iʿtisam* 16 Muharram 1367/30 November 1947, 14–15, at 14.

38. Khattab, "al-Fiqh al-Islami," 15.

39. Khattab, "al-Fiqh al-Islami," 15.

BETWEEN JALLABIYYA AND SUIT: SARTORIAL PRACTICE UNDER ʿABD AL-NASIR

The history of Islamic movements under ʿAbd al-Nasir is often narrated as one of repression, and rightfully so. While Ansar al-Sunna weathered this period more effectively than their counterparts in either the Muslim Brotherhood or the Jamʿiyya Sharʿiyya,[40] the organization's mosque expansion, vibrant in the 1930s and 1940s, slowed significantly. Most pertinent to the question of *isbal*, however, would be the intersection of longer-term trends of bureaucratic expansion and urbanization with a secular-nationalist understanding of modernity. The Egyptian state had begun to assert greater control over rural areas beginning in the mid-nineteenth century through schooling, architecture, and sanitation.[41] It was only in 1922, though, that the state absorbed previously independent village *kuttab* (Quranic elementary schools) into the national educational system and, by 1930, the number of students under state supervision had risen from 23,000 to roughly 253,000.[42] This was a story not merely of an expanded governmental footprint within society but also of urbanization. Finally, as discussed in chapter 4, the period between 1950 and 1975 saw a significant expansion of the proportion and number of Egyptians living in urban areas.[43]

The ʿAbd al-Nasir period would be pivotal to the rise of a cadre of religious student activists in the 1970s. Under ʿAbd al-Nasir, both primary and higher education continued to expand, with the number of students enrolled increasing by 234 and 325 percent, respectively.[44] During this period, the number of government employees with at least a secondary school degree grew from 310,000 to 770,000 in 1960 to 1.035 million in 1966–67.[45] In 1964, ʿAbd al-

40. Ansar al-Sunna and the Jamʿiyya Sharʿiyya retained their mosques up until nearly the end of the ʿAbd al-Nasir period. By contrast, Brotherhood members, having lost access to independent mosques, often attended Friday prayer at Ansar al-Sunna and Jamʿiyya Sharʿiyya-affiliated sites of worship. Abu-l-Futuh, *ʿAbd al-Munʿim Abu-l-Futuh*, 35–36.

41. Omnia al-Shakry, *The Great Social Laboratory: Subjects of Knowledge in Colonial and Postcolonial Egypt* (Stanford, CA: Stanford University Press, 2007), 116.

42. Starrett, *Putting Islam to Work*, 68.

43. For statistics based on the successive censuses, see Ibrahim, *Egypt, Islam and Democracy*, 99.

44. Wickham, *Mobilizing Islam*, 25.

45. Khaled Ikram, *Egypt: Economic Management in a Period of Transition: The Report of a Mission Sent to the Arab Republic of Egypt by the World Bank* (London: John Hopkins Press, 1980), 145.

Nasir ensured that this newly enlarged generation of college graduates would continue their daily lives within state institutions when he passed decree 185, which guaranteed a white-collar government job for all college graduates.[46] Crucially, ʿAbd al-Nasir's call to social change included clothing, mandating that students and government employees shed the traditional garb of the countryside, the *jallabiyya*, and don pants and a button-down shirt.[47]

Though writers in *al-Hadi al-Nabawi* did not initially discuss this challenge, a member of Ansar al-Sunna confronted the implementation of a secular-nationalist sartorial change in the pages of *al-Iʿtisam*. In a 21 September 1952 article, ʿAbd al-Qadir Shayba al-Hamd, an Azhari who headed the Ansar al-Sunna branch in the Delta city of Zaqaziq and would leave in 1376/1956 for Saudi Arabia,[48] rejected the efforts of "Westernized Egyptians" (*al-Mustaghribīn fi Miṣr*) to define a "single clothing style" (*tawḥīd al-ziyy*). Instead, al-Hamd insisted that this effort proceeded on the false premise that Egypt was the only nation in which "multiple forms of dress existed" (*tataʿaddad fihi al-azyāʾ*).[49]

The issue was not merely unnecessary homogenization but also origin. Al-Hamd argued that the basis of Egypt's national dress under ʿAbd al-Nasir was not "Arab clothing" (*ziyy^an ʿarabiyy^an*) but rather the "brimmed hat" (*al-qubʿa*) and the "Mexican top hat" (*al-būrnīṭa al-maksīkiyya*), presumably a sombrero. Indeed, what these westernized Egyptians sought to do was to "erase what remained of our Islamic appearance. . . ." (*maẓāhirinā al-Islāmiyya*).

46. Wickham, *Mobilizing Islam*, 27.

47. *Al-Ahram* featured advertisements for this outfit. For example, see "al-Asʿar al-Muwahhada li-l-Malabis," *al-Ahram*, 7 July 1963, 8; "al-Asʿar al-Muwahhada li-l-Malabis," *al-Ahram*, 22 July 1963, 8; "al-Asʿar al-Muwahhada li-l-Malabis," *al-Ahram*, 4 August 1963, 6. It appears, however, that at the price of 49 Egyptian pounds, this suit was too expensive: the 12 July 1976 issue of *al-Ahram* chronicled efforts to import raw materials from China in order to sell a suit to white-collar workers and students for a price between eight and twelve pounds. See "Wazir al-Tijara wa'l-Tamwin Yaʿlin ʿan Istirad," *al-Ahram*, 12 July 1976, 6.

48. Al-Hamd would first work at the ʿUnayza Institute, where he taught Salih al-Fawzan, before moving on to the Faculty of Shariʿa and Arabic Language in Riyadh in 1379 /1959. In 1382/1962, he joined the faculty of the recently-established Islamic University of Medina, apparently at the express request of Ibn Baz, and taught there until retirement in 1404/1984. See "Tarjamat al-Shaykh ʿAbd al-Qadir Sahyba al-Hamd," *The Salafi Center*, Markaz al-Salafli-l-Buhuth wa'l-Dirasat, https://salafcenter.org/wp-content/uploads/2019/05 /ترجمة-شيبة-الشيخ-الحمد.pdf, accessed 10 February 2020.

49. ʿAbd al-Qadir Shayba al-Hamd, "Tawhid al-Ziyy," *al-Iʿtisam*, 1 Muharram 1372/21 September 1952, 2.

While al-Hamd initially addressed the threat posed by Westernized Egyptians, he also noted the history of (secular-nationalist) military revolutions in both Iran and Turkey, here referring to Reza Shah (r. 1925–41) and Mustafa Kamal Ataturk (r. 1923–38), who in their respective efforts to standardize and modernize dress had been "waging war on religion" (*ḥārib*^an^ *ʿan al-dīn*). He then concluded by making the target of his address crystal clear: "the servants of the West and followers of the Orientalists should know that we will not shed the turban and wear the [European] brimmed hat (*al-burnīṭa*) and we hope that the current government will rebuild the state based on Islam (*ʿalā asās min al-Islām*) rather than fighting Islam (*an tuḥārib al-Islām*)."[50]

Roughly a month later, two leading members of the Egyptian religious establishment intervened in this debate. The Shaykh of al-Azhar, whose name is not specifically mentioned in the ruling but based on the date of publication would have been Muhammad al-Khidr Husayn (d. 1958), tackled the question of a standardized national dress of "pants and shirts" (*al-banṭalūn waʾl-qamīṣ*) directly. Noting that he had learned "that it had been recommended that the unified dress (*al-ziyy al-muwaḥḥad*) be European dress because the latter had become global dress (*ziyy*^an^ *ʿālamiyy*^an^)," this leading state religious functionary questioned the factual accuracy of this claim.[51] Instead, he explained, current efforts to standardize national dress were akin to imitating non-Muslims, analogous to the cummerbund (*zunnār*) that was understood to constitute conversion to Christianity.[52] Along similar lines, the Egyptian Mufti Hasanayn Muhammad Makhluf (r. 1946–50, 1952–54) emphasized the impermissibility of replacing the *tarbush* with a brimmed hat (*al-qubʿa*).[53]

The question of national dress was not merely one of the broader body politic but also cut to the heart of al-Azhar's visual distinctiveness. In a March 1955 article, Muhammad Kamil Hasan, the Rector (*Wakīl*) of the Faculty of Arabic Language at al-Azhar, laid claim to the necessity of a distinct scholarly uniform. While such a concern was far from novel—debates over the *tarbush* at al-Azhar roughly a quarter century prior underscore a slow-moving process

50. ʿAbd al-Qadir Shayba al-Hamd, "Tawhid al-Ziyy," *al-Iʿtisam*, 1 Muharram 1372/21 September 1952, 2.

51. "Raʾi Shaykh al-Azhar," *al-Iʿtisam*, 1 Safar 1372/20 October 1952, 3.

52. "Raʾi Shaykh al-Azhar," *al-Iʿtisam*, 1 Safar 1372/20 October 1952, 3, 6.

53. "Raʾi al-Mufti," *al-Iʿtisam*, 1 Safar 1372/20 October 1952, 6.

of sartorial contestation—Hasan's specific concern was an article in the popular cultural magazine *al-Ithnayn*, in which the author questioned the religious significance of the turban (*al-ʿimāma*) specifically and of Azhari dress (*al-ziyy al-Azharī*) more generally. Noting that the turban was not "merely a custom" (*mujarrad ʿādat*[an]) but rather a praiseworthy practice (*sunna*), Hasan also extolled the moral and health benefits of the loose-fitting robe donned by Azharis.[54] Neither would the battle over the dress of Azhari scholars die down as the decade progressed. In a November 1959 article in *al-Iʿtisam*, entitled "the Turban and al-Azhar," Bayyumi Muhammad Muhammad Suqi, a professor at al-Azhar's Faculty of Arabic Language, bemoaned the unfortunate reality that many graduates of al-Azhar had taken off the turban.[55] The conversation had shifted and the *ʿulamaʾ* now saw it necessary to debate matters that had little direct connection to *fiqh*.

Egypt's defeat in the 1967 Arab-Israeli war punctured ʿAbd al-Nasir's secularizing ambitions, both national and regional. Following his death in September 1970, Anwar al-Sadat would embrace an alternative vision—the fusion of science and faith (*al-ʿilm waʾl-īmān*)—while also opening up new spaces for Islamic activists both within and beyond mosques. It is to this story, and the new styles of clothing that its main actors wore, that we now turn.

THE RISE OF ISLAMIC STUDENT ACTIVISTS AND GRASSROOTS RELIGIOUS MOBILIZATION, 1970–1990

The 1973 Arab-Israeli war was supposed to bring deliverance from the disappointments, military and ideological, of 1967. For al-Sadat and those that supported his rule, the crossing of the Bar Lev line, a chain of fortified positions established by Israel on the eastern bank of the Suez Canal following the 1967 war, was seen as a religious miracle. Indeed, Azhari scholar Ahmed Musa Salim noted that an "Awakening had come to Egypt on the tenth of Ramadan" (*fī al-ʿāshir min Ramaḍān jaʾat Ṣaḥwa*), propelling the Egyptian army to what was popularly perceived as a victory on the opening day of the

54. Muhammad Kamil Hasan, "Mawduʿ al-Hadith," *al-Iʿtisam*, Rajab 1374/March 1955, 31–33, at 32.

55. Bayyumi Muhammad Muhammad Suqi, "al-ʿImama waʾl-Azhar," *al-Iʿtisam*, Jumada al-Ula 1379/November 1959, 38.

war.[56] Furthermore, in the months that followed, thousands of Muslims and Copts sought to glimpse the Virgin Mary after she was said to have appeared in the Zeitoun neighborhood of Cairo.[57]

The concern of Salafis during this period, however, was the persistence of *impiety* within Egyptian society. Most notably, a 1974 article in *al-Tawhid*, authored by the Egyptian Principal at Dar al-Hadith in Mecca—a key gathering point for Egyptian Salafis in Saudi Arabia—complained that, as Egyptian youth and even some Shaykhs celebrated the 1973 victory, "we see them wearing pants (*al-banṭalūn*) and bareheaded (*ḥāsiray al-ruʾūs*) . . . . [as they are affected by] the customs of colonialism (*ʿādāt al-istiʿmār*)."[58] Pants thus constituted a key symbol of religious devotion for Salafis.

Though the Jamaʿa Islamiyya did not lay claim to the prohibition against *isbal*, its members articulated a powerful model of visibility. While women in this movement often wore either the *hijab* or *niqab*, its men distinguished themselves not only through their bushy beards but also through long flowing robes. In a 1980 article, Jamaʿa Islamiyya activist (and later Muslim Brotherhood leader) ʿIssam al-ʿAryan (d. 2020) spelled out the key defining practices of university youth: the head covering (*ḥijāb*) among women, the popularization of beards and long robes (the *jilbāb*, also referred to as the *jallābiyya*) among men, and the performance of the twice-yearly Eid prayers at open-air sites throughout Egypt.[59] Similarly, a discussion in *al-Iʿtisam*, now a Salafi-Islamist periodical, noted that the white robe (*al-jilbāb al-abyaḍ*) constituted a mark of piety.[60]

This neo-traditional robe, however, was far more than a straightforward sign of devotion: this stylistic turn both reflected and contested a sartorial

56. Ahmad Musa Salim, "al-Maʿraka wa Isharatuha: Haqaʾiq al-Iman," *al-Azhar*, Dhu al-Hijja 1393/January 1974, 888.

57. Fadwa el-Guindi, "Veiling Infitah with a Muslim Ethic," *Social Problems* 28, no. 4 (1981): 476.

58. Muhammad ʿUmar ʿAbd al-Hadi, "Farha wa Ya Laha min Farha," *al-Tawhid*, Rabiʿ al-Awwal 1394/~March 1974, 31:1.

59. ʿIssam al-ʿAryan, "al-Mudd al-Islami fi al-Jamiʿat," *al-Daʿwa*, Muharram 1400/November 1980, 72–74, at 73.

60. ʿAbd al-Latif Mustahiri, "Aqwal al-Suhuf," *al-Iʿtisam* Dhu al-Hijja 1396/December 1976, 40. The privileged status of white reflects a hadith report in which Muhammad enjoined Muslims to wear white (and the related understanding of this practice as praiseworthy). For example, see "Bab Istihbab al-Thawb al-Abyad," in Abu Zakariyya Yahya b. Sharaf al-Nawawi, *Riyad al-Salihin min Kalam Sayyid al-Mursalin*, ed. Mahir Yasin al-Fahl (Beirut: Dar Ibn Kathir, 2007), 247–49.

vision of secular nationalism. As a matter of materiality, it was identical to the robe worn by Egyptians for generations and remains widespread to this day in the countryside. In the specific context of the 1970s, however, the employment of this garment in highly urbanized settings, especially on university campuses, visibly challenged state efforts to articulate a modern Egyptian identity that contrasted itself with a traditional political and religious order that prized continuity with the past. It was in this context that the state Mufti, Jadd al-Haqq ʿAli Jadd al-Haqq, reaffirmed in a 14 January 1981 fatwa that clothing fell into the category of "custom" (*al-ʿurf wa'l-ʿāda*) and disputed the claim that the robe (*al-jilbāb*) held an elevated religious status.[61]

It does not appear, however, that the activists of the Jamaʿa Islamiyya—some of whom identified as Salafi, other as Muslim Brothers[62]—observed *isbal*. This question did not arise in the "Youth and University News" (*Akhbār al-Shabāb wa'l-Jāmiʿāt*) of the Muslim Brotherhood's official magazine, *al-Daʿwa*, nor in the fatwa section of this periodical and its Salafi-Islamist counterpart *al-Iʿtisam*. While one explanation of this silence is that this practice was already observed widely, the limited photographic evidence from this period does not support this view. Specifically, an image of an ʿEid procession, dated by the Islamist website *Islamiyyun* to the 1970s or early 1980s, shows a group of young men many (though not all) of whom are dressed in robes with full beards, the white skullcap (known as a *Ṭāqiya*) and sandals, carrying signs that declare: "The Jamaʿa Islamiyya Offers Greetings upon the ʿEid."[63] Most striking, however, is that these men's robes appear to come down past the ankle. Collectively, this evidence suggests that those who wore the *jilbab* were not concerned with its length.

The Salafi scene beyond Egypt, however, had begun to change. Our earliest evidence of Salafi adoption of the prohibition against *isbal* is to be found in a fatwa issued by Permanent Committee member Ibn al-ʿUthaymin on 26 May 1979. This fatwa's contents would have been unremarkable to Mahmud Muhammad Khattab al-Subki or to Muhammad b. Ibrahim, as it states that

61. *al-Fatawa al-Islamiyya min Dar al-Ifta' al-Misriyya*, 3469–77. Indeed, Haqq even suggested that, if university administrators declared that this robe was inappropriate for the university, then students must not wear it (*al-Fatawa al-Islamiyya min Dar al-Ifta' al-Misriyya*, 3677).

62. Al-Arian, *Answering the Call*, 152–56.

63. "Tayyar al-Jamaʿa al-Islamiyya fi al-Jamiʿat al-Misriyya," *al-Islamiyyun*, published 4 February 2016, https://tinyurl.com/y6dutbyf.

anyone whose dress (*izār*) extended below their ankles would be punished by hellfire, with the severity of punishment depending on whether the intention was arrogance (*khuyalāʾ*).[64]

This ruling first appears in an Egyptian context in 1981, in a pamphlet published by Umar b. Ghurama b. ʿUmar al-ʿAmrawi, a Yemeni transplant to Saudi Arabia and then Egypt who previously appeared in chapter 3. Al-ʿAmrawi's main contribution to the development of Salafi practice lay in his 1981 work, entitled *Clarifying the Prophet's Views Regarding Praying in Shoes.* In this text, however, the author goes beyond his main discussion to note with some frustration that men are harassed for praying in shoes, but not for "observable sins" (*maʿāṣi ẓāhira*) such as neglecting prayer, shaving their beards, or "letting their clothing extend down" (*isbāl al-thiyāb*).[65] As a migrant unaffiliated with a particular Salafi organization, al-ʿAmrawi was hardly representative of Egyptian Salafis during this period. Crucially for the debates that would follow, however, he had raised the longstanding, yet socially marginal, legal position that long robes were forbidden whatever their intent.

For Egyptian Salafis at this time more broadly, the challenge was fighting the perception of radicalism. This perception, though arguably unfair to Ansar al-Sunna, had not emerged in a vacuum: since the mid-1970s, the Jamaʿa Islamiyya had taken advantage of the latitude offered by al-Sadat to enforce public morality through coercive means of commanding right and forbidding wrong.[66] For example, at the University of Minya in Upper Egypt, members of the Jamaʿa Islamiyya pressured professors into granting them time during the lecture to preach to students, while also seeking to enforce gender segregation in the classroom. As tensions escalated, members also vandalized local Coptic churches, closed down plays, pressured the university to cancel a proposed café, and even attacked and took hostages from the local Coptic Christian population.[67]

While the duty to command right and forbid wrong was pursued most aggressively by the Jamaʿa Islamiyya, it was not, in theory, limited to them. In the April

64. Ibn al-ʿUthaymin, *al-Risala fi Sifat Salat al-Nabi Sala Allah ʿAlayhi wa Salam*, 35–36. While this book was published some eight years later, it included this fatwa dated to 26 May 1979.

65. Al-ʿAmrawi, *Fasl al-Maqal fi Kalam Sayyid al-Anam ʿAlayhi al-Salat waʾl-Salam fi Hukm al-Salat fi al-Niʿal*, 5.

66. Muhammad Jumʿa al-ʿAdawi, "al-Amr bi-l-Maʿruf waʾl-Nahi ʿan al-Munkar fi Nazar al-Mutahadirin," *al-Tawhid*, Rajab 1400/~May 1980, 102:1–6, at 102:1.

67. Gaffney, *The Prophet's Pulpit*, 94–107.

1979 issue of *al-Tawhid*, Muhammad Jamil Ghazi noted that every Muslim must command right and forbid wrong, which pertains to everything from positive encouragement to engage in prayer, zakat, fasting and obligatory pilgrimage to Mecca to counseling oppressive rulers, to forbidding engagement in illicit sexual relations (*zinā*), the consumption of alcohol, and usury.[68] The issue at hand, instead, was one of capability: in May 1980, Ansar al-Sunna's Muhammad Jumʿa al-ʿAdawi noted that the issue with the efforts by youth within the Jamaʿa Islamiyya was not, as opponents claimed, that it was forbidden to coercively correct wrongdoing (*taghyīr al-munkar bi-l-yad*). Instead, the central question was whether these youth possessed the "ability" (*al-istiṭāʿa*) to productively do so.[69]

As Ansar al-Sunna's leaders worked to thread a needle between the theoretical legitimacy of the duty to command right and forbid wrong and its practical complications, they also faced the public perception that their position and that of the Jamaʿa Islamiyya were indistinguishable. In this vein, Ahmad Fahmi Ahmad penned an August 1980 editorial, roughly a year prior to al-Sadat's assassination and the mass roundup of activists, Islamist and Leftist, that preceded it,[70] in which he complained that an unnamed former Minister of Endowments had recently described donning the *jilbab* as a mark of "radicalism" (*al-taṭarruf*).[71] Al-Sadat's October 1981 assassination would further fragment the opportunities for distinct performances of piety.

The years immediately following al-Sadat's assassination led to the consolidation of shifts already underway among Islamic movements in Egypt. For the Brotherhood, it further underscored the strategic value of expanding its activism from one site previously protected from harsh state repression—the university—to another, the professional syndicate.[72] The Jamaʿa Islamiyya itself experienced a three-fold split as college graduates fanned out among

68. Muhammad Jamil Ghazi, "Kitab al-Futuhat," *al-Tawhid*, Jumada al-Ukhra 1399/April 1979, 80:92.

69. al-ʿAdawi, "al-Amr bi-l-Maʿruf waʾl-Nahi ʿan al-Munkar fi Nazar al-Mutahadirin," 102:5.

70. Kepel, *Muslim Extremism in Egypt*, 191–222.

71. Ahmad Fahmi Ahmad, "Kalimat al-Tahrir," *al-Tawhid*, Shawwal 1400/~August 1980, 1–3, at 2.

72. As Carrie Wickham notes, "in 1984, the Brotherhood-affiliated Islamic trend entered the Doctors' Association elections as an organized bloc for the first time. Shortly thereafter, it ran its own list of candidates in the Engineers', Dentists', Scientists', Agronomists', Pharmacists', Journalists', Commercial Employees', and Lawyers' Associations" (*Mobilizing Islam*, 184).

Quietist Salafi organizations, Muslim Brothers, and jihadis, with the last group retaining the movement's name as it targeted both military and civilian targets up through the mid-1990s.[73] Those who turned to Quietism, on the other hand, often joined Ansar al-Sunna.

Despite significant ideological and strategic difference with the reconstituted Jamaʿa Islamiyya, Ansar al-Sunna found itself under siege based on presumed association with its competitor. In a January 1983 article, *al-Tawhid's* editor noted that "the government officials and decision makers who are discussing radicalism and radicals (*al-taṭarruf wa'l-mutaṭarrifīn*) . . . [are] casting blame on Salafism (*yalqūn bi-l-lawm ʿalā al-Salafiyya*)." His demand was clear: "Take your hands off Salafism!" (*kaffū aydikum ʿan al-Salafiyya*).[74]

Beyond Ansar al-Sunna, a transnational sphere of Salafi debate had come to focus on *isbal*. Most notably, between 1977 and 1986, leading Saudi Arabia-based Salafis who were affiliated with the Permanent Committee tackled the question of pants and *isbal*. The first fatwa from this period, signed by Ibn Qaʿud, Ibn Ghadyan, al-ʿAfifi, and Ibn Baz, distinguished between the permissibility of pants (which constituted a custom, or *ʿāda*) and the beard, which represented a religious obligation.[75] The authors further make clear the shift at which al-ʿAmrawi had previously hinted: "Those who limit the reasons for the prohibition of *isbal* to [an intention of arrogance or muddy or unclean roads] are mistaken. Rather . . . it is [in and of itself] a manifestation of arrogance and extravagance" (*innahu maẓhar min maẓāhir al-kibr wa'l-isrāf*). During this period, the Permanent Committee would issue two more fatwas, signed by the same scholars, which made clear that *isbal* is forbidden without consideration of intent.[76]

73. Roel Meijer, "Commanding Right and Forbidding Wrong as a Principle of Social Action: The Case of the Egyptian Jamaʿa Islamiyya," in *Global Salafism: Islam's New Religious Movement*, ed. Roel Meijer (New York: Columbia University Press, 2009), 198–200.

74. Ahmad Fahmi Ahmad, "Kalimat al-Tahrir," *al-Tawhid*, Rabiʿ al-Thani 1403/~January 1983, 1–3, at 1.

75. *Fatawa al-Lajna al-Da'ima li-l-Buhuth al-ʿIlmiyya wa'l-Ifta': Kitab al-Jamiʿ*, ed. Ahmad b. ʿAbd al-Razzaq al-Duwaysh (Riyadh: Ri'assat Idarat al-Buhuth al-ʿIlmiyya wa'l-Ifta', N.D.) 11:7, fatwa #7881.

76. *Fatawa al-Lajna al-Da'ima li-l-Buhuth al-ʿIlmiyya wa'l-Ifta'*, 11:5–7. The first fatwa (#1583) declares all clothing that extends beyond the ankle (*al-kaʿb*) to be "absolutely forbidden" (*ḥarām muṭlaqan*) because it is "presumed to be an act of arrogance" (*li-kawnihi maẓinna li-dhalik*). See 11:5–6. In the latter fatwa (#4679), the authors simply ignore the question of intent. See 11:6.

Popularization of this prohibition even appears to have reached the point where it aroused opposition. A July 1985 article in *al-Mujtamaʿ* included an article noting the importance of shortening the robe (*taqṣīr al-thawb*) yet, in a manner that echoed longstanding legal debates on this matter, questioned the exclusive association of arrogance (*khuyalāʾ*) with this particular practice.[77] As when the Islamic University of Medina's social supervisor ʿAbd Allah al-Qadiri cautioned students not to place all their emphasis on outward signs of piety like the beard, so too had *isbal* become a powerful visual marker in Gulf-based Salafi circles.

At the tail end of this period, a fatwa signed by Ibn Baz appeared in *al-Daʿwa*, a monthly magazine published by the Saudi Ministry of Endowments.[78] The questioner inquired as to whether one was required to grow one's beard and to "shorten the tunic" (*taqṣīr al-thawb*) or whether such practices were mere "shells" (*qushūr*) of religion and thus not obligatory. In response, Ibn Baz rejected the notion that religious practice could be divided into "shells" and a core (*lubb*). Yet, such practices, while far from superficial, did not belong to the category of the roots of faith (*uṣūl al-dīn*) but rather to the "branches" (*furūʿ*), actions in Islam that have been legislated yet about which scholars can legitimately disagree. He then clarified that the prohibition against *isbal* applies not only to the Saudi tunic (*thawb*) but also to trousers (*sarāwīl*) and the cloak (*busht*) popular in Central Arabia, Bahrain, and Iran. Ibn Baz further explained that the preferable length of one's garment is such that it falls between the mid-shin (*niṣf al-sāq*) and the ankle (*al-kaʿb*).[79]

Ibn Baz's ruling is notable for his introduction of a second reference point: the mid-shin (*niṣf al-sāq*). This point on the leg, which was significantly higher than the ankle and far easier to pinpoint, is mentioned in canonical hadith reports used to justify the prohibition against *isbal*. In this context, however, it is *only* the robe that extends beneath the ankle that leads man to hellfire; the garment that stops at the mid-shin simply is described as the "robe of the

77. Faysal al-Zamil, "A-Huwa Taqsir al-Thawb Am Madha?," *al-Mujtamaʿ*, 20 Shawwal 1405/9 July 1985, 48.

78. *Al-Daʿwa* should not be confused with its Egyptian counterpart of the same name, published by the Muslim Brotherhood from 1951–54 and 1976–81.

79. ʿAbd al-ʿAziz b. Baz, "al-Fatawa," *al-Daʿwa*, 22 Rabiʿ al-Awwal 1407/24 November 1986, 26–27.

believer" (*izrat al-muʾmin*).[80] By defining the area between the mid-shin and ankle as an acceptable range, Ibn Baz's ruling created a margin of error for those who sought to follow this ruling.

The growing normativity of this expanded definition of *isbal* in transnational Salafi circles is also evident in the association of the obligation to grow a beard and the prohibition against long pants. In February 1989, Ibn al-ʿUthaymin noted in a fatwa published in the Saudi daily *al-ʿUkaz* that it is forbidden to shave the beard, just as it is forbidden to wear clothes to extend "below the ankles" (*mā asfal al-kaʿbayn*). Indeed, the latter practice leads to hellfire (*al-nār*) regardless of whether the intention was arrogance or not (*siwāʾ kāna fihi khuyalāʾ am ghayr khuyalāʾ*), though the former motive incurs greater punishment.[81] By the end of the 1980s, the prohibition against *isbal* appears widespread among Saudi Salafis.[82] Yet it would be up to an Egyptian Salafi to directly tie this debate to questions of religious identity and internal Muslim communal boundaries.

THE TURN OF EGYPTIAN SALAFIS TO *ISBAL*, 1988–1992

As with Muhammad b. Ismaʿil al-Muqaddam of the Alexandria-based Salafi Call (*al-Daʿwa al-Salafiyya*) in the case of the beard, the earliest adopter of the prohibition against *isbal* in Egypt would also come from outside Ansar a-Sunna. Around 1988,[83] a native of the Delta governorate of Sohaj, Abu-l-Mundhir ʿAbd

80. Muslim b. al-Hajjaj al-Qushayri, *Sahih Muslim maʿa Sharh Sahih Muslim al-Musamma Ikmal al-Muʿallim wa Ikmal Ikmal al-Muʿlim*, ed. Muhammad b. Yusuf Sanusi et al. (Beirut: Dar al-Fikr al-ʿIlmiyya, 1994), 5:384–85.

81. Ibn al-ʿUthaymin, "Fatawa," *al-ʿUkaz*, 11 Rajab 1409/17 February 1989, 8.

82. One explanation for the prohibition against *isbal* catching on earlier in Saudi Arabia is the supportive position of the Wahhabi-Hanbali elite, and specifically Muhammad b. Ibrahim, on this question.

83. *Tanbihat Hamma ʿala Malabis al-Muslimin al-Yawm* does not contain a date of publication. The back cover, however, includes a list of recently published titles of Maktabat al-Tawʿiyya al-Islamiyya. While the majority are not extant in library databases, three are: Muhammad Nasir al-Din al-Albani's *Talkhis Ahkam al-Janaʾiz* (1984, held by Princeton, Cornell, Columbia, and New York Universities), an edited edition of Ibn Taymiyya's *Idah al-Dalala fi ʿUmum al-Risala* by Muhammad Shakir (1986, held by the libraries of Princeton, Cornell, Columbia, and New York Universities) and Ibn Qayyim al-Jawziyya's *al-Risala al-Tabukiyya* (1987, held by the Israeli National Library). Furthermore, the text itself cites fatwas from the Saudi *al-Daʿwa* magazine, which appeared in issues 855, 913, 920 and 935. While I do not have access to these

al-Haqq b. ʿAbd al-Latif (d. 2012) published *Important Warnings Regarding Muslims' Clothing Today* (*Tanbihat Hamma ʿala Malabis al-Muslimin al-Yawm*). Abu-l-Mundhir who would also publish a book entitled *The Beard: Worship or Custom* (*al-Lihya: ʿAda am ʿIbada*) in 2011,[84] was a purist even within Purist Salafism: a biography preserved on a leading Saudi Salafi website states that he left Ansar al-Sunna because he believed that it too often placed "reason over the revealed text" (*al-ʿaql ʿalā al-naṣṣ al-sharʿī*).[85] In the specific case of *isbal*, though, he addressed himself to a sartorially diverse audience:

> To every Muslim who believes in God
> To every Muslim who fears God
> To every Muslim who takes pride in his clothing
> To every Muslim who extends his clothing beyond the ankles (*yuṭīl thiyābahu taḥta al-kaʿbayn*)
> To every Muslim who extends his clothing in prayer
> To every Muslim who extends his pants below the ankles (*yuṭīl al-banṭalūn taḥta al-kaʿbayn*)
> To every Muslim who prays in pants
> To every Muslim who resembles the infidels (*yatashabbah bi-l-kuffār*)
> To every Muslim who inquires as to the most virtuous clothing (*afḍal al-thiyāb*).[86]

This opening acknowledgment is notable for the variety that it assumes: pants and implicitly the *jallabiyya*, Salafi and non-Salafi. It invokes belief in and fear of God on the one hand, and pride in one's clothing, on the other. In these pages, Abu-l-Mundhir banishes any doubt as to his position on pants: he is making an argument not only against *isbal* generally but about pants in particular because the latter is a foreign invention whose popularization, like the shaving of the beard, is linked to the spread of colonial rule in the Middle East.[87]

---

issues' dates, issue #1067 appeared on 22 Rabiʿ al-Awwal 1407/24 November 1986. Given this information, it is likely that the volume was published sometime fairly soon after 1987.

84. Abu-l-Mundhir ʿAbd al-Haqq b. ʿAbd al-Latif Athri, *al-Lihya: ʿAda am ʿIbada?* (Cairo: Maktabat al-Balad al-Amin, 2011).

85. "Abu-l-Mundhir ʿAbd al-Haqq ʿAbd al-Latif," *Multaqa Ahl al-Hadith*, published 6 December 2013, https://www.ahlalhdeeth.com/vb/archive/index.php/t-285981.html.

86. Abu-l-Mundhir ʿAbd al-Haqq b. ʿAbd al-Latif, *Tanbihat Hamma ʿala Malabis al-Muslimin al-Yawm wa maʿahu Fatawa fi al-Isbal li-l-Shaykh ʿAbd al-ʿAziz b. Bāz waʾl-Shaykh Ibn ʿUthaymin wa Adab al-Libas li-baʿd Talaba al-ʿIlm* (Cairo: Maktabat al-Tawʿiyya al-Islamiyya, ~1988), 2.

87. Abu-l-Mundhir, *Tanbihat Hamma ʿala Malabis al-Muslimin al-Yawm*, 4.

Neither is Abu-l-Mundhir exclusively concerned with these two practices, highlighting everything from women's makeup, to jewelry for men and women, to smoking and long hair for men popularized by the "Beatles" (*al-khanāfis*) and the "Hippies" (*al-Hībīz*).[88] Along with this imitation of non-Muslim styles and practices, he laments that Muslims spend their free time watching television, visiting the cinema, and listening to the radio rather than listening to Quranic recitation or commanding right and forbidding wrong.[89] Accordingly, Abu-l-Mundhir's ambitions for this pamphlet were none other than to save Muslims from "catastrophe" (*muṣība*).[90] To achieve this end, the pamphlet proceeds to lay out the prohibitions against *isbal* and pants alike based on authenticated hadith reports.

In the course of this case against *isbal* and pants, an intended audience not explicitly acknowledged in the opening lines of the book comes into focus: the "many Brothers who wear the short shirt" (*qamīṣ^{an} qaṣīr^{an}*) along with "long pants" (*banṭalūn^{an} ṭawīl^{an}*). To clarify this practice, Abu-l-Mundhir cites a mid-1980s conversation between leading Egyptian Salafi Abu Ishaq al-Huwayni (b. 1956) and Muhammad Nasir al-Din al-Albani.[91] In this conversation, al-Albani rejects the notion, characteristic of the longer *madhhab*-based legal tradition, that any motivation other than "arrogance" (*khuyalā'*) can account for excessively long clothing.[92] To further buttress his case against pants, Abu-l-Mundhir cites an additional al-Albani recording in which the latter distinguishes between wider trousers (*sarāwīl*) that had long been worn in the Middle East and pants (*al-banṭalūn*), which arrived with colonialism.[93] The identity of those men who wear a shirt and long pants is not hard to discern: Abu-l-Mundhir is referring to the identifying uniform of activists in the Jamaʿa Islamiyya.

Unlike the obligation to pray in shoes or grow the beard, but like the adoption of gender segregation, Abu-l-Mundhir's call to adopt *Isbal* carried with it implicit class dimensions. Unlike its countryside cousin, the properly Salafi robe required either custom production or a visit to the tailor to amend it.

88. Abu-l-Mundhir, *Tanbihat Hamma ʿala Malabis al-Muslimin al-Yawm*, 5.

89. Abu-l-Mundhir, *Tanbihat Hamma ʿala Malabis al-Muslimin al-Yawm*, 5.

90. Abu-l-Mundhir, *Tanbihat Hamma ʿala Malabis al-Muslimin al-Yawm*, 7.

91. The author dates the conversation between al-Huwayni and al-Albani to 1407 H, which would fall in either 1986 or 1987.

92. Abu-l-Mundhir, *Tanbihat Hamma ʿala Malabis al-Muslimin al-Yawm*, 15–16.

93. Abu-l-Mundhir, *Tanbihat Hama ʿala Malabis al-Muslimin al-Yawm*, 27.

Furthermore, the behaviors that Abu-l-Mundhir identifies as harmful, ranging from allegedly excessive time spent enjoying television, cinema, and the radio, to makeup and jewelry, to replicating foreign hairstyles, would not have been as available to Egyptians of more limited means and literacy. A seemingly modest form of dress carried hidden costs.

Just as importantly, Ansar al-Sunna was still struggling to disassociate itself from the Jamaʿa Islamiyya's coercive style of commanding right and forbidding wrong. Most notably, in 1988, a group of members of Ansar al-Sunna had attacked a music festival in an attempt to prevent a band from playing. Chastising this excess, the group's leadership reiterated that commanding right and forbidding wrong involved "gentle preaching" (*al-mawʿiẓa al-ḥasana*).[94] Triangulating between these young men and the implicit threat of repression by security forces, the author of the article noted:

> The excess and radicalism (*al-ghūlū wa'l-taṭarruf*) [of these youth] did not emerge out of a vacuum . . . but rather from seeing a society distant from Islam. . . . We must understand the causes that lead to [radicalism] . . . . Oh people . . . know that wisdom (*al-ḥikma*) is necessary to guide the comprehensive Islamic Revival (*al-Ṣaḥwa al-Islāmiyya al-shāmila*) through which our society is currently living.[95]

Seven months later, a second editorial note elaborated on the prior diagnosis of the causes of radicalism, citing everything from limited religious education within the public school system to the immorality of the Egyptian media to the "application of the emergency law (*qānūn al-ṭawārīʾ*) . . . which threatens those preachers who are society's virtuous elite (*al-nukhba al-fāḍila*). . . ."[96]

In the face of these challenges, Ansar al-Sunna formally adopted the prohibition against *isbal*. Ahmad Fahmi Ahmad's ruling discussed in the chapter's opening, which came suddenly and without clear cause, can be best understood not only in light of broader Salafi winds, but also in the context of the same issue's introductory statement, which sought to understand the causes of radicalism (*al-taṭarruf*) and offer solutions to fight it. Ahmad was no state lackey: he made it clear that he resented the claim that actions such as men growing the beard and donning "short dress" (*al-thiyāb al-qaṣīra*) and women

94. Ahmad, "Kalimat al-Tahrir," *al-Tawhid*, Dhu al-Hijja 1408/July 1988, 1–4, at 1–2.

95. Ahmad, "Kalimat al-Tahrir," 4.

96. Ahmad, "Kalimat al-Tahrir," *al-Tawhid*, Rajab 1409/February 1989, 1–5, 12, at 2–5.

wearing the *niqab* qualify them as radicals.[97] But he was deeply concerned about the careless and widespread use of *takfir* by the Jamaʿa Islamiyya.[98] Here, however, we see *isbal* as not merely a marginal practice popularized by Salafi scholars, but also a key marker of a broader movement that sought to visibly distinguish itself from its religious competitors who wielded violence against the state and society alike.[99]

In turning to *isbal*, Ahmad was joined by Salafis further afield. In February 1990, a fatwa by the Permanent Committee was published in *al-Mujahid*, a magazine published by Jamil al-Rahman, who led a Salafi state in the Kunar Province in the Northeast of Afghanistan. It specified that the "short robe" (*al-qamīṣ al-qaṣīr*) stops at the mid-shin (*niṣf al-sāq*).[100] Similarly, in April 1992, the *Sahwa*-affiliated *al-Bayan* published a fatwa affirming that those who extend their garment lower than the ankle will be punished with hellfire (*fī al-nār*).[101]

In 1993, al-Albani would also extend the argument attributed to him by Abu-l-Mundhir in a lesson given in Amman, Jordan. Though the main topic of this particular lesson was the permissibility of combining prayers (*al-jamʿ bayna al-ṣalawāt*) and trimming the beard when it exceeded the length of the fist (*al-qabḍa*), he arrived at the topic of the robe and pant length some thirty-three minutes into his remarks. The question at hand was not the basic pre-

97. Ahmad Fahmi Ahmad, "Kalimat al-Tahrir," *al-Tawhid*, Shawwal 1409/~May 1989, 1–5, at 2.

98. Ahmad, "Kalimat al-Tahrir," 5.

99. That same year, the Saudi daily newspaper *ʿUkaz* published an interview with ʿAtiyya Salim, previously mentioned in chapter 4. A native of the Egyptian governorate of Sharqiyya, Salim had moved to Saudi Arabia in the 1960s to teach in the Ministry of Education and later, based on a connection to Ibn Baz, had begun teaching at the Islamic University of Medina. The topic of the interview was ostensibly the wave of Islamic Revival that had swept the Middle East in the previous two decades, but Salim appeared to have a specific target, noting that "religious commitment is not just about shortening the robe (*taqṣīr al-thawb*) or wearing one's watch on the right hand" (See "al-Fikr al-Islami," *al-ʿUkaz*, 10 Shawwal 1410/5 May 1990, 14).

100. al-Lajna al-Daʾima, "Fatawa," *al-Mujahid*, Rajab 1410/February 1990, 43–5, at 44.

101. Khalid b. Salih al-Sayf, "Qiraʾa li-Fikr al-Sihafi Fahmi Huwaydi, *al-Bayan*, Shawwal 1412/~April 1992, 50:76. In November 1996, *al-Bayan* featured an additional explanation of *isbal*, which specified that while the Sunnaic practice was to let one's garment hang down to the shin it was permitted (*mubāḥ*) to wear one's clothing between the mid-shin and ankle (*mā dūn niṣf al-sāq ilā al-kaʿbayn*), while it was forbidden for it to reach "lower than the ankle" (*mā asfal min al-kaʿbayn*). Most egregious, though, was the act of dragging one's robes out of arrogance (*an yajirruhu khuyalāʾ*). See ʿAbd Allah Ismaʿil, "Min Ahkam al-Libas," *al-Bayan*, Rajab 1417/~November 1996, 107:16.

scription of how to observe the prohibition against *isbal*, that one's clothing could only extend between the mid-shin (*niṣf al-sāq*) and ankles (*kaʿbayn*), but rather a specific hadith report in which the Prophet's Companion and the first Caliph, Abu Bakr, had said to Muhammad: "'Oh Messenger of God, my robe (*izār*) slips down and I do not pay attention to it.' He responded: '[but] you are not one of those who do it out of pride (*khuyalāʾ*).'" In response, al-Albani explained that the issue in Abu Bakr's violation is that his robe falls without him intending for it do so (*al-mukhālafa bi-suqūt al-izār dūna al-qaṣd minhu*). Rather, while only God knows a man's intentions—whether he has let his robe hang down out of arrogance or not—such a person has "clearly violated his Prophet's model" (*khālafa Sunnat Nabīhi*).[102] The legal question had morphed from whether one could wear long robes or pants without seeking to express arrogance to why a long robe violated Muhammad's model: because it *communicated* disregard.

Though a product of textual deliberation, the question of *isbal* also carried political sensitivities and functions in Egypt related to the rise of jihadi groups that donned the *jallabiyya* but did not observe *isbal*. To be clear, the length of one's robes was not the primary site of textual debate: between 1989 and 1992, Badawi Muhammad Khayr, a prominent scholar within Ansar al-Sunna, had laid out the question of commanding right and forbidding wrong over the course of sixteen linked essays, touching on the requirements, key ideas, and situational judgment required to successfully perform this duty. While not directly related to *isbal*—the targets of forbidding wrong were far more likely to be the neglect of prayer or the consumption of alcohol—this question cut to the core of the organization's commitment to quietism insofar as it explicitly challenged the capacity and will of the Mubarak government to uphold public morality.

It was in this context that Khayr sought to reassert control over the duty to command right and forbid wrong. Instead of subsuming it within the obligation to render advice to the ruler, he offered an alternative argument based on the Sunni tradition: the performance of this duty "by the hand" (*bi-l-yad*) was limited to those under one's authority (*wilāya*). A man had authority over his wife and children, while the ruler possessed such authority over the

102. al-Albani, "al-Jamʿ Bayna al-Salawat li-l-Musafir wa'l-Muqim/al-Insaf ʿInda al-Imam al-Albani bi-Wujub al-Akdh min al-Lihya ma Zad ʿan al-Qabda/Tasmiyyat al-Shaykh al-Albani li-Bint Abi Layla bi-Burayda," 8 September 1993, 65 min at 37:30 and 39:50, respectively.

population at large.[103] The practice of burning down nightclubs or bars practiced by the Jamaʿa Islamiyya, then, not only represented an unlawful claim to authority over others, but also had the effect of increasing, rather than halting, corruption by entrenching those who owned or frequented such institutions in their sinful practices.[104]

Just as important, however, was Khayr's prescription for engaging with the ruler effectively and ethically. Emphasizing the importance of speaking truth to an unjust ruler (*kalimat al-ḥaqq ʿinda al-sulṭān al-jāʾir*), Khayr noted that one must do so without needlessly clashing (*tajannub bi-qadar istiṭāʿatihi*).[105] Indeed, although a tyrant (*ṭāghiya*) like Pharaoh differs little across time and place (*fī kull ʿaṣr wa-kull zamān*), one should never accuse such rulers of disbelief (*kufr*). Instead, the wise path is to "describe the characteristics of infidels (*ṣifāt al-kāfirīn*) in a general fashion . . . lest the ruler accuse you of making this accusation."[106] Ethical engagement with power, as envisioned by Khayr, was a religio-political tightrope.

The question that remained, for Khayr, was how to provide space for commanding right and forbidding wrong consistent with at least some deference to an impious ruling elite. To square this circle, this Salafi scholar argued that, while the highest form of the duty is that which is performed by hand (*bi-l-yad*), this is reserved for the rulers who are themselves judged by God.[107] The failure of rulers to fulfill this duty, however, necessitates that individual Muslims command right and forbid wrong verbally in their presence, just as they do to their fellow Muslims outside the halls of power.[108] Pushing back against the Jamaʿa Islamiyya's claim to religious duty as a justification for attacking state and society alike, Khayr sought to guide quietist Salafis to peaceful forms of religious exhortation, while guarding them against accusations of radicalism and extremism. Just as striking, however, is Khayr's attempt to then *exclude*

103. Badawi Muhammad Khayr, "al-Amr bi-l-Maʿruf waʾl-Nahi ʿan al-Munkar," *al-Tawhid*, Shawwal 1411/~April 1991, 30–4. Badawi Muhammad Khayr may have been drawing on Ibn Taymiyya's views on commanding right and forbidding wrong. See Cook, *Commanding Right and Forbidding Wrong in Islamic Thought*, 174.

104. Khayr, "al-Amr bi-l-Maʿruf waʾl-Nahi ʿan al-Munkar," 33.

105. Khayr, "al-Amr bi-l-Maʿruf waʾl-Nahi ʿan al-Munkar," *al-Tawhid* Jumada al-Ukhra 1411/~December 1990, 36–40, at 36.

106. Khayr, "al-Amr bi-l-Maʿruf waʾl-Nahi ʿan al-Munkar," 37–39.

107. Khayr, "al-Amr bi-l-Maʿruf waʾl-Nahi ʿan al-Munkar," *al-Tawhid*, Shawwal 1411/~April 1991, 30–4, at 31.

108. Khayr, "al-Amr bi-l-Maʿruf waʾl-Nahi ʿan al-Munkar," 33.

mixing between men and women or unveiled women from the domain of legitimate targets for the fulfillment of this obligation.[109] Although Salafis had adopted gender segregation as a key position over the previous decade and a half, this call had had failed to convince the Mubarak government to institute gender segregation within either state institutions or public spaces. As such, Khayr sought to thread the needle between a condemnation of gender mixing and an effort to distance Ansar al-Sunna from the efforts of the Jama'a Islamiyya to target such spaces as part of claim to command right and forbid wrong.

In the concluding article of this sixteen-part series, Khayr noted that the path to "greatness, victory and dignity" (*al-ʿizza waʾl-naṣr waʾl-karāma*) depended on the successful performance of the duty to command right and forbid wrong by both the population and ruler alike. Crucial to this campaign was substantive engagement with radical youth, yet up to this point, state-aligned scholars had only driven further polarization.[110] The problem of confusion among radical youth, however, remained. An early fall 1992 article in *al-Tawhid*, written by Muhammad b. ʿAli al-Gharmawi, a teaching assistant at Cairo University, responded to an article that appeared in the 24 July 1992 edition of the Egyptian daily newspaper *al-Akhbar*. Al-Gharmawi's objection was that article's author had claimed that those who wore the beard, "short jilbabs" (*al-jalābīb al-qaṣīra*) and *niqab* were guilty of "excessive religiosity" (*al-mughalāʾ fī al-tadayyun*) and "radicalism" (*al-taṭarruf*).[111] Instead, he argued, this dress choice for men represented no less than the "guidance of the Prophet of God" (*hadī Rasūl Allāh*), as God had command Muslims to "wear the *jilbab* and to shorten it" (*lubs al-jilbāb wa taqṣīrihi*).[112] Yet at the time when al-Gharmawi argued that the shortened robe was none other than Prophetic guidance and Badawi Muhammad Khayr argued for greater engagement with radical youth, Egypt saw a particularly severe wave of terrorist attacks; in 1993, over one hundred police officers died in this string of jihadi attacks.[113]

109. Khayr, "al-Amr bi-l-Maʿruf waʾl-Nahi ʿan al-Munkar," 33.

110. Khayr, "al al-Amr bi-l-Maʿruf waʾl-Nahi ʿan al-Munkar," *al-Tawhid*, Rabiʿ al-Akhar 1412/~October 1991, 26–31, at 30.

111. Muhammad b. ʿAli al-Gharmawi, "Jahhalu al-Islam wa Qalu," *al-Tawhid*, Rabiʿ al-Awwal 1413/~August 1992, 24–27, at 24.

112. Muhammad b. ʿAli al-Gharmawi, "Jahhalu al-Islam wa Qalu," *al-Tawhid*, Rabiʿ al-Awwal 1413/~August 1992, 26–27.

113. David Sagiv, *Fundamentalism and the Intellectuals in Egypt, 1973–1993* (London: Frank Cass, 1995), 155–6.

The challenge that the Salafis faced was not merely one of confusion with radical groups in the eyes of the security forces, but also one of broader cultural trends. The next year saw the release of a film entitled *The Terrorist* (*al-Irhabi*) starring the prominent Egyptian comedy movie star ʿAdil Imam (b. 1940). While Imam's rendition of *jihadi* fashion was far from exact—his mustache was shaven, rather than trimmed[114]—Ansar al-Sunna's leaders were concerned: a May 1994 article described how this film had depicted the protagonist wearing "the short *jilbab* (*al-jilbāb al-qaṣīr*), growing his beard, wearing a skullcap (*ṭāqiya*), and carrying a machine gun" (*al-bunduqiyya*).[115] The claim to properly practice the prohibition against *isbal*, in turn, constituted both a show of the broader Salafi movement's commitment to emulating the Prophet Muhammad's model and an effort to distinguish Ansar al-Sunna in the eyes of both the population and the security forces alike vis-à-vis their (and the state's) jihadi challengers.

CONCLUSION

In 1992, ʿUqayl b. Muhammad Zayd al-Maqtari, a Yemeni Salafi scholar and preacher who had studied with Muqbil b. Hadi al-Wadiʿi, published a critical edition of Muhammad b. Ismaʿil al-Sanʿani's (d. 1768) *Setting Forth the Opinions Regarding the Forbidden Nature of Isbal for Men* (*Istifaʾ al-Aqwal fi Tahrim al-Isbal ʿala al-Rijal*). Based on a manuscript held in the Library of the Great Mosque (*Maktabat al-Jāmiʿ al-Kabīr*) in Sanaa and published in both Yemen's capital and in Jerusalem, this short work sets forth the basic prohibition against letting one's garments hang down belong the ankle. To underline the contemporary significance of this text, al-Maqtari notes with considerable concern that "letting one's clothes hang down (*isbāl al-thiyāb*) below the ankles (*asfal min al-kaʿbayn*) has become widespread among people in recent times. . . ."[116] Neither is this merely an issue of less-learned Muslims: al-Maqtari takes

114. The 1992 film *al-Irhab waʾl-Kabab* also depicted Jihadis with shaved mustaches. Though there is basis within the Hadith corpus to justify shaving the mustache, the perception that Salafis do so appears to largely be a creation of the Egyptian film industry.

115. "al-Iʿlam al-Misri wa Muharabat al-Tatarruf," *al-Tawhid*, Dhu al-Hijja 1414/~May 1994, 59–63, at 62.

116. Muhammad b. Ismaʿil al-Sanʿani, *Istifaʾ al-Aqwal fi Tahrim al-Isbal ʿala al-Rijal*, ed. ʿUqayl b. Muhammad Zayd al-Maqtari (Sanaa, Yemen, and Jerusalem: Maktabat Dar al-Quds, 1992), 5.

aim at scholars (*man yantasib ʿilā al-ʿilm*), particularly graduates of al-Azhar University, who take this position and then are followed by Muslims more broadly.[117]

That a Yemeni Salafi scholar in the early 1990s would take aim at non-Salafis, particularly those at internationally influential institutions such as al-Azhar, is hardly noteworthy; tensions with al-Azhar had been found among Salafis both within and beyond Egypt since the 1930s. Nor is the reproduction of classical works by modern scholars remarkable; this editorial process was a common feature of the Salafi movement more broadly. Instead, what is striking about al-Maqtari's introduction is the claim that the practice of letting one's clothes hang below the ankles is a product of "these recent times" (*hadhihī al-azmān al-mutaʾakhkhira*).[118] On the contrary, it was during this period that the practice of *refusing* to let one's garments hang down had become a point of distinction.

Al-Maqtari, and before him, al-Sanʿani, had a strong basis for the claim that *isbal* is prohibited in Islamic law. As in previous chapters, however, our question here is not whether this practice is novel—in its basic articulation, it is not—but rather *how* Salafis came to privilege a definition of *isbal* that pivoted on length rather than intent at a time when few observed the letter of this law. As this chapter has shown, long robes or pants were not a product of "recent times," or not of the recent century, at any rate. Instead, a focus on shortened robes arose out the efforts of Salafis from Egypt to Saudi Arabia to transform *isbal* into a powerful social symbol at the intersection of an ethical commitment to following the Prophet Muhammad's model, nationalist visions of subject formation, and new clothing styles.

117. al-Sanʿani, *Istifaʾ al-Aqwal fi Tahrim al-Isbal ʿala al-Rijal*, 5.
118. al-Sanʿani, *Istifaʾ al-Aqwal fi Tahrim al-Isbal ʿala al-Rijal*, 5.

Conclusion

In December 2018, I had the pleasure of attending a conference on "The Future of Salafism" organized by Masooda Bano and Saud Al Sarhan and sponsored jointly by Oxford University and the King Faisal Center for Research and Islamic Studies. On one of the panels, Dr. Saad Aljloud, an Associate Professor at Qassim University in Saudi Arabia, presented a paper authored jointly with Shaykh ʿAbd Allah al-Muniʿ (b. 1930), a Wahhabi-Hanbali scholar member of the Kingdom's Committee of Grand ʿUlamaʾ. Dr. Aljloud explained that Salafis derive their entire approach to Islam from the Quran and Sunna.

During the Q&A portion of the talk, I asked why, if the Salafi beard could be derived clearly and unequivocally from the Quran and Sunna, it had taken until the 1970s for Salafis to define the parameters of a proper beard? When Dr. Aljloud responded that all Salafis had to do was look at the Prophet Muhammad's model, I pushed further, noting that it was a hadith regarding the practices of Ibn ʿUmar, not those of Muhammad, that served as a proof-text for the minimal length of the fist (*al-qabḍa*). His response was that my timeline was off, and that I was making a simple matter far too complicated. I do not recount this anecdote to single out Dr. Aljloud but to highlight a broader tendency among scholars of Salafism to take this movement's self-understanding as an analytical framework through which to study it.

This conference also included fascinating papers on varied Salafi movements, whether in Saudi Arabia, Europe, South Asia, or Southeast Asia. The vast majority of studies across this geographical expanse, however, focused on Salafi-Islamist (also known as Politico) or jihadi groups. This distribution was far from random, reflecting the broader makeup of the subfield of "Salafism Studies," even as the vast majority of Salafis globally embrace political quietism and focus on social activism.[1]

This approach that privileges politics exists alongside that of scholars of Salafi intellectual history who focused primarily on the movement's neo-Hanbali theological tenets (known as *ʿaqīdat al-Salaf*) and its textual methodology. Such a lens has the undeniable merit of taking seriously the continued resonance of longstanding Islamic theological and textual approaches, as well as casting light on the centrality of theology to Salafi movements. Salafism's significance as a twentieth-century project that melds neo-Hanbali theology and a commitment to deriving all law from the Quran and Sunna, however, emerges primarily not from the way that its intellectual approach has shaped the Arab world and beyond, but rather from its social impact. Like the research on Salafism and politics, that on Salafi intellectual history has revealed little about what has made this movement socially significant or of how society (and states) have shaped its origins and the course of its history.

This story of the rise of distinctly Salafi social practices in the twentieth-century Middle East, by contrast, charts how this movement's adherents have used their bodies to shape themselves and the society around them. Centered in Egypt but splaying out to the Levant and Gulf alike, it traces the roots and consolidation of Salafism's signature practices. My approach might appear idiosyncratic and painstaking: rather than relying on Salafi legal compendia and pamphlets to analyze these practices, I turn to journals and magazines, Salafi and non-Salafi, to excavate the process by which particular bodily practices became religiously significant. By reorienting the study of Salafism towards the social, I show the centrality of visible daily practice to this movement's development and influence alike.

A focus on the social also casts light on Salafis who engage in neither political competition or armed conflict. Though this "origins story" of distinct practices tells us little about the intersection of theological reasoning on the one hand and political policy and *jihad*, on the other, it does reveal Salafism to be a movement intimately shaped by the world around it. A potential objection would be that social environments shape daily practice far more than they

1. An edited volume, based on the conference, has a similar focus. See Masooda Bano, ed., *Salafi Social and Political Movements* (Edinburgh, UK: Edinburgh University Press, 2021).

do theology or political strategy. This, however, obscures the basic fact that the broader intellectual and social world influences not only models of social organization but also theological and political visions. Here I have shown how a basic component of Salafi theology, an expansive definition of worship (*ʿibāda*), was structured by challenges of both secular nationalism and social competition. My contribution to the study of Islamist/Politico- and Jihadi-Salafis, in turn, is the inversion of the assumptions that generally define analysis of such groups. Instead of foregrounding theological reasoning as it relates to political participation and *takfir,* I argue that we must explore the historical circumstances—political, social and intellectual—that have rendered the claims made by these branches of Salafism possible and plausible in the twentieth and twenty-first centuries.

I have shown not only that Salafism is a project best understood within the ideological contestation of the twentieth century, but also that the defining logic of its social practices, specifically the emphasis on self-regulation and linkage between ethics and communication through visibility, are inextricably related to and products of the emergence of powerful states and modern mass societies. Far from politicizing daily life, Salafism *responds* to this politicization by offering a distinctly modern ethics of communication. At the same time, though, such projects are often incomplete or ambiguous; multiple practices must be performed simultaneously precisely because a concern with individual practices of facial hair, shortened pants, or gender segregation is not exclusive to Salafism, and because practices that distinguish Salafis in one country may not serve this function in other countries.

An emphasis on practice also reveals the material and perceptual conditions that have transformed Islamic scholarly reasoning in the twentieth century. Building on previous scholarship that dissects the subtle yet significant transformation of longstanding tools of *fiqh,* this book explores practices of citation as transmitted through Islamic print media and embodied by men and women in daily practice. My emphasis on Salafism as a project of historical reconstruction through an ostensibly straightforward textual approach also challenges the assumption, sometimes implicit and other times explicit, that contemporary Islamic piety movements rely on a discursive tradition of embodied ethical practice. This approach, most prominent in anthropological scholarship on Islam, valuably casts light on adherents' engagement with pre-modern religious texts. Yet, as the story of Salafi social practices reveals, citation of past authorities is not *necessarily* a discursively continuous act; indeed, it can both represent and produce profound rupture.[2] As such, contemporary forms of Islamic piety are shaped primarily by the communicative conditions of modernity and the social worlds of their participants, and only secondarily by a discursive Islamic ethical tradition.

Finally, this is a story of Islamic law that relies on media sources generally considered secondary, if not unimportant, to understanding the development of this tradition. Previous studies that foreground landmark religious texts valuably illustrate the logic that defines these works and their relationship to previous interpretation. By complement, my focus on periodicals and pamphlets, and to a lesser extent lessons and lectures recorded by audiocassette, reveals the indispensability of contemporary media to understanding the *process* by which significant legal rulings arise.

While this story is historical, its core dynamics continue to shape the Salafi movement. Whether in Egypt, Saudi Arabia, Kuwait or Yemen, let alone Iraq and Syria, Salafi scholars, organizations, and movements remain influential claimants to the right to define the relationship between religion and politics across the Middle East and beyond. As scholars track these movements, a deep knowledge of Islamic history will remain important for comprehending how Salafis understand themselves. Yet it is only by reorienting our analytical gaze away from the Quran and Sunna that scholars can move past this normative claim to understand the ways in which Salafism has been molded by a world of non-Islamic influences that it abhors. In sum, this is a story of the ways in which a movement that rejects a myriad of the innovations (*bidʿa*) of modern life is deeply shaped by them.

2. For an example, see Moulie Vidas, *Tradition and the Formation of the Talmud* (Princeton, NJ: Princeton University Press, 2014), 14–15.

BIBLIOGRAPHY

PERIODICALS

al-Ahram. 1926–94, Egypt.
al-Da'wa. 1951–56, 1976–81, Egypt, Muslim Brotherhood.
al-Fath. 1926–43, Egypt, Muhibb al-Din al-Khatib.
al-Hadi al-Nabawi. 1936–66, Egypt, Ansar al-Sunna al-Muhammadiyya.
al-Hadi al-Nabawi. 1993–2000, Egypt, Jama'at Da'wat al-Haqq.
al-Ikhwan al-Muslimun. 1933–38, 1943–46, Egypt, Muslim Brotherhood.
al-I'tisam. 1939–81, 1984–90, Egypt, Ahmad 'Isa 'Ashur.
al-Jami'a al-Islamiyya bi-l-Madina al-Munawwara. 1968–80, Saudi Arabia, Islamic University of Medina.
al-Tamaddun al-Islami. 1935–81, Syria, Islamic Civilization Association.
al-Tawhid. 1973–2000, Egypt, Ansar al-Sunna al-Muhammadiyya.
al-'Ukaz. 1976–90, Saudi Arabia.

BOOKS AND ARTICLES

'Abd al-Aziz, Jum'a Amin. *Fahm al-Islam fi Zilal al-Usul al-'Ishrin li-l-Imam Hasan al-Banna*. Cairo: Dar al-Da'wa li-l-Tiba'a wa'l-Nashr, 1990.

'Abd al-Hadi, Fatima. *Rihlati ma'a al-Akhawat al-Muslimat: Min al-Imam Hasan al-Banna ila Sujun 'Abd al-Nasir*, edited by Hussam Tammam and Farid 'Abd al-Khaliq. Cairo: Dar al-Shuruq, 2011.

'Abd al-Rahim, Ya'qub. *Taysir al-Wusul ila Manhaj al-Usul min al-Manqul wa'l-Ma'qul*. Riyadh: Maktabat 'Ubaykan, 2010.

'Abd al-Salam, Siham. *Khitan al-Dhukur: Bayna al-Din, al-Tibb, al-Thaqafa, al-Tarikh*. Cairo: Ru'ya li-l-Nashr wa'l-Tawzi', 2006.

al-ʿAmrawi, ʿUmar b. Ghuarama. *Fasl al-Maqal fi Kalam Sayyid al-Anam ʿAlayhi al-Salat wa ʾl-Salam fi Hukm al-Salat fi al-Niʿal*. Riyadh: Matabiʿ wa-Iʿlanat al-Sharif, 1988.

al-ʿAsqalani, Ibn Hajar. *Fath al-Bari bi-Sharh Sahih al-Bukhari*, edited by ʿAbd al-ʿAziz b. Baz, Muhammad Fuʾad ʿAbd al-Baqi, and Muhibb al-Din al-Khatib. Beirut: Dar al-Maʿrifa, 1959?.

———. *Fath al-Bari Bi-Sharh Sahih al-Bukhari*, edited by ʿAbd al-Qadir Shayba al-Hamd. Riyadh: Maktabat al-Malk Fahad al-Wataniyya, 1421/~2001.

———. *Fath al-Bari bi-Sharh Sahih al-Bukhari*, edited by ʿAbd al-ʿAziz b. Baz and Muhammad Fuʾad ʿAbd al-Baqi. Beirut: Dar al-Kutub al-ʿIlmiyya, 2017.

al-ʿAyni, Badr al-Din Mahmud b. Ahmad. *ʿUmdat al-Qari: Sharh Sahih al-Bukhari*, edited by ʿAbd Allah Mahmud Muhammad ʿUmar. Beirut: Dar al-Kutub al-ʿIlmiyya, 2001.

Abbasi, Rushain. "Did Pre-Modern Muslims Distinguish the Religious and Secular? The Dīn-Dunyā Binary in Medieval Islamic Thought." *Journal of Islamic Studies* 31, no. 2 (2020): 185–225.

Abdel-Fadil, Mahmoud. *The Political Economy of Nasserism: A Study in Employment and Income Distribution Policies in Urban Egypt, 1952–72*. Cambridge, UK: Cambridge University Press, 1980.

Abou el Fadl, Khaled. *And God Knows the Soldiers: The Authoritative and Authoritarian in Islamic Discourses*. Lanham, MD: University Press of America, 2001.

Abugideiri, Hibba. *Gender and the Making of Modern Medicine in Colonial Egypt*. New York: Routledge, 2016.

Abu-l-Futuh, ʿAbd al-Munʿim. *ʿAbd al-Munʿim Abu-l-Futuh: Shahid ʿala Tarikh al-Haraka al-Islamiyya fi Misr, 1970–1984*, edited by Hussam Tammam. Cairo: Dar al-Shuruq, 2012.

Abu Shadi, Ibrahim. *al-Ikhtiyarat al-Fiqhiyya li-l-Imam al-Albani*. Mansura, Egypt: Dar al-Ghadd al-Jadid, 1427/2006.

Aflaq, Michel. *Dhikra al-Rasul al-ʿArabi*. Beirut: al-Muʾassasa al-ʿArabiyya li-l-Dirasat waʾl-Nashr, 1972.

Agrama, Hussein Ali. *Questioning Secularism: Islam, Sovereignty, and the Rule of Law in Modern Egypt*. Chicago: University of Chicago Press, 2012.

Ahmed, Chanfi. *West African ʿulamāʾ and Salafism in Mecca and Medina: Jawāb Al-Ifrīqī—The Response of the African*. Leiden: Brill, 2015.

al-Albani, Muhammad Nasir al-Din. *Hijab al-Marʾa al-Muslima fi al-Kitab wa ʾl-Sunna*. Cairo: al-Matbaʿa al-Salafiyya, 1954.

———. *Sifat Salat al-Nabi Min al-Takbir ila al-Taslim ki-Annaka Taraʾha*. Damascus, Syria: al-Maktab al-Islami, 1381/1961.

———. *Tadhir al-Sajid min Ittikhadh al-Qubur Masajid*. Damascus, Syria: al-Maktab al-Islami, 1983.

———. *Tamam al-Minna fi al-Taʿliq ʿala Fiqh al-Sunna*. Amman, Jordan: Dar al-Raya, 1988?

———. *Sahih al-Jamiʿ al-Saghir wa-Ziyadatuhu*, edited by Zuhayr al-Shawish. Damascus, Syria: al-Maktab al-Islami, 1988.

———. *Sifat Salat al-Nabi Min al-Takbir ila al-Taslim ki-Annaka Tara'ha*. Riyadh: Maktabat al-Maʿarif li-l-Nashr wa'l-Tawziʿ, 1410 H.

———. *Silsilat al-Ahadith al-Daʿifa wa'l-Mawduʿa wa Atharuha al-Sayyi' fi-l-Umma*. Riyadh: Maktabat al-Maʿarif, 2001.

Al-Rasheed, Madawi. *A History of Saudi Arabia*. Cambridge, UK: Cambridge University Press, 2010.

Armbrust, Walter. *Mass Culture and Modernism in Egypt*. Cambridge, UK: Cambridge University Press, 1996.

Anderson, Benedict. *Imagined Communities: Reflections on the Origin and Spread of Nationalism*. New York: Verso, 1991.

Andunisiyya, Fatriyya Wardi. *ʿInayat al-Shariʿa al-Islamiyya bi-Nazafat al-Fard wa 'l-Biʾa*. Beirut: Dar al-Kutub al-ʿIlmiyya, 2014.

Ansari, Ali M. *Modern Iran: The Pahlavis and After*. New York: Routledge, 2007.

al-Arian, Abdullah. *Answering the Call: Popular Islamic Activism in Sadat's Egypt*. Oxford: Oxford University Press, 2014.

Antoun, Richard. *Muslim Preacher in the Modern World: A Jordanian Case Study in Comparative Perspective*. Princeton, NJ: Princeton University Press, 1989.

———. "On the Modesty of Women in Arab Muslim Villages: A Study in the Accommodation of Traditions," *American Anthropologist* 70, no. 4 (August 1968): 671–97.

Asad, Talal. "The Idea of an Anthropology of Islam." Washington, DC: Georgetown University Center for Contemporary Arab Studies, 1986.

———. *Genealogies of Religion: Discipline and Reasons of Power in Christianity and Islam*. Baltimore, MD: Johns Hopkins University Press, 1994.

———. *Formations of the Secular: Christianity, Islam, Modernity*. Stanford, CA: Stanford University Press, 2003.

Ayalon, Ami. *Reading Palestine: Printing and Literacy, 1900–1948*. Austin: University of Texas Press, 2004.

Ayubi, Zahra. *Gendered Morality: Classical Islamic Ethics of the Self, Family and Society*. New York: Columbia University Press, 2019.

Badr, Badr Muhammad. *al-Jamaʿa al-Islamiyya fi Jamiʿat Misr: Haqaʾiq wa Wathaʾiq*. Cairo: N.P., N.D.

al-Banna, Hasan. *Mudhakkirat al-Daʿwa wa 'l-Daʿiyya*. Kuwait City: Maktabat Afaq, 2012.

Bano, Masooda, ed. *Salafi Social and Political Movements: National and Transnational Contexts*. Edinburgh, UK: Edinburgh University Press, 2021.

Barak, On. *On Time: Technology and Temporality in Modern Egypt*. Berkeley: University of California Press, 2013.

Baron, Beth. *Egypt as a Woman: Nationalism, Gender and Politics*. Berkeley: University of California Press, 2005.

———. *The Orphan Scandal: Christian Missionaries and the Rise of the Muslim Brotherhood*. Stanford, CA: Stanford University Press, 2014.

al-Barnahaburi, Nizam al-Din. *al-Fatawa al-Hindiyya al-Maʿrufa bi-l-Fatawa al-ʿAlamkiriyya fi Madhhab al-Imam al-Aʿzam Abi Hanifa al-Nuʿman*. Beirut: Dar al-Kutub al-ʿIlmiyya, 2000.

Bauer, Thomas. *A Culture of Ambiguity: An Alternative History of Islam.* Translated by Hinrich Biesterfeldt and Tricia Turnstall. New York: Columbia University Press, 2021.

Bell, Catherine. *Ritual Theory, Ritual Practice.* Oxford: Oxford University Press, 1992.

Beránek, Ondřej, and Pavel Ťupek. *The Temptation of Graves in Salafi Islam: Iconoclasm, Destruction and Idolatry.* Edinburgh, UK: Edinburgh University Press, 2019.

Berkey, Jonathan P. *Popular Preaching and Religious Authority in the Medieval Islamic Near East.* Seattle: University of Washington Press, 2001.

Blecher, Joel, and Josh Dubler. "Overlooking Race and Secularism in Muslim Philadelphia." In *Race and Secularism in America,* edited by Vincent Lloyd and Jonathan S. Kahn, 122–50. New York: Columbia University Press, 2016.

Bier, Laura. *Revolutionary Womanhood: Feminisms, Modernity, and the State in Nasser's Egypt.* Stanford, CA: Stanford University Press, 2011.

Bonnefoy, Laurent. *Salafism in Yemen: Transnationalism and Religious Identity.* Oxford: Oxford University Press, 2012.

Brown, Jonathan A. C. *The Canonization of al-Bukhārī and Muslim: The Formation and Function of the Sunnī Ḥadīth Canon.* Leiden: Brill, 2007.

Brooke, Steven, and Neil Ketchley, "Social and Institutional Origins of Political Islam." *American Political Science Review* 112, no. 2 (2018): 376–94.

al-Bukhari, Muhammad b. Isma'il. *Sahih al-Bukhari.* Damascus, Syria: Dar Ibn Kathir, 1423/2002.

Bunzel, Cole. "Manifest Enmity: The Origins, Development, and Persistence of Classical Wahhābism. 1153–1351/1741–1932." Ph.D. diss, Princeton University, 2018.

Bursey, Scott. "Finding Muhammad Qutb: Praising Ghosts Online, a Different Qutbian legacy and Islamic Revivalism in the Gulf." M.A. thesis, Simon Fraser University, 2017.

Calvert, John. *Sayyid Qutb and the Origins of Radical Islamism.* Oxford: Oxford University Press, 2013.

Central Agency for Public Mobilization and Statistics. *1976 Population and Housing Census.* Cairo: Central Agency for Publication Mobilization and Statistics, 1980.

Commins, David. "From Wahhabi to Salafi." In *Saudi Arabia in Transition: Insights on Social, Political, Economic and Religious Change,* edited by Bernard Haykel, Thomas Hegghammer, and Stéphane Lacroix, 151–66. Cambridge, UK: Cambridge University Press, 2015.

Cook, Michael. *Commanding Right and Forbidding Wrong in Islamic Thought.* Cambridge, UK: Cambridge University Press, 2001.

Cook, Michael. *Ancient Religions, Modern Politics.* Princeton, NJ: Princeton University Press, 2014.

Commins, David Dean. *Islamic Reform: Politics and Social Change in Late Ottoman Syria.* New York: Oxford University Press, 1990.

Coppens, Pieter. "Jamāl al-Dīn al-Qāsimī's Treatise on Wiping over the Socks and the Rise of a Distinct Salafi Method." *Die Welt Des Islam* (2021, first view): 1–34.

Cordesman, Anthony H. *Saudi Arabia Enters the Twenty-First Century: The Political, Foreign Policy, Economic and Energy Dimensions.* Westport, CT: Praeger, 2003.

al-Dasuqi, Muhammad b. Ahmad b. ʿArafa. *Hashiyyat al-Dasuqi ʿala al-Sharh al-Kabir li-l-Shaykh Abi al-Barakat Sidi Ahmad b. Muhammad al-ʿAdawi al-Shahir bi-l-Dardir.* Beirut: Dar al-Kutub al-ʿIlmiyya, 2010.

Dorril, Stephen. *Blackshirt: Sir Oswald Mosley and British Fascism.* London: Thistle Publishing, 2006.

Dorroll, Phil. *Islamic Theology in the Turkish Republic.* Edinburgh, UK: University of Edinburgh Press, 2021.

al-Dimyati, Abu Bakr ʿUthman b. Muhammad Shatta. *Hashiyat Iʿanat al-Talibin ʿala Hall Alfaz Fath al-Muʿin bi-Sharh Qurrat al-ʿAyn bi-Muhimmat al-Din.* N.P.: Dar al-Fikr 2019.

Duderija, Adis. *Constructing a Religiously Ideal 'Believer' and 'Woman' in Islam: Neo-Traditionalist Salafi and Progressive Muslims' Methods of Interpretation.* New York: Palgrave Macmillan, 2011.

Eickelman, Dale, and James Piscatori. *Muslim Politics.* Princeton, NJ: Princeton University Press, 2004.

Eickelman, Dale, and Jon W. Anderson. *New Media in the Muslim World: The Emerging Public Sphere.* Bloomington: Indiana University Press, 2003.

Euben, Roxanne L., and Muhammad Qasim Zaman. *Princeton Readings in Islamist Thought: Texts and Contexts from al-Banna to Bin Laden.* Princeton, NJ: Princeton University Press, 2009.

Farquhar, Michael. *Circuits of Faith: Migration, Education, and the Wahhabi Mission.* Stanford, CA: Stanford University Press, 2016.

Fahmy, Khaled. *All the Pasha's Men: Mehmed Ali, his Army, and the Making of Modern Egypt.* Cairo: American University in Cairo Press, 1997.

———. *In Quest of Justice: Islamic Law and Forensic Medicine in Modern Egypt.* Berkeley, CA: University of California Press, 2020.

Fahmy, Ziad. *Ordinary Egyptians: Creating the Modern Nation Through Popular Culture.* Stanford, CA: Stanford University Press, 2011.

al-Fanari, Muhammad b. Hamza. *Fusul al-Badaʾiʿ fi Usul al-Sharaʾiʿ.* Beirut: Dar al-Kutub al-ʿIlmiyya, 2006.

al-Fatawa al-Islamiyya min Dar al-Iftaʾ al-Misriyya, edited by Zakariyya al-Bari, Jadd al-Haqq ʿAli Jadd al-Haqq, and Jamal al-Din Muhammad Mahmud. Cairo: Supreme Council for Islamic Affairs, 1400/1980.

Fatawa al-Lajna al-Daʾima li-l-Buhuth al-ʿIlmiyya wa'l-Iftaʾ, edited by Ahmad b. ʿAbd al-Razzaq al-Duwaysh. Riyadh: al-Muʾayyad li-l-Nashr wa'l-Tawziʿ, 1411/1991.

Fatawa al-Lajna al-Daʾima li-l-Buhuth al-ʿIlmiyya wa'l-Iftaʾ: al-Majmuʿa al-Thaniyya, edited by Ahmad b. ʿAbd al-Razzaq al-Duwaysh. Riyadh: al-Riʾasa al-ʿAmma li-l-Buhuth wa'l-Iftaʾ, 2006.

Frisken, Amanda. *Victoria Woodhull's Sexual Revolution: Political Theater and the Popular Press in Nineteenth-Century America.* Philadelphia, PA: University of Pennsylvania Press, 2004.

Fuchs, Simon Wolfgang. "Failing Transnationally: Local intersections of science, medicine, and sectarianism in modernist Shiʿi writings." *Modern Asian Studies* 48, no. 2 (2014): 433–67.

———. "Glossy Global Leadership: Unpacking the Multilingual Religious Thought of the Jihad." In *Afghanistan's Islam*, edited by Nile Green, 180–206. Berkeley, University of California Press, 2017.

———. "A Direct Flight to Revolution: Maududi and the 1979 Moment in Iran." *Journal of the Royal Asiatic Society* (2021, first view): 1–22.

Gaffney, Patrick D. "The Changing Voices of Islam: The Emergence of Professional Preachers in Contemporary Egypt." *Muslim World* 81, no. 1 (1991): 27–47.

———. *The Prophet's Pulpit: Islamic Preaching in Contemporary Egypt*. Berkeley, CA: University of California Press, 1994.

Gauvain, Richard. *Salafi Ritual Purity: In the Presence of God*. London: Routledge, 2013.

———. "Egyptian Sufism Under the Hammer: A Preliminary Investigation into the Anti-Sufi Polemics of ʿAbd al-Rahman al-Wakil. 1913–1970." In *Sufis and Salafis in the Contemporary Age*, edited by Lloyd Ridgeon, 33–57. London: Bloomsbury Academic, 2015.

Geertz, Clifford. *The Interpretation of Cultures: Selected Essays by Clifford Geertz*. New York: Basic Books, 1973.

Gelvin, James. *Divided Loyalties Nationalism and Mass Politics in Syria at the Close of Empire*. Berkeley: University of California Press, 1993.

Gershoni, Israel, and James P. Jankowski. *Redefining the Egyptian Nation, 1930–1945*. Cambridge, UK: Cambridge University Press, 1995.

Gesink, Indira Falk. *Islamic Reform and Conservatism: Al-Azhar and the Evolution of Modern Sunni Islam*. London: I. B. Tauris, 2009.

Goldziher, Ignac. *Muhammedanische Studien*. N.P.: Halle A. S., Max Niemeyer, 1889.

Golinkin, David. "Ha-im Mutar Le-Hitpalel Yakhef?," *Schechter Institute of Jewish Studies*, 16 August 2020, accessed 4 May 2021. https://schechter.ac.il/article/praying-barefoot/?fbclid=IwAR14Fw-glg_j_7dsE2jvdQZkh_oaFPeo-rUNMhdV8_vKDXz_KKCOSZn2qsc.

Graham, William A. "Traditionalism in Islam: An Essay in Interpretation." *The Journal of Interdisciplinary History* 23, no. 3 (1993): 495–522.

Griffel, Frank. "What Do We Mean by 'Salafi'? Linking Muhammad 'Abduh with Egypt's Nur Party in Islam's Contemporary Intellectual History." *Die Welt des Islams* 55, no. 2. (2015): 186–220.

———. "Rejoinder: What is the Task of the Intellectual (Contemporary) Historian?—A Response to Henri Lauzière's "Reply." *Die Welt des Islams* 56, no. 2 (2016): 249–55.

El-Guindi, Fadwa."Veiling Infitah with a Muslim Ethic." *Social Problems* 28, no. 4 (1981): 465–85.

Hadith Dhikrayat maʿa Khalid ʿAbd Al-Qadir ʿAwda, al-Juzʾa al-Awwal. Perf. Khalid ʿAbd al-Qadir ʿAwda. Ikhwantube, 2010.

Hakami, Hafiz b. Ahmad b. ʿAli. *Maʿarij al-Qubul bi-Sharh Sullam al-Wusul ila ʿAlam al-Usul fi al-Tawhid*, edited by ʿUmar b. Mahmud Abu ʿUmar. Dammam, Saudi Arabia: Dar Ibn al-Qayyim, 1415/1995.

al-Halabi, ʿAli. *Hukm al-Din fi al-Lihya wa'l-Tadkhin*. Amman, Jordan: al-Maktaba al-Islamiyya, 1984.

Halevi, Leor. *Modern Things on Trial: Islam's Global and Material Reformation in the Age of Rida, 1865–1935*. New York: Columbia University Press, 2019.

Halkin, A. S. "The Hashawiyya." *Journal of the American Oriental Society* 54 (1934): 1–28.

Hamdeh, Emad. "Qur'an and Sunna or the *Madhhabs*?: A Salafi Polemic Against Islamic Legal Tradition." *Islamic Law and Society* 24, no. 3 (2017): 211–53.

———. *Salafism and Traditionalism: Scholarly Authority in Modern Islam*. Cambridge, UK: Cambridge University Press, 2020.

al-Hanafi, Abu al-Hasan al-Maʿruf bi-l-Sindi. *Sunan Ibn Maja bi-Sharh al-Sindi wa Misbah al-Zujaja fi Zawaʾid Ibn Maja*. Beirut: Dar al-Maʿrifa, 1996.

al-Harani, Ahmad b. Taymiyya. *ʿAqidat Ahl a-Sunna wa'l-Firaq al-Najiyya*, edited by ʿAbd al-Razzaq al-ʿAfifi. Cairo: Matbaʿat Ansar al-Sunna al-Muhammadiyya, 1358/~1939–40.

Hasan, Salah al-Din. *al-Salafiyyun fi Misr*. Giza, Egypt: Awraq li-l-Nashr wa'l-Tawziʿ, 2013.

al-Haskafi, Muhammad b. ʿAli b. Muhammad b. Ahmad b. ʿAbd al-Rahman al-Hanafi. *Al-Durr al-Mukhtar: Sharh Tanwir al-Absar wa Jamiʿ al-Bahhar*, edited by ʿAbd al-Munʿim Khalil Ibrahim. Beirut: Dar al-Kutub al-ʿIlmiyya, 2002.

Hatina, Meir. *ʿUlamaʾ, Politics, and the Public Sphere: An Egyptian Perspective*. Salt Lake City: University of Utah Press, 2010.

Haykel, Bernard. *Revival and Reform in Islam: The Legacy of Muhammad al-Shawkānī*. Cambridge, UK: Cambridge University Press, 2003.

———. "On the Nature of Salafi Thought and Action." In *Global Salafism: Islam's New Religious Movement*, edited by Roel Meijer, 33–57. New York: Columbia University Press, 2009.

Hegghammer, Thomas. *The Caravan: Abdallah Azzam and the Rise of Global Jihad*. Cambridge, UK: Cambridge University Press, 2020).

———, and Stéphane Lacroix. "Rejectionist Islamism in Saudi Arabia: The Story of Juhayman al-ʿUtaybi Revisited." *International Journal of Middle East Studies* 39 (2007): 103–22.

Hilmi, Mustafa. *Qawaʾid al-Manhaj al-Salafi fi al-Fikr al-Islami*. Beirut: Dar al-Kutub al-ʿIlmiyya, 2005.

Hirschkind, Charles. *The Ethical Soundscape: Cassette Sermons and Islamic Counterpublics*. New York: Columbia University Press, 2006.

Hourani, Albert. *Arabic Thought in the Liberal Age: 1798–1939*. Cambridge, UK: Cambridge University Press, 1983.

Hunter, F. Robert. *Egypt Under the Khedives, 1805–1879: From Household Government to Modern Bureaucracy*. Cairo: American University in Cairo Press, 1984.

Ibn ʿAbd al-Birr, al-Hafiz. *al-Tamhid lima fi al-Muwatta min al-Maʿani waʾl-Asanid*, edited by Muhammad al-Taʾib al-Saʿidi. N.P.: N.P., 1971.

Ibn ʿAbidin, Muhammad b. ʿUmar. *Radd al-Muhtar ʿala al-Durr al-Mukhtar li-Khatimat al-Muhaqqiqin Muhammad Amin al-Shahir bi-Ibn ʿAbidin*, edited by ʿAdil Ahmad ʿAbd al-Mawjud and ʿAli Muhammad Muʿawwad. Riyadh: Dar ʿAlam al-Kutub, 2003.

Ibn al-ʿArabi, Abu Bakr. *Aridat al-Ahwadhi bi-Sharh Sahih al-Tirmidhi*. Beirut: Dar al-Kutub al-ʿIlmiyya, 2011.

Ibn Abd al-Latif, Abu-l-Mundhir ʿAbd al-Haqq. *Tanbihat Hamma ʿala Malabis al-Muslimin al-Yawm wa maʿahu Fatawa fi al-Isbal li-l-Shaykh ʿAbd al-ʿAziz b. Bāz waʾl-Shaykh Ibn ʿUthaymin wa Adab al-Libas li-baʿd Talaba al-ʿIlm*. Cairo: Maktabat al-Tawʿiyya al-Islamiyya, c. 1988.

———. *al-Lihya: ʿAda am ʿIbada?* Cairo: Maktabat al-Balad al-Amin, 2011.

Ibn ʿAsakir. *Tabyin Kidhb al-Muftari fi-ma Nusiba ila al-Imam Abi al-Hasan al-Ashʿari*, edited by Muhammad Zahid al-Kawthari. Cairo: al-Maktaba al-Azhariyya li-l-Turath, 2010.

Ibn Baz, ʿAbd al-ʿAziz. *al-Tabarruj wa Khatar Musharakat al-Marʾa li-l-Rajul fi Maydan ʿAmalih*. Cairo: Maktabat al-Salam, 1980.

———. *al-Tabarruj wa Khataruh*. Riyadh: Dar ʿAlam al-Kutub, 1992.

———. *Majmuʿat Fatawa wa Maqalat Mutanawiʿ*, edited by Muhammad b. Saʿd al-Shuwayʿir. Riyadh: Dar al-Qasim li-l-Nashr, 1420/~2000~.

———. *Fatawa Nur ʿala al-Darb li-Samahat al-Imam ʿAbd al-ʿAziz b. ʿAbd Allah b. Baz*, edited by Abd Allah b. Muhammad al-Tayyar and Muhammad b. Musa b. ʿAbd Allah Al Musa. Riyadh: Dar al-Watan li-l-Nashr, N.D.

Ibn Hanbal, Ahmad. *al-Fath al-Rabbani li-Tartib Musnad al-Imam Ahmad b. Hanbal al-Shaybani wa maʿahu Kitab Bulugh al-Amani min Asrar al-Fath al-Rabbani*, edited by Ahmad ʿAbd al-Rahman al-Banna. Cairo: Dar Ihyaʾ al-Turath al-ʿArabi, 1976.

———. *Musnan al-Imam Ahmad*, edited by Hamza Ahmad al-Zayn. Cairo: Dar al-Hadith, 1416/1995.

Ibn Ibrahim, Muhammad. *Fatawa wa Rasaʾil Samahat al-Shaykh Muhammad b. Ibrahim*, edited by Muhammad b. ʿAbd al-Rahman b. Qasim. Mecca, Saudi Arabia: Matbaʿat al-Hukuma, 1399.

Ibn Maja, Abu ʿAbd Allah Muhammad b. Yazid. *Sunan al-Hafiz Abi ʿAbd Allah Muhammad Ibn Yazid al-Qazwini Ibn Maja 207–275 H*, edited by Muhammad Fuʾad ʿAbd al-Baqi. Cairo: Dar Ihyaʾ al-Kutub al-ʿArabiyya, 1952–3.

Ibn al-Jawzi, Abu al-Faraj ʿAbd al-Rahman b. ʿAli. *Kashf al-Mushkil min Hadith al-Sahihayn*. Riyadh: Dar al-Watan li-l-Nashr, 1997.

Ibn Taymiyya. *Iqtidaʾ al-Sirat al-Mustaqim: Mukhalafat Ashab al-Jahim*, edited by Muhammad Hamid al Fiqi. Cairo: Matbaʿat al-Sunna al-Muhammadiyya, Dhu al-Qaʿda 1369 H/~August 1950.

Ibn Taymiyya, Taqi al-Din Ahmad. *Majmuʿa Fatawa Shaykh al-Islam Ibn Taymiyya*, edited by ʿAmir al-Jazzar and Anwar al-Baz. Mansura, Egypt: Dar al-Wafaʾ li-l-Tibaʿa waʾl-Nashr waʾl-Tawziʿ, 1997.

Ibrahim, Saad Eddin. *Egypt, Islam and Democracy: Twelve Critical Essays.* Cairo: American University of Cairo Press, 1996.

Ikram, Khaled. *Egypt: Economic Management in a Period of Transition: The Report of a Mission Sent to the Arab Republic of Egypt by the World Bank.* London: John Hopkins Press, 1980.

Inge, Anabel. *The Making of a Salafi Muslim Woman.* Oxford: Oxford University Press, 2016.

Ingram, Brannon. *Revival From Below: The Deoband Movement and Global Islam.* Berkeley, CA: University of California Press, 2018.

Ismail, Raihan. *Rethinking Salafism: The Transnational Networks of Salafi 'Ulama in Egypt, Kuwait, and Saudi Arabia.* Oxford: Oxford University Press, 2021.

Issawi, Charles. *The Fertile Crescent, 1800–1914: A Documentary Economic History.* New York: Oxford University Press, 1988.

Ivanyi, Katharina Anna. *Virtue, Piety and the Law: A Study of Birgivī Meḥmed Efendī's al-Ṭarīqa al-muḥammadiyya.* Leiden: Brill, 2020.

Inside Mecca. New York: National Geographic, 2006.

'Illayash, Muhammad b. Ahmad b. Muhammad. *Minah al-Jalil Sharh 'ala Mukhtasar al-'Allama al-Khalil,* ed. 'Abd al-Jalil 'Abd al-Salam. Beirut: Dar al-Kutub al-'Ilmiyya, 2003.

Jacob, Wilson Chacko. *Working Out Egypt: Effendi Masculinity and Subject Formation in Colonial Modernity, 1870–1940.* Durham, NC: Duke University Press, 2011.

Jakes, Aaron. *Egypt's Occupation: Colonial Economism and the Crises of Capitalism.* Stanford, CA: Stanford University Press, 2020.

Jankowski, James P. "The Egyptian Blue Shirts and the Egyptian Wafd." *Middle Eastern Studies* 6, no. 1 (1970): 77–95.

———. *Egypt's Young Rebels: "Young Egypt" 1933–1952.* Stanford, CA: Hoover Institution Press, 1975.

al-Jazari, 'Ali 'Izz al-Din b. al-Athir. *al-Nihaya fi Gharib al-Hadith wa 'l-Athar,* edited by Mahmud Muhammad al-Tanahi. N.P: al-Maktaba al-Islamiyya, 1383/1963.

al-Jawziyya, Ibn Qayyim. *Tuhfat al-Mawdud bi-Ahkam al-Mawlud,* edited by 'Uthman b. Jum'a Dumayriyya. Jedda, Saudi Arabia: Dar 'Alam al-Fawa'id, 1431/2011.

al-Jawziyya, Muhammad b. Abi Bakr b. Qayyim. *Ighathat al-Lahfan fi Masayid al-Shaytan,* edited by Muhammad 'Aziz Shams and Muhammad b. Sa'id Itim. Mecca, Saudi Arabia: Dar 'Alam al-Fawa'id li-l-Nashr wa'l-Tawzi', 2010.

———. *al-Tibb al-Nabawi,* edited by 'Abd al-Ghani 'Abd al-Khaliq, 'Adil Zuhri and Mahmud Faraj al-'Uqda. Beirut: Dar al-Fikr, N.D.

al-Jaziri, 'Abd al-Rahman. *al-Fiqh 'ala al-Madhahib al-Arba'a.* Beirut: Dar al-Fikr, 2019.

Jones, Linda G. "'He Cried and Made Others Cry': Crying as a Sign of Pietistic Authenticity or Deception in Islamic Preaching." In *Crying in the Middle Ages,* edited by Elina Gertsman, 103–35. London: Routledge, 2012.

Jouili, Jeanette S. *Pious Practice and Secular Constraints.* Stanford, CA: Stanford University Press, 2015.

Kalmbach, Hilary. *Islamic Knowledge and the Making of Modern Egypt*. Cambridge, UK: Cambridge University Press, 2020.

Kamali, Mohammad Hashim. *Principles of Islamic Jurisprudence*. Cambridge, UK: The Islamic Texts Society, 2011.

al-Kandhalawi, Muhammad Zakariya. *Wujub I'fa' al-Lihya*, edited by 'Abd al-'Aziz b. Baz. Mecca: Maktabat al-Ma'arif, 1981.

Kane, Ousman. *Muslim Modernity in Postcolonial Nigeria: A Study of the Society for the Removal and Reinstatement of Tradition*. Leiden: Brill, 2003.

Katz, Marion H. *Women in the Mosque: A History of Legal Thought and Social Practice*. New York: Columbia University Press, 2014.

———. "'Azīma and rukhṣa." In *Encyclopedia of Islam*, edited by Kate Fleet, et al. Accessed 23 July 2018, http://dx.doi.org/10.1163/1573-3912_ei3_SIM_0261.

al-Kawthari, Muhammad Zahid b. Hasan. *Raf' al-Ishtibah 'an Mas'alatay Kashf al-Ru'us wa Lubs al-Ni'al fi al-Salat*. Cairo: al-Sayyid 'Izzat al-'Attar al-Husayni, 1947.

Kepel, Gilles. *Muslim Extremism in Egypt: The Prophet and Pharaoh*. Translated by Jon Rothschild. London: al-Saqi Books, 1985.

Kerr, Malcolm. *Islamic Reform: The Political and Legal Theories of Muhammad 'Abduh and Rashīd Riḍā*. Berkeley: University of California Press, 1966.

al-Khamis, Muhammad b. 'Abd al-Rahman. *al-Jami' fi Alfaz al-Kufr*. Kuwait: Dar Ilaf al-Dawliyya li-l-Nashr wa'l-Tawzi', 1999.

Khan, Ahmad. "Islamic Tradition in an Age of Printing: Editing, Printing and Publishing the Classical Heritage." In *Reclaiming the Islamic Tradition: Modern Interpretations of the Classical Heritage*, edited by Elisabeth Kendall and Ahmad Khan, 52–99. Edinburgh, UK: Edinburgh University Press, 2016.

Khan, Arsalan. "Pious Sociality: The Ethics of Hierarchy in the Tablighi Jamaat in Pakistan." *Social Analysis: The International Journal of Anthropology* 60, no. 4 (2016): 96–113.

Khoja-Moojli, Shenila. *Sovereign Attachments: Masculinity, Muslimness, and Affective Politics in Pakistan*. Berkeley: University of California Press, 2021.

Khuri-Makdisi, Ilham. "Fin de siècle Egypt: a Nexus for Mediterranean and Global Radical Networks." In *Global Islam in the Age of Steam and Print, 1850–1930*, ed. James Gelvin and Nile Green, 78–100. Berkeley: University of California Press, 2013.

Kister, M.J. "'Do Not Assimilate Yourselves . . .': *Lā Tashabbahū*." *Jerusalem Studies in Arabic and Islam* 12 (1989): 321–71.

Krämer, Gudrun. *Hasan al-Banna*. Oxford: Oneworld, 2010.

Lacroix, Stéphane. *Awakening Islam: The Politics of Religious Dissent in Contemporary Saudi Arabia*. Translated by George Holoch. Cambridge, MA: Harvard University Press, 2011.

Lacroix, Stéphane, and Thomas Hegghammer. *The Meccan Rebellion: The Story of Juhayman al-'Utaybi Revisited*. Bristol, UK: Amal Press, 2011.

Lauzière, Henri. "The Construction of Salafiyya: Reconsidering Salafism from the Perspective of Conceptual History." *International Journal of Middle East Studies* 42, no. 3 (2010): 369–89.

———. *The Making of Salafism: Islamic Reform in the Twentieth Century*. New York: Columbia University Press, 2016.

———. "Rejoinder: What We Mean Versus What They Meant by "Salafi": A Reply to Frank Griffel." *Die Welt des Islams* 56, no 1 (2016): 89–96.

Lav, Daniel. *Radical Islam and the Revival of Medieval Theology*. Cambridge, UK: Cambridge University Press, 2012.

——— "Radical Muslim Theonomy: A Study in the Evolution of Salafi Thought." Ph.D. diss, Hebrew University of Jerusalem, 2016.

Salafi Political Theology. Cambridge, UK: Cambridge University Press, forthcoming.

Le Renard, Amelie. *A Society of Young Women*. Stanford, CA: Stanford University Press, 2014.

Lebkicher, Roy. *Aramco Handbook*. N.P: ARAMCO, 1960.

Lia, Brynjar. *The Society of the Muslim Brothers in Egypt: The Rise of an Islamic Mass Movement, 1928–1942*. Ithaca, NY: Ithaca Press, 1999.

Levy-Rubin, Milka. *Non-Muslims in the Early Islamic Empire: From Surrender to Co-Existence*. Cambridge, UK: Cambridge University Press, 2011.

Lockman, Zachary. "Exploring the Field: Lost Voices and Emerging Practices in Egypt, 1882–1914." In *Histories of the Modern Middle East*, edited by Israel Gershoni, Y. Hakan Erdem, and Ursula Wokock, 137–54. London: Lynne Rienner Publishers, 2002.

Macleod, Arlene. *Accommodating Protest: Working Women, the New Veiling, and Change in Cairo*. New York: Columbia University Press, 1991.

Mahmood, Saba. *The Politics of Piety: The Islamic Revival and the Feminist Subject*. Princeton, NJ: Princeton University Press, 2005.

———. "Rehearsed Spontaneity and the Conventionality of Ritual: Disciplines of Salat." *American Ethnologist* 28, no. 4 (2001): 827–53.

Martin, Kevin W. *Syria's Democratic Years: Citizens, Experts, and Media in the 1950s*. Bloomington: Indiana University Press, 2015.

Mattelart, Armand. *The Invention of Communication*. Translated by Susan Emanuel. Minneapolis: University of Minnesota Press, 1996.

Maqalat Kibar al-ʿUlamaʾ fi al-Suhuf al-Saʿudiyya, edited by Ahmad b. ʻAbd al-ʻAziz Jamaz and ʻAbd al-ʻAziz b. Salih Tawil. Riyadh: Dar Atlas li-l-Nashr waʾl-Tawziʿ, 2010/1431.

al-Maqdisi, Ibn Qudama. *al-Mughni*, edited by ʿAbd Allah b. ʿAbd al-Muhsin al-Turki and ʿAbd al-Fattah Hulw. Riyadh: Dar ʿAlam al-Kutub, 1997.

al-Maqdisi, Muhammad b. Muflih b. Shams al-Din. *Kitab al-Furuʿ*, edited by ʿAbd Allah b. al-Muhsin al-Turki. Beirut: Muʾasasat al-Risala, 2003.

———. *al-Adab al-Sharʿiyya*, edited by Shuʿayb Arnaʾut and ʿUmar Qiyyam. Beirut: Dar al-Risala al-ʿAlamiyya, 2014.

McLarney, Ellen. "Freedom, Justice, and the Power of *Adab*." *International Journal of Middle East Studies* 48 (2016): 25–46.

———. *Soft Force: Women in Egypt's Islamic Awakening*. Princeton, NJ: Princeton University Press, 2015.

Melchert, Christopher. "Whether to Keep Women Out of the Mosque: A Survey of Medieval Islamic Law." In *Authority, Privacy and Public Order in Islam: Proceedings of the 22nd Congress of L'Union Européenne des Arabisants et Islamisants*, 59–70. Dudley, MA: Orientalia Lovaniensia Analecta, 2006.

Meijer, Roel. "Commanding Right and Forbidding Wrong as a Principle of Social Action: The Case of the Egyptian Jamaʿa Islamiyya." In *Global Salafism: Islam's New Religious Movement*, edited by Roel Meijer. New York: Columbia University Press, 2009, 189–220.

Messick, Brinkley. *The Calligraphic State: Textual Domination and History in a Muslim Society*. Berkeley: University of California Press, 1993.

——— *Shariʿa Scripts: A Historical Anthropology*. New York: Columbia University Press, 2018.

Messick, Brinkley, Muhammad Khalid Masud, and David Powers, eds. *Islamic Legal Interpretation: Muftis and Their Fatwas*. Cambridge, MA: Cambridge University Press, 1996.

Mestyan, Adam. *Arab Patriotism: The Ideology and Culture of Power in Late Ottoman Egypt*. Princeton, NJ: Princeton University Press, 2017.

Metcalf, Barbara. "Living Hadith in the Tablighi Jamaʿat." *The Journal of Asian Studies* 52, no. 3 (1993): 584–608.

al-Misnid, Muhammad b. ʿAbd al-ʿAziz. *Fatawa Islamiyya*. Riyadh: Dar al-Watan, 1414/1994.

Mitchell, Richard P. *The Society of the Muslim Brothers*. New York: Oxford University Press, 1993.

Mitchell, Timothy. *Colonising Egypt*. Berkeley: University of California Press, 1988.

Mobatagani, Mazin S. "Islamic Resurgence in the Hijaz Region (1975–1990)." *Journal of West Asian Studies* 23 (2009): 46–61.

Morton, Michael Quentin. *Buraimi: The Struggle for Power, Influence and Oil in Saudi Arabia*. London: I. B. Taurus, 2013.

Moll, Yasmin. "The Idea of Islamic Media: The Qur'an and the Decolonization of Mass Communication." *International Journal of Middle East Studies* 52 (2020): 623–42.

Mouline, Nabil. *The Clerics of Islam: Religious Authority and Political Power in Saudi Arabia*. Translated by Ethan S. Rundell. New Haven, CT: Yale University Press, 2014.

Muhammad, Saʿd Sadiq. *Siraʿ Bayna al-Haqq wa 'l-Batil*. Cairo: Matbaʿat al-Sunna al-Muhammadiyya, 1964.

AlMunajjed, Mona. *Women in Saudi Arabia Today*. London: Macmillan Press Ltd, 1997.

al-Muqaddam, Muhammad b. Ismaʿil. *Adillat Tahrim Halq al-Lihya*. Huli, Kuwait: Dar al-Arqam, 1405/1985.

al-Najdi, ʿAbd al-Rahman b. Muhammad b. Qasim al-ʿAsimi al-Qahtani. *Kitab al-Durar al-Saniyya fi al-Ajwiba al-Najdiyya*. Mecca, Saudi Arabia: Matbaʿat Umm al-Qurra, 1352/~1933.

Najmabadi, Afsaneh. *Women With Mustaches and Men Without Beards: Gender and Sexual Anxieties of Iranian Modernity.* Berkeley: University of California Press, 2005.

Nakissa, Aria. *The Anthropology of Islamic Law: Education, Ethics, and Legal Interpretation at Egypt's al-Azhar.* Oxford: Oxford University Press, 2019.

al-Nawawi, Abu Zakariyya Muhi al-Din Yahya b. Sharaf. *al-Minhaj bi-Sharh Sahih Muslim Ibn al-Hajjaj.* Cairo: al-Matba'a al-Misriyya bi-l-Azhar, 1930.

———. *Kitab al-Majmu' Sharh al-Muhadhdhab li-l-Shirazi*, edited by Muhammad Najib al-Muti'i. 23 vols. Jeddah, Saudi Arabia: Maktabat al-Irshad, 1980.

———. *Riyad al-Salihin min Kalam Sayyid al-Mursalin*, edited by Mahir Yasin Fahl. Beirut: Dar Ibn Kathir, 2007.

Nimr, 'Abd al-Mun'im. *al-Thaqafa al-Islamiyya Bayna al-Ghazw wa'l-Istighza'.* Cairo: Dar al-Ma'arif, 1987.

Olidort, Jacob. "In Defense of Tradition: Muḥammad Nāṣir al-Dīn al-Albānī and the Salafī Method." Ph.D. diss., Princeton University, 2016.

Pall, Zoltan. *Salafism in Lebanon: Local and Transnational Movements.* Cambridge, UK: Cambridge University Press, 2018.

Patel, Youshaa. "Muslim Distinction: Imitation and the Anxiety of Jewish, Christian and Other Influences." Ph.D. diss., Duke University, 2012.

———. "The Islamic Treatises against Imitation (Tašabbuh): A Bibliographical History." *Arabica* 65 (2018): 597–639.

———. "'Whoever Imitates a People Becomes One of Them': A Hadith and its Interpreter." *Islamic Law and Society* 25 (2018): 359–426.

Peter-Hartung, Jan. "Making Sense of 'Political Quietism': An Analytical Intervention." In *Political Quietism in Islam: Sunni and Shi'i Perspectives*, edited by Sarhan al-Saud, 15–32. London: I. B. Tauris, 2020.

al-Qaradawi, Yusuf. *al-Halal wa'l-Haram fi al-Islam.* Cairo: Maktabat Wahba, 2012.

———. *Dirasa fi Fiqh Maqasid al-Shari'a Bayna al-Maqasid al-Kulliya wa'l-Nusus al-Juz'iyya.* Cairo: Dar al-Shuruq, 2006.

Quadri, Junaid. *Transformations of Tradition: Islamic Law in Colonial Modernity.* Oxford: Oxford University Press, 2021.

al-Qushayri, Muslim b. al-Hajjaj. *Sahih Muslim ma'a Sharh Sahih Muslim al-Musamma Ikmal al-Mu'allim wa Ikmal Ikmal al-Mu'lim*, edited by Muhammad b. Yusuf Sanusi et al. Beirut: Dar al-Fikr al-'Ilmiyya, 1994.

———. *Sahih Muslim*, edited by Nazar b. Muhammad al-Faryabi Abu Qutayba. Riyadh: Dar Tayba, 2006.

Qutb, Sayyid. *Ma'alim fi al-Tariq.* Cairo: Dar al-Shuruq, 1979.

Reid, Megan. *Law and Piety in Medieval Islam.* Cambridge, UK: Cambridge University Press, 2013.

Rheins, Richard S. "Asu Seyag LaTorah: Make a Fence to Protect the Torah." In *Re-Examining Progressive Halakhah*, edited by W. Jacob and M. Zemer, 91–110. New York: Berghahn Books, 2002.

Riexinger, Martin. "Ibn Taymiyya's Worldview and the Challenge of Modernity: A Conflict Among the Ahl-i Ḥadīth in British India." In *Islamic Theology, Philosophy and Law: Debating Ibn Taymiyya and Ibn Qayyim al-Jawziyya*, edited by Birgit Krazietz and Georges Tamer, 493–517. Berlin: Walter de Gruter, 2013.

Rock-Singer, Aaron. *Practicing Islam in Egypt: Print Media and Islamic Revival*. Cambridge, UK: Cambridge University Press, 2019.

———. "Prayer and the Islamic Revival: A Timely Challenge." *International Journal of Middle East Studies* 47 (2016): 293–312.

Ryad, Umar. "A Printed Muslim 'Lighthouse' in Cairo al-Manār's Early Years: Religious Aspiration and Reception (1898–1903)." *Arabic* 56 (January 2009): 27–60.

Ryzova, Lucie. *The Age of the Efendiyya: Passages to Modernity in National-Colonial Egypt*. Oxford: Oxford University Press, 2014.

Rinaldo, Rachel. *Mobilizing Piety: Islam and Feminism in Indonesia*. New York: Oxford University Press, 2013.

Rizq, Jabir. *Madhabih al-Ikhwan fi Sujun Nasir: Asrar Rahiba Tudha ʿli-Awwal Marra*. Cairo: Dar al-Iʿtisam, 1978.

El-Rouayheb, Khaled. *Before Homosexuality in the Arab-Islamic World, 1500–1800*. Chicago: University of Chicago Press, 2005.

al-Sadhan, ʿAbd al-ʿAziz b. Muhammad b. ʿAbd Allah. *al-Imam al-Albani Rahimahu Allah: Durus wa Mawaqif wa ʿIbar*. Riyadh, KSA: Dar al-Tawhid li-l-Nashr, 1429/2008.

Sagiv, David. *Fundamentalism and the Intellectuals in Egypt, 1973–1993*. London: Frank Cass, 1995.

Saiman, Chaim. *Halakhah: The Rabbinic Idea of Law*. Princeton, NJ: Princeton University Press, 2018.

al-Sanʿani, Muhammad b. Ismaʿil. *Istifaʾ al-Aqwal fi Tahrim al-Isbal ʿala al-Rijal*, edited by ʿUqayl b. Muhammad Zayd al-Maqtari. Sanaa, Yemen, and Jerusalem: Maktabat Dar al-Quds, 1992.

Saqr, Shahata Muhammad ʿAli. *al-Ikhtilat Bayna al-Rijal waʾl-Nisaʾ: Ahkam wa Fatawa, Thimar Murra Qisas Mukhziyya, Kashf 136 Shubha li-Duʿat al-Ikhtilat*. Cairo: Dar al-Yusr, 2011.

al-Shatibi, Abu Ishaq. *al-Iʿtisam*, edited by Salim b. ʿAbd al-Hilali. Khobar, Saudi Arabia: Dar Ibn ʿAffan, 1992.

Shechter, Relli. "From effendi to infitahi? Consumerism and Its Malcontents in the Emergence of Egyptian Market Society." *British Journal of Middle Eastern Studies* 36, no. 1 (2009): 21–35.

al-Sibaʿi, Mustafa. *al-Marʾa Bayna al-Fiqh waʾl-Qanun*. Beirut: Dar al-Warraq, 1420/1999.

al-Silmi, ʿUbayd b. ʿAbd al-ʿAziz b. ʿUbayd. *al-Tabarruj waʾl-Ihtisab ʿAlayhi*. Medina, Saudi Arabia: N.P, 1987.

Simens, Daniel. *Stormtroopers: A New History of Hitler's Brownshirts*. New Haven, CT: Yale University Press, 2017.

Smith, Charles D. *Islam and the Search for Social Order in Modern Egypt*. Albany: State University of New York Press, 1983.

Soloveitchik, Haym. "Rupture and Reconstruction: The Transformation of Contemporary Orthodoxy." *Tradition* 28, no. 4 (1994): 64–130.

Starrett, Gregory. "The Hexis of Interpretation: Islam and the Body in the Egyptian Popular School." *American Ethnologist* 22. no. 4 (1995): 953–69.

———. *Putting Islam to Work: Education, Politics and Religious Transformation in Egypt.* Berkeley, CA: University of California Press, 1998.

Sabiq, al-Sayyid. *Fiqh al-Sunna.* Beirut: Dar al-Kutub al-ʿArabi, 1973.

al-Safi, ʿUthman b. ʿAbd al-Qadir. *Hukm al-Sharʿ fi al-Lihya waʾl-Azya waʾl-Taqalid waʾl-ʿAdat.* Beirut/Damascus: al-Maktab al-Islami, 1403/1983.

Scott, James C. *Seeing Like a State: How Certain Schemes To Improve the Human Condition Have Failed.* New Haven, CT: Yale University Press, 1998.

Shabana, Ayman. *Custom in Islamic Law and Legal Theory: The Development of the Concepts of ʿUrf and ʿĀdah in the Islamic Legal Tradition.* New York: Palgrave Macmillan, 2010.

Schayegh, Cyrus. *Who is Knowledgeable is Strong: Science, Class, and the Formation of Modern Iranian Society, 1900–1950.* Berkeley: University of California Press, 2009.

al-Shakry, Omnia. *The Great Social Laboratory: Subjects of Knowledge in Colonial and Postcolonial Egypt.* Stanford, CA: Stanford University Press, 2007.

El Shamsy, Ahmed. *The Canonization of Islamic Law: A Social and Intellectual History.* Cambridge, UK: Cambridge University Press, 2013.

———. *Rediscovering the Islamic Classics: How Editors and Print Culture Transformed an Intellectual Tradition.* Princeton, NJ: Princeton University Press, 2020.

Shahrokni, Nazanin. *Women in Place: The Politics of Gender Segregation in Iran.* Berkeley: University of California Press, 2020.

al-Shawkani, Muhammad. *Nayl al-Awtar min Ahadith Sayyid al-Akhyar Sharh Muntaqa al-Akhbar.* Beirut: Dar al-Kutub al-ʿIlmiyya, 2011.

al-Shinqiti, Muhammad b. Habib Allah b. ʿAbd Allah b. Ahmad al-Maliki. *Zad al-Muslim fi-ma Ittafaq ʿalayhi al-Bukhari wa Muslim.* 6 vols. Cairo: Dar Ihyaʾ al-Kutub al-ʿArabiyya, 1967.

Sidqi, Niʿmat. *al-Tabarruj.* Cairo: Dar al-Iʿtisam, 1975 [1951].

al-Sijistani, Abu Daʾud Suliman b. al-Ashʿath. *Sunan Abi Daʾud wa Maʿalim al-Sunan,* edited by ʿIzzat ʿUbayd al-Daʿas and ʿAdil al-Sayyid. Beirut: Dar Ibn Hazm, 1997.

Siyam, ʿImad. "al-Haraka al-Islamiyya waʾl-Jamʿiyyat al-Ahliyya fi Misr." In *al-Jamʿiyyat al-Ahliyya al-Islamiyya fi Misr,* edited by ʿAbd al-Ghafar Shukr, 73–150. Cairo: Dar al-Amin 2006.

Skovgaard-Petersen, Jakob. *Defining Islam for the Egyptian State: Muftis and Fatwas of the Dār Al-Iftā.* Leiden: Brill, 1997.

Spadola, Emilio. *The Calls of Islam: Sufis, Islamists, and Mass Mediation in Urban Morocco.* Bloomington: Indiana University Press, 2014.

———. "The Call of Communication: Mass Media and Reform in Interwar Morocco." zin *Middle Eastern and North African Societies in the Interwar Period,* edited by Kate Fleet and Ebru Boyar, 97–122. Leiden: Brill, 2018.

Stolz, Daniel A. *The Lighthouse and the Observatory: Islam, Science and Empire in Late Ottoman Egypt*. Cambridge, UK: Cambridge University Press, 2018.

al-Subki, Mahmud Muhammad Khattab. *al-Din al-Khalis aw Irshad al-Khalq ila Din al-Haqq*, edited by Amin Mahmud Khattab. Cairo: al-Maktaba al-Mahmudiyya al-Subkiyya, 1986.

Tarrow, Sidney. *Power in Movement: Social Movements and Contentious Politics*. New York: Cambridge University Press, 2011.

al-Tahir, Ahmad Muhammad. *Jama'at Ansar al-Sunna al-Muhammadiyya: Nash'atuha –Ahdafuha –Manhajuha –Juhuduha*. Cairo/Riyadh: Dar al-Hadi al-Nabawi li-l-Nashr wa'l-Tawzi'/Dar al-Fadila li-l-Nashr wa'l-Tawzi', 2004.

Thanvi, Ashraf 'Ali. *Imdad al-Fatawa*. Karachi, Pakistan: Maktabat Dar al-'Ulum, 2010.

Thurston, Alexander. *Salafism in Nigeria: Islam, Preaching and Politics*. Cambridge, UK: Cambridge University Press, 2016.

Tignor, Robert L. *State, Private Enterprise and Economic Change in Egypt, 1918–1952*. Princeton, NJ: Princeton University Press, 1984.

Tucker, Judith. *Women, Family and Gender in Islamic Law*. New York: Cambridge University Press, 2008.

al-Turayqi, 'Abd Allah b. Muhammad b. Ahmad. *Mu'jam Musannafat al-Hanabila*. Riyadh: Maktabat al-Malik Fahd al-Wataniyya, 2001.

al-Tuwayjiri, Hammud. *al-Radd 'ala Man Ajaza Tahdhib al-Lihya*. Riyadh: Maktabat al-Ma'arif.

al-'Uthaymin, Muhammad b. Salih. *al-Risala fi Sifat Salat al-Nabi Sala Allah 'Alayhi wa Salam*. N.P: N.P, 1987.

———. *Majmu' Fatawa wa Rasa'il Fadilat al-Shaykh Muhammad b. Salih al-'Uthaymin*, edited by Fahd b. Nasir al-Suliman. Riyadh: Dar al-Thurya li-l-Nashr wa'l-Tawzi', 1419/1998.

———. *Tawjihat li-l-Mu'minat Hawl al-Tabarruj wa'l-Sufur*. Riyadh: Dar Ibn Huzayma, 1998.

———. *al-Sharh al-Mumti' 'ala Zad al-Mustaqni'*. Dammam, Saudi Arabia: Dar Ibn Jawzi, 1425.

'Uqayl, 'Abd Allah. *Min A'lam al-Da'wa wa'l-Haraka al-Islamiyya al-Mu'asira*. Amman, Jordan: Dar al-Bashir, 2008.

Vandermeulen, Ian. "Electrosonic Statecraft: Technology, authority, and latency on Moroccan Qur'ānic radio." *American Ethnologist* 48, no. 1 (2021): 80–92.

Varisco, Daniel Martin. *Islam Obscured: The Rhetoric of Anthropological Representation*. New York: Palgrave Macmillan, 2005.

Vidas, Mouli. *Tradition and the Formation of the Talmud*. Princeton, NJ: Princeton University Press, 2014.

Vishanoff, David R. *Islamic Hermeneutics: How Sunni Legal Theories Imagined a Revealed Law*. New Haven, CT: American Oriental Society, 2011.

al-Wad,i'i Muqbil b. Hadi. *Majmu'at Rasa'il 'Ilmiyya*, edited by Sa'id b. 'Umar. Sana', Yemen: Dar al-Athar, 1420/1990.

Wagemakers, Joas. *A Quietist Jihadi: The Ideology and Influence of Abu Muhammad al-Maqdisi*. Cambridge, UK: Cambridge University Press, 2012.

———. *Salafism in Jordan: Political Islam in a Quietist Community*. Cambridge, UK: Cambridge University Press, 2016.

Ware, Rudolph T. *The Walking Qur'an: Islamic Education, Embodied Knowledge and History in West Africa*. Chapel Hill: University of North Carolina Press, 2014.

Wegenstein, Bernadette. "Body." In *Critical Terms for Media Studies*, edited by W. J. T. Mitchell and M. Hansen, 19–34. Chicago: University of Chicago Press, 2010.

Weismann, Itzchak. *Taste of Modernity: Sufism, Salafiyya, and Arabism in Late Ottoman Damascus*. Leiden: Brill, 2001.

———. "New and Old Perspectives in the Study of Salafism." *Bustan* 8, no. 1 (2017): 22–37.

Weiss, Max. *In the Shadow of Sectarianism: Law, Shi'ism, and the Making of Modern Lebanon*. Stanford, CA: Stanford University Press, 2010.

White, Jenny. *Muslim Nationalism and the New Turks*. Princeton, NJ: Princeton University Press, 2013.

Wickham, Carrie Rosefsky. *Mobilizing Islam: Religion, Activism, and Political Change in Egypt*. New York: Columbia University Press, 2002.

Willi, Victor. *The Fourth Ideal: A History of the Muslim Brotherhood in Egypt, 1968–2018*. Cambridge, UK: Cambridge University Press, 2021.

Wishnitzer, Avner. *Reading Clocks, Alla Turca*. Chicago: University of Chicago Press, 2015.

Yunus, Khalid Muhammad. "al-Qarn al-'Ishrin wa Juhud al-Harakat al-Da'wiyya fi Misr." Ph.D. diss., Karachi University, 2006.

Yusuf, Muhammad Khayr Ramadan, and Khayr al-Din Zirkili. *Tatimmat al-A'lam li-l-Zirkili*. Beirut: Dar Ibn Hazm, 1998.

Zaman, Muhammad Qasim. *The Ulama in Contemporary Islam*. Princeton, NJ: Princeton University Press, 2002.

———. *Modern Islamic Thought in a Radical Age: Religious Authority and Internal Criticism*. Cambridge, UK: Cambridge University Press, 2012.

———. "The Sovereignty of God in Modern Islamic Thought." *Journal of the Royal Asiatic Society* 25, no. 3 (July 2015): 389–418.

Zaydan, 'Abd al-Karim. *Mufassal fi Ahkam al-Mar'a wa'l-Bayt al-Muslim*. Beirut: Mu'asassat al-Risala, 1994.

Zemmin, Florian. *Modernity in Islamic Tradition: The Concept of 'Society' in the Journal al-Manar (Cairo, 1898–1940)*. Berlin: De Gruyter, 2018.

Zerubavel, Eviatar. *Hidden Rhythms: Schedules and Calendars in Social Life*. Berkeley: University of California Press, 1985.

INDEX

Abu-l-A'la al-Mawdudi, 87, 149
Abu Hamid al-Ghazali, 84, 113n49
Abu Hanifa, 112
Abu-l-Mundhir 'Abd al-Haqq b. 'Abd al-Latif, 219–20, 222
Abu-l-Wafa' Muhammad Darwish, 55; facial hair, 177; human representation, 61–62; lectures, 50; political participation, 63; prayer, 57, 102, 115–16; publications, 49
Ahl al-Hadith (Pre-Modern), 13
Ahl al-Hadith (Saudi Arabian), 119–20, 150
Ahmad 'Ali Taha al-Rayyan, 183–84
Ahmad b. Hanbal. *See* Ibn Hanbal
Ahmad b. Taymiyya al-Harrani. *See* Ibn Taymiyya
Ahmad Fahmi Ahmad, 186, 196, 215–16, 221–22
Ahmad Muhammad al-Tahir, 66–67
Ahmad Taha Nasr, 165, 186, 195
Amin Muhammad Khattab, 59, 178, 207
Amin Muhammad Rida, 116–17, 128, 133, 141
al-amr bi-l-ma'ruf wa'l-nahi 'an al-munkar, 59, 82n60, 145, 166, 199, 214–15, 224–25
Anwar al-Sadat, 64; assassination, 215; gender segregation, 162n117; Islamic activism, 150, 153; Islamic Revival, 179; Jihadism, 99; science and faith, 211
Association for the Revival of the Islamic Heritage, 89
Association of Social Reform, 155
al-Azhar University, 25, 39, 40, 52, 104, 119; al-Azhar Scholars' Front, 53; educational institutions, 39, 51, 56, 109; facial hair, 170n4, 175, 178, 191; Islamic Research Academy, 99, 179; pants, 210–11; publications, 54n125, 81, 149, 158; public outreach, 181–82; Salafi scholars, 4, 59, 74, 87, 94n117, 105, 183, 227; student protests, 38
'Abd al-'Aziz b. Al al-Shaykh, 131
'Abd al-'Aziz b. Baz, 1, 2; *'awra*, 152; double *adhan*, 99; facial hair, 97, 170, 182–83, 185, 187, 189, 191–94; gender segregation, 1,2, 153, 156–59, 161–66; *isbal*, 216–18, 222n99; Islamic University of Medina, 154–55; al-Jama'a al-Salafiyya al-Muhtasiba, 180; Neo-Hanbali theology, 191–92; Permanent Committee on Religious Scholarship and Fatwas, 126; praying in shoes, 127–32; *Sahwa*, 150, 153; Wahhabi-Hanbalism, 16, 120, 194
'Abd al-'Aziz b. Rashid, 49, 105–6, 205–6
'Abd Allah 'Azzam, 86–88
'Abd Allah b. 'Abd al-Rahman b. Ghaydyan, 126–28, 216
'Abd Allah b. Qa'ud, 127–28, 216
'Abd Allah b. 'Umar, 173n8, 175–76, 183, 190–93, 229
'Abd al-Halim Qatit, 78–82, 206
'Abd al-Latif al-Mushtahiri, 80, 84n72, 153n79, 181
'Abd al-Majid Salim, 104, 105, 106, 107, 108, 112n41, 116. *See also* State Mufti
'Abd al-Mun'im Abu-l-Futuh, 149
'Abd al-Mun'im Nimr, 99–100, 119
'Abd al-Qadir 'Awda, 150

ʿAbd al-Rahman al-Wakil, 59, 134
ʿAbd al-Razzaq al-ʿAfifi, 16n46, 105n10; fatwas, 127, 128, 216; lectures, 63; political participation, 59; publications, 48n91; Saudi Arabia, 106, 126; upbringing, 39, 40
ʿAbd al-Razzaq al-Baytar, 47n82
ʿAbd al-Razzaq Hamza, 154
ʿAbd al-Zahir Abu-l-Samh, 55, 74–75, 178
ʿAli Hasan Hulwa: facial hair, 177; gender segregation, 144–45; *isbal*, 206–7; praying in shoes, 114–15; turbans, 58
ʿAtiyya Salim, 154, 222n99

Baʿth party, 3, 76
Bakr Abu Zayd, 131
bidʿa, 32, 46, 54n125, 68, 69, 82, 121, 232; *bidʿa haqiqiyya*, 193n99; *bidʿa idafiyya*, 170, 193
Blue Shirts, 44. *See also* Wafd Party
boy scouts, 43
burnita, 76, 201n15, 210

Classical Islamic ethics, 18, 34
colonialism: fashion, 178, 219–20; gender and sexuality, 70, 140, 146; hygiene, 103n4; Islamic law, 140n11; Ismaʿiliyya square, 51; order, 33; professionalization, 203; protests, 38; religious education, 41; rural governance, 37; subjectivity, 20–21, 32, 41–43; textual authority, 34–36
Committee of Grand ʿUlamaʾ, 120, 126, 130, 229
communication, 31; imitation, 22–23; modern states, 6; social performance, 11, 13, 171, 195; uniforms, 35; visibility and ethics, 3, 9, 24–25, 65, 98, 101, 231; worship, 68, 83

Dar al-Daʿwa waʾ-l-Irshad, 51
Dar al-ʿUlum, 42
Day of Annunciation, 71, 173
Discursive tradition, 10, 16–21, 24–25, 232. *See also* Talal Asad

efendiyya/efendi: clothing, 40–43, 201; facial hair, 175; performance, 14, 74; self-regulation, 41; shirts movement, 44. *See also* Mustafa Kamil

Fakhr al-Din al-Razi, 84
Fatima ʿAbd al-Hadi, 152, 176
fiqh (See *Usul al-Fiqh*)
fitna, 2; facial hair, 188; gender mixing, 156; praying in shoes, 111, 116, 126, 129
Free Officers, 59; religious legitimacy, 63, 84; repression, 117

Geertz, Clifford, 19n61, 21
General Presidency for the Management of Religious Scholarship, Preaching, and Guidance, 120, 132
Great Mosque of Mecca, 45, 55, 105n10, 129, 226
Green Shirts, 44. *See also* Young Egypt Party

Hanbalism: facial hair, 175n18, 194; leading scholars, 39, 83n66, 93n109, 140; legal approach, 15; *najasa*, 103; neo-Traditionalism, 13; opponents, 113, 152n75; praying in shoes, 28, 108, 119, 130; public sin, 34; *shirk*, 49; theology, 3, 12, 16, 46n76, 48, 54n125, 90, 230. *See also* Wahhabi-Hanbalism
hhiyar code, 22, 70n10

ʿIsa ʿAbduh, 159–60
ʿIssam al-ʿAryan, 212
Ibn ʿAbd al-Wahhab: *madhhab*, 15; Salafism, 13, 47; *tawhid*, 73, 75
Ibn Hanbal, 113n49; facial hair, 205n29; *Musnad*, 49, 76; Salafism, 47, 189
Ibn Kathir, 90
Ibn Qayyim al-Jawziyya, 31, 50, 90, 93n109, 108n20
Ibn Taymiyya, 31, 39; *al-amr bi-l-maʿruf waʾl-nahi ʿan al-munkar*, 224–25; *manhaj*, 88n87; publications, 48, 50, 204n25, 218n83; Salafism, 47, 189
al-Islah (journal), 45–46
Islamic Association, 53–55
Islamic Civilization Association, 86
Islamic Education Association, 53
Islamic Jurisprudence (See *Usul al-Fiqh*)
Islamic Modernism, 16, 77
Islamic Morals Association, 53
Islamic Revival (Egyptian), 149, 179, 221
Islamic University of Medina: facial hair, 183, 187, 217; faculty, 222n99; gender segregation, 152–56, 159, 166; *isbal*, 217; politics, 120; praying in shoes, 129; worship, 95

Jadd al-Haqq ʿAli Jadd al-Haqq, 186–87, 213. *See also* State Mufti
jahiliyya, 56, 90, 117, 157. See also *takfir*
al-Jamaʿa al-Diniyya, 149

al-Jama'a al-Islamiyya, 149–50, 162, 165, 172, 179–80, 212–13, 220; political violence, 197, 214, 215, 221–22, 224–25
Jama'at al-Muslimin, 99, 149, 180n40
al-Jama'a al-Salafiyya al-Muhtasiba, 120, 129, 180–81
Jama'at Shabab al-Islam, 149
Jamal 'Abd al-Nasir, 28; attempted assassination, 60, 178; dress, 198, 208–9; education, 85, 208; Free Officers' revolution, 59; gender, 146, 178; ideological vision, 64, 74; Islamic activism, 84–86, 117, 144n30, 150n64. *See also* Free Officers
Jamal al-Din al-Afghani, 4, 12, 46, 200n12
Jamal al-Din al-Qasimi, 13, 47, 68n6, 102n2
jallabiyya: neo-traditional, 29, 212, 219, 223; traditional, 198, 200–201, 205, 207, 209
jubba, 42–43, 71
Juhayman al-'Utaybi, 120, 180, 181. *See also* al-Jama'a al-Salafiyya al-Muhtasiba

Khedive 'Abbas Hilmi, 38
Khedive Sa'id, 35
King Faruq, 53, 59, 102, 108, 117, 206
kuttab system, 39, 104, 208

Literalism, 1, 205
Literacy, 27, 47, 221

madhhab: anti-*madhhab* sentiment, 117; eponyms, 38, 40; institutional role, 112, 194; legal approach, 5–6, 15, 38, 58, 75, 129, 171, 189, 220; *madhhab al-salaf*, 3, 16,46, 48, 191; ritual cleanliness, 103
Mahmud 'Abd al-Wahhab Fayyad: Jam'iyya Shar'iyya, 153; *manhaj*, 85; relationship to 'Abd al-Nasir, 84; Salafism, 80n54
Mahmud Muhammad Khattab al-Subki: facial hair, 94, 173–74; *isbal*, 199; neo-Hanbalism, 54n125; politics, 81n56; praying in shoes, 106; religious decline, 71–72
Mahmud Mukhtar, 60
al-Manar (journal): gender segregation, 158; *isbal*, 200, 201; Muslim distinction, 69, 70, 71, 204; praying in shoes, 106–7; religious print media, 46, 49
manhaj, 68, 69, 85, 100; Islamic activism, 88; Sayyid Qutb, 90; textual methodology, 88n87; worship, 86, 89, 90, 95
maqasid al-shari'a, 156n97
al-maslaha al-'amma, 11n27, 15, 28, 81, 100, 169
mass politics, 37, 40
mawlid, 36, 115, 139
Michel Foucault, 10, 32
Military (Egyptian), 20, 29; 1967 war, 85; facial hair, 174; Jama'a Islamiyya, 216; prisons, 179; uniforms, 41, 128
Ministry of Education (Egyptian), 25, 191, 222n99; curriculum, 60
Ministry of Endowments (Egyptian), 25, 44, 52; mosques, 124, 133; publications, 109; public dialogues, 181, 182
Ministry of Hajj and Endowments (Saudi Arabian), 121–22
Muhammad 'Abd Allah al-Qahtani, 180. *See also* al-Jama'a al-Salafiyya al-Muhtasiba
Muhammad 'Abd al-Majid al-Shafi'i, 52, 105
Muhammad 'Abduh: al-Azhar, 40, 104; conceptual framework, 70; *isbal*, 200n12; print media, 46, 49; Salafism, 4, 12
Muhammad 'Ali (Ottoman), 35
Muhammad 'Ali 'Abd al-Rahim, 98, 133, 185, 187–88
Muhammad 'Ali Mahjub, 124. *See also* Ministry of Endowments (Egyptian)
Muhammad Aman al-Jami, 47n82, 164n123
Muhammad Amin al-Shinqiti, 129, 185n67
Muhammad Bahjat al-Baytar: clothing, 76–78, 204–5; education, 111; gender, 141; prayer, 110; Salafism, 47
Muhammad b. 'Abd al-Wahhab. *See* Ibn 'Abd al-Wahhab
Muhammad b. 'Ali al-Sabuni, 191–92
Muhammad b. Ibrahim: gender mixing, 145, 156–57; *isbal*, 199, 218n82; Muhammad Nasir al-Din al-Albani, 152; praying in shoes, 119; Egypt, 52n115
Muhammad b. Isma'il al-Muqaddam, 133, 185
Muhammad b. Kamal al-Khatib, 79–80, 82, 204
Muhammad b. Salih al-'Uthaymin: approach, 16n46; facial hair, 98, 187, 218; gender segregation, 167; *isbal*, 213, 218; Permanent Committee on Religious Scholarship and Fatwas, 126; praying in shoes, 130
Muhammad Hamid al-Fiqi: Ansar al-Sunna, 4, 39; clothing, 204; employment, 44, 45; facial hair, 94, 172–73, 175; *madhhab* system, 112; politics, 60; praying in shoes, 107; print media, 46; Salafism, 46
Muhammad Jamil Ghazi, 215. See also *al-amr bi-l-ma'ruf wa'l-nahi 'an al-munkar*

Muhammad al-Khidr Husayn, 210. *See also* al-Azhar University
Muhammad Mahmud Pasha, 44
Muhammad Makhluf, 210. *See also* State Mufti
Muhammad Najib, 59. *See also* Free Officers
Muhammad Nasir al-Din al-Albani: Abu Hanifa, 112; Ahl al-Hadith, 119–20; facial hair, 170, 190-93; graves, 62n158; Hanbalism, 152; human representation, 60; *manhaj*, 68n6, 102n2; modesty, 137, 142, 153, 167n133; pants, 205, 218n83, 220, 222–23; politics, 13; prayer, 112n45, 117, 136; students, 184; turbans, 57, 71, 83
Muhammad Qutb, 87n80, 90
Muhammad Rashid Rida: al-Azhar, 40; gender, 205; *isbal*, 200–201; Mahmud Muhammad Khattab al-Subki, 54n125; Muhammad Hamid al-Fiqi, 4;Muslim distinction, 69–71, 74, 79, 93; prayer, 106; print media, 46, 49
Muhammad al-Shawkani: facial hair, 94n117, 189n82, Salafism, 16, 47n82
Muhammad Yusri Ibrahim, 166
Muhammad Zahid b. Hasan al-Kawthari, 111–13
Muhammad Zakariyya al-Kandhalawi, 182–83
Muhammad's Youth, 53, 55
Muhibb al-Din al-Khatib, 109n29, 203
Muqbil b. Hadi al-Wadi'i, 128–30, 226
Muslim Brotherhood (Egyptian): 'Abd Allah 'Azzam, 88; 'Abd al-Nasir, 60, 117, 178, 208; categorization, 13; clothing, 42–43; establishment, 3; facial hair, 175–76, 178–79, 212; gender, 143, 146, 153, 155, 159, 162; historiography, 8; ideology, 74, 85, 89; *isbal*, 213; Islamic Association, 53–54; missionaries, 108; prayer, 57–58, 106, 111; publications, 46, 109; structure, 26, 36, 45, 63, 149, 150
Muslim Brotherhood (Syrian), 158
Muslim Sisters, 152, 176. *See also* Fatima 'Abd al-Hadi
Mustafa Hilmi, 89–90
Mustafa Kamil, 41, 60. See also *efendiyya*)

Najdi Call (*See* Wahhabi-Hanbalism)
nationalism: 'Abd al-Nasir, 179; clothing, 203, 213; custom, 68, 75, 101, 231; ethnicity, 14; gender, 146; media, 36; mobilization, 37; modernity, 74, 174; religious nationalism, 25; representation, 60; theory, 7–8, 78n45
neo-Traditionalism, 13
Ni'mat Sidqi, 116, 137, 141–44, 148, 152, 160–61
Nu'man Khayr al-Din al-Alusi, 47

Ottoman Empire, 35–36, 40, 51, 82, 103n4, 111–12, 140

Permanent Committee on Religious Scholarship and Fatwas: *da'wa*, 121; facial hair, 188; *isbal*, 213, 216, 222; media, 127; praying in shoes, 128, 131–32; Salafism, 126

qub'a, 58, 76, 78, 203n22, 206, 209
quietism, 13, 32, 60, 62–63, 88n85, 104, 180, 188, 197, 223

race, 14, 76
Rashad al-Shafi'i. *See* Muhammad 'Abd al-Majid al-Shafi'i

Sa'ad Zaghlul, 60
sadd al-dhari'at, 15n43, 194
Sahwa (Saudi Arabian): facial hair, 96, 186; gender, 150, 153, 155; mobilization, 120; politics, 132, 170, 189; print media, 86, 222
Salafiyya Bookstore, 48, 203
Salih 'Ashmawi, 54
Salih b. Ibrahim al-Bulayhi, 167
Salih al-Fawzan, 126, 131, 191–92, 209n48
Salih al-Lahidan, 127
al-Sayyid 'Abd al-Halim Malaqi, 84, 88,
Sayyid Qutb: divine sovereignty, 182n48; execution, 63; gender, 143; *'ibada*, 87; *manhaj*, 90, 95; *takfir*, 53n119
al-Sayyid Sabiq, 143–44, 151, 175–76
Shahata Muhammad 'Ali Saqr, 166,
shirk, 45, 49, 56, 115, 121, 134
Siddiq Hasan Khan al-Qannuji, 47n82, 189
State Feminism, 146, 165. *See also* Nationalism
State Mufti, 36–37, 104, 108, 186, 187, 213

tafsir, 42, 103
Tahir al-Din al-Jaza'iri, 47n82
takfir, 53, 182, 197, 222, 231. *See also* Jama'at al-Muslimin
al-Takfir wa'l-Hijra. *See* Jama'at al-Muslimin
Talal Asad, 17, 19n61
Taqi al-Din al-Hilali, 129
taqlid, 15n43, 38, 74, 78

tarbush, 35, 40, 42, 201, 203, 210. See also *efendiyya*
tawhid, 12, 67, 73, 75–76
turban: *efendiyya*, 42; Islamic identity, 56, 70, 71n14, 200–201, 203, 210; prayer, 57n135, 58, 71, 83; religious status, 211

uniforms: boy scouts, 43–44; Jamaʿa Islamiyya, 220; military and school, 35, 41, 98; Salafism, 29; scholars, 210; theory, 21, 24
urbanization, 24n82, 36, 37, 208
usul al-fiqh, 39, 67n5
ʿUmar b. Ghurama b. ʿUmar al-ʿAmrawi: *isbal*, 214, 216; prayer, 124, 125, 126, 128, 130
ʿUmar b. al-Khattab, 175, 183
al-ʿUrwa al-Wuthqa (journal), 46

Wafd Party, 40, 43–44, 46, 53, 108
Wahhabi-Hanbalism: definitions, 14, 15n43; *al-Durar al-Saniyya fi al-Ajwiba al-Najdiyya*, 118; gender segregation, 138, 153, 156; Gulf war, 189; methodology, 16n46; najd, 105, 118; praying in shoes, 119; scholarly establishment, 52, 229; Shiʿism, 121; theology, 3, 16, 46n76, 48–49, 191
Wahhabism. *See* Wahhabi-Hanbalism

Young Egypt Party, 44, 46, 74. *See also* Green Shirts
Young Men's Muslim Association, 4, 45n73, 46, 108–9

Zaynab ʿAwad Allah Hasan, 160
Zaynab al-Ghazali, 176n23
zunnar, 70, 73, 210

Founded in 1893,
UNIVERSITY OF CALIFORNIA PRESS
publishes bold, progressive books and journals on topics in the arts, humanities, social sciences, and natural sciences—with a focus on social justice issues—that inspire thought and action among readers worldwide.

The UC PRESS FOUNDATION
raises funds to uphold the press's vital role as an independent, nonprofit publisher, and receives philanthropic support from a wide range of individuals and institutions—and from committed readers like you. To learn more, visit ucpress.edu/supportus.